# Media and Religion
# in American History

## On the cover:

Variation on "Eliza Crossing the Ice," a lithograph (1853) that served as the model for artwork used to illustrate Harriet Beecher Stowe's *Uncle Tom's Cabin*. The novel originally appeared in serialized form in the abolitionist *National Era* newspaper. Mrs. Stowe said that she wrote the story, which had a strong Christian moral basis, from an irresistible spiritual inspiration. *Uncle Tom's Cabin* was the most widely read literature of the time and exercised a leading influence in mobilizing opinion in support of abolition.

# Media and Religion in American History

## EDITED BY

## Wm. David Sloan

VISION V PRESS

# Media and Religion in American History

Some chapters in this book originally appeared as articles in other publications. We appreciate the permission given us to include the following works:

Bruce J. Evensen, "The Evangelical Origins of the Muckrakers." © *American Journalism*, 1989. Reprinted by permission.

David Paul Nord, "The Evangelical Origins Of Mass Media In America, 1815-1835." © *Journalism Monographs*, 1984. Reprinted by permission.

Marvin N. Olasky, "When World Views Collide: Journalists and the Great Monkey Trial." © *American Journalism*, 1987. Reprinted by permission.

Stephen J. Whitfield, "The Jewish Contribution to American Journalism." © *American Journalism*, 1986. Reprinted by permission of *American Journalism: A Journal of Media History*.

## Media and Religion in American History

**Library of Congress Cataloging-in-Publication Data**

Media and religion in American history/editor, Wm. David Sloan.
    p. cm.
    ISBN 1-885219-14-8
    1. Religion and the press--United States--History. 2. Journalism, Religious--United States--History. 3. Mass media--United States--Religious aspects. I. Sloan, W. David (William David), 1947-

PN4888.R44 M43 1999
070.4'49200973--dc21

99-045313

# CONTENTS

# Introduction

## Media History and Religion

RELIGION, PARTICULARLY CHRISTIANITY, has played a prominent role throughout the history of America's mass media. It was integral to the founding and development of the media during the formative stages, and much of the essential character of the media has religious underpinnings.

That religion should be so important in the history of America's mass media is not surprising, since American society itself was based in large part on religious foundations. And for the most part, the relationship between religion and the media was positive. That relationship began to cool with the appearance of mass newspapers in the first half of the nineteenth century, but journalists generally tended still to be favorable toward Christianity. It was only in recent years that there appeared what could be described as antagonism between them.

One of the most common misconceptions about the history of mass communication is that the media and religion have always been natural enemies. That error portrays the early press as struggling to free itself from repressive clerical authorities and has journalists of later generations moving toward enlightened, responsible service to readers. In fact, from the beginning, religious leaders were at the forefront of encouraging the publication of newspapers. American publishers were almost invariably Christians, and generation after generation of journalists were motivated to higher ideals of public service based in large part on their understanding of the Christian faith. Much of the journalistic effort toward improving society throughout American history gained its impetus from Christians and Judeo-Christian values.

If not telling an erroneous story, many historical works have simply neglected the important role that religion often played in the mass media. For much of media history, religion was instrumental in determining their nature. It is fair to say that Christian concepts provided a key factor in shaping the beneficial public role that the media played. Many reasons have probably contributed to historians' neglect of religion — which would require an entirely different essay from this one — but suffice it here to say that of the several thousand books and articles that have been written about the history of mass communication, the number giving substantive treatment to religion is fewer than a hundred. Many of those, furthermore, deal not with religion and the mainstream media but with the religious press *per se*.

In the modest efforts presented in this book, the authors have provided accounts of a variety of episodes to attempt to help correct the picture. Focusing mainly on journalism, their accounts begin with the origins of printing in America and chronicle recent efforts in religious publishing aimed at countering secular trends in the mainstream press. The general trend that one will find in history is that religion exercised a decreasing influence on the media with the passage of time. From colonial times through the 1800s, religion played a positive and often a strong role in the development and operation of mass communication. Then, mainly in the twentieth century, one will find an increasingly hostile treatment of religion in the media.

The chapters in this book focus mainly on the relationship of Christianity to the media. Christianity is the focus for the simple historical reason that historically it was, and continues to be, Christianity that was the dominant religion of America. Thus, it was Christianity that played the most important role in mass communication. Stephen Whitfield's provocative essay (chapter 11) makes clear that there has been a major Jewish influence on American journalism but that, as he points out, the influence was not the result primarily of Jewish religious beliefs.

Recent media attitudes toward religion, particularly mainstream Christianity, seem to mirror a declining religiosity on the part of journalists. Surveys vary in their findings about journalists' religious beliefs. None, however, indicates that journalists are as religious as the rest of the American population. For example, a survey in the early 1990s found that only 54.4 per cent of journalists have a Protestant background. In another recent survey to determine journalists' values, one-half, when asked to indicate their religion, answered "none," and only 20 per cent identified themselves as Protestants. That compares with a general population that is overwhelmingly Christian and mainly Protestant. Even though many newspapers have increased coverage of religion in recent years, various studies have shown that religion is underrepresented in both newspaper and television news and that portrayal of Christians is more negative than for most other groups. One study found that only about 1 per cent of news stories on national television networks deal with religion. Another study found that prime-time television presents "non-Christian values" more than twice as often as "Christian values" and that Christian characters are portrayed unfavorably almost as often as they are favorably. In such a media mindset, it therefore does not surprise one to read a religion columnist for the *New York Times* declaring that Baptists, the largest Protestant group in the nation, are "small-minded" and "obstreperous." Journalists' expressions of such views are commonplace. It was not always so. Only in the last few decades did the profession of journalism and the entertainment media become non-religious (some critics would claim "anti"-religious), particularly skeptical toward America's traditional faiths, especially Christianity but Judaism also.

That attitude has been mirrored in the bulk of the work of those few historians who have written about the relationship of religion to the mainstream media. It is not surprising therefore that their work is critical of religion's (particularly Christianity's) relationship to the mass media. The problem with the studies, though, is that most are based on inferior scholarship and show little familiarity with the true historical record. They reflect the historians' bias rather than the evidence. In explaining colonial journalism, for example, one historian gave this account of the motives of Samuel Keimer, publisher of Philadelphia's second newspaper. He was, according to the historian, simply a deist advocating a "liberal spirit." His deism was obvious from his peculiar plan to reprint the entire contents of an encyclopedia in his newspaper — since interest in the natural world is incompatible with religious faith. The problem with the account is that Keimer in fact was a member of the French Prophets, a Christian sect. His reason for reprinting the encyclopedia, according to his own explanation, was his great reverence for God's creation. Such errors are not uncommon when historians have dealt with religion. Some of their explanations have been exactly the opposite of the meaning of the records.

There existed, in fact, between the media and religion a positive, supportive role from the beginning. Yet even a cursory familiarity with the media and religion in our own time makes it clear that such a relationship no longer exists across the board. The faithful more often can be heard criticizing the media than praising them, and the media — from newspapers to motion pictures — tend to present a picture of America's traditional faiths, Christianity and Judaism, that is less than favorable. How did such a change occur?

It did not happen all at once. Rather, individuals made small cracks here and there, and with time the cracks became a wide fissure. Occasionally in the long years before the American Civil War, isolated journalists such as James Gordon Bennett of the *New York Herald* made disparaging remarks about organized religion (in Bennett's case, Catholicism), but skepticism did not become generally acceptable until the latter part of the nineteenth century. Some journalists' newfound animosity toward religion can be seen readily in coverage of the evolution trial of teacher John Scopes in the 1920s. Yet, it was not until the last half century that the American media could be called truly secular.

A variety of causes brought about the change. Commercialization of the media was one, as owners became more interested in material affairs and placed them ahead of achieving ideals. Another was the increasing dichotomy of science vs. faith as a worldview, with the division gathering momentum particularly in the late nineteenth century through the influence of Darwinism. In journalism one can see the influence of a scientific worldview through the emphasis placed on objectivity. In its purest form, objectivity is a way of knowing that places primacy on the physical, objective world instead of on the internal, subjective perspective of the journalist. Related to both commercialization and the contest to determine the dominant worldview — and to many other causes, no doubt — was a general secularization of society. As a part of society, the media reflected that changed attitude toward the supremacy of religion. Another cause was the professionalization of journalism. As journalists came to see themselves as part of their own, insulated fraternity, they tended to think of themselves as in opposition to other institutions such as the government, the military, and big business. Eventually, that attitude extended to the church. Religion, particularly evangelical Christianity, fell to their skepticism.

Despite the media's coolness, it should be mentioned that the relationship is not universally negative even today. Many newspapers, for example, still run weekly pages devoted to news of church activities; and some newspapers, influenced no doubt by the particular attitudes of their staff members, still are visibly favorable toward religion. Likewise, it is unmistakable that religion still works a positive influence on the media. Despite the secularization of the profession of journalism, for example, Christian morals and ethics provide a foundation for thinking in American culture and for many practices of journalism.

The chapters in this book fill in much of the story. In them the reader can discern the contours of the general history of the relationship between religion and the media. Although the relationship today often is rocky, one can also recognize in its history the debt that America's mass media owe to religion. The purpose of this book is not to take sides in today's debate about media and religion but simply to provide a documented history of the essence of their relationship in the past. In the process, the authors believe that readers will find a vibrant — and sometimes surprising — story.

# Media and Religion
# in American History

# Evangelism and the Genesis
# of Printing in America
by Julie Hedgepeth Williams

IT WAS STILL NIGHT, but a hint of light was beginning to glow. Jacob Amsden and three friends were waiting on Boston Common, their breath puffing in the darkness, trumpets at their sides. Judge Samuel Sewall watched. He had hired the trumpeters, and his friend Mr. Bellman was clutching a piece of paper, on which Sewall had written a poem appropriate to the occasion. Just before the sun peeked over the horizon, Amsden and his friends raised the trumpets and blew a fanfare for the new year. It was not just any new year. It was the dawn of a new century, the seventeenth giving way to the eighteenth, and a new era stretched before them. Bellman read Sewall's poem aloud. It hailed the possibilities of the new century:

> Once more! our God vouchsafe to shine:
> Correct the Coldness of our clime.
> Make haste with thy Impartial Light,
> And terminate this long dark night.
>
> Give the poor Indians Eyes to see
> The Light of Life: and set them free.
> So Men shall God in Christ adore,
> And worship Idols rain, [sic] no more.
>
> So Asia, and Africa,
> Eurôpa, with America
> All Four, in Consort join'd shall sing
> New Songs of Praise to Christ our King.[1]

---

[1]Journal entry of 1 January 1700/01 by Samuel Sewall in M. Halsey Thomas, ed., *The Diary of Samuel Sewall, 1674-1729*, vol. 1 (New York: Farrar, Straus and Giroux, 1973), 440. Thomas quotes the poem, 441-2 note.

Sewall's celebration for the new century was a praise of evangelistic action — a call to spread true religion to Indians, to Europe, to Asia, and to Africa. It was indicative of American thought in general and Puritan thought in particular. The early Americans were evangelists, bent on spreading God's word. The next step that Sewall took filled in the other half of the evangelism equation: he had the poem printed and given out as a guideline for the new century, a tangible set of suggestions that readers could consult for as long as the paper lasted.[2] Evangelism was high on the American agenda, and printing was one important vehicle for evangelism.

Colonial America was a religious haven. From earliest times, groups as diverse as Puritans, Quakers, Catholics, and Huguenots came to the New World, eager for the safety of isolation. Europe and her persecutions were an ocean away. In America, religious groups could practice their faith in peace. At least that was the idea many emigrating Europeans treasured. In reality there were sometimes feuds and distrust between sects, and hand in hand with that there was evangelism — the attempt to convert worshippers of other faiths to another point of view. Religious Europeans came to America armed with Bibles and devotional literature, many committed to spreading God's word. That commitment not only accounted for some vigorous intellectual activity, but it also helped launch the American publishing industry.

## TO CHRISTIANIZE THE HEATHEN

From the start, newcomer Americans were determined to convert the native Americans, whom they called "Indians." The Virginians, not particularly remembered in history as religious zealots, left behind abundant evidence of both their desire to convert Indians and the role of literature in doing so. They did not have their own press, but that did not stop them from using books in the work of God. True, conversations, speeches, and sermons were extremely important and were the basis for much religious communication, but the press was another important evangelical tool. Once a piece of writing or a spoken word was converted to type and ink and paper, it did not suffer in the retelling. The word was passed from hand to hand with no distortion, save misinterpretation or wear and tear on the paper. Thus, the earliest American colonists thought of books as a way to carry and preserve religious ideas.

Early Virginians were no exception. They were driven to convert the Indians to Christianity, and they used tracts both to persuade Indians and to garner support for the effort from readers back home in Europe. To John Rolfe, who wanted to wed the Indian Pocahontas, such a marriage would be an opportunity to Christianize. To make that idea plain to European readers, he published his reasoning in a tract in 1614. "[W]hy dost not thou indevour to make her a Christian?... What should I doe?" he wrote. "[S]hall I be of so untoward a disposition, as to refuse to lead the blind into the right way? Shall I be so unnaturall, as not to give bread to the hungrie? or uncharitable, as not to cover the naked? Shall I despise to actuate these pious dueties of a Christian?... God forbid."[3]

---

[2]Journal entry of 1 January 1700/01 by Sewall in ibid., 440. Thomas says Sewall indicated that he paid for the trumpet blasts, 442 note.

[3]John Rolfe to Sir Thomas Dale, 1614, in Ralph Hamor, *A True Discourse of the Present Estate of Virginia, and the Successe of the Affaires there* (London: 1615), letter only reprinted in Lyon Gardiner Tyler,

The fact that he published his ideas was significant. Why should readers in England (or in Virginia, for that matter) be interested? Aside from satisfying natural curiosity about the mysterious Indians, Rolfe was mirroring the common interest of the day in the possibility of converting the Indians, who were ignorant of the Europeans' God.

The theme of Christianizing the Indians sounded often in colonial writings published for European readers. In a 1624 book about America, adventurer John Smith recounted the story of an Indian chief named Wamanto, who was impressed with the Bible. "Hee much wondered at our Bible, but much more to heare it was the Law of our God," Smith wrote. Wamanto found Genesis interesting, since he, like Adam, had only one wife at a time. Smith's book was designed to attract settlement; obviously Smith perceived that the possibility of Christian Indians was a positive thing that might induce settlement.[4] Smith reported in another publication that Indians were ready to be converted, for the natives considered the Englishmen's God to be more powerful than their own deities. Smith pitied the Indians, so long ignorant of God. "And in this lamentable ignorance doe these poore soules sacrifice themselves to the Divell [Devil], not knowing their Creator," he wrote. He added that colonies would bring wealth to the king of England, but the true worth of colonies was in their religious mission. "... [R]educing Heathen people to ciuilitie and true Religion bringeth honour to the King of Heaven,"[5] he wrote. It was clear that Smith was hoping to stir up a sense of Christian duty in his readers, giving them a sort of spiritual authority to settle in America.

In the same 1624 book, Englishman Thomas Hariot noted that Indians found the Anglican religion to be superior to theirs. The Bible played a dramatic role in the Indians' outlook. As Hariot put it :

> ... through conversation with vs [us], they were brought into great doubts of their owne, and no small admiration of [our religion]: of which many desired to learn more then [*sic*] we had meanes for want of vtterance in their Language to expresse.
>
> Most things they saw with vs as ... Bookes, writing, Guns, and such like; so far exceeded their capacities, that they thought they were rather the workes of gods then men; or at least the gods had taught vs how to make them, and loued vs so much better then them, & caused many of them [to] giue credit to what we spake concerning our God.

In fact, the Indians were so amazed by the Bible that they wanted to touch, kiss, and embrace it, and "to hold it to their breasts, and heads, and stroke all their body over with it," Hariot reported.[6] As Hariot noted, Indians were attracted by argument and example, but it was also true that Englishmen used books to evangelize them.

---

ed., *Narratives of Early Virginia, 1606-1625* (New York: Barnes & Noble, 1907), 240.

[4] John Smith, *Generall Historie of Virginia, New England, and the Summer Isles* (London: Printed by I.D. and I.H. for Michael Sparkes, 1624), reprinted in Tyler, ed., *Narratives of Early Virginia*, 352.

[5] John Smith, "A Preface of foure Poynts," in Smith, *Generall Historie of Virginia, New England, and the Summer Isles* (London: Printed by I.D. and I.H. for Michael Sparkes, 1624; facsimile reprint, Ann Arbor, Mich.: University Microfilms, 1966), unnumbered preface.

[6] Thomas Hariot, "*The Observations of Master* Thomas Heriot," ibid., 11.

In early Virginia, evangelism was important work. Through it, settlers would not only reap the benefits of an Indian population sympathetic to white men's ways, but they would also have the joy of knowing they had given the unChristian damned an opportunity for Christianity and salvation. Tracts written about America were often calculated to attract European interest and investment in the colonies, and it is significant that some of them used religion to turn readers' heads.

Evangelism gave legitimacy to colonizing the New World. It was a deliberate appeal, for publicists realized that religion was a strong motivating force in Europe. Protestantism was growing and dynamic as different interpretations of the Bible led to new sects. Many new churches felt the need to proclaim the gospel, and colonial promoters keyed into that popular concern about church and spirituality. In 1608 and 1616 pamphlets, John Smith and his editor both suggested that newcomers to America could convert the Indians.[7] Touting "New Brittaine" (now part of the Carolinas) as having temperate air and fertile soil, pamphleteer Edward Bland and co-authors suggested that by European settlement, "those poor Indians" might be converted to Christianity. In the 1650 pamphlet, Bland personally addressed readers with his concept of conversion:

> WHO ever thou art that desirest the Advancement of Gods glory by conversion of the Indians, the Augmentation of the English Common-wealth, in extending its liberties; I would advise thee to consider the present benefit and future profits that wil arise in the wel setling [of] ... that happy Country of New Brittaine....[8]

John Archdale, in a 1707 pamphlet, cited Daniel 12 in the Bible as a reason for Christianizing the New World. The chapter urged readers to increase religious knowledge in all the Earth.[9]

Clearly, the settlers in Virginia and nearby colonies took conversion of the Indians to be a divinely inspired goal. They saw published material as a vehicle for evangelism. Yet, despite that religious focus, Virginia did not have its own press for many years. From the founding of Jamestown in 1608 to the establishment of William Parks' press in 1733, Virginians who wished to spread the word of God among Indians had to rely on material printed elsewhere, usually overseas.[10]

---

[7]John Smith, *A Description of New England* (1616), reprinted in George Parker Winship, ed., *Sailors' Narratives of Voyages along the New England Coast, 1524-1624* (Boston: 1905; reprint, New York: Burt Franklin, 1968), 247. (Page numbers refer to reprint edition.) See also an editorial note by I.H. in John Smith, *A True Relation* (1608), reprinted in Tyler, ed., *Narratives of Early Virginia, 1606-1625*, 32.

[8]Edward Bland, Abraham Wood, Sackford Brewster, and Elias Pennant, *The Discovery of new Brittaine, Began August 27, Anno Dom., 1650*, reprinted in Alexander S. Salley, Jr., ed., *Narratives of Early Carolina, 1650-1708* (New York: Charles Scribner's Sons, 1911), 6.

[9]John Archdale, *A New Description of that Fertile and Pleasant Province of Carolina* (London: Printed for John Wyat, 1707), reprinted in Salley, ed., *Narratives of Early Carolina*, 284.

[10]There may have been a press set up briefly in Virginia in 1681-1682 to print the colonial laws. It was ordered to print nothing more and was apparently disbanded. Isaiah Thomas, *The History of Printing in America*, 2d. ed., Marcus A. McCorison, ed. (1810; reprint, New York: Weathervane Books, 1970), 551-2. (Page numbers refer to reprint edition.)

*ENTER THE PURITANS; ENTER THE PRESS*

The Puritans, however, had a different outlook. They were members of the Church of England, too, like the Virginians were, but unlike the Virginians they had grave differences with the church. To them, the church was corrupt, and they hoped their example would purify it. They also had a deep belief in the power of the printed word to help transform the church into a purer, more godly institution. They were determined evangelists, if one accepts the definition of evangelism as being "the spreading of God's word." Puritans did not believe man had the power to save souls. That was God's privilege. Thus, they never claimed to offer salvation through evangelism. Their evangelism instead was meant to open thinking toward God, to direct people to the will of the Almighty. Due in part to their interest in evangelizing both Indians and Europeans, it was the Puritans who would bring the first press into English America.

Puritans' commitment to printing did not diminish their interest in other forms of communication. Sermons were the heart of Puritan religious life, and examples of godly living were inspirational. But the printing press acted as a magnifier for both sermon and example, for printing could cover a large area. A reader in Connecticut could "hear" a sermon given in Boston by reading it. Books and pamphlets also preserved the character of good men and women, and those publications could circulate over great geographic distances. They could also bridge temporal differences. Via the printed word, a saintly person could still have an influence after his or her death, and a sermon could be fresh long after it was spoken. Thus, the printing press was a useful tool — it gave *permanence* to an evangelical message.

Puritans' love of the printed word was tied to the fact that they were Protestants. The Bible was central to them. Roman Catholicism of the era granted the right to read the Scriptures only to clergymen. Puritans adamantly believed that was the wrong approach. It was important to them to read the Scriptures themselves, to hold the actual Bible in their hands, not just to hear it read by a clergyman. The text was a necessity, for through reading it, each individual might come to an understanding of God. God's word was all-important, but the physical book was the vehicle that brought that word to spiritually hungry readers.

Puritans, along with their Protestant brethren around Europe, feared that their right to read the Bible would be swallowed up in a renewal of Catholic power and influence. The first complete English-language Bible had been printed by Miles Coverdale in 1535,[11] and at the time America was being settled, the English Bible was still a fairly new phenomenon. Thus, Puritans jealously guarded the right to read the Bible free from the influence of clergymen. The very presence of the Bible in a home was a tangible symbol of the right to worship as one pleased.

So that each person, male or female, might read the Bible, Puritans emphasized education, which also nurtured the ability to interpret the word of God appropriately. Such reading and reasoning was a necessity in Puritan New England,[12] and thus it is no surprise that Puritans were well-educated and literacy

---

[11]Paul Alfred Pratte and Frank J. Krompak, "Communication Before America" in Wm. David Sloan and James D. Startt, eds., *The Media in America: A History* (Northport, Ala.: Vision Press, 1996), 15.

[12]David D. Hall, *Worlds of Wonder, Days of Judgment: Popular Religious Belief in Early New England* (Cambridge, Mass.: Harvard University Press, 1990), 34.

was fairly high. One scholar estimates that 60 per cent of New England white males were literate in 1660. The number had grown to 70 per cent in 1710 and to 85 per cent in 1760. Before 1670 in New England, 33 per cent of women were apparently literate; by the end of the colonial era, the number had risen to 45 per cent.[13] In fact, when asked about youth literacy in 1668, officials in the town of Beverly, Massachusetts, could find no child over age nine who could not read.[14]

The goal of universal Bible-reading in New England accounted for high literacy, and that literacy, in turn, shaped Puritans' intellectual outlook. They valued reading, thinking, and reasoning about the Bible — and about religion in general. Interpretation, discussion, and argument were crucial to awaken the heart to Christ, and those discussions and arguments took place both in spoken form and in the form of publications.

Thus, many Puritans saw an evangelical mission for themselves in the New World. One was the great Puritan leader John Winthrop, who in 1629 cited evangelism in his decision to help found Massachusetts Bay Colony. "It wilbe [*sic*] a service to the Churche of great Consequence to carrye the Gospell into those partes of the world," he wrote, "and to rayse a bullwarke against the kingdom of the Antichrist which the Jesuits labour to reare vp [*sic*] in all places of the world." The Bible showed that the gospel must be preached to all nations, and that, he felt, morally obligated the Puritans to preach the gospel to the Indians in America.[15] Jesuits sent their best missionaries to the Indians, he complained, while the Anglicans sent only a handful of their dullest missionaries. Reasoning from the basis of the Bible, Winthrop concluded that the Anglicans' missionary practices were unwise and violated biblical commands, for in the book of Acts, Jesus' apostles left their own country to preach the word. Therefore, Puritans in Massachusetts should give the gift of the word to those who so desperately needed it — the Indians.[16] It was just one argument of many that Winthrop gave for founding a colony, but it was one his fellow Puritans would earnestly act upon.

It is never easy to found a colony, especially when land must be cleared, new ways learned, and old ways modified, and the Puritans of Massachusetts were not exempt from such pressures. However, the challenges did not dull their evangelistic fervor. The nearest press was in England, but Puritan writers turned to the English press whenever they needed to publish, and Puritan friends and family left behind in England continually shipped religious books published in London to New Englanders.[17]

Books and tracts were so important to Puritans, however, that a number of them thought that a top priority for the colony was the establishment of a printing press. After all, as Winthrop had so eloquently put it in a sermon aboard ship as his new colony travelled to America, Massachusetts was to be "a city on

[13]Kenneth A. Lockridge, *Literacy in Colonial New England: An Enquiry into the Social Context of Literacy in the Early Modern West* (New York: W.W. Norton, 1974), 13, 21, 38. Lockridge based his estimations on the number of people who could sign their names to their wills, instead of just leaving their mark.

[14]Hall, *Worlds of Wonder*, 33-4.

[15]John Winthrop, signed draft entitled "General Observations," May 1629, in Stewart Mitchell, ed., *Winthrop Papers*, vol. 2 (Boston: Massachusetts Historical Society, 1931), 114, 116.

[16]Untitled manuscript document in John Winthrop's handwriting, 1629, in ibid., 126-7.

[17]See, for instance, John Humfrey to Isaac Johnson, 9 December 1630, postscript, in ibid., 30. Many other Puritan diarists and letter-writers mentioned receiving books from England.

a hill," one that everyone could see and imitate.[18] The Atlantic, however, was a wide ocean, and if the city on a hill were to be visible in Europe, it seemed urgent to Puritans on both sides of the great ocean that printing play a role. The printed page could convey messages from Massachusetts back to England with clarity and accuracy. That was not all. The printed word could also help solidify the faith in Massachusetts, as invariably backsliders and the unconverted would need guidance. Massachusetts, after all, was going to be the proof that God's true church was not just an ideal, but a reality. Every means should be employed to that end, including the most current communications technology.

Various Puritans felt so strongly about this that church members in England, as well as fellow believers who had fled to Holland to escape persecution, joined forces and finances to secure an American press as quickly as possible. Just nine years after Winthrop had convinced himself that Puritans had a duty to spread God's word to Indians, European backers had raised enough money to purchase a press and related materials for Massachusetts. Reverend Joseph Glover, who had led the drive to raise funds for the press, would himself escort the newly purchased printing materials across the Atlantic in 1638, and he would set up the print shop. He was bringing a printer with him, one Stephen Daye, and he was also bringing the prayers and well-wishers of a throng of Puritans. Glover died at sea, but his widow Elizabeth delivered the press to Cambridge, where it was set up at Harvard College. The press was not strictly to be used for Harvard's business, although that was one goal.[19] Mrs. Glover and the European contributors primarily expected the press to aid church and state.[20] After some legal wrangling over Glover's estate,[21] in 1638 or 1639, Daye produced the first item from the new press: *The Oath of a Free-man.* It was the governmental oath repeated by all voting members of the colony. The press next produced two almanacs, and then Daye completed his first religious publication, the now-famous *Bay Psalm Book.*[22]

The new press had only limited capabilities, and the majority of printed matter circulating in Massachusetts came from England. However, the local press was still a boon to Puritan churches, especially in their endeavor to spread the word of God throughout New England. In 1641, the Massachusetts General Court announced plans to agree upon and publish a catechism that would help readers of all ages take the beginning steps toward understanding true Christianity.[23] The publishers would see to it that the catechism was distributed among Indian children, who needed to understand Christ if they were to pave the way

---

[18]"A Modell of Christian Charity," sermon preached by John Winthrop aboard the *Arabella*, 1630, excerpts reprinted in Giles Gunn, ed., *Early American Writing* (New York: Penguin Books, 1994), 107-12.

[19]Thomas, *The History of Printing in America*, 5, 42-5.

[20][Edward Johnson], *A History of New-England From the English planting in the Yeere 1628. [sic] untill the Yeere 1652* (London: Nathaniel Brooke, 1654), reprinted as J. Franklin Jameson, ed., *Johnson's Wonder-Working Providence, 1628-1651* (New York: Charles Scribner's Sons, 1910), 183. (Page numbers refer to reprint edition.)

[21]Thomas, *The History of Printing in America*, 45-9.

[22]According to Charles Evans, *American Bibliography*, vol. 1: 1639-1729 (New York: Peter Smith, 1941), no original copies of *Oath of a Free-man* survive. However, scholars are sure that Daye printed the work in Cambridge in March of either 1638 or 1639. See Evans entry #1. For information on the next three items from the press, see items #2 to #4. The actual title of the *Bay Psalm Book* was *The VVhole Booke of Psalmes* ([Cambridge, Mass.]: Printed by [Stephen Daye], 1640).

[23]Journal entry of 21 June 1641 by John Winthrop in James Kendall Hosmer, ed., *Winthrop's Journal, "History of New England," 1630-1649*, vol. 2 (New York: Charles Scribner's Sons, 1908), 37.

for future generations of Indians to accept Christianity. The catechism apparently did find its way into Indian children's hands. John Winthrop asked Indian leaders in 1643 whether they allowed their children "to read God's word, that they may have knowledge of the true God and to worship him in his own way." The Indians were less than enthusiastic, but they replied that they approved of such reading.[24]

## THE INDIAN BIBLE: A BEACON FROM THE CITY ON A HILL

One of the most visible Puritan evangelical efforts was the work of John Eliot, who preached to the Indians. Furthermore, he perceived that the printing press could play a role in converting Indians. It was Eliot's publications and evangelism, perhaps more than any other religious efforts in Puritan New England, that made Europeans notice the city on a hill. As a result, English groups financed Eliot's publications in order for him to convert more Indians. In Englishmen's mind, Christianizing the Indians was linked with the technology of the press.

Eliot, a Massachusetts resident, learned the Algonquin dialect of the local Indian tribe. From that starting point, he began evangelizing the Indians by preaching to them in their own tongue. Edward Johnson, a fellow Massachusetts Puritan, wrote in a work published in London, "[Eliot was] apt to teach, as by his indefatigable paines both with his own flock, and the poore Indians ... whose Language he learned purposely to helpe them to the knowledge of God in Christ, frequently Preaching in their Wigwams, and catechizing their children."[25] To publicize Eliot's work, Thomas Shepard published *The Day-Breaking if not the Sun-Rising of the Gospell with the Indians in New England* in 1647 and, in 1648, *The Clear Sunshine of the Gospel breaking forth upon the Indians in New England*, both intended for London audiences. Other books praising Eliot's holy work among the heathens were also distributed in London, and they indeed created excitement. The Lord's work was being done in America. As Johnson reported in his contemporaneous history book, Parliament was so amazed about the evangelical work among the Indians that it agreed to incorporate the Company for Propagating the Gospel in New England.[26] The Company would offer financial support for further attempts to lead the savage race toward God.

To the Company and Eliot, preaching was not enough. Spreading the gospel to the Indians would be complete only if Indians could read the gospel in their native language. The Puritans themselves cherished the ability to read the Bible, and by logical extension, the Indians should cherish reading the Scriptures, too. Rounding out his life's work as a missionary, Eliot translated the holy book into the Algonquin dialect. The New Testament was published in 1661 and the Old Testament in 1663.[27] It was the first Bible ever published in America.

The Indian Bible was Eliot's masterpiece, but he also translated other works

---

[24]Journal entry of 12 June 1643 by Winthrop in ibid., 124.

[25]Jameson, ed., *Johnson's Wonder-Working Providence*, 72.

[26]Ibid., 264 note. Johnson called it the Society for Propagating the Gospel, while all others substituted "Company" for "Society." There was later a Society for Propagating the Gospel sponsored by the Anglican Church.

[27]John Eliot, trans., *The New Testament in the Algonquin Indian Language* (Cambridge, Mass.: Printed by Samuel Green, 1661). The Old Testament followed in 1663.

into the Indian dialect. Among those was a psalter that featured columns in the Indian language alongside a translation in English. Like the Bible, the Indian hymnbook was made at the request of the Company. Two Indians, John Nees-nummin and James Printer, worked on the printing of the psalter. Printer shared credit for producing the work — it bore the imprint of Bartholomew Green and James Printer.[28]

Indian-language evangelism sparked much interest among religious-minded Europeans. Dutch traveler Jasper Danckaerts, for example, was still hearing about the Indian Bible some twenty years after it was first published. A religious man himself, he was quite anxious to purchase the Indian Bible when he visited Massachusetts. His persistent efforts to locate a copy illustrate how Puritans' efforts to convert the Indians impressed Europeans. The city on a hill was truly shining brightly on the other side of the Atlantic.

Danckaerts was a member of the Labadist sect, which was at the time based in Holland. The group had suffered much persecution, and America looked like a good place to them to retreat from the fight, nurse their wounds, and build up their church. Thus, Danckaerts and friend Peter Sluyter were travelling through America in 1680 and searching for possible locations for a Labadist colony. That was the major goal of the trip, but Danckaerts had a personal goal: he wanted to purchase a copy of the famous Indian Bible. He and Sluyter searched Boston booksellers in vain for a copy. The only hope, they decided, was to find John Eliot himself, who lived a forty-five minute ride away in Roxbury.[29] Persisting until they located Eliot, Danckaerts and Sluyter realized that they could not communicate with him. The aged minister did not speak Dutch, and the travelers could speak only broken English. But Danckaerts was determined. After inquiring, he found out that both he and Eliot spoke Latin. The two conversed in the ancient language, and it was a conversation Danckaerts never forgot. Eliot told him that he had converted numerous Indians to Christianity, but unconverted Indians despised the church and the Bible. Recognizing the Bible as the moving force behind Christianity, heathen Indians had carried away all existing copies of the Indian Bible in a recent war. Undaunted, Eliot was preparing a new edition, which was in press.[30]

Eliot did not want to disappoint his guests. There were no complete copies of the new edition Indian Bible available yet, but he still had his own copy of the first-edition Old Testament and most of the New Testament from that edition. Eliot was able to add a few sheets of the New Testament from the new printing, thus making a complete Bible. He gave it to Danckaerts.[31] Danckaerts was awed and thankful for such a gift. He wrote lovingly in the front of the book:

> All the Bibles of the Christian Indians were burned or destroyed by these heathen savages. This alone was saved; and from it a new edition, with im-

---

[28]*Massachuset* [sic] *Psalter...in Columns of Indian and English* (Boston: Bartholomew Green and James Printer, 1709).

[29]Journal entries of 7 and 8 July 1680 by Jasper Danckaerts, reprinted in Bartlett Burleigh James and J. Franklin Jameson, eds., *Journal of Jasper Danckaerts, 1679-1680* (Netherlands, 1687; translated and reprinted by Henry C. Murphy, 1867; reprint of translation, New York: Charles Scribner's Sons, 1934), 263-4. (Page numbers refer to 1934 edition.)

[30]Journal entry of 8 July 1680 by Danckaerts, ibid., 264.

[31]Ibid.

provements, and an entirely new translation of the New Testament, was undertaken. I saw at Roccsberri [Roxbury], about an hour's ride from Boston, this Old Testament printed, and some sheets of the New. The printing-office was at Cambridge, three hours' ride from Boston, where also there was a college of students, whether of savages or of other nations. The Psalms of David were added in the same metre.

At Roccsberri dwelt Mr. Haliot [Eliot], a very godly preacher there. He was at this time about seventy years old.... He was the principal translator and director of the printing of both the first and second editions of this Indian Bible. Out of special zeal and love he gave me this copy of the first edition, for which I was, and shall continue, grateful to him.[32]

In order to make the Bible more useful to him, Eliot also gave Danckaerts two or three small grammar books explaining the Indian language, again authored by Eliot. The evangelist would not take money for the books, so Danckaerts gave Eliot a copy of a publication from the Labadist church. Eliot praised God to see the reformation of Holland's church as discussed in the tract.[33]

Danckaerts' determination to locate a copy of the Bible illustrated the fact that Puritan evangelical efforts were catching attention in Europe. Impressed by Eliot's work, Parliament had already formed the Company for Propagating the Gospel to aid in evangelizing the Indians, and Danckaerts made clear that news of the Indian Bible was inspirational to other nonPuritans, too. Puritans had set out to be a city upon a hill, a model for other Christians to follow. As intended, Danckaerts and Sluyter had seen much good in Puritan efforts, even though they were of a different sect.

*THE WORD TO ANYONE*

No matter how successful Eliot was with the Indians, it was obvious to any Puritan that many other people also needed evangelizing. Englishmen needed to be upbraided and shown a better way so that they might purify the corrupt Anglican Church. Other Europeans also needed the clear thinking of Puritan religious men and women, whether to avoid Catholicism or to cure corrupt churches in general. Added to those goals, not everyone in New England was a covenanted member of the church, and certainly people in other colonies needed to understand the nature of God's religion. Unconverted New Englanders might hear Puritan sermons, but it was unlikely that many people from other colonies or other nations would have a steady diet of in-church sermon and personal example from Puritan New England. They were simply too far away. However, the printing press could bridge the gap between Puritans and humanity in need.

Sometimes those in need were cousins, at least in matters of the spirit. Presbyterians, like Puritans, were dissenters from the Church of England, eager for the church's reform. But when the Westminster Assembly convened in July

---

[32]Handwritten passage at beginning of Danckaerts' copy of the Indian Bible. The text is given in ibid., 264-5.

[33]The book was *Protestation Sincera Purae at Verae Reformatae Doctrinae Generalisque Orthodoxiae Johnnis de Labadie*, which was part of Jean de Labadie, Pierre Yvon, Pierre du Lignon, Henry Sluiter, and Peter Sluiter, *Veritas sui Vindex* (Herford, Germany: 1672). See Danckaerts' journal entry for 8 July 1680, in James and Jameson, eds., *Journal of Jasper Danckaerts*, 265-6 and 265 note.

of 1643 to debate how best to reconstruct church government, Presbyterians attacked Puritans' congregational-style churches. Presbyterian writers claimed that the "New England way" had led to immorality and false teachings.[34] The charges were alarming, especially since, to Puritans, Presbyterians favored far too lax standards in admitting church members.[35] The elders of New England churches met in 1645 and worked out answers to offending Presbyterian tracts that had reached America. They ordered their replies sent to London for immediate publication.[36] It was imperative that the truth reach London. When the Reverend Peter Bulkley published *The Gospel Covenant* in London in 1646 to illustrate Puritan thought, Massachusetts reader Edward Johnson lauded him in verse: "Thy Tongue, and Pen doth to the World declare/ Christ's covenant with his flock shall firmly stand...."[37] As Johnson had pointed out, books reached the *world*, not just neighbors. Acting on that notion of wide-reaching evangelism, American Puritans such as John Cotton often published tracts in London.[38] The Puritans were not shy about dictating their wisdom to any branch of the polluted English church. The model city on a hill needed to be seen an ocean away, and the press helped make the church visible.

Unfortunately, sometimes the polluted churches that New Englanders so earnestly wanted to evangelize were local Puritan ones. Doctrinal differences began to develop very early in New England. Puritan leaders could scarcely tolerate that. They were the city on a hill; they needed to project unity, not sectarianism. Puritan divines worked out their differences in a 1648 synod, and then, as was customary in Puritan evangelism, they turned to the press to make their decisions clear to any who might question them. There was no doubt that sermons, conversations, and letters would spread the news of the synod, but the pastors spoke eloquently for the value of the press as a tool for correcting their own straying congregations. In print, the pastors said, the new rules "might be better scanned and tried of every particular person in the several congregations or churches."[39]

Puritans were so used to the printed word, so convinced of its power, that some of them carried copies of religious tracts or books wherever they went and spread them to likely readers. Samuel Sewall took religious publications with him when he visited England in 1689. He stopped at Winchester College and donated two books to the students' library. One was a copy of Eliot's Indian Bible, and the other a booklet about the successful evangelical work being done to Christianize Indians. That book happened to be published in London, but its topic was indicative of how the word was being spread in the New World.[40] On

---

[34]David D. Hall, ed., *The Antinomian Controversy, 1636-1638: A Documentary History*, 2d. ed. (Durham, N.C.: Duke University Press, 1990), 3-23, 200, 396.

[35]Francis Dillon, *The Pilgrims* (Garden City, N.Y.: Doubleday, 1975), 209.

[36]Journal entry of 5 March 1645 by John Winthrop in Hosmer, ed., *Winthrop's Journal*, 257.

[37]Jameson, ed., *Johnson's Wonder-Working Providence*, 110-11. The book Johnson praised was Peter Bulkley, *The Gospel Covenant* (London: 1646).

[38]Jameson, ed., *Johnson's Wonder-Working Providence*, 88-9.

[39]Ibid., 242. The work was Synod of 1648, *A Platform of Church Discipline* (Cambridge, Mass.: Printed by Samuel Green, 1649).

[40]Journal entry for 25 February 1688/89 by Samuel Sewall, in Thomas, ed., *The Diary of Samuel Sewall*, vol. 1, 197. Thomas says the Bible is still in the college library, although the Mather work has disappeared. Thomas speculates it was Increase Mather, *De Successu Evangeli; apud Indos in Novâ-Angliâ* (London: 1688).

the same trip, he visited Dr. Nehemia Grew in Fleet Street, London, and gave him a psalm book, most likely the famous *Bay Psalm Book*, which was an American product. As such, it spoke well for American religious efforts.[41] He also distributed books on this side of the Atlantic. He gave his own locally published religious book, titled *Phaenomena quaedam Apocalyptica*, to a church deacon. The man was grateful for the gift and commented that he hoped it would help uplift him. "This day I prayed for it ...," Sewall wrote in his diary, adding that he hoped the book would have a life-altering effect.[42] Soon after, Sewall donated a copy of *Phaenomena* to the library at Harvard College, along with other religious publications that addressed problems plaguing youths at the college — including the sinful practice of swearing.[43] Turning his attention to colonies to the South, Sewall was excited to hear of a Scottish settlement heading for the American Isthmus (now Panama) in 1698. Sewall sent the new colony twelve copies of *Phaenomena*, along with six sermons by a Reverend Noyes, "to welcom them into the New World."[44] The Scotsmen were pleased about the gift; they wrote to Sewall that they enjoyed the "Spirit and Hand of Almighty God" outstretched to them.[45] Encouraged, Sewall sent a copy of *Phaenomena* and other tracts to Nathanael Higginson, a former Massachusetts resident living in Ceylon. Sewall hoped the godly publications would convince Higginson to return to be elected governor of Massachusetts.[46] Apparently, in Sewall's eyes, the tracts indicated the good work of God being performed in Massachusetts. He hoped Higginson would agree. Sewall never doubted that the printed word could carry God's word accurately and convincingly to readers. He, like so many Puritans, was sure that the message in tracts could be understood and imitated.

## COTTON MATHER'S EVANGELISM

The most ardent publisher of Puritan evangelism was Cotton Mather. The idea to use the press to spread God's word came to him early, when he was a young man, in 1683. Someone gave him a book profiling the lives of excellent Christians, one of whom was his own grandfather. "In reading hereof, I would particularly take notice of such passages as rendered other Persons excellent; and vigorously endeavour to follow them," Mather wrote in his diary. The gift made him think about how such books had directed him. Surely they could be of use to other readers. He had an inspiration — an acquaintance who was an old book hawker might be able to "fill this Countrey with devout and useful Books, if I will direct him."[47]

   That idea became a lifelong theme with Mather. He sought diligently to fill the country with "devout and useful Books." Not surprisingly, he exhorted his

---

[41]Journal entry of 4 April 1689 by Sewall in Thomas, ed., *The Diary of Samuel Sewall,* vol. 1, 207.

[42]Journal entry of 5 February 1697/8 by Sewall in ibid., 387.

[43]Journal entry of 16 March 1697/8 by Sewall in ibid., 390.

[44]Journal entry of 20 December 1698 by Sewall in ibid., 401.

[45]William Paterson to John Borland, 18 Feb. 1699, quoted in journal entry of 8 May 1699 by Sewall in ibid., 409. Borland was the agent through whom Sewall sent the books, according to the editor.

[46]Journal entry of 30 June 1699 by Sewall in ibid., 411.

[47]Diary entry of 4 June 1683 by Cotton Mather in *Diary of Cotton Mather,* vol. 1, in *Massachusetts Historical Society Collections,* 7th series, vol. 7 (Boston: Massachusetts Historical Society, 1911), 65. Vol. 2 of the diary is found in vol. 8 of the *Historical Society Collections.*

congregation to read and apply the Bible each day.[48] However, not everyone understood or followed the Bible, and that was when inspired authors needed to step in. When soldiers went to war with Canada in 1690, Mather sent religious tracts to a friend with the hope that a bookseller would reprint them for soldiers to read.[49] In 1700, someone asked Mather to compose a primer for Indian children, and he wrote it so that it included advice against sins young people and Indians were tempted to commit.[50] Seven years later, when he heard that Massachusetts frontier settlers were turning to Catholicism, Mather published a short catechism to teach them a better way. He was so sure that the booklet would counteract the Catholic influence that he had one hundred copies printed and passed out in predominantly Catholic Maryland.[51] To Mather, books were a fine way to spread the word of God. Mather could not be everywhere at once, but books could.

Through books, Mather could also target his sermons to specific audiences. Reading published words was not at all the same experience as attending a sermon, but Mather realized that his potential "congregations" were not always traditional. A traditional church congregation included people from all walks of life, but groups within that congregation might need special help. Sailors needed spiritual encouragement, for instance; so in 1709 he wrote *The Mariners Companion and Counselor,* which was "designed first of all, to awaken the unregenerate Sailour, out of his dangerous Condition, sleeping on the Top of a Mast in the midst of the Sea." He gave copies to naval officers in each port in New England for distribution to sailors. "Who can tell, what may be done?" he bubbled in his diary. "Whether some of the Elect of God may not be found out upon the Waters!"[52] Such targeting of readers continued. There were many widows in Mather's community, so he wrote, preached, and then published a sermon specifically directed to widows. He planned to give a copy to each of them.[53] He also planned to give religious books to poor gentlewomen who were confined to their homes by illness. He thought they might benefit from such material,[54] since they could not attend church. After a 1711 fire destroyed much of Boston, Mather published a book for distribution to all fire victims. It warned that moral decay would result in a demonstration of God's wrath, such as the fire. "It may be very seasonable to lodge these Admonitions with them, while the Sense of their Calamity is yett fresh upon them," he wrote.[55] He had no doubt that sin had caused the fire. Over a year later, sin was flaming through the Southern colonies in the form of "Antinomian Troublers." A pamphlet circulating in the South reportedly advocated licentious behavior, which Puritans associated with Antinomians. Disturbed, Mather sought God's advice on the matter, and he was thereafter inspired to write *Adversus Libertinos* for distribution in the South.

---

[48]Diary entry of 4 May 1686 by Mather in ibid., 127.

[49]Cotton Mather to James Brown, 30 June 1690, in Kenneth Silverman, comp., *Selected Letters of Cotton Mather* (Baton Rouge: Louisiana State University Press, 1971), 27.

[50]Diary entry of 31 January 1699/1700 by Cotton Mather in *Diary of Cotton Mather*, vol. 1, 328.

[51]Diary entry of 13 July 1707 by Mather in ibid., 594-5.

[52]Diary entry of 20 August 1709 by Mather in ibid., vol. 2, 14.

[53]Diary entry of 26 July 1711 by Mather in ibid., 92.

[54]Diary entry of 2 September 1711 by Mather in ibid., 105.

[55]Diary entry of 7 October 1711, by Mather in ibid., 116, 118. The book was Mather, *Advice from Taberah* (Boston: Printed by B. Green, 1711).

Mather was positive that God had directed him to the press to counteract the sinful effects of Antinomianism.[56] Later that year when "knotts of riotous Young Men ... [o]n purpose to insult Piety" came to Mather's window several nights and serenaded him with "profane and filthy Songs," Mather turned to the press again.[57] He tried to counter obnoxious ballads such as the ones they sang by publishing pious poetry. He hoped the publication would cure corrupt minds and manners.[58]

### QUAKER MISSIONS

While Cotton Mather and his fellow Puritans were distributing literature throughout America, so were other sects. The difference, however, was that most other sects imported their religious literature from Europe. As time wore on, writers of various denominations did seek out the American press. But besides Massachusetts' Puritan press, the only other seventeenth-century American press that had a significant religious bent was the Quaker press of Philadelphia.

In the seventeenth century, Quakers were bold evangelicals. They loved peace, but they did not shrink from carrying on a verbal war against antagonists.[59] They set up a press in Philadelphia in 1687, and the formula of competing presses, antagonistic doctrines, and evangelical attitudes was powerful enough to erupt in a war of words with Puritans. Puritans used pamphlets as a weapon against Quakers, and Quakers fought back in kind. Samson Bond, a Puritan minister, published *A Publick Tryal of the Quakers in Barmudas*, in which he headed up a mock "trial" (actually a debate) with Quakers in Bermuda. At the end, he wrote, a panel of listeners declared that he had won. The Quakers were found "guilty" and sentenced to *"Execution* [by] the *Presse"*; that is, publication of a pamphlet against them, which was the very one he was writing.[60] Other Puritan ministers joined in the fray over the years. About 1689, Increase Mather published antiQuaker literature in hopes of counteracting any influence of the sect. Quaker evangelist George Keith replied hotly in a pamphlet that it was *Puritans* who were unChristian. He claimed that the Bible backed him up on that assessment.[61] The charge drew angry counterattacks, again in printed form. Four writers got together to make a reply as an "antidote" to Keith's writings,[62] and Keith then replied with a tract called *The Pretended antidote proved poy-*

---

[56]Diary entry of 28 February 1712/13 by Cotton Mather in Mather, *Diary of Cotton Mather*, vol. 2 (New York: Frederick Ungar, [1957?]), 184. The editor notes that *Adversus Libertinos* was printed by B. Green for Samuel Gerrish in 1713.

[57]Diary entry of 24 June 1713 by Mather in *Diary of Cotton Mather*, vol. 2, Massachusetts Historical Society edition, 216-7.

[58]Diary entry of 27 September 1713 by Mather in ibid., 242.

[59]Contrary to our notion of Quakers in the late twentieth century, seventeenth- and early-eighteenth century nonQuaker sources described Quakers as forceful proselytizers. One writer, for example, commented that "nothing but Controversy" will appeal to Quakers, whom he called "a sharp and Inquisitive People." The anonymous writer is quoted in Edgar Legare Pennington, ed., *Apostle of New Jersey: John Talbot, 1645-1727* (Philadelphia: The Church Historical Society, 1938), 30.

[60]Samson Bond, *A Publick Tryal of the Quakers in Barmudas* (Boston: Printed by Samuel Green, 1682), 50, 75.

[61]George Keith, *The Presbyterian and independent visible churches in New-England and else-where, brought to the test* (Philadelphia: Printed and sold by Will. Bradford, 1689). Keith mentioned Mather's attacks on the title page.

[62]James Allin, Joshua Moodey, Samuel Willard, and Cotton Mather, *The Principles of the Protestant Religion Maintained* (Boston: Printed by Richard Pierce, 1690).

*son.*[63] Puritans were not to be beaten, however. An author of a Puritan children's book disputed the Quaker doctrine of "inner light," or divine inspiration passing to individuals. Puritan writer Pardon Tillinghast published a booklet challenging the same doctrine, and then Cotton Mather published a piece that defended his father for abusing Quakers. Answering all three of the works, Keith wrote *A Refutation of three opposers of truth.*[64] The Quaker Church itself went on the defensive and published *The Christianity of the People commonly Called, Quakers Asserted.*[65]

The Quakers had a feisty champion in George Keith — until Keith suddenly converted to Anglicanism. He turned on Quakers and Anabaptists with rage. He attacked Anabaptists by traveling great distances, distributing books he wrote and printed "mostly att his own Charge & Cost & giving them out freely, which has been very expensive to him," Anglican John Talbot observed in 1703. "By these Means People are much awaken'd, & their Eyes open'd to see the good Old Way and they are very well pleased to find the Church att last take such Care of her Children for it is a sad thing to Consider the years that are past."[66]

Keith knew that Quakers had a stronghold in Jersey, so in that colony he attacked Quaker publications, which Quakers held so dear in winning converts. As Keith described it, he "detected the Quakers errors out of their great Authors, *George Fox* his great Mystery, and *Edward Burroughs* Folio Book, and others...."[67] Keith proceeded to Boston to do battle with his old nemeses, the Puritans, who were Anglican dissenters and thus unsatisfactory to an Anglican missionary. Anglicans in Boston published a Keith sermon against Puritans, igniting a pamphlet war with Increase Mather. Thereafter the Puritans who operated the presses in the colony began refusing works by Church of England writers — but the Anglicans sent material to New York for publication instead.[68]

*WAR FOR SOULS/WAR OF THE PRESS*

Certainly the war for souls in America was a war of sermon, example, and conversation — but it was also a war of the press. Evangelists of many sects saw printing as a tool in helping the word of God linger in people's libraries for years as a refreshment to the soul and a stirrer of faith.

In seventeenth-century America, settlers had practical and spiritual reasons for committing to evangelism. To all European settlers, Christianization of the Indians would tend to subdue the Indian population and also offer the heathen race a chance for salvation. Thus, Europeans were actually acting the role of a spiritual Moses — they were leading a lost people toward a sort-of spiritual

---

[63]George Keith, *The Pretended antidote proved poyson* (Philadelphia: Printed by William Bradford, 1690).

[64]George Keith, *A Refutation of three opposers of truth, by plain Evidence of the holy Scripture* (Philadelphia: Printed and sold by William Bradford, 1690).

[65]Society of Friends, *The Christianity Of the People commonly Called, Quakers Asserted, Against the Unjust Charge of their being No Christians* (Philadelphia: Printed by William Bradford, 1690).

[66]John Talbot to John Chamberlayne, 1 September 1703, in Pennington, ed., *Apostle of New Jersey*, 95.

[67]Journal entry of 3 November 1702 by George Keith, in Keith, *A Journal of Travels from new-Hampshire to Caratuck* (London: Printed by Joseph Downing for Brab. Alyner, 1706), excerpts reprinted in ibid., 173.

[68]The print war is summed up in Pennington, ed., *Apostle of New Jersey*, 25.

Promised Land. Settlers embraced evangelism as an important and God-inspired activity in the New World, portraying it as a way to please God by adding the Indians to His worshippers. Of course, there was other evangelical work to be done in America. There was also a great need for any number of newcomer sects to set up a spiritual bulwark in America, to construct a haven of religious safety and thus allow true religion (however each viewer saw it) to flourish. Evangelical work was a key in that effort, as Americans of various sects attempted to target settlers who needed comfort, edification, conversion, or guidance.

And if evangelism were to be carried out effectively, early Americans reasoned, the printing press must play a role. Time and again evangelists tried to impress Indians or Christians of other faiths with books. Over and over writers turned to the press to give their ideas permanence, so that readers both near and far, both contemporary and future, could read and understand something about religion in the New World.

The Puritans embraced that idea and imported a press less than ten years after Massachusetts was founded — a lightning pace, really, compared to other colonies, which all grew far more established before supporting a press. Why did the Puritans set up a press so quickly? It could be that they simply had a deep love of technology. The historic evidence shows no such interest, however. The interest seems to have been not in the means, but in the end. Printing was a way to achieve great things. Puritans writers indicated that the press held a special place in their effort to be a city on a hill. They had a vision of the press as a mouthpiece for God, speaking to everyone. It can justly be said that one strong reason that the Puritans hastened to establish printing in New England was to help spread true religion. The printing presses of early Massachusetts were mechanical missionaries.

For the first half-century of American printing, the entire colonial American press output was from the Puritans. Then the Quakers set up their own press, and they, too, used it in a war of words to try to battle detractors and to win converts. Other presses would follow, and over time the religious evangelical focus would grow less distinct. All colonies would one day get a press, and much effort would be devoted to religious writings, but to other writings, too.

Although religious evangelism grew less central in America over time, the concept of the press as an evangelist only grew stronger throughout the colonial period. Americans continued to think of the press as having an evangelical aura, a persuasive edge. As the colonial era drew to a close, the press would still practice evangelism — but not of a religious nature. It would evangelize souls to the cause of protest, revolution, and liberty.

The sense that the press had evangelical powers to bring a message, leave a message, and spark imitation of a message, remained paramount in the American concept of the press. The American publishing industry, born in the seventeenth century to help evangelize readers to Christianity, never really gave up its evangelical identity, even though the goals of printed evangelism shifted. The press remained a persuasive tool of whomever was writing and for whatever purpose, much as it had originally been a tool for godly men seeking a more Christian continent. The American publishing industry was born as an evangelist, and so it remained.

2

# Puritans and Freedom of Expression /
## *1638-1690*
## by Julie Hedgepeth Williams

IT WAS AN EXCITING MOMENT in the brand new print shop at Harvard College. On an invigorating day in March of 1638,[1] printer Stephen Daye was at last ready. The types were set for the first time; the press had been freshly inked for its premier performance; and soon Cambridge readers would be holding a crisp, new broadside in their hands. It would be the first item ever printed in English America.

That first printed broadside, titled *The Oath of a Free-man,* explained the rights and duties of citizens in the Puritan haven of Massachusetts. For the New England Puritans who were busy constructing their city on a hill for all the world to see,[2] the oath was a reminder of the ideal relationship between a man and his government.

With the printing of the oath, Americans were forced to begin the long examination of their concept of free expression. Massachusetts Puritans already cherished the printed word, for Protestants everywhere — Puritans included — treasured the right to read the Bible and then to publish their own interpretations of it. Puritans had been persecuted in England for publishing their own ideas, both in manuscript and printed form. One of their great writers in England, John Milton, had argued for a free press so that all ideas might be heard, including ideas of minorities such as the Puritans.[3]

---

[1]Charles Evans' bibliography of American prints was an excellent guide to locating most of the early prints mentioned in this chapter. See Charles Evans, *American Bibliography,* Vol. 1: 1639-1729 (Chicago: Blakely Press, 1903). Evans made comments on some works, noting their fate or their significance. According to Evans, no original copies of Daye's first print survive. Thus, the exact date of publication is unknown, but Evans is sure that Daye printed the work in March of either 1638 or 1639. See Evans entry #1. Extant prints to which Evans refers are preserved on Readex Microprint in Clifford K. Shipton, ed., *Early American Imprints, 1639-1800* (Worcester, Mass.: American Antiquarian Society).

[2]Puritan leader John Winthrop adopted the "city on a hill" phrase from Matthew 5:14 in a lay sermon he delivered aboard the ship *Arabella* while it was still at sea in 1630. See John Winthrop, "A Model of Christian Charity," in Alan Heimert and Andrew Delbanco, eds., *The Puritans in America* (Cambridge, Mass.: Harvard University Press, 1985), 91.

[3]John Milton, *Areopagitica* (London: 1644), reprinted in Merritt Y. Hughes, ed., *John Milton: Complete*

Although the American Puritans would continue to rely on presses in London to publish many of their works, with the establishment of local printing in 1638 they had the means to publish their own religious, educational, civic, and other materials. The fact that printed material had now been brought forth on Massachusetts soil plunged the Puritans of the new colony into the struggle to define free expression. As the printing industry unfolded from Daye's first broadside in 1638 to America's first newspaper in 1690, Massachusetts Puritans sculpted their ideas about what information should be freely expressed and what information should be kept private. As the evidence shows, the Puritans came down strongly in favor of free expression as a means of expressing their religion.

In general, modern people have inherited a negative opinion of the Puritans as strict theocrats who allowed no breathing space, no freedom to think and disagree. Yet, Puritans were the first by nearly fifty years to embrace printing and publishing in America. They welcomed the circulation of ideas via the press. As shown by some of their publications during that early period, the Puritans of Massachusetts Bay believed that they had a right — in fact, a *duty* — to discuss ideas openly, providing those discussions did not blatantly detract from God. As long as they avoided heresy, Puritans enjoyed a lively exchange of ideas on religious and secular topics. Their laws guaranteed such an exchange, and most of their leaders encouraged it. Before 1690, one scholar says, there were only three legal cases published in Massachusetts regarding free expression.[4] That number compares with some 549 works published in Massachusetts from 1638 to 1690.[5] Clearly there were more publications than legal arguments about them; people were apparently free to publish without legal challenge.

As it turned out, Stephen Daye unwittingly set forth the argument to come over freedom of expression as he pressed his types into the rough rag paper to create *The Oath of a Free-man*. Freemen took the oath upon becoming voting members of Massachusetts Bay colony. The oath-taker promised that he would be true and faithful to the government of Massachusetts. The freeman also vowed to "truly endeavour to maintain and preserve all the liberties and priviledges thereof, submitting my self to the wholesome Lawes and Orders made and established by the same. And further, that *I* will not plot or practice any evill against it." The oath went on:

> Moreover, *I* doe solemnly bind my self in the sight of God, that when *I* shal be called to give my voyce touching any such matter of this State, in which Freemen are to deal, *I* will give my vote and suffrage as *I* shall judge in mine own conscience may best conduce and tend to the publike weal of the body, without respect of persons, or favour of any man.[6]

---

*Poems and Major Prose* (Indianapolis, Indiana: Bobbs-Merrill, 1957), 732-3. (Page numbers refer to reprint edition.)

[4]See Wilfred J. Ritz, compiler, *American Judicial Proceedings First Printed Before 1801: An Analytical Bibliography* (Westport, Conn: Greenwood Press, 1984). Ritz's bibliography of all published law cases in America before 1801 lists only eight cases published in Massachusetts before 1690, and three of those relate to free expression. The bibliography includes all non-newspaper writings about court cases, but it is does not mention unpublished cases.

[5]The number is derived from Evans' work, *American Bibliography*. Evans missed some publications in his bibliography, but it is a good indication of approximate numbers.

[6]Massachusetts Bay Colony. *The Oath of a Free-man* (Cambridge: Printed by Stephen Daye, 1638 or 1639). Although the *Oath* does not survive in its original form, a copy does survive. It is quoted here.

Obviously, Massachusetts expected and even encouraged its freemen to give their opinions as they saw fit. The colony counted on those opinions to help build the public good. Massachusetts Bay also valued liberty of conscience and an accompanying liberty of expression, at least in political voting. Clearly, the oath offered a liberal policy toward free expression. And yet, the oath maintained that a man must never do evil against the government. That set up a predicament for freemen who ever wanted to disagree with the government.

But in 1638, disagreement with the government was perhaps less of a problem than disagreement with God. Puritans saw their religion as the very foundation of the Massachusetts colony. They had fled England to worship God in their own way. As the dominant group in Massachusetts Bay, they felt a religious obligation to uphold rightful reverence for God. That fundamental devotion to God, however, did not diminish their political obligations as Englishmen. In fact, the Puritans' understanding of God figured into their concept of their governmental loyalties. They were still citizens of Great Britain and loyal to the king. The king was the defender of the Anglican church, and the Puritans were sure that the church could be reformed by their example.[7] As a result of that Puritan outlook, Massachusetts Bay had an acute awareness of God in its laws, both from English tradition and from Puritan fervor.[8]

That religious intensity shone in the book of Massachusetts laws of 1647. Among other topics, the lawbook addressed free expression, and that expression could not displease God. Any Christian, the law warned, proved his unChristianity if he committed such horrors as interrupting a preacher in church or falsely charging a minister with "any errour which he hath not taught in the open face of the Church." The law warned that any Christian who dared reproach a preacher or in any other way made "Gods wayes contemptible and ridiculous" faced the wrath of the General Court. First-time offenders would be chastised by a magistrate and bound to their good behavior. If caught a second time, the guilty party had to pay a £5 fine or suffer public humiliation. To be humiliated, the offender would stand on a stool four feet high with a paper affixed to his breast announcing he was "AN OPEN AND OBSTINATE CONTEMNER OF GODS HOLY ORDINANCE." Such an embarrassing punishment, the court reasoned, would made sure that "others may fear and be ashamed of breaking into the like wickedness."[9]

None of the offenses as spelled out in the law specifically mentioned speech

---

[7]The Puritans' desire to reform the church is apparent in a number of John Winthrop's writings. See Winthrop, "Reasons to be Considered for...the Intended Plantation in New England" (1629), in Heimert and Delbanco, 71. See also Winthrop, "A Model of Christian Charity," ibid., 89-90, and quotes from Winthrop's personal papers in Loren Baritz, *City on a Hill: A History of Ideas and Myths in America* (New York: John Wiley and Sons, 1964), 13 and 35.

[8]The Puritans' understanding of their loyalty to the king and the importance of both their role and the king's role in defending Christianity was illustrated in a 1661 declaration of the Massachusetts colonists' rights, derived from the original charter that allowed them to settle in the New World. See "The Court's Declaration of their Rights by Charter, in 1661," (1661), reprinted in Thomas Hutchinson, *The History of the Colony and Province of Massachusetts-Bay*, ed. Lawrence Shaw Mayo (Cambridge, Mass.: Harvard University Press, 1936), 439-40.

[9]Massachusetts Bay Colony. *The Book of the General Lauues and Libertyes concerning the Inhabitants of Massachusetts.* (Cambridge: 1648), 19-20. Due to the colonial habit of writing paragraphs upon paragraphs of information into titles, titles of most works mentioned in this chapter have been shortened to their obvious primary title. The material in the passages quoted below are found in the same source on pp. 26, 29, 1-2, 35-6, and 35.

or writing, but obviously, a person would have to use some form of communication in order to be caught breaking the laws. A person who kept ungodlike thoughts to himself would only be discovered by God, not man. But man could and did restrict unholy speech and writing.

To underline that distinction between public speech and private thoughts, the same set of laws spoke to Jesuits, Indians, and Anabaptists, who were not to display their religions publicly. The restrictions were for the colony's survival. The court announced gravely:

> THIS Court taking into consideration the great wars, combustions and divisions which are this day in Europe: ... the same are observed to be raysed and fomented chiefly by the secret underminings, and solicitations of those of the Jesuiticall Order....

Jesuits' ability to speak freely was therefore restricted. Likewise, Indians could not "at any time *powaw*, or performe outward worship to their false gods: or to the devil in any part of our jurisdiction." Disobedient Indians had to pay £5. Anabaptists were also forbidden to display their religion openly. They could not publicly condemn infant baptism or try to persuade people to their point of view. Clearly, Massachusetts defenders of the church were worried about the communication of heretical beliefs to the flock. It is significant that there was no restriction against Indians, Anabaptists, and Jesuits conducting private worship, but the open attempt to convert anyone was a grave sin.

Other restrictions flatly prevented the colonists from breaking the ninth commandment against bearing false witness. Anyone over age fourteen was mature enough to have the understanding of truth and falsity. By law, therefore, teens and adults could never lie, either in voice or in published form. Liars who harmed anyone "with false news or reports" could be fined, put in the stocks, or whipped.

But the lawbook was not a sour list of "thou shalt nots." It also offered some bold protections for free expression. Under 1647 law, every man, whether an inhabitant of Massachusetts or a "Forreiner," whether free or bond, had the right to come to any public court, council, or town meeting. He could either speak his mind or present his views in writing. He could make a motion, complaint, or petition. If he wished, he could just seek information, or he could move any lawful question.

Every legal restriction on free expression in the 1647 laws tied somehow into religion. Men had broad freedom in political expression, but no one had the freedom to condemn God. In the city on a hill, it was only natural that God come first in the writing of the human law. In that spirit, the court had defeated a 1646 petition that called for general religious toleration. The court had cited the petitioners for seditious proposals.[10] But reflecting the notion that man's earthly needs were no solid reason to clamp down on expression, magistrates in 1649 turned down a request that sought licensing of the press in order to eliminate any inconvenience to the commonwealth.[11] Political inconvenience was not a

---

[10]Clyde Augustus Duniway, *The Development of Freedom of the Press in Massachusetts* (New York: Longmans, Green, and Co., 1906), 31.

[11]General Court action, May 1649, in *Massachusetts Archives* (manuscripts in the office of the Secretary

strong enough reason to restrict free expression. That policy would not always be consistent across time, but the Puritans would steadfastly think twice before allowing politics to burden expression. For example, at one point the General Court felt it should excuse an author who opposed the method of electing council members, because his intentions weren't evil. However, the court finally made the author acknowledge his mistake.[12] Another publication criticizing the form of the government made the error of attacking the Christianity of both king and Parliament; for *that* reason, the General Court censored it without a second thought. The court, however, did not seem to be disturbed by the writer's speculations on governmental structure.[13]

Because they were extremely concerned about annoying God in their speech and press, Puritans struggled with the fear that their published words were but a dull substitute for the Almighty. Although the majority of Massachusetts prints were religious tracts, authors continually apologized for putting their ecclesiastical words into print. The Reverend Richard Mather, for one, objected to publishing his 1652 pamphlet, *The Summe of Certain Sermons Upon Genes.: 15.6.* He didn't want to flaunt his knowledge of God. Fellow Christians had begged him to have the piece printed. At first he turned them down, but they begged all the harder. Mather finally considered relenting because his work might glorify God and help God's servants. But printing was far too brash, too intense, too public. Instead the minister made a handwritten copy for the interested brethren, *"with renuall of my former objections against printing"* and told them *"to let the printing alone."* But still they insisted. Mather finally printed the sermon, but only after thorough apology.[14]

Mather's modest objections (which were fairly typical of authors in the era) showed that Puritans considered printing a very public matter for the public's benefit, not a private one for individual glorification. That view of printing reflected the colonists' concept of free expression. An item was most properly expressed in public if it truly would be of help or interest to the public. Expression of ideas via printing was a public matter, a matter of education and enlightenment.

Despite their embarrassment at attempting to put God into print, Puritans felt that printing was a mighty tool for discussion. Religious heresy was the outer boundary of free speech, with Jesuits, Anabaptists, and heathen Indians falling outside the boundary. But within that limit, Massachusettsans enjoyed reading printed argument about religious topics. Every view deserved a hearing, as long as it was not so deviant as to be sinful or heretical. In fact, the Puritans had an extremely liberal outlook about opposition prints. A tract titled *Propositions Concerning the Subjects of Baptism and Consociation of Churches* made a dramatic statement on the importance of free discussion. The court had read over the pamphlet, which detailed the controversial findings of a church synod in 1662. The court said emphatically that it would be folly to tolerate damnable

---

of the Commonwealth), lviiii, II. Quoted in Duniway, ibid., 25.

[12]General Court action, May 1642, *Massachusetts Records*, II, 5, 20, 21. Cited in Duniway, ibid, 29.

[13]General Court action, 22 May 1661, *Massachusetts Records*, IV, pt. ii, 5-6. Quoted in Duniway, *The Development of Freedom of the Press in Massachusetts*, 38-9.

[14]Richard Mather, *The Summe of Certain Sermons upon Genes.: 15.6* (Cambridge: Printed by Samuel Green, 1652), preface. As was customary, the pages of the preface were not numbered. This chapter will cite references from unnumbered prefaces as "preface."

heresies. Aside from that, however, the court was willing to let various factions publish their understanding of religious matters. As long as heretical discussion was not allowed, the court said:

> ... to bear one with another in lesser differences, about matters of a more difficult and controversial nature, and more remote from the Foundation, and wherein the godly-wise are not like-minded, is a Duty necessary to the peace and welfare of Religion.... In such things let not him that practiseth despise him that forbeareth, and lot not him that forbeareth judge him that practiseth, for God hath received him.

The court added hastily that it did not speak of the need to consider both sides because it doubted the truth of the synod's decision.[15] The court felt the synod knew God's will on the matter. But certainly it recognized that someone other than the synod might offer a new light on baptism that would be valuable. After all, as the pamphlet so eloquently put it, free discussion of religion was an actual *duty*.

That call by the court for public discussion in print was not just a one-time fluke. Instead it was a theme. In 1663 *Another Essay for the Investigation of Truth* called for toleration of printed opinions, even those out of the mainstream. The pamphlet offered opinions on baptism that dissented with the synod of 1662. The synod had adopted a proposal that the church baptize children of godly adults who had not attained fully covenanted church membership. The hard-line minority complained that the move watered down church principles.[16] Justifying the minority opinion, the tract's "Apologetical Preface to the Reader" said pointedly that even in the early Christian church, the apostles themselves disagreed with one another. The preface writer added a note on behalf of the dissenters. Pointing out that they were few in number, he asked, "Is *Truth bound up to Number?*" The author also said:

> *Variety of Judgements may stand with* Unity of Affections. He that judgeth a Cause before he hath heard both parties speaking, although he should judge rightly, is not a righteous Judge. *[Thus] We are willing that the World should see what is here presented.*

In fact, the writer said, he had a moral responsibility to make the information public so that he would not accidentally withhold the truth from mankind. The preface insisted that anything might be put before the public for discussion as long as it did not damage peace and the oneness of affection for God.[17]

*Another Essay for the Investigation of Truth* was a sterling call for free expression as an out-and-out obligation of mankind. It is significant that Samuel

---

[15]Synod of Elders and Messengers of Churches in Massachusetts Colony, *Propositions Concerning the Subject of Baptism and Consociation of Churches* (Cambridge: Printed by Samuel Green for Hezekiah Usher, 1662), preface.

[16]John Davenport, *Another Essay for the Investigation of Truth* (Cambridge: Printed by Samuel Green and Marmaduke Johnson, 1663), 9-23. The title page of "Another Essay" is missing. Evans, *American Bibliography*, gives its title. See Evans, *American Bibliography*, entry #78.

[17]Ibid., preface, which was not written by Davenport. The author of the preface was anonymous, although scholars generally think it was Increase Mather, the famous Puritan cleric.

Green and Marmaduke Johnson, printers of the piece, operated the press at Harvard College and thus were in the direct employment of mainstream Puritans.[18] As publishers controlling the press, those mainline Puritans had every chance to suppress the opposition piece, but they allowed it. After all, as the tract explained, suppression might inadvertently mask the truth. The fact that the prominent Reverend Increase Mather sided with the minority in this case[19] proved that perhaps God wished the majority to think hard about the truth. The Puritans, who were quite convinced of their human imperfection,[20] could not, in good conscience, deny honest discussion of religious ideas. They were all too aware that human reasoning, even the majority's reasoning, could be wrong. Thus, they accepted religious discussion, as long as it did not tear apart the church at its most fundamental points.

Truth to tell, *Another Essay* bothered the elders of the church. But they sat quietly, willing to let the other side have its say — for awhile, anyway. Finally, they made their move to continue the argument. They did not squash *Another Essay,* nor did they chastise the pamphlet as blasphemy or heresy. Instead, the elders lumped *Another Essay* together with a tract called *Antisynodalia* for comment and fought them gently with another publication. John Allin, writing for the elders, said:

> When the Antisynodalia of our Brethren came to our hands, and Another Essay of the same nature was here Published, some godly and wise Christians advised the Elders to let them pass in silence; conceiving that they would not so take with the People, as to hinder the Practice of the Doctrine of the Synod: and that a Reply would occasion farther Disputes and Contests. But, upon serious consideration of the matter by divers Elders met to that End, the Reasons on the other side did preponderate.

Allin added that silence would be sinful, for many followers were inquiring about the ideas on baptism expressed in the pamphlets. Likewise, an existing ordinance said that people should consult the Assembly of Elders in disputes, but the practice was not well-established. The elders felt obliged to set a precedent for such behavior by getting into the fray. They also worried that silence on the tracts would ultimately cause enough confusion to allow the Anabaptist sect to convert Puritans.[21] Clearly, the elders who responded to *Another Essay* and *Antisynodalia* had a sense of toleration of other opinions. To them, printing was a fair tool of debate, as opposed to authoritarian ranting and raving that would only cause louder dissent and deeper stubbornness.

---

[18]The first press that the Puritans did not control did not arrive for several more years. Duniway, *The Development of Freedom of the Press in Massachusetts,* gives the timeline on 42 and 47.

[19]Duniway, ibid., 43.

[20]That theme is constant in Puritan writings. Baritz, on p. 5, discusses the Puritans' Synod of Dort in 1618-1619, which outlined the theological point that man is basically corrupt. Individual Puritans such as Michael Wigglesworth constantly berated themselves for their lack of godliness. See journal entries of 23 March and 5 October 1653, March 1654, and 10 January 1656, in Edmund S. Morgan, ed., *The Diary of Michael Wigglesworth, 1653-1657: The Conscience of a Puritan* (New York: Harper and Row, 1946), 14, 49, 81, and 98.

[21]John Allin, *Animadversions Upon the Antisynodalia Americana, A Treatise printed in Old England: in the Name of the Dissenting Brethren* (Cambridge: Printed by Samuel Green and Marmaduke Johnson for Hezekiah Usher, 1664), preface.

A healthy printed debate on the baptism question continued, with the Reverend Jonathan Mitchel publishing a tract in favor of the synod. "How loth we are to enter the Lists of publick Debate with the *Brethren*," he moaned, "and such Brethren as we love and honour in the Lord, with whom we are Exiles in the same Wilderness for the same Truth...."[22] Mitchel's outlook and tone were gentle. Dissenters, he felt, deserved respect, even if he disagreed with them. To Puritans such as Mitchel and the elders in 1664, freedom of expression meant a gentlemanly debate, not a suppression of ideas.

That attitude of toleration on the part of church elders extended to other realms. Even government-appointed licensers of the press tried to be broad-minded. The General Court had finally passed an ordinance for licensing to prevent "irregularitjes & abuse ... by the printing presse" in 1662,[23] an act that mirrored the fact that licensing was in place in England.[24] Reflecting a liberal philosophy, Massachusetts licensers approved the printing of Thomas à Kempis' *The Imitation of Christ* in 1667, in spite of the title's clear indication that the work offered an earthly imitation of the Savior. Kempis even happened to be a Catholic priest. But the licensers allowed it. Ultimately, it was the court that criticized both *The Imitation of Christ* and the licensers. Kempis, the court scoffed, was "a Popish minister." The court ruled that the work "contayned some things that are lease safe to be infused amongst the people of this place," and ordered that the press licensers look over the work more carefully.[25]

The court was exasperated with the licensing system. It did not always work perfectly. A year later the court had to fine printer Marmaduke Johnson £5 for producing a romantic and coarsely-written book about free sex without first getting the approval of the licensers.[26] Johnson must have taken the fine to heart, because shortly after that he printed a straight news account of the eruption of Mount Ætna "by authority."[27] Of course, Johnson was known as something of a scalawag around town; he had a terrible reputation as a romancer not too unlike the featured character in the offensive romance.[28] When Johnson had brought the first private press into Boston, the General Court had been frightened about what

---

[22]Jonathan Mitchel and Elders, *A Defence of the Answer and Argument of the Synod Met at Boston in the Year 1662* (Cambridge: Printed by Samuel Green and Marmaduke Johnson for Hezekiah Usher, 1664), preface.

[23]*Massachusetts Records* IV, pt. ii, 62. Quoted in Duniway, *The Development of Freedom of the Press in Massachusetts*, 41-2.

[24]13 & 14 Charles II, chapter 33. Cited in Duniway, ibid., 45-6.

[25]Thomas à Kempis, *The Imitation of Christ* (Cambridge: Printed by Samuel Green, 1667). Evans gives the work's legal history. See Evans, *American Bibliography*, entry #114.

[26]Henry Nevile, *The Isle of Pines, or a late discovery of a fourth Island in Terra Australis, Incognita, By Henry Cornelius Van Sloetten* (Cambridge: Printed by Marmaduke Johnson, 1668). Nevile's name may actually have been spelled "Neville." The romance is quoted in Felice Flanery Lewis, *Literature, Obscenity, and Law* (Carbondale: Southern Illinois University Press, 1976), 3. The story involved a shipwrecked white man who had a large number of illegitimate children with four women, one of them a Negro slave. Johnson confessed to printing the work in Marmaduke Johnson, "To the honorable Councill of the Commonwealth," September 1668, *Massachusetts Archives*, lviii, 63. Quoted in Duniway, *The Development of Freedom of the Press in Massachusetts*, 52-3.

[27]Earl of UUinchilsea, *A True and Exact Relation of the Late Predigious Earthquake & Eruption of Mount Ætna, or Monte-Gibello* (Cambridge: Printed by Samuel Green and Marmaduke Johnson, 1669).

[28]From Middlesex County, Massachusetts, *Records of the County Court* I (manuscripts in the office of the clerk, Cambridge) and *Massachusetts Records* IV, pt. ii, 93, cited in Duniway, *The Development of Freedom of the Press in Massachusetts*, 44; and Samuel Green, Sr., to John Winthrop, Jr., 6 July 1675, in *Collections of the Massachusetts Historical Society*, 5th series, I (Boston: 1792-1905), 422-4. Cited in Duniway, *Ibid.*, 57 note.

kind of licentious filth he might turn out. The court had reacted by restricting printing to Cambridge and reminding printers of the licensing process.[29] After Johnson had spent a great deal of the court's time promising to be good, the court granted him the right to print in Boston,[30] and it appointed a couple of Boston licensers.[31]

With the court showing discontent over licensing practices, licensers felt obliged to let readers in the colony know exactly what was acceptable for print and what was not. Approving *A Narrative of the Trouble with the Indians* by William Hubbard in 1677, the licensers explained:

> The worthy *Author* of this *Narrative* (of whose Fidelity we are well assured) by his great pains, and industry in collecting and compiling the several Occurrences of this *Indian Warre*, from the Relations of such as were present in the particular Actions, hath faithfully, and truly performed the same, as far as best information agreeing could be obtained, which is therefore judged meet for publick view....[32]

The licensers valued truth and accuracy in printed matter. Proving it did have teeth, the licensing board did check up on Hubbard's reports to ascertain their correctness. As far as the licensers were concerned, their job was quality assurance. Licensing was not a matter of personal favor or arbitrary whim, but almost an editorial function of assuring that a mistaken or lying piece of writing did not find its way into print.

Although the licensing board made it look like any reputable work would be approved, authors found the licensing process distasteful. Hubbard, for one, was afraid colonial governors would censor *A Narrative of the Troubles with the Indians.* He was desperate to have the pamphlet published. He would try anything, even begging and flattery. He implored the governors of Massachusetts, Plymouth, and Connecticut to allow him to print the narrative. Hubbard praised the governors' faithfulness and courage in managing their power and asked them to let the narrative "pass into publick view under the umbrage of your Protection." He assured them everything in the piece was accurate, and he was confident the pamphlet would "meet with a ready Welcome, and suitable entertainment in every honest mind...." In a firm statement for the responsibility of free expression, Hubbard added that he had taken "great care ... to give all and every one, any way concerned in the subject of the discourse, their just due, and nothing more or less...." Although confident his careful reporting technique would be to his benefit, Hubbard did worry that "yet perhaps some critical Leader will not let every sentence pass without some censure or other." However, he was willing to have the authorities' stamp of approval, for it was better to catch any errors before publication. After all, Hubbard pointed out ingratiatingly, a publication

---

[29]General Court action [May?] 1665, *Massachusetts Records*, IV, pt. ii, 141. Quoted in Duniway, *Ibid.*, 48.

[30]Petitions by Marmaduke Johnson, various dates, and answers by the General Court, various dates. *Massachusetts Archives*, lviii, 58, 60, 63, and 91. Quoted in Duniway, *The Development of Freedom of the Press in Massachusetts*, 50-3, 54-6.

[31]General Court action, 1674, *Massachusetts Records*, V, 4. Quoted in Duniway, ibid., 56.

[32]William Hubbard, *A Narrative of the Troubles with the Indians* (Boston: Printed by John Foster, 1677), prefatory statement by the licensers.

was a record to posterity.[33]

Although Hubbard showed that grovelling may have had something to do with acceptance of a work for public printing, he also illustrated the prevailing thought in 1677 about what type of pieces should make it into print. As the licensing process indicated, a literary work had to be truthful and accurate, not only for truth's sake, but also for posterity. As Hubbard pleaded, a news report should also show all sides of the story.

Licensing was accepted in part because Puritans were convinced that the press wielded a tremendous influence. In 1682, Puritan Reverend Samson Bond wanted to attack the Puritans' perennial enemy, the Quakers. Bond had had a debate about Quakerism with some Quakers in Bermuda, and he had (in his eyes, anyway) won. Bond said that his impatient opponents were exposed as unChristian and were "sentenced" to "execution" — that is, to publication of a pamphlet against them, which he wrote himself.[34] Thus, Bond made plain that the Puritan concept of free expression included the right to unearth and humiliate any wrongdoing, especially in the realm of religion. The press was strong enough to "execute" the unChristian.

That attitude was indicative of an advance in Puritan toleration. In 1659, Massachusetts had executed two Quakers for persistent proselytizing in the colony.[35] By 1682, Puritans had come to realize that the press had poison in its ink, available to clever authors. The colony allowed that poisonous ink to flow. It was part of the privilege of having a press. It was also more forgiving than executions. Thanks to their thought on freedom of expression, the Puritans were growing more tolerant.

In 1683, the Anglican governor of Massachusetts, Sir Edmond Andros, revoked the colony's charter. After that, Andros did not have the laws printed, and without a charter or laws to guide them, citizens were in legal limbo. Resentment grew. After five years of pressure, the time was ripe for an opposition political press. Religious dissenters had been tolerated for years. Now, religious leaders called for dissent against the government.

Puritan leader Increase Mather led the way. He complained bitterly in a 1688 pamphlet that "the people are at a great loss to *know what* is *Law and what not.* "[36] As far as Mather was concerned, printing and distribution of certain information such as the law was a basic necessity. Massachusetts residents had long since come to rely on the printing press for the smooth conduct of their everyday affairs. Andros, however, had come to Massachusetts with royal instructions to watch over the press and allow only prints that he approved.[37] In Math-

---

[33]Ibid., Hubbard's "Epistle Dedicatory."

[34]Samson Bond, *A Publick Tryal of the Quakers in Barmudas* (Boston: Printed by Samuel Green, 1682), title page and 50 and 75.

[35]*A Declaration of the General Court of Massachusetts Holden at Boston in New-England, October 18, 1659. Concerning the Execution of Two Quakers* (Cambridge: Printed by Samuel Green,1659). Ritz cites the broadside on p. 159. The publication is no longer extant.

[36]Increase Mather, *A Narrative of the Miseries of New-England, by Reason of an Arbitrary Government Erected there, Under Sir Edmond Andros* (Boston: Printed by Richard Pierce, 1688). This was actually a reprint; the first edition appeared in London, according to *The Andros Tracts, Being a Collection of Pamphlets and Official Papers Issued During the Period Between the Overthrow of the Andros Government and the Establishment of the Second Charter of Massachusetts* I (New York: Burt Franklin, Research and Source Works Series #131, 1868), 5.

[37]Commissions to Massachusetts Governors, *Massachusetts Historical Society Proceedings* (June 1893): 273.

er's eyes, Andros had carried out his instructions in the wrong spirit, with far too many restrictions. The press was meant to help the people. It was not a means of keeping people in the dark.

Mather didn't stop there. Andros, he charged, had tried to clamp down on free speech by prohibiting town meetings except for once a year, when people wanted to meet once a week. "But it is easie to penetrate into the Design of this Law, which was (no Question) to keep them in *every Town* from complaining to *England*, of the Oppression they are under...," Mather said.[38]

In his 1688 *Memorial of the Dissenters,* Mather brought shocking charges against the governor of a Puritan colony. Andros did not allow Massachusettsans to worship as they pleased. "As to matters of religion, [the inhabitants] are inhibited the free exercise thereof, for they are not allowed to set dayes for prayer or Thanksgiving...," Mather reported. Andros had actually "told them that hee should then send souldiers to guard them and their meeting-houses too. The worship of the Church of England has been forced into several of their [Puritan] meeting-houses."[39] Such charges were scandalous in the city on a hill. While religion was the boundary that free expression could not cross in Massachusetts, citizens were now using free expression to demand free religion.

Other Massachusettsans read, repeated, and reprinted Mather's complaints. Gentlemen of the colony published a 1689 tract protesting once again that laws had not been published.[40] A group of colonists took up arms against the governor. Fifteen men then published a broadside addressed to Andros, advising the governor to surrender for his own good. If he didn't conform, the petitioners warned, the people would take the governmental fortifications by storm.[41]

The opposition prints caused a stern reaction from Andros. He needed to come down hard on rampant anti-governmental expression. Late in 1689, his administration issued an order against seditious publications. It thundered:

> WHEREAS many papers have beene lately printed and dispersed tending to the disturbance of the peace and subversion of the government of this theire Majesties Colonie
> ... It is therefore ordered that if any person or persons within this Collony be found guilty of any such like Misdemeanour of printing, publishing or concealing any such like papers or discourses, or not timely discover such things to Authority, ... they shall be accounted enemies to their Majesties present Government and be proceeded against as such with uttermost severity.[42]

The government's threat notwithstanding, dissenters imprisoned Andros. They were not to be thwarted by an unjust governor who denied them their God.

Meanwhile, Increase Mather had gone to England to plead for a new Massachusetts charter. He saw the press as a means to inform the people back home of exactly how their complaints were playing in London. Without such informa-

---

[38]Increase Mather, *A Narrative of the Miseries of New England,* in *Andros Tracts* II, 5.

[39]Increase Mather, "Memorial of Grievances Presented by Increase Mather to James II," part of *Memorial of the Dissenters of New England* (1688), in *Andros Tracts* III, 139, note.

[40]*The Declaration of the Gentlemen, Merchants, and Inhabitants of BOSTON, and the Country Adjacent* (1689), in *Andros Tracts* I, 14.

[41]*At the Town-House in Boston: April 18th, 1689* (Boston: Printed by Samuel Green, 1689).

[42]*Order against seditious publications* (1689), in *Andros Tracts* III, p.107.

tion, rumors were spreading wildly. In 1689 he issued *The Present State of the New-English Affairs.* "This is published," the pamphlet announced dramatically, "to prevent false reports." The press, after all, had a longstanding goal in Massachusetts of spreading truth. *The Present State* proclaimed, among other things, that the king was well pleased with the overthrow of Andros and would have colonists' rights and charter restored.[43]

The Andros affair created much discussion of press freedom. While Massachusettsans had revolted against the government in part for denying them the right to speak freely in both politics and religion, Andros' supporters felt they, too, were denied the right to freedom of expression. In 1690 John Palmer had *An Impartial Account of the State of New England* printed in London as a response to a publication by Mather about the situation in New England. Palmer was disgusted about the attacks on free expression in Massachusetts. He accused:

> There was so much Industry used in New England, by those who had taken upon themselves the Government, that nothing should come abroad which might undeceive the People, already wrought to such a pitch of Credulity, easily to believe the most monstrous Lyes and Follies, that the ensuing Letter could not be Printed without excessive Charge and Trouble; the Press being forbid to any that were injur'd, to justifie themselves, though open to all that would calumniate, and abuse them....

The searing indictment of prevailing Massachusetts press policy went on. Palmer said he had first circulated the now-published piece as a manuscript, which authorities deemed libelous and treasonable. If anyone were caught reading it, he would be severely punished.[44]

Not surprisingly, "John Palmer" was not his real name. He described himself as a maligned citizen who merely wanted to vindicate Andros. Palmer said he had been held ten months in prison without cause in the Andros incident and then was banished to London. He went on the public record *"that the World may see how barbarously we have been used, and most unmercifully dealt withal, by those* Professing People...."[45]

It was a scathing attack. Massachusetts had rarely restricted any but ungodlike speech for fifty-two years, but under pressure of popular hatred of the government, it appeared the operators of the press were restricting access based on politics. Publishers had once tolerated dissenters so that people might better judge the nature of truth, but now it seemed that political dissenters had to resort to the English press.

But Palmer underestimated the liberalism of the Massachusetts press. A few months later his tract was reprinted in Boston under a slightly different title, despite his claim that Boston would never allow it.[46]

---

[43]Increase Mather, *The Present State of the New English Affairs* (Boston: Printed by Samuel Green, 1689), in *Andros Tracts* II, 15-8. Some scholars have thought of *The Present State* as the first newspaper, for it took the form of a newspaper. Although it did contain news, it was apparently not intended to be a periodical.

[44]John Palmer, *An Impartial Account of the State of New England* (London: 1690), preface, in *Andros Tracts* I, 21-4.

[45]Ibid., 24.

[46]Editorial note in *Andros Tracts* I, 23. The notes to the *Andros Tracts* were supplied by W.H. Whitmore.

Perhaps the opposition to Andros helped pry open the attitude toward religious opposition in Massachusetts, because by 1690, even prints attacking the Puritan church were more tolerated. Henry Glover published *Mr. Cotton Mather opposed by a Son of the Church.* Glover brashly took on one of Puritanism's most respected ministers. The Mathers had been church leaders for generations. But unlike so many religious writers before him, Glover did not apologize for attempting to explain the word of God. Instead he said brazenly that Mather had misinterpreted the sacraments. Glover insisted the sacraments had the power to convert the unsaved. Mather thought the opposite.[47]

Likewise, a Boston Anglican had written against the Puritan church in New England, claiming that most Puritans were lax about attending church and were really not interested in being Puritans. Such scandalous words might have brought on the wrath of the council in years past, but by now, Massachusetts thinkers were accustomed to using the public press to fight their wars. Increase Mather lashed back in a piece that was "printed with Allowance." It had some sort of official sanction, although clearly licensers who would allow the opposition piece to get through had long since toned down their degree of control over free expression.[48] Mather's *Vindication of New England* said bluntly that the scandalous opposition print was garbage. He said the piece was "a Libell (A *Lie* because False, and a *Bell* because *Loud), this whole Paper being One Loud *Lie* (sounding from *America* to *Europe*)...." Mather felt that the libelous material was not true, and he offered his opinion that the truth, as explained in his work, would cure the evil work done by libel.[49] By 1690, legal penalties for libel may have been available, but the most obvious cure for libel was now the truth, expressed for all the world to see in print.

Mather emphasized that his antagonism toward libel was not mere prudishness. Libel, he said emphatically, violated the ninth commandment restriction against bearing false witness. He accused the writers of the Anglican tract of making light of the commandment.[50] Mather's statement that libelous speech was fundamentally a denial of God pointed out that Massachusetts society, at its roots, still based its outlook about free expression on God.

The religious texture of New England philosophy explained a renewed restriction on free expression in 1690. In March of that year, the governor and General Court issued a broadside ordering enforcement of existing vice laws. Particularly, the law clamped down on blasphemy, cursing, profane swearing, and lying, as well as gambling and drunkenness.[51]

---

[47]Henry Glover, *Mr. Cotton Mather opposed by a Son of the Church* (Boston: 1690). It is not certain that Glover was the author, and the piece was undated. However, Evans and at least one other bibliographer record the piece as a tract by Glover in 1690. See Evans, *American Bibliography*, entry #510.

[48]Increase Mather, *A Vindication of New England* (1690), in *Andros Tracts* II. According to Evans, *American Bibliography*, entry #542, *A Vindication* was the duplicate of Evans, *American Bibliography*, entry #452. The #452 entry was "printed with Allowance." *Early American Imprints* simply does not repeat the tract at entry #542, instead referring the reader to #452. The *Andros Tracts* version does not include the "printed with Allowance" line. Thus, it may be true that there was no licensing at all on the second version of *A Vindication.* However, the two versions appeared only about two years apart, and it is clear that the Puritans of this time frame were tolerating both "pro" and "con" pieces relating to church, whether the licensing system was firmly in operation or not. *A Vindication* was not signed, but scholars feel that Mather was its author. See Evans, *American Bibliography*, entry #542.

[49]Ibid., 32-3, 43-4.

[50]Ibid., 39.

[51]*By the Governour & General Court of the Colony of Massachusetts Bay* (Boston: 1690).

The act was neither an arbitrary power grab nor a groundless attempt to squelch unpleasant speech. In sad truth, the act was needed because God was punishing the sinning people of Massachusetts. The French had incited repeated Indian attacks against the colony. As if that were not enough, London authorities were renewing their resistance to the negotiations for a new charter. The Massachusetts treasury, meanwhile, was so stressed that the government took the scary step of issuing paper money.[52] Massachusetts governmental officials sincerely attributed those calamities to people's immoral behavior. God was punishing their sins.[53] To cure the problem, the government felt it *had* to clamp down on unholy speech. The action mirrored a restriction against Quakers in the late 1670s; leaders of Massachusetts had considered the growing toleration of Quakers to be a sin that God had punished by sending an Indian war.[54] To the governor and General Court of Massachusetts Bay, the colony's very survival depended on curbing any sin, including deviant speech, which would offend God. It was an old, old theme in Puritan-dominated Massachusetts, but an important and sincerely held one.

A half a year after the renewal of the vice laws, Benjamin Harris issued America's first newspaper, *Publick Occurrences, both Forreign and Domestick.* Harris intended the Boston newspaper to be a monthly,[55] but the governor and council squelched the newspaper after one issue. The council was offended that the newspaper was not licensed. *Publick Occurrences* also offered "Reflections of a very high nature" and "sundry doubtful and uncertain Reports."[56] Cotton Mather recorded that the specific "uncertain Reports" were about the Mohawk Indians and about the French king seducing his daughter-in-law.[57] The Mohawks, who were Massachusetts' allies, suffered harshly in *Publick Occurrences;* Harris called them savages and said the colony was foolish to rely on them too heavily. As for the report from France, the short tidbit was a shocking rumor that the king *"used to lie with [his] Sons Wife."*[58]

Only six months earlier, the government had declared that God had punished sinful speech with Indian wars. Now *Publick Occurrences* had actually printed a rumor on incest in the French royal family, which might be called sinful speech. The newspaper had also derided the colony's Indian allies. Given the fear of sinful expression as shown in March's vice law, perhaps the governor and council were at least partly afraid that *Publick Occurrences* would bring a renewal of God's wrath against sinful expression, because in this case, sinful expression was potentially dangerous.

The problems surrounding *Publick Occurrences* ran deeper than just that one fear; the officials mentioned licensing, for instance, and the Mohawk story criti-

---

[52]The broadside only cited unnamed calamities that had hit Massachusetts, but Hutchinson detailed the numerous Indian attacks, the treasury experiment, and the ongoing charter disputes all happening about that time. See Hutchinson, *The History of the Colony and Province of Massachusetts-Bay,* 335.

[53]*By the Governor & General Court of the Colony of Massachusetts Bay.*

[54]Hutchinson, *The History of the Colony and Province of Massachusetts-Bay,* 270.

[55]*Publick Occurrences, both Forreign and Domestick* (Boston) 25 September 1690 (printed by Richard Pierce).

[56]*By the Governour & Council* (Boston: 1690).

[57]Cotton Mather to John Cotton, 17 October 1690, in Kenneth Silverman, compiler, *Selected Letters of Cotton Mather* (Baton Rouge: Louisiana State University Press, 1971), 27-8. The Mohawks in this era were called "Maquas."

[58]*Publick Occurrences, both Forreign and Domestick,* 25 September 1690.

cized official policy. Other underlying problems existed as well.[59] But it is not unreasonable to believe that the governor and council had a genuine concern that their duty to the colony included suppression of sin, even in a printed newspaper. The law called for it. So did propriety, and so did God.

As is obvious from their prints from 1638 to 1690, the Puritans were not arbitrary oppressors of free speech. Clearly, they believed that public expression was valuable and necessary. They restricted only ungodlike prints or speeches by heretics and blasphemers. Within the boundaries of godlike expression, Puritans encouraged discussion for the better enlightenment of mankind.

The Puritans were human, of course. Their rule that free expression should be a blessing to society occasionally backfired as people such as John Palmer accused them of silencing free speech. But then again, Palmer was supporting a governor whose basis for governing was the squelching of political expression and the silencing of Puritan religious ministry. Thus, the concept of free speech fell back once again on the necessity for free religion, which was the basis upon which Massachusetts was founded.

Many of today's historians, applying today's concepts of free expression to their explanation of the seventeenth-century press, see that Puritans licensed the press and that *Publick Occurrences* disappeared at the hands of the censor after just one issue. In modern terms, licensing and censorship indicate oppression. Thus, historians often jump to the conclusion that Puritans had no interest in free expression.

But that picture of the Puritans is highly flawed. They showed a toleration and encouragement of free speech and free press within certain limits. Those limits were the boundaries that they sincerely felt were imposed by Almighty God, for whom their colony was built. To the Puritans, religion had to be fundamentally protected. So long as free speech did not abridge religion, free expression was both a treasure and a prize, a tool for learning and a means of debate — and, in fact, a valuable way to clarify, sharpen, and purify concepts of religion. The Puritans, who so dearly cherished their religion, were therefore also champions of free expression, for only by free expression could true religion be realized.

---

[59]Wm. David Sloan, "Polemics, Chaos, and America's First Newspaper," *Journalism Quarterly* 70 (1993): 666-81.

# The Origins of the American Newspaper
by Wm. David Sloan

MASSACHUSETTS IN 1690 teetered on the brink of anarchy. The royal government had been overthrown, and the governor thrown into jail. Under his policies, taxes had become onerous; and now taxpayers revolted. "This people are now so very poor," declared an official, "that many profess they have not corn for their families, and those to whom wages are due, cry, that if they have them not, they and their families must starve."[1] Mohawk Indians, who had renewed hostilities two years earlier, destroyed frontier communities. "Sundry plantations easterly, in the province of Maine," the official reported, "are utterly ruined and depopulated."

A provisional government, hoping to impress the new English king, had mounted a military expedition against the Indians and their French allies in Canada, but the expedition was going badly. Its revenue depleted, the government was unable to pay soldiers, and they refused to perform their duties. Amid this chaos, the colonies' agents were in London attempting to negotiate a new charter, and factions had sprung up over the question of what form a new government should take. Compounding the problem, rumors spread, and publications appeared critical of the authorities. It was in this chaotic situation that Benjamin Harris decided to publish America's first newspaper.

*BOSTON*

The town of Boston, the home of the paper, had nurtured the conditions that made the situation ripe for such a venture. Indeed, one of the most evident features of America's earliest journalism was the prominent role of Boston. Not only were the first three newspapers printed there; but of the fifteen American newspapers published in the period ending in 1735, eight — slightly more than

---

[1]Dep. Gov. Thomas Danforth to Sir Henry Ashurst, 1 April 1690, quoted in Thomas Hutchinson (1711-1780), *The History of the Colony and Province of Massachusetts-Bay*, 2 vols. (Cambridge, Mass.: Harvard University Press, 1936), 1: 337n.

half of the total — were in Boston. Why was it so prolific?

The easiest answer – assumed by several historians — is population. Boston was the colonies' largest town in the seventeenth century, with approximately 5,500 inhabitants in 1690, and retained that status until Philadelphia overtook it in the 1750s. Population offered a number of advantages for newspaper publication, including a body of potential readers, cosmopolitanism, businesses needing to advertise, systems such as shipping and postal services for the reception of information, printing establishments and booksellers, and potential writers. By 1700 Boston was shedding its wilderness image and becoming a small model of London. Population alone, however, did not guarantee that a newspaper would appear. New York City, for example, attained a population of 5,000 around the year 1710, but it did not have its first newspaper until 1725 when its population was more than 8,000. Its second newspaper appeared only in 1733, by which time its population had grown to approximately 9,400.

Along with population, the publication of newspapers was related to other particular circumstances. Of special importance were political situations — ones that either provided a supportive climate or were so controversial as to provoke publishers into action. Furthermore, the role of the individual publisher should not be overlooked.

But why did Boston provide opportunities so much more frequently than other towns? The main reason lies in the fact that it was the leading town in the most Puritan colony in North America. As such it had developed a vigorous intellectual environment. No other colony presented a climate that encouraged freedom of inquiry to the extent that Massachusetts did or was so favorable to freedom in printing. Puritans, as compared to their opponents in England and the settlers in other colonies, had created an intellectual environment that encouraged inquisitiveness and free expression. It was from the interest in inquiry and knowledge that they established Harvard College in 1638 and required parents to send their children to schools. Similarly, the first printing presses in the colonies were imported into Massachusetts; and they did a voluminous business, mainly in producing religious tracts but also in publishing political, scientific, and other material as well.[2] In the English-speaking world, by 1700 Boston was second only to London as a center for book publishing and selling. By 1719, when the first colonial newspaper outside Massachusetts appeared, Boston was home to five presses.

The Puritans' intellectual outlook grew directly out of their theology. In migrating to America, Puritans were especially eager to remove themselves as far as possible from Anglicanism, thus gaining the ability to take ecclesiastical and spiritual authority from the central church heirarchy, to emphasize the freedom of the individual believer, and to place church matters in the hands of the local autonomous congregation. Because they emphasized the individual, rather than the established church, as having the authority to interpret God's word, they declared that the individual must be free to inquire and that diversity of views had

---

[2]Increase Mather wrote, for example, "Believe not those that would perswade you that Schools of Learning, Colleges, &c. are Antichristianism, or late Popish Inventions.... Books are Talents in God's service. They are a weariness to the flesh, but a testimony to be produced." Mather, *Some Important Truths*, 1674. Norwood Marion Cole ("The Origin and Development of Town-School Education in Colonial Massachusetts, 1635-1775," Ed.D. dissertation, University of Washington, 1957) concluded that Puritan leaders believed that education was "essential ... for good citizenship and world accomplishment."

to be tolerated.

The foregoing is not intended to argue that Puritans were unwavering libertarians.[3] At times they objected, as other groups did, to opposition printing; and they did not have the same toleration for views, such as Anglicanism and Catholicism, extremely different from their own that they had for disagreements among themselves. For their age, however, they were at the forefront in arguing for the right of the individual to inquire into ideas and to express them freely;[4] and one does not find in Puritan Massachusetts the severity of punishment for offensive printing as elsewhere. When Benjamin Harris, for example, offended the colony's governing council, he was not fined or imprisoned, as he had been in England, but was simply told to desist from publishing.[5]

With, however, the revocation of the colony's charter in 1685, the British monarchy, in effect, expropriated everything that the Puritans had built. The intellectual climate that Puritans had created was altered. The monarchy assumed the authority to appoint the colony's governor, the authority to regulate the press was placed in his hands, and the new charter that was issued in 1691 continued that policy. With the exception of William Phips and William Stoughton, whose administrations covered the period from 1692 to 1697, the appointed governors were Anglicans in religion and Tories in politics. The strongest efforts at repression in Massachusetts, where Anglicans never made up more than one-fifth of the population, came when royal Anglican authorities controlled the government. Actions to prosecute for publishing offenses increased. Increase Mather, for example, was being hunted by the government of Edmund Andros when he escaped to England to serve as Massachusetts' agent in 1688; and his son Cotton faced a variety of legal proceedings for his writings.

The government philosophy of restriction collided, however, with the tradition of expression that the Puritans had established. Authorities never were completely successful at preventing critical publications. Pamphlets abounded, written by both Puritans and their Anglican opponents. The idea that one should be free to publish spilled over into politics. Thus, Massachusetts, which had the most dynamic political situation in the colonies, had spawned a vibrant printing atmosphere by the early 1700s.

## THE RELIGIOUS HERITAGE

One cannot account for America's earliest newspapers without a recognition that religion was the key ingredient. Indeed, throughout the whole history of colonial Massachusetts, religion played a chief, perhaps even the central role. One of the most distinctive features was an ongoing struggle between Puritans and Anglicans, centering on the issue of the freedom of the individual believer and the local congregation versus the authority of the church. In that debate, Puritans' ef-

---

[3]Clyde Augustus Duniway, whose *The Development of Freedom of the Press in Massachusetts* (New York: Longmans, Green, 1906) is the most detailed study on the subject, takes the ideological view that Puritans were intolerant. One is tempted to conclude, however, that he neglects the statements Puritans made supportive of freedom and exaggerates those that can be read as suppressive.

[4]Cotton Mather, for example, wrote, "No man may be Persecuted, because he is Conscienciously not of the same Religious Opinion, with those that are uppermost." (*Theopolis Americana* [Boston, 1692], 29.)

[5]Walter Franklin Terris found that Puritans never inflicted punishment that exceeded that allowed by the common law. Terris, "The Right to Speak: Massachusetts, 1628-1685" (Ph.D. dissertation, Northwestern University, 1962).

forts were aimed at establishing local autonomy, while the Church of England aimed its energies at exerting its control. Anglicans argued that authority rested ultimately with the British monarch, exercised through the crown-appointed Archbishop of Canterbury.

Massachusetts Puritans had managed to keep their religious freedom by aggressively opposing the efforts of the Church of England and the English monarchy to establish Episcopacy in the colony. The Puritans' efforts had the effect of helping to assure both political and religious independence in Massachusetts. In defending their religious freedom, Puritans, it is true, did attack Anglicanism energetically, but still they permitted the Anglicans and members of other minority churches to practice their faith. Anglicans' efforts, on the other hand, were aimed at officially establishing the Church of England and displacing Puritanism. In those colonies where Anglicanism was established, it worked toward conformity in both religion and politics and toward a joining of the two. In New Hampshire, for example, Governor Cranfield wrote to England to propose "that it will be absolutely necessary to admit no person into any place of trust, but such as will take the sacrament and are conformable to the rites of the Church of England." Opposing clergy and views had to be quieted. "I utterly despair," Cranfield added, "of any true duty and obedience paid to his Majesty until their college be suppressed and their ministers silenced."[6]

Owing largely to popular opposition and to the ministers' talents, Puritans successfully resisted the intrusions of Anglicanism throughout most of the seventeenth century. Massachusetts, and particularly the town of Boston, remained safe from Anglican threats until the colony was made a royal province and on May 16, 1686, a ship brought Joseph Dudley to be president of Massachusetts, New Hampshire, and Maine. Arriving on the same passage was the Rev. Robert Ratcliffe to conduct Episcopal services in Boston — the equivalent, Puritans believed, of worshipping Baal.[7] The Puritan leaders refused the Anglican churchmen's request that one of the local church buildings be made available for Anglican services. The issue was soon forced with the arrival of Edmund Andros as royal governor of New England and his order that a Puritan church be turned over for Anglican use.

Shortly thereafter, the Anglicans began construction of their own building, King's Chapel, "the Church of England as by law established." Inspired by that success, Edmund Randolph, one of the royal commissioners and a devout Anglican, proposed to King James that the costs of supporting the church and its minister be paid by the Puritan congregations.[8] It was as if being allowed to exist conferred on Anglicans special status. The Puritans unremittingly opposed that attitude.[9]

---

[6]Quoted in George Hodges, "The Episcopalians," in *The Religious History of New England*, 213.

[7]Expressing, for example, the Puritans' common abhorrence of Anglicanism, Cotton Mather wrote in his diary in November of that year: "The Common-Prayer-Worship [is] being sett up in this Country. I would procure and assist the Publication of a Discourse written by my Father, that shall enlighten the *rising Generation*, in the *Unlawfulness* of that Worship, and antidote them against Apostasy from the Principles of our First Settlement." 11 November 1686, *Diary of Cotton Mather*.

[8]"I humbly represent to your Grace," he wrote, "that the three meeting houses [Puritan churches] in Boston might pay twenty shillings a week a piece, out of their contributions, towards defraying our Church charges." Hutchinson, *Collections*, 549.

[9]In Randolph's earlier proposal to the Puritans themselves, they had rebuffed him. "They tell us," he explained to the king, "those that hire him [the Anglican minister] must maintain him, as they maintain their

With the founding of King's Chapel, its members at once became energetic in the attempts to establish Anglicanism in Massachusetts. Their view was that the colonies were possessions of Britain and were therefore subject to that government in all matters civil and religious. Since the Anglican church was the official church of England, it therefore automatically was the established church in England's colonies. They were at the forefront of efforts to tie church matters to political ones and thus gain success.

## AMERICA'S FIRST NEWSPAPER

The founding of America's first newspaper, Harris' *Publick Occurrences*, was the upshot of the strong religious and political influences that had been at work in English life for the past century and in Massachusetts since the founding of the colony. The political chaos that confronted the colony in 1690 was instrumental in both the newspaper's founding and its suppression. Playing active roles in its brief life and death were some of the most important personalities in the colonies. They included, among others, Increase Mather's son Cotton, a supporter of the newspaper; and the Mathers' adversary, council member Elisha Cooke. The key player, however, was Harris. Although he was influenced greatly by strong religious motivations, the newspaper's suppression was not, as some historians have implied, the handiwork of Massachusetts' Puritan clergy. On the contrary, the government's action was motivated in part by efforts of an energetic faction opposed to the leading clergyman, Increase Mather. Nor was it a simple matter of a defiant journalist being silenced as he tried to strike a blow for freedom of the press.[10]

With conditions growing more chaotic daily in 1690, the provisional governing council found itself helpless to control the situation. Officials proposed a variety of remedies, ranging from warning people not to make false reports to asking the British crown to take over the government. Harris, a confident Bostonian experienced in London journalism, decided a newspaper was needed and conferred with a few knowledgeable townspeople. He was especially concerned that the newspaper carry nothing but accurate reports. Meeting the young Puritan cleric Cotton Mather on the street, he obtained from him suggestions on how to prepare a detailed account of the military expedition into Canada. Despite Harris' good intentions, the governing council suppressed the paper almost imme-

---

own minister, by contributions." Hutchinson, *Collections*, 549.

[10]The most familiar assumptions — nearly all inaccurate — about the suppression of *Publick Occurrences* come mainly from general survey histories. George Henry Payne, for example, characterized Harris as a bold advocate of "humanity and progress" who opposed the "authorities" and "was an exceptional figure in the fight for a free press." Cotton Mather, Payne declared, "cried out against" *Publick Occurrences*. (*History of Journalism in the United States* [New York: D. Appleton and Company, 1920], 21, 22, 12, and 30.) Frank Luther Mott described Harris as a publisher who "presumptuously ... defied the ... government" in a colony that was a "Puritan theocracy." (*American Journalism* [New York: Macmillan, 1941], 9 and 18.) More recently Edwin and Michael Emery have described Harris as a "troublemaker" with "progressive views" and declared that "the Puritan clergy was scandalized" by the contents of *Publick Occurrences*. They equate the clergy with the "licensers" of the press. (*The Press and America* 5th ed. [Englewood Cliffs, N.J.: Prentice-Hall, 1984], 28, 29, and 30.) Sidney Kobre, in *The Development of the Colonial Newspaper* (Pittsburgh: Colonial Press, 1944), wrote that the "ruling governmental officials and the Puritan clergy did not like the tone" of the contents of *Publick Occurrences* (p. 16). For a fuller account of the life and death of the paper, see Wm. David Sloan, "Chaos, Polemics, and America's First Newspaper," *Journalism Quarterly* 70 (1993): 666-81.

diately after publication. Thus this first American newspaper, titled *Publick Occurrences, Both Forreign and Domestick*, lasted but one issue, prohibited for a variety of reasons.

Harris was a man of deeply held beliefs and determined action, and his experiences in the fierce British political battles of the 1670s and '80s had prepared him particularly well for his career in America. Born in London, he was an ardent Anabaptist in religion and Whig in politics.[11] He set up as a printer and bookseller in London in 1673 and immediately rose to prominence with publication of the tract *War with the Devil* by the bold Anabaptist preacher and anti-Catholic Benjamin Keach. He soon became the leading printer and publicist for the Anabaptist cause. Even more than most Anabaptists, he was embroiled in politics. Although based fundamentally on religious tenets, Anabaptism became involved in the political arena because of its radical beliefs in the authority of the individual (rather than church leaders) in spiritual matters and the total separation of church and state.[12] In these matters of faith, Anabaptists found themselves not only in opposition to Roman Catholicism but to the Church of England as well.

Harris was bold in presenting these dissident views — "a brisk Assertor of English Liberties," a fellow publisher called him.[13] In politics, he supported the Earl of Shaftesbury and the Whig parliament in their opposition to King Charles II, and he was ardent in advocating the efforts of the parliament to exclude the Duke of York (James II), Charles' Catholic brother, from succession to the throne.[14]

Because of his vigorous and visible support of the Whig and dissident Protestant side,[15] the Tory/Anglican authorities made him a continuing target for prosecution. Between 1680 and 1683 they proceeded against him three times and imprisoned him twice.[16] Despite the legal difficulties, he continued to sell books and pamphlets on the superiority of Protestantism to Catholicism and on

---

[11]Harris is the subject of a number of brief, mainly encyclopedic biographies. They generally tend to be critical of him because of his strong anti-Catholic views.

[12]Anabaptism was a complicated movement with a variety of adherents who held to various beliefs. Most of them, however, had a combination of both social and religious concerns. In his Anabaptism, Benjamin Harris' was violently anti-Catholic and gave particular emphasis to the role of faith in political affairs, where he was a staunch Whig and advocate of parliamentary rule.

[13]John Dunton, *The Life and Errors of John Dunton* (1705, printed for S. Malthus, London; reprint ed., New York: Garland Publishing, 1974), 293. In a letter to George Larkin, Dunton added that Harris' works, including the *Book of English Liberties* and the *Protestant Tutor*, had met strong opposition. The latter, Dunton declared, was "not at all relished by the Popish party, because it is the design of that little book to bring up children in an aversion to Popery." Dunton to Larkin, 25 March 1686, *Letters from New England* (1687), quoted in George Emery Littlefield, *Early Boston Booksellers, 1642-1711* (New York: 1900; reprint ed., New York: Burt Franklin, 1969), 148. Harris spoke of himself as being "vigorous" in arguing for his side. (*Intelligence Domestick and Foreign* [London], 14 May 1695.)

[14]At the height of the struggle between Charles and the Whigs, Harris, at Shaftesbury's urging, in July of 1679 began publication of the first Whig newspaper, *Domestick Intelligence.*

[15]"Dissident Protestant" is a term that refers to Protestant churches opposed to the Church of England.

[16]His trials are recorded in *A Compleat Collection of State Trials*, 2 vols. (London: 1719), 2: 476-8, 560; *Protestant [Domestick] Intelligence*, 20 January 1680; *London Gazette*, 5-9 February 1680; Nathaniel Thompson's Tory *Domestick Intelligence*, 27 January and 7 February 1680; W. H. Hart, *Index Expurgatorius Anglicanus* (London, 1872), 206-8; Narcissus Luttrell, *A Brief Historical Relation of State Affairs*, 2 vols. (Oxford, 1857), 1: 34-6; Dunton, *Life and Errors* , 294; *Calendar of State Papers, Domestic Series, of the Reign of Charles II, 1660-1685*, Mary Anne Everett Greene, ed. [London: Longman, 1860], 1679-1680: p. 397; *Moderate Intelligencer* (London), 23 October 1682; andHenry Muddiman (the leading Tory publisher), newsletter, 7 August 1683, quoted in J. G. Muddiman's critical "Benjamin Harris, the First American Journalist," *Notes and Queries*, part II, 27 August 1932, 150.

English liberties. With, however, the defeat in 1685 of the Duke of Monmouth, whose rights to the throne Harris had advocated, he fled England, probably with the purpose of escaping retribution for his support of the rebellion and publication of a book titled *English Liberties*.[17]

Harris sailed first to Holland in 1685 and then to the Puritan refuge of Massachusetts in the fall of 1686. Boston was the North American colonies' largest city, the home to 5,000 inhabitants, and one of only two towns with its own printing trade, the other being Cambridge, site of the press at the Puritan Harvard College. In Boston, Harris entered printing and bookselling, his familiar occupations. He soon had a prosperous business going, issuing in December of 1686 the first of a series of annual almanacs. Part of his motivation was simply to make a living. There was, however, more behind his work than mere occupation, for much of it was distinctive for its emphasis on political and dissident Protestant works.

Because of his publishing experience and his capacity for supporting the Whig/Protestant cause, Harris was able to exercise a visible public role. Through his publishing activities, soon after arriving in Boston he became acquainted with the activist Puritan leadership and helped advocate their political goal of autonomy for Massachusetts. He was on speaking terms with Cotton Mather, the Puritan cleric, for whom he printed several volumes. Mather also assisted him in compiling material for publications.[18]

Harris' escape from the authority of the British crown was, however, short-lived. In 1684 Charles II had revoked the Massachusetts charter, and in 1686 James II appointed the staunch Anglican and Tory Sir Edmund Andros as governor of the colony. Andros arrived in Boston in December 1686, bringing with him a communication from the king that "[w]e do here will and require and command that ... all persons ... especially [those] as shall be conformable to the rites of the Church of England be particularly countenanced and encouraged."[19] The new governor immediately demanded that Anglicans be allowed the use of the Old South Church building, but the Puritan ministers would agree only to permit the use of the Town House. Andros would not willingly submit to this affront to his faith, and in March, on Good Friday, of the following year commanded that the South Church be opened. On Easter Sunday, the Anglicans took the building for their service and did not vacate it for the church's Puritan congregation until after 2 p.m.[20] Finally, the two sides reached an understanding

---

[17]After returning to England in 1695, Harris gave this explanation of his reasons for leaving: "[U]pon all occasions I vigorously asserted the Laws and Liberties of England against the bold and open violators of both; which procured me so many and inveterate enemies that, to save my life and family from ruin, I was compell'd to be an exile from my native country...." (*Intelligence Domestick and Foreign*, 14 May 1695). John Dunton gave this explanation: "Old England is now so uneasie a Place for honest Men, that those that can will seek out for another Countrey: And this I suppose is the Case of Mr. Benjamin Harris and the two Mr. Hows.... Mr. Ben Harris, you know, has been a noted Publick Man in England, and I think the Book of English Liberties that you [George Larkin] Printed, was done for him and Mr. How. No wonder then that in this Reign they meet with Enemies...." Dunton to Larkin, 25 March 1686, *Letters from New England* (1687), quoted in Littlefield, *Early Boston Booksellers*, 144.

[18]Mather's contribution to *Publick Occurrences* is discussed later. He also is believed to have provided material for Harris' most famous publication, *The New England Primer*.

[19]Massachusetts Historical Society, *Collections* 3: 7 and 148.

[20]The diarist Sewall recorded, "'Twas a sad sight to see how full the street was with people gazing and moving to and fro, because they had not entrance into the house." (29 March 1687, *The Diary of Samuel Sewall, 1674-1729*, M. Halsey Thomas, ed. [New York: Farrar, Straus and Giroux, 1973], 136.)

by which the Puritans offered one of their churches for use of Anglican services on Sunday afternoons. Throughout Andros' brief administration, Harris supported the Puritan side and acted as a public opponent of Andros.

Andros' power to oppress Puritan Massachusetts lasted only briefly. James II was overthrown in 1688 in the Glorious Revolution, and shortly thereafter colonists seized Andros and confined him and several other officials to jail. Increase Mather and other dissenting clergy were suspected of being the main instigators of the revolt.[21] Revolting against a crown-appointed governor raised great possible danger, and Harris was one of few supporters of the rebellion not afraid of letting his stance be known. While most, such as the "council of safety" that assumed formal control of the political situation, took steps to protect themselves, he published a pamphlet favorably detailing the revolution.[22] He then supported Increase Mather in the debate over his attempts to negotiate a new charter for Massachusetts.

Following the overthrow of Andros, the colony began to sink into a period of anarchy. The council that had been elected in 1686 reassumed office, but it was ineffectual in bringing order to the situation. Under this interim government and while Massachusetts was waiting for a new charter, internal order began to disintegrate.

It was in this political situation that on September 25, 1690, Harris published the first issue of what he intended to be a periodic newspaper, naming it *Publick Occurrences, Both Forreign and Domestick.* His primary purpose was to provide a medium that the public could rely on for accurate information amidst chaotic conditions. He also intended to use the paper to speak out on issues.

The internal disorder that Massachusetts was facing was of utmost concern to Harris. Political stability in the colony was breaking down, factions had arisen, and the chaos fed a variety of rumors, many of them false. Harris hoped that *Publick Occurrences* could serve as an antidote. In his statement of purpose at the head of the first column on page one, he went to considerable lengths to emphasize his concern that reports be accurate. He would take, he explained to readers, "*what pains he can to obtain a* Faithful Relation *of all such things; and will particularly make himself beholden to such Persons in* Boston *whom he knows to have been for their own use the diligent Observers of such matters.*" Furthermore, he declared, he would make a point of exposing falsehoods. He hoped that *Publick Occurrences* might serve as a cure for the "Spirit of Lying, *which prevails among us.*" To that end, he promised that "*nothing shall be entered, but what we have reason to believe is true, repairing to the best fountains for our Information. And when there appears any* material mistake *in any thing that is collected, it shall be corrected in the next.*" He would attempt, he promised, to expose in print anyone found guilty of maliciously providing false information for publication in the paper.[23]

As for providing news, Harris stated that the purpose of *Publick Occurrences*

---

[21]Edward Randolph to Boards of Trade, 5 September 1689, *Calendar of State Papers, Colonial Series. America and West Indies* (London), 13: #407.

[22]Harris shortly afterwards published a pamphlet favorably detailing the revolution: "An Account of the Late Revolutions in New-England by A.B." Boston: 1689. Reprinted in *The Andros Tracts: Being a Collection of Pamphlets and Official Papers* ..., 6 vols. (Boston: Prince Society, 1868-1874), 6: 189-201.

[23]This and the following quotations are taken from *Publick Occurrences.*

was to furnish "the Countrey ... once a month (or if any Glut of Occurrences happen, oftener,) with an Account of such considerable things as have arrived unto our Notice," so that "Memorable Occurrents of Divine Providence may not be neglected or forgotten, as they too often are." In carrying out that plan, Harris filled the pages of the newspaper with domestic reports of such items as Christianized Indians planning a "day of Thanksgiving to God for his Mercy in supplying their extream and pinching Necessities," the abduction of two children by Indians, a recently widowed man hanging himself, the status of a smallpox epidemic that was then on the decline in Boston, and the damages caused by a local fire. He devoted the greatest amount of space to the expedition of a Massachusetts militia against the French and their Indian allies in Canada.

Despite Harris' evident efforts to assure that the reports he included were accurate, the governing authorities moved to suppress the newspaper almost immediately upon publication. Some reacted negatively as soon as they saw it,[24] and only four days after *Publick Occurrences* appeared the governing council issued an order forbidding Harris to continue publication.[25]

The reasons for the suppression of *Publick Occurrences* were complex. One thing is clear, though. The suppression had nothing to do with the opposition of the Puritan clergy, as some historians have argued. In fact, the council membership, rather than being under the clergy's control, represented a diversity of interests and of political and religious views. Cotton Mather opposed the council's action, claiming that some of its members had used the *Publick Occurrences* issue to attack him by implying that he was responsible for the newspaper's publication. Harris and Mather were acquainted well enough that Harris relied on Mather for advice in producing some of the contents. Mather praised the paper as "a very Noble, useful, & Laudable Design." In discussing the suppression of *Publick Occurrences*, he declared that council members — instead of trying to make him "odious" — instead "might do well to endeavour themselves to do something that may render them worthy to bee accounted *Serviceable*, before they discourage such Honest men, as those [responsible for *Publick Occurrences*]."[26] He did not specify why certain councilors were opposed to him, but evidence points to the dispute involving Increase Mather's efforts to negotiate a new charter for the colony. Although a number of the councilors, most of whom were judges, were close friends of the Mather family, others formed an opposing faction that believed staunchly that the old charter should be restored. The negotiations that Increase Mather, Elisha Cooke, and two other agents were conducting in England for a new charter formed the burning issue in Massachusetts in 1690. Cooke, the most politically active member of the council, was a vocal advocate of keeping the old charter in unaltered form; and when he found Mather and the other agents prepared to agree to a new charter, he refused to continue to work with them. The new charter altered or eliminated several items from the old one. Cooke blamed Mather for what he considered to be a number of shortcomings of the new charter, and he was joined by a consider-

[24]Samuel Sewall, a member of the council, recorded on 25 September objections to the newspaper. *The Diary of Samuel Sewall*, 267.

[25]"*Whereas Some have lately presumed to Print and Disperse a Pamphlet ... Without the least Privity or Countenance of Authority ...* Boston, September 29th. 1690."

[26]Mather to John Cotton, 17 October 1690, in Victor Hugo Paltsits, "New Light on 'Publick Occurrences': America's First Newspaper," *American Antiquarian Society* (April 1949): 87-8.

able body of sympathizers. Indicating how deep his opposition to Mather ran, he later was at the forefront of efforts to remove Mather from the presidency of Harvard.[27]

Whatever their personal allegiances, the council members were men of diverse views; and each one likely had his own particular reasons for voting for or against suppressing *Publick Occurrences*. No such thing as unanimity or perfect harmony existed. The cause of the demise of *Publick Occurrences* was not, it is clear, opposition from the Puritan clergy, but a combination of factors working in the political environment. The *Publick Occurrences* episode offers evidence that religious commitment was a strong ingredient in the mix. Contrary to general assumptions, however, the Puritan clergy were on the side of America's first newspaper as it opposed Royal authority. They had comparatively little interest in restricting or suppressing newspaper expression.

## THE BOSTON NEWS-LETTER

Following the suppression of *Publick Occurrences*, it was fourteen years before anyone attempted to published another colonial newspaper. Like the first, the second also had Boston as its home. Unlike *Publick Occurrences*, though, it was tied closely to the royal governorship.

One of the goals of Boston's Anglicans was to get a governor appointed who was an adherent of the Church of England and therefore would assist in the establishment efforts of the church. As one of the first official acts of King's Chapel, its minister, the Rev. Samuel Myles, and the church wardens petitioned the crown, who "has bin graciously pleased to have particular regard to the religion of the Church of England," to appoint a new colonial governor and council so that the Church might "grow up and flourish, and bring fruites of religion and loyalty, to the honour of Almighty God, and the promotion and increase of Your Majesty...."[28] Their hopes were satisfied with the appointment of Joseph Dudley, the Puritans' old nemesis, as governor.

Dudley was the son of Thomas, one of the most respected of the first generation of Massachusetts settlers. The younger Dudley, however, had been suspect ever since his mission as colonial agent to England in 1682. Having placed his own interests above those of the colonists, he returned to tell them that they must submit to the monarchy. In 1685 James II named him governor of New England in the interim before Andros assumed the position. Under Andros, he served as chief justice of the superior court and acted as overseer of the press. Along with Andros he was imprisoned by Bostonians during the 1689 rebellion. Appointed governor of Massachusetts in 1702, he adhered uncompromisingly to a doctrine of submission to royal prerogative and, having converted to the Anglican church, to episcopal authority. His duty of enforcing unpopular British laws combined with the enmities created during his first administration to make him the most disliked man in Massachusetts. He was, Cotton Mather

---

[27]*Calendar of State Papers, America and West Indies*, Vol. 14: 23 March 1693.

[28]"The humble Address of Your Majesty's most loyal and dutiful Subjects of the Church of England in Boston...," quoted in Henry Wilder Foote, *Annals of King's Chapel*, 2 vols. (Boston: Little, Brown, and Company, 1896), 1: 102.

declared, a "wretch."[29]

It was under him that Boston acquired its first continuing newspaper, published by the Anglican John Campbell. He began the paper, the *Boston News-Letter*, without any conception of its being a true newspaper or of exercising any publishing independence. Producing a quasi-official report in the form of a newspaper was, he believed, one of the responsibilities required by his position as postmaster. He thus looked on himself not as an energetic editor but as an official conduit of information and on the newspaper as a formal, chronological record of news items. Tied so plainly to the unpopular Dudley administration, he never gained the confidence of the populace, and he found that his life as a publisher was an ongoing, tiresome struggle for mere existence.

The situation, difficult as it was, grew worse in 1718. Campbell was replaced with another postmaster, William Brooker. Campbell's philosophy about operating the *News-Letter* as if it were an official journal led his successor to assume that the newspaper was a part of the postmaster's position. When Campbell refused to give the paper to Brooker, the latter began a new newspaper, the *Boston Gazette*, in late 1719.

*JOHN CHECKLEY*

Because of their moderation, neither the *News-Letter* nor the *Gazette* could satisfy the combative High Church faction in King's Chapel, and it was that small group's dissatisfaction that provided the motive for a third newspaper, the *New-England Courant*. It brought the differences between radical Anglicanism and Boston Puritanism to a head. Ever since the founding of King's Chapel, its members had hoped Anglicanism would be established as the official church in Massachusetts. Thus, one finds continual contention between the Boston Anglicans and their Puritan neighbors' efforts to restrain them. Since Anglicans were greatly outnumbered and their presumptions and practices held in contempt by most of the populace, they had found it necessary to act with a degree of prudence. When John Checkley burst onto the scene, however, they gained a zealous spokesman who did not shrink from controversy but relished it. Seeking a forum from which he could attack Puritanism, in 1721 he decided upon the tack of founding the *Courant*.

Checkley was Boston's leading voice for the most extreme positions of the High Church party in the Anglican Church. That faction believed that the Anglican Church was the only legitimate church and that there was no salvation outside of it. Staunchly Tory in politics, the High Churchers tended to tie religion to state. Checkley himself still held to the view that kings ruled by divine right and subjects must be passively obedient — although that notion had been outdated in England since the Glorious Revolution. While other Boston Anglicans shared Checkley's dogma, they were circumspect in making their beliefs known. Checkley, in contrast, declared them fiercely.

He began the polemics in 1719 when he published a tract by the Charles Leslie, with the implication that Puritans were as misguided in their religious faith as were deists. In that and other tracts published over the next few years, he declared that ecclesiastical authority rested in bishops; that Puritans were "Car-

---

[29]*Diary of Cotton Mather*, 16 June 1702.

nal Libertines" and Christianity's enemies; that "the Church of England, and NO OTHER, is established" in New England; that sacraments, ordinances, and baptisms administered by dissenting clergy, specifically Boston's Puritan clergy, were a "Sacrilege, and Rebellion against Christ"; and that any Puritan parent having a child baptized by the Puritan clergy was "guilty of the blood of [the] child."[30]

Checkley's arguments were so strident that they created dissension in his own church and animosity from without. While some Anglicans wished he would desist, a High Church faction coalesced around him. Although small in number, its aggressive members dominated the affairs of King's Chapel for awhile.[31] It was this faction that served as the original group of writers for the *New-England Courant*. By 1721, as Checkley's attacks intensified, the contention between that faction and Puritan leaders had taken on the nature of a personal feud between Checkley and Cotton Mather. Possessing the best mind and most articulate pen in the colonies, Mather had been especially vigilant in opposing Anglican maneuvers. He therefore became the prime target for the High Churchers.

*THE INOCULATION CONTROVERSY*

The unpopularity of their theological views with the general populace had prevented the Anglican advocates from making much headway in their efforts to advance the Church of England. A plague that entered Boston in 1721, however, gave the High Church faction an opportunity to attack Mather and his fellow Puritan clergymen in a way that, on the surface, seemed unrelated to Anglicanism. Although members of the faction used religious doctrine for part of their assault, their arguments were not framed in Anglican theology, and for the most part they never rose above personalized invective. Their intent, though, was to persecute Mather and the Puritan clergy in order to destroy their popularity. It was all part of a strategy to establish the Anglican Church on the ruins of Puritanism. Having failed to carry the theological argument in their earlier encounters, they now resorted to vilification based on the Puritan clergymen's unpopular advocacy of inoculation for smallpox.

In the early 1700s in Europe and America, more deaths resulted from smallpox than from any other cause. The mortality and the loathsome nature of the disease made it the most dreaded. Boston itself had experienced six outbreaks be-

---

[30]"The Religion of Jesus Christ the only True Religion; or, A Short and Easie METHOD with the DEISTS, Wherein the Certainty Of The Christian Religion Is demonstrated by Infallible Proof from FOUR RULES, which are Incompatible to any Imposture that ever yet has been, or that can possibly be...." Boston: Printed by Thomas Fleet, 1719; "Choice Dialogues Between A Godly Minister and an Honest Country Man Concerning Election and Predestination." Boston: 1720; "Modest Proof of the Order & Government Settled by Christ and his Apostles in the Church." Boston: 1723. "A Defence of ... A Modest Proof." Boston: 1724; "A DISCOURSE Shewing Who is a true Pastor of the Church of Christ," and "The Speech of Mr. John Checkley upon his Tryal at Boston, in New England, for publishing the Short and Easy Method with the Deists, etc." London: 1730. Clergy who had not been ordained by proper bishopic authority, Checkley declared, acted as a "vile Prostitution" of the true priesthood of Christ. They "outdid the wickedness of [the Jews] in persecuting" the apostles. "[E]very Tag, Rag, and Long-tail call themselves [Christ's] Ambassadors by a call from the People! Good God! — Good God! — How has the Priesthood been vilify'd of late!"Appendix to Charles Leslie, "A Short and Easie Method...." (8th ed.). Boston and London: 1723.

[31]Dr. William Douglass to Cadwallader Colden, 13 February 1728 and 18 March 1728, in Massachusetts Historical Society, *Collections* 2: 179 and 182.

fore 1721, with the epidemic of 1677-1678 taking the lives of 700 residents, 12 per cent of the population. In April 1721, smallpox again entered Boston. By June it was out of control. Hundreds of residents fled the town, and of those who remained virtually every household experienced the contagion. By September the number of deaths was so great that the selectmen limited the length of time that funeral bells could toll. By the time it had receded the following year, 6,000 of Boston's 10,500 residents had contracted the disease, and more than 800 had died.

Soon after authorities learned of the presence of smallpox, Mather — who had learned of the experimental method of inoculation from reading accounts in the journal *Philosophical Transactions* and from his African slave — proposed to Boston's physicians that they attempt the procedure. Only one of the ten physicians, Dr. Zabdiel Boylston, a neighbor of Mather, agreed to try the procedure.

The other physicians, along with the public, responded ferociously. Injecting a disease into a healthy person seemed to most laymen, and to most physicians also, not only a ludicrous strategy but hazardous as well. Mather, however, had not foreseen how intense the public reaction would be; and he had not expected that his Anglican adversaries would take advantage of his goodwill to unleash a withering and prolonged attack on him. This being the first attempt at immunology in the English-speaking world, word quickly spread around the little town of Boston, already in hysteria because of the pervasive danger of smallpox, that Boylston was deliberately spreading the disease. The populace was furious at both Boylston and Mather.[32] The public case against inoculation was led by the physicians,[33] with William Douglass at the forefront, and it gained government support through the selectmen. Whether the opponents and the proponents divided along religious lines is unclear,[34] but it is notable that none of the seven most visible advocates of inoculation was Anglican.[35] A number of the prominent opponents, including Douglass, were members of King's Chapel.

It was Douglass' sense of superiority to Boston's other physicians that led him to attack Boylston publicly, thus starting the newspaper war over inocula-

---

[32]"The Destroyer," Mather recorded in his diary for 16 July, "being enraged at the Proposal of any Thing, that may rescue the Lives of our poor People from him, has taken a strange Possession of the People on this Occasion. They rave, they rail, they blaspheme; they talk not only like Ideots but also like Franticks, And not only the Physician who began the Experiment, but I also am an Object of their Fury; their furious Obloquies and Invectives." 16 July 1721, *Diary of Cotton Mather*. There is no record of exactly what proportion of the population was opposed to his effort; but only about 240 of Boston's 10,500 residents received inoculation, and the strength of the opposition suggests that it was a substantial majority.

[33]Mather wrote that "our unhappy physicians ... poisoned and bewitched our people with a blind rage." Mather to Hans Sloane, 10 March 1722, in Kenneth Silverman, comp., *Selected Letters of Cotton Mather* [Baton Rouge: Louisiana State University Press, 1971], 347. He wrote in 1724 that the physicians played "the part of butchers or tools for the destroyer to our perishing people, and with envious and horrid insinuations infuriated the world against [Boylston]." Mather to Dr. James Jurin, 15 December 1724, in Silverman, *Selected Letters of Cotton Mather*, 402.

[34]Later, after the epidemic had abated, Cotton Mather wrote Dr. James Jurin of the Royal Society of London that the opposition had been contrived by a "political or ecclesiastical" party whose main purpose was to discredit the Puritan clergy. "It is with the utmost indignation," he wrote, "that some have sometimes beheld the practise made a mere party business, and a Jacobite, or High-flying party, counting themselves bound in duty to their party to decry it, or perhaps the party disaffected unto such and such persons of public station and merit, under the obligations of a party to decline it." 21 May 1723, in Silverman, *Selected Letters of Cotton Mather*, 361.

[35]Dr. Boylston was a member of Brattle Street Church, and the others were all clergymen in dissenting Protestant churches. Along with Increase and Cotton Mather, they were Benjamin Colman and his associate pastor William Cooper of Brattle Street Church, Thomas Prince of Old South Church, and John Webb of New North Church.

tion. In a letter to the *Boston News-Letter*, signed with the pseudonym "W. Philanthropos," Douglass called Dr. Boylston a "Cutter for the Stone," a "quack," "Ignorant," and "unfit" and challenged his professional competence in administering inoculations. He argued that using inoculation was theologically wrong, for it attempted to place the cure of a disease in man's ability rather than leaving it in God's providence.[36] The proponents of inoculation responded to the attack with a letter of their own to the *Boston Gazette*. Written mostly by Benjamin Colman, Boylston's pastor, but signed by inoculation's other five clerical supporters, the letter defended Boylston as a skilled and tender physician, criticized Douglass' conceit, called for more charity than Douglass' letter exhibited, and refuted his religious argument against inoculation.[37] Throughout the following months of the controversy, the High Churchers frequently repeated the argument that inoculation violated man's requirement to depend on God,[38] thus paradoxically requiring the faithful clergy to defend medical science from theological attacks.

## THE NEW-ENGLAND COURANT

Conditions were ripe for the Anglican opposition to found a newspaper. The *New-England Courant* began publication on August 7. The key figure was Checkley, who was supported by a group of affluent Anglicans, all members of the High Church party in King's Chapel, including Douglass. Checkley originated the idea and approached Douglass about it. After they had laid the plans, they arranged with James Franklin to print it and recruited their fellow High Churchmen into the enterprise.[39]

The lead article on page one of the two pages was an essay Checkley wrote introducing himself as the "Author" of the paper and lampooning the Puritan clergy for their advocacy of inoculation. The remainder of the front page was filled with an essay by Douglass arguing against inoculation, which included personal attacks on Dr. Boylston and the clergy, "Six Gentlemen of Piety and Learning, profoundly ignorant of the Matter."[40] The focus on anti-inoculation was made clear in the August 21 issue, in which Checkley wrote that the "chief

---

[36]*Boston News-Letter*, 24 July 1721.

[37]*Boston Gazette*, 31 July 1721.

[38]See, for example, William Cooper, *A Letter to a Friend in the Country, Attempting a Solution to the Scruples & Objections of a Conscientious or Religious Nature, Commonly Made against the New Way of Receiving the Small-Pox.* Boston: 1721.

[39]It quickly became clear in the small town of Boston, where such things were easy to discover, who the operators were. Two weeks following the appearance of the *Courant*, a letter published in the *News-Letter* lamented that "what likewise troubles us is, That it goes Currant among the People, that the Practitioners of Physick in Boston, who exert themselves in discovering the Evil of Inoculation and its Tendencies (several of whom we know to be Gentlemen by Birth, Learning, Education, Probity and good Manners that abhors any ill Action) are said, esteem'd and reputed to be the Authors of that Flagicious and wicked paper." *Boston News-Letter*, 21 August 1721. Checkley referred to himself as author of the newspaper. Judging from printing arrangements for pamphlets and other publications of the time, the arrangement provided either for Checkley to pay Franklin for the printing or for Franklin to print the *Courant* at his own expense and retain whatever income he could derive through copy sales and advertising. Considering that Franklin continued to print the newspaper after Checkley's departure, it appears likely that the second arrangement was the one he and Checkley entered into. Wm. David Sloan, "The New-England Courant: Voice of Anglicanism," provides more information on the operations of the newspaper. (*American Journalism* 7 [1991]: 108-41).

[40]*New-England Courant*, 7 August 1721. The authorship of articles in the first forty-three issues of the *Courant* is indicated in Benjamin Franklin's marked files.

design of the *New-England Courant* is to oppose the doubtful and dangerous practice of inoculating the small pox."

Douglass' motive in starting the *Courant* was, likewise, to fight inoculation and attack Mather. He opposed inoculation for a variety of reasons, ranging from his belief that it was an unsound medical procedure and interfered with God's providential working in human affairs to the fact that he was irritated at Mather for having used information about inoculation from copies of *Philosophical Transactions* borrowed from Douglass. The latter therefore believed he had a proprietary right to the work.[41] Furthermore, he was angry at Mather for presuming to offer advice in the field of medicine, Douglass' domain.[42]

The underlying implication of the *Courant's* content was that the Puritan clergy could not be trusted.[43] With the clergy's stature eroded, a void might be created that the Anglican church could fill. In his writings in the *Courant*, Checkley avoided his normal strident Anglican theology and instead emphasized ridicule of the Puritan leaders, apparently hoping to diminish their standing with the public. Abrasive in his style, he upset even the Anglicans when in the third issue of the *Courant* he called the Rev. Thomas Walter, Cotton Mather's nephew, an "obscene and fuddling Merry-Andrew" and accused him of drunkenness and debauchery.[44]

Along with Douglass and Checkley, the other main figures in the founding of the *Courant* were two physicians in King's Chapel, George Steward and John Gibbins, both members of the High Church party and close associates of Checkley.[45] These two wrote all essays in the first three issues of the *Courant* not authored by Douglass or Checkley. Steward's contribution to the *Courant* criticized inoculation on the grounds that reports from Turkey indicated unfavorable reactions to the procedure; that inoculation, while it might benefit some people, resulted in some deaths; and that Boylston inoculated in a way that resulted in the inoculees' spreading the disease to other people. He charged Boylston and the Puritan clergy of violating the Sixth Commandment against murder.[46] Gibbins' writing, on the other hand, dealt solely in personal attacks. His major contribution was an assault in the third issue on Cotton Mather's nephew, Thomas Walter. He repeated a rumor that Walter drank excessively, although he claimed in different parts of his essay that the drink was rum, wine, cider, and dram.[47]

---

[41]Douglass, "Inoculation of the Small-Pox as practised in Boston...." Boston: 1722; *Boston News-Letter*, 17 July 1721; Douglass to Cadwallader Colden, 20 February 1722, Massachusetts Historical Society, *Collections*, 4th series, 2: 164. Benjamin Colman, pastor of Brattle Street Church, later claimed that some physicians opposed inoculation "because it would have saved the Town Thousands of pounds that is now in their pockets." Douglass himself, explaining to a colleague in the medical field why he had not had time to record his medical observations, wrote that he found it "more natural to begin by reducing my smallpox accounts into bills and notes for the improvment of my purse." Quoted in Kenneth Silverman, *The Life and Times of Cotton Mather* (New York: Harper & Row, Publishers, 1984), 345.

[42]In a letter to a medical colleague in England, he referred contemptuously to "a certain credulous Preacher of this place called Mather ... [who] preached up Inoculation." (Douglass to Dr. Alexander Stuart, 24 September 1721, Royal Society, quoted in Otho T. Beall Jr. and Richard H. Shryock, *Cotton Mather: First Significant Figure in American Medicine* [Baltimore: The Johns Hopkins Press, 1954], 112).

[43]The *Courant*, wrote a grandson of Increase Mather, was "written on purpose to destroy the Religion of the Country." (*Boston Gazette*, 8 January 1722. This letter frequently has been attributed to fifteen-year-old Mather Byles, but it more likely was written by his older cousin Samuel Mather.)

[44]*New-England Courant*, 21 August 1721.

[45]Rev. Thomas Harward to Bishop of London, 19 July 1731, in Foote, *Annals of King's Chapel*, 414.

[46]*New-England Courant*, 14 August and 11 December 1721.

[47]*New-England Courant*, 21 August 1721.

Having converted from Congregationalism to Anglicanism, Gibbins exhibited the marks of someone who simply wanted to attack the ministers of his former faith and had no goal of helping advance any useful discussion.

Following Gibbins' and Checkley's two-pronged attack on Walter, uneasiness about the direction the *Courant* was taking intensified. The pastors of King's Chapel were disturbed. Checkley, they thought, had gone overboard. The rector, perhaps with the support of the church's other members who produced the *Courant*, directed him to desist from such writings and "reprove[d]" Franklin for printing them.[48] Thereafter, Checkley dropped his association with the paper, refusing even to subscribe to it.[49]

In order to continue publishing the newspaper, King's Chapel's assistant rector, the Reverand Henry Harris, took over writing duties for the issue of August 28. More moderate than the High Churchmen, he showed more civility than Checkley. Still, his essay, which filled most of the non-news space in the paper, argued that it was a religious duty and a requirement of the Sixth Commandment that inoculators avoid spreading smallpox deliberately.[50]

After the *Courant's* fourth issue, the newspaper passed out of the hands of its original operators. Without Checkley's leadership, the High Churchmen Steward and Gibbins apparently had no burning desire to continue with the paper. Douglass was more interested in his medical practice than in producing a newspaper each week, and the Rev. Harris' Anglican passion was not hot enough to induce him to continue the project. Steward, Douglass, and Harris would write other articles, but no longer were they involved in operating the paper. With the fifth issue, that duty passed into the hands of printer James Franklin, and the responsibility for providing the content was taken up by a "Mr. Gardner."[51]

Despite the change in management, the *Courant's* content did not change significantly. Members of King's Chapel continued to have a dominant hand in writing its content.[52] Although claiming to be neutral on inoculation and

---

[48]James Franklin, recounting the episode, in *New-England Courant*, 27 November 1721.

[49]*New-England Courant*, 15 January 1722. Checkley's Puritan opponents, however, continued to believe for some time that he directed the *Courant*, as shown by a letter from Mather Byles, a grandson of Increase Mather, published in the 8 January 1722 issue of the *Boston Gazette*. Checkley, although no longer writing for the *Courant*, increased his other activities aimed at promoting the Anglican cause and, as one of his critics declared, "with an uncharitable and bitter Zeal contend[ed] for the Episcopal Pre-eminence" (Edward Wigglesworth, *Sober Remarks on a Book late reprinted at Boston, Entituled "A Modest Proof of the Order and Government settled by Christ and his Apostles in the Church."* Boston: 1724). Almost incessantly contentious, he provoked his opponents inside and outside the Anglican church.

[50]*New-England Courant*, 28 August 1721.

[51]Historians have disagreed about the identity of Gardner.

[52]All but three of the paper's contributors can be identified as Anglicans. Of the ten writers who, along with the original High Church group, contributed to the paper between the fourth and forty-third issues, six can be identified as members of King's Chapel, one can be identified as an Anglican and therefore a probable member of King's Chapel, one ("Mr. Gardner") cannot be identified, and one writer perhaps was not an Anglican, although he was a friend of the Reverand Henry Harris. The other writer was sixteen-year-old Benjamin Franklin, whose first "Silence Dogood" essay was printed in the issue of 2 April 1722. Since he was an apprentice in James' shop, religious motives may have been irrelevant to his desire to write for the *Courant*. Eliminating his articles and those by Gardner, one can calculate that about nine-tenths of the remainder were written by people who can be identified as members of King's Chapel. Along with Gardner and James and Benjamin Franklin, the writers were the following: Matthew Adams, a member of King's Chapel; Thomas Fleet, the printer for King's Chapel and member of the church; Thomas Lane, a member of and generous contributor to King's Chapel; John Williams, a member of King's Chapel and proprietor of a "tobacco-cellar"; John Eyre, a member of King's Chapel whose parents had been members of the Old South Church; John Valentine, a leading lawyer in Boston and a warden at King's Chapel; and Capt. Christopher Taylor, whose church membership is unknown but who owned the rental housing where Harris lived.

"promis[ing] that nothing for the future shall be inserted, anyways reflecting on the Clergy ... and nothing but what is innocently Diverting,"[53] the newspaper still opposed inoculation,[54] fought Puritanism, attacked opponents with ridicule, used theological grounds as a basis for much of the attack, and attempted satire. The opposition clergy continued to believe that the *Courant's* "main intention ... [was] to Vilify and abuse the best Men we have, and especially the principal Ministers of Religion in the Country,"[55] with Cotton Mather believing the purpose was to "lessen and blacken the Ministers of the Town, and render their Ministry ineffectual."[56]

That the *Courant* should continue a strong Anglican tenor under Franklin is not surprising. A devout Christian, he was a member of King's Chapel.[57] Nevertheless, he was not in the social or intellectual circle of the High Churchers who ran the *Courant*. Having gained his printing knowledge through an apprenticeship, he was not as well educated as they. Young (twenty-five years old in 1721) and struggling in his printing business, neither did he possess their social standing. His younger brother, Benjamin — admittedly biased because of the treatment he received as James' apprentice — described him as demeaning, envious, passionate, and hot-headed.[58] His writing in the *Courant* was prone to be petty and capricious, often revealing him sulking over criticism he received from people he had first attacked. The clearest personality that emerges is that of an immature, rash young man unable to handle the criticism and pressure that his own actions provoked.

The *Courant's* targets responded in several ways. Friends of the Puritan clergymen and Dr. Boylston defended them. The most devastating charge they made was that the *Courant's* writers were the equivalent of the sacrilegious and infamous Hell-Fire Club of England,[59] and the *Courant's* writers went to great lengths to refute the charge.[60] For the most part, the pro-inoculators were more restrained than the *Courant* writers. Since the key public issue in the contro-

---

[53]*New-England Courant*, 4 September 1721.

[54]Of all items, approximately fifty in number, related to inoculation that the *Courant* published by the end of 1721, only one, a report from London, was slightly favorable toward the practice.

[55]*Boston Gazette*, 15 January 1722. The author probably was Mather Byles, nephew of Cotton Mather.

[56]9 December 1721, *Diary of Cotton Mather*. Typical of the religious ridicule was James Franklin's "Essay against Hypocrites" in the issue of 14 January 1723. The only notable change in the *Courant's* content after the fourth issue was more occasional publication of essays on public and private manners. A favorite topic was relationships between spouses. The *Courant* also published a considerable number of attacks on Philip Musgrave, who in 1720 had taken the printing contract for the *Boston Gazette* from James Franklin and given it to Samuel Kneeland.

[57]When challenged for the *Courant's* attacks on the Puritan clergy, he responded that he was confident of his own salvation. "I expect and Hope to appear before God," he declared, "with safety in the Righteousness of Christ." (*New-England Courant*, 29 January 1722.) In responding to a charge that he used the *Courant* to "Banter and Abuse the Ministers of God," he asserted that "*My own pastors* are as faithful to their Flock as [Cotton Mather] can be to his" (italics added for emphasis). (*New-England Courant*, 27 November 1721.) King's Chapel records contain this account of funds donated for improvements: "A List of the Well disposed Gentlemen and other Persons that Contributed their assistance for the Building a Gallery, a New Pulpit, and adorning the Kings Chappel in Boston, and the Paving before it in the Year 1718." The list includes "J: Franklyn," who along with "Capt. Richd. Quick" made a contribution of £10. (King's Chapel records, reprinted in Foote, *Annals of King's Chapel*, 265.)

[58]Benjamin Franklin, *Autobiography* (New York: Modern Library, 1944), 24-5.

[59]*Boston News-Letter*, 21 August 1721.

[60]There is no evidence to suggest, as some historians have claimed, that the *Courant* writers accepted the name as a badge of pride. To the contrary, the *Courant's* response indicates that the charge was unsettling to them. See, for example, *New-England Courant*, 28 August 1721 and 15 January 1722.

versy was inoculation, they argued for the efficacy of the practice, relying more on medical knowledge and facts. They produced a number of pamphlets and newspaper articles attempting to show the evidence in support of inoculation. In the long run, their argument worked because of the demonstrated success of the practice. Especially effective was their use of mortality figures. Dr. Boylston reported that he had inoculated 242 patients, of whom six died.[61] The fatality rate for inoculees was 2.5 per cent, whereas among people who contracted the disease naturally, the rate was 14.8 per cent.

Another ingredient in the pro-inoculators' ultimate victory was their demonstrated concern for those who contracted smallpox. At the height of the epidemic, when scores were dying weekly and the *Courant* was running satire on women's fashions, the clergy were visiting the sick, providing the poor with firewood for the winter, trying their best to comfort them and their families, and in their visits facing the possibility of contracting a disease themselves.[62]

With the end of the smallpox epidemic, the *New-England Courant* lost the public issue that had provided the immediate cause for its founding. Although the public did not immediately change its views on inoculation, Mather and Boylston soon were to be widely recognized for their achievements, the first in preventive medicine in the English-speaking world. By contrast, the *Courant's* opposition to the practice made its writers look credulous and reactionary. Thereafter, it resorted to petty personal attacks on Mather and other Puritan clergy. Its original High Church group no longer wrote for the paper, but theological differences with Puritanism continued to provide material for its group of newer contributors. Although promising readers to be bright and entertaining, it continued to publish only for four years after the smallpox epidemic ended, outlived by both the *Boston Gazette* and *News-Letter*.

The main reason for the *Courant's* quick death was the unpopularity of Anglicanism in Boston. Even though the inoculation hysteria for a time had led to outrage against the clergy, Puritanism remained the faith of the vast majority of the populace. The continuing arguments of Anglicanism's most belligerent advocates, that no other church had any validity, annoyed rather than persuaded. Because of that narrow view, combined with the Anglican church's ties to the British monarchy, Anglicanism made itself repugnant to most Massachusetts inhabitants.[63] Although the *Courant* stayed away from arguing the unpopular dogma of Anglican preeminence, it did take positions that Anglican authorities held. One, for example, was the large amount of space it devoted in late 1722 to the defection to Anglicanism of the Congregational administrators of Yale College. In a town as overwhelmingly Puritan as Boston was, the *Courant's* position was far from popular.

The *Courant* also suffered when its methods were contrasted with those of its opponents. The *Courant's* writers and its critics described the paper in many ways, but one word they did not use was "moderation." With an avowed purpose of "expos[ing] the Vices and Follies" of people with whom it disagreed,

---

[61]Zabdiel Boylston, *Historical Account*, 50, in John B. Blake, "The Inoculation Controversy in Boston: 1721-1722," *New England Quarterly* 25: 4 (1952): 496-7.

[62] For examples, see *Diary of Cotton Mather*, 26 and 29 September; 7, 8, 14, 15, and 16 October 1721.

[63]Of the eleven Boston churches in 1721, seven were Congregational and one was Anglican. The other three were Anabaptist, Quaker, and Huguenot.

the paper was unlikely to set an example of propriety. The objects of its darts, on the other hand, while sometimes responding in kind, tried to resist meanness and pettiness. Cotton Mather, as the most obvious example of their temperate approach, left in his diary frequent reminders to himself to "Exercise ... a forgiving Spirit."[64] In the passion of the smallpox epidemic, some newspaper readers may have welcomed the *Courant's* language, but in calmer times they recognized the superior value of the opponents' moderation.

Likewise, the genuine concern that Mather and other pro-inoculators showed for those suffering with smallpox spotlighted the *Couranteers'* egocentered and querulous nature. While the *Courant* published lampoons, the clergy were working with the sick and the poor.[65] The due regard Bostonians had for Mather's benevolence was attested to best, in terms of the *Courant*, when Benjamin Franklin near the end of his life told Mather's son, "I have always set a greater value on the character of a *doer of good*, than on any other kind of reputation; and if I have been, as you seem to think, a useful citizen, the public owes the advantage of it to that book [Mather's *Bonifacius*]."[66]

With his benevolence, Mather combined the best mind in colonial America. The *Courant's* aspersions, made during the inoculation controversy, that he was naive and ill-informed did not hold up in calmer times. His was the first colonial work to gain wide recognition in Europe. Upon his death in 1728, he was eulogized as the most learned mind and the most prolific writer the colonies had produced.

A large share of the blame for the death of the *Courant* can be placed, however, directly on the paper's operators. There is no reason to assume that Bostonians in the 1720s liked scurrility or awkward style any more than readers do today. The entire tenor of the *Courant* was off-key for it to be a popular or respected newspaper.[67] In the *Courant's* early issues, essays and news items each

---

[64]Although the main target of the town's anger and the *Courant's* sarcasm, Mather was cautious about using intemperate language. When he succumbed to the human desire to retort publicly, he usually chided himself. Even as the *Courant's* contumely was most vicious at the height of the smallpox epidemic, he wrote, "I must beware, that I don't harbour or admitt, any Tendency towards the least Wish of Evil, unto such as may have displeased me.... I must beware, that upon the Provocations ... my Speeches be not intemperate and unadvised, or any Ebullitions of Impatience; and Trespasses upon the Rules of Meekness and Wisdome. I must beware, that I don't spread any false Reports." 3 December 1721, *Diary of Cotton Mather*. For similar statements during the same period, see diary entries of 29 October, 3 and 12 November, 3, 17, and 24 December 1721; and 14 and 17 January 1722.)

[65]Writing of Dr. Boylston almost three years after the epidemic, Mather observed that "When the rest of our doctors ... with horrid insinuations infuriated the world against him, this worthy man had the courage and conscience to enter upon the practise [of inoculation]; and ... he alone, with the blessing of Heaven, saved the lives of I think several hundreds.... With an admirable patience he slighted the allatrations of a self-destroying people, and the satisfaction of having done good unto mankind made him a noble compensation for all the trouble he met withal." Mather to Dr. James Jurin, 15 December 1724, in Silverman, *Selected Letters of Cotton Mather* 2: 402. In a similar tone, he wrote the same correspondent: "[W]e that cry with a loud voice to them, *Do yourselves no harm*, and show them how to keep themselves from the paths of the destroyer, are conscious of nothing but of a pity for mankind under the rebukes of God ... a desire to have our neighbors *do well*, and a solicitude for a better state of the world. And all the obloquies and outrages we suffer for our charity, we shall entertain as persecutions for a good cause, which will not want its recompenses." Mather to Jurin, 21 May 1723, in Silverman, *Selected Letters of Cotton Mather* 2: 367.

[66]Quoted in Ronald W. Clark, *Benjamin Franklin: A Biography* (New York: Random House, 1983), 19.

[67]In his autobiography, Benjamin Franklin recalled that the High Church group of writers for the *Courant* said their compositions were received with "approbation" (p. 23). Several considerations related to their reports make it virtually impossible to verify or refute their accuracy. It may be that during the inoculation controversy a considerable number of members of the public agreed with the *Courant's* approach, or that the *Couranteers* repeated comments from selected readers. On the other hand, it also is possible that Cotton Mather's later comment was true that anti-inoculators were of such disreputable character that some people

occupied about half of its space. The essays either attacked opponents, especially the Puritan clergy, or commented on contemporary behavior, such as male-female relationships. Some attacks were simply heavy-handed and direct, while others attempted to use satire for their ridicule.[68] Most of the essays come across as sarcastic, gratuitously insulting, unsophisticated in style, dull, and devoid of wit. In addressing issues, they tended to ignore facts and concentrate on minor points that opponents raised. Over time they decreased in number and finally disappeared, leaving the *Courant* as a compiler, like its competitors, of brief news items.

The characteristic that finally doomed the *Courant* perhaps was its own pretentiousness and hypocrisy, the exact features it condemned in the Puritan clergy. It opposed inoculation because the clergy favored it. Rather than consider the arguments for and against the practice out of a concern for saving lives from smallpox, it was more eager to attack. While hundreds of Boston residents were dying, it went on with its satire, its abusiveness, and its self-centeredness. Then, as the final paradox, it decried the clergy's sanctimony in berating other people's sins.

Benjamin Franklin provided evidence that the general public was getting annoyed with the *Courant* when it was less than a year and a half old. After the government ordered James to stop printing the newspaper because of his criticism of officials' slowness in pursuing pirates, he substituted Benjamin's name as printer beginning in the issue of February 4, 1723. Benjamin's salutary address began: "Long has the press groaned in bringing forth an hateful brood of pamphlets, malicious scribbles and billingsgate-ribaldry." He described the new operator as having morals that were "clearly Christian" and as a "man of good temper, courteous Deportment, sound judgment, a mortal Hater of Nonsense, Foppery, Formality, and Endless Ceremony."

Benjamin Franklin, who wrote the youthful series of "Silence Dogood" letters for the *Courant*, remained with the paper only a short time until he seized the opportunity to escape his apprenticeship and fled Boston. The *Courant* from then on went downhill. No records exist of its circulation figures, but its advertising diminished. After the inoculation controversy ended, its share of advertising shrank to one-fifth of the total published in all three Boston newspapers.[69] No financial records of the *Courant* are available, but it does not appear from the advertising figures that James Franklin was doing well. He published the *Courant's* final issue on June 25, 1726, and thereafter moved to Rhode Island.

---

came to support inoculation because "they were ashamed of their [anti-inoculaton] company." Mather to Dr. James Jurin, 21 May 1723, in Silverman, *Selected Letters of Cotton Mather,* 362.

[68]John Eyre's essay from 23 October 1721, criticizing Cotton Mather for dealing with medical matters, provides an example: "Doubtless, a Clergyman ... when he shall degenerate from his own Calling, and fall into the Intriegues of State and Time-Serving, he becomes a Devil; and from a Star in the Firma-Ment of Heaven, he becomes a sooty Coal in the blackest Hell, and receiveth the greatest damnation."

[69]During the inoculation controversy, from August 1721 through May 1722, it averaged 7.9 column inches of advertising per issue. That gave it 30 per cent of the advertising published in Boston's three newspapers. The *Gazette* averaged 10.4 column inches for 40 per cent of the total, and the *News-Letter* 7.8 inches for 30 per cent. After the May 1722 issue, the *Courant's* advertising shrank to an average of 3.8 inches per issue and 21 per cent of the total. While all three newspapers published ads for pamphlets and other items they printed and sold, such house-ads accounted for a larger amount of space in the *Courant* than in either the *Gazette* or the *News-Letter.*

THE NEW ENGLAND WEEKLY JOURNAL

Most of Boston's populace probably was happy to see the *Courant* go, but the newspaper during its short life left a mark on the town's journalism. The *News-Letter* and the *Gazette* had emphasized news, but the *Courant* devoted its space mainly to essays. Shortly after the *Courant's* demise, Boston gave birth to a new newspaper, the *New England Weekly Journal*, whose intentions were literary. It was, however, better at playing the role than the *Courant* had been, and neither was it guilty of the *Courant's* excessive violations of moderation and tact. It enjoyed a considerably longer and more successful life, employing literary essays better than the *Courant* had done and publishing works on science and history for the edification of readers.

The printer Samuel Kneeland, a pious member of the Old South Church, and his pastor, the Reverend Thomas Prince, most likely conceived of the enterprise. Prince then recruited his friend Mather Byles, nephew of Cotton Mather. Although only twenty years of age, Byles already was the colonies' best-known poet, and he agreed to join the newspaper as chief writer. The first issue of the *Weekly Journal*, published March 20, 1727, announced that several of the "most knowing and ingenious Gentlemen" in the colony had agreed to contribute material. They had "the happiness of a liberal Education," and some had improved their talents "by Travels into distant Countries."[70] The *Weekly Journal's* group of writers was more respectable than the *Courant's* club had been and came from the best traditions that the colony had to offer.

One of the men was the Rev. Prince, who was considered "the most learned scholar, with the exception of Cotton Mather, in New England."[71] During his entire ministerial career, he was a leading advocate of Puritanism in New England and forceful opponent of Anglicans' continuing efforts to win a favored place for their church. His interests included history, geography, medicine, and science. He had been one of the advocates of inoculation during Boston's smallpox epidemic of 1721-1722, and he carried on his own experiments in medicine. His extensive collection of historical works and the latest books on science were later to become the nucleus for the Boston Public Library. He was at the forefront of marrying religious faith to natural science. He refuted the deistic belief that God stood distant from His creation, while he argued that the Holy Scriptures were "but very brief Abridgments of large Histories."[72] His special concerns dealt with cosmology, disease, natural disasters, and the role of the clergy as scientists. Along with his scientific endeavors, he was a prolific author of works on colonial and European history,[73] and he frequently published articles on geography in the *Weekly Journal*.

Admirers claimed that Mather Byles, who had turned twenty only one week before the newspaper appeared, was America's Alexander Pope. His father having died shortly after Mather's first birthday, he came under the care and tutelage of

---

[70]*Weekly Journal*, 20 March 1727.

[71]The Reverend Charles Chauncy, quoted in "Thomas Prince," *National Cyclopaedia of American Biography*, 7: 144. See similar remarks in Massachusetts Historical Society, *Collections*, 1st series, 10: 164.

[72]Thomas Prince, *Christ Abolishing Death* (Boston, 1736), 7.

[73]His most ambitious historical work was the *Chronological History of New-England*, 2 vols. (Boston, 1736-1755), and he was co-founder with his son of *Christian History*, the colonies' first religious periodical.

his uncle Cotton Mather, who freely shared his encyclopedic knowledge. Byles became friends with Benjamin Franklin, another young visitor to the Mather study. At the age of fourteen, he was ready for college, and his uncle enrolled him at Harvard, where he prepared for the ministry. While he was still a student, several of his poems, modeled after the extremely popular work of Pope, were published in London. By the time he graduated at the age of eighteen he had gained a reputation as the colonies' best poet and essayist.[74] His prose was noted for its use of pun.

Byles and Prince, assisted by Judge Samuel Danforth, a Harvard graduate whose interests were law, medicine, and science, provided original essays for the *Weekly Journal* for its first full year of operation. Under their guidance, it devoted a substantial portion of its space to poetry, literary essays, and scholarly discussions of such subjects as geology, astronomy, and natural curiosities, mixed with short news items. It was characterized more by wit than diatribe, as the *New-England Courant* had been; and its purpose was information and entertainment rather than public controversy. Polemical discussion was not absent from its columns, as demonstrated in its first issue by a satire on Elisha Cooke and his "Brahmin Club." Generally, however, its tenor mirrored Byles' later description of an ideal clergyman, possessing "universal Knowledge ... understand[ing of] the Controversies of the Polemical Systems ... Good Taste for Writing," while being "truly Learned, without Pedantry; and truly Eloquent, without Stiffness and Affectation."[75]

With the *Weekly Journal*, early Boston journalism had reached a ripe maturity. Along with its predecessors, it had been made possible by the fertile soil of Massachusetts. They were the fruits of the intellectual and theological heritage that Puritanism made possible.

---

[74]He still enjoys a stature surpassed only by Anne Bradstreet and Edward Taylor among poets whom Puritan America produced. Of the three, only Byles was born in the American colonies. His collected works included *Poems on Several Occasions* (1744) and *A Collection of Poems by Several Hands* (1745).

[75]Mather Byles, *The Man of God* (New London, 1758).

# 4

# Religion and Colonial Newspapers
by David Copeland

IN 1690, BENJAMIN HARRIS hoped the newspaper he was planning would be a regular publication for the citizens of Massachusetts. Calling his creation *Publick Occurrences Both Forreign and Domestick*, the immigrant English printer issued his prospectus as part of the three pages of news. Foremost in his reasoning was his desire "That Memorable Occurrents of Divine Providence may not be neglected or forgotten, as they too often are."[1] In his first and only American newspaper issue, Harris reported news about war between English colonists and the French and Indians, a smallpox epidemic in Boston, an accident, plentiful harvests, fires, shipping woes the French caused in the Caribbean, and related political news from Europe. Within those news stories, Harris referred to Christians, Huguenots, and Papists. He spoke of the Devil, God, and merciful providence. He reported about Meeting-Houses, congregations, the Lord's Day, and a pious man.

Religion itself was not a topic in *Publick Occurrences*. It was, however, an integral part of the news and a motivator of events. After "a Sober and Pious Man" buried his wife, Harris explained, "The Devil took advantage" and led the man to hang himself. "Merciful Providence" fed troops attacking the French in Canada who ran low on supplies. Likewise, if Canada could be reduced, Harris promised that from all of New England "God alone will have all the Glory."

The relationship between newspapers and religion in colonial America cannot be underestimated because of the prominent role religion played in eighteenth-century American society. As Patricia Bonomi has noted, religion and eighteenth-century life were so entwined that religion left its mark on all parts of life,[2] and that included newspapers. Similarly, Wm. David Sloan and Julie Hedgepeth Williams say that, with few exceptions, the Christian faith played a

---

[1]*Publick Occurrences Both Forreign and Domestick* (Boston), 25 September 1690, 1.
[2]Patricia U. Bonomi, *Under the Cope of Heaven: Religion, Society, and Politics in Colonial America* (New York and Oxford: Oxford University Press, 1986), 3.

part in newspapers produced up to 1740.[3] This is not to say that every piece of news that appeared from 1690-1776 was tinged with religious implications or on religious   subjects.[4] It was most emphatically not, but news about religious events or with religious overtones appeared in colonial newspapers more than news about almost any other subject.[5] And as others have pointed out, religious leaders had a hand in the formation of America's first newspapers.[6]

This chapter looks at the relationship between religion and news in colonial America. America's eighteenth-century newspapers printed news about religion, which included sermons, scripture passages, and baptisms, and this chapter will discuss this news. But the chapter will focus upon how religious beliefs influenced what was printed and the way in which religious issues and controversy became news, the concept of religious toleration being one example. The chapter will also provide background on religion in the eighteenth century, which should help in understanding why religion and news became entwined.

Colonial newspapers tell us something about their readers' religious beliefs. They were for the most part Protestants with a strong distrust — if not outright dislike — for Catholics. They could find God's hand in almost all types of events, especially acts of nature. They viewed religion as a foundation for political events and believed God could effect change within the political realm if people so desired. And most readers of colonial newspapers probably understood what they read through a theological lens, seeing a medical breakthrough as a divine gift or the ability to develop that cure as God's providence, not as humankind acting alone.[7] Religious beliefs as they developed in American society were often at the root of the explanation of events, and this fact is reflected in newspapers. The discussion begins with religion in eighteenth-century America.

## THE RELIGIOUS CLIMATE OF COLONIAL AMERICA

While some British emigrants to America in the seventeenth and eighteenth centuries may have come for financial or political reasons, religion served as a great motivator for most. Immigrants often sought religious toleration, and they often viewed America as a Promised Land, a place of new beginnings. Once colonies were established, however, some intolerance for differing religious viewpoints arose, although not to the same degree as in England. Most people in both England and America were convinced that their understanding of religion was correct

---

[3]Wm. David Sloan and Julie Hedgepeth Williams, *The Early American Press. 1690-1783* (Westport, Conn.: Greenwood Press, 1994), 206.

[4]David Paul Nord, "Teleology and the News: The Religious Roots of American Journalism, 1630-1730," *Journal of American History* 77 (1990): 37, says that around 1730 news with divine influence gave way to being "simply the news" with little religious influence.

[5]David A. Copeland, *Colonial American Newspapers: Character and Content* (Newark: University of Delaware Press, 1997), 199.

[6]Nord, "Teleology and the News...," reaches the same conclusion, as does Wm. David Sloan in "Chaos, Polemics, and America's First Newspaper," *Journalism Quarterly* 70 (1993): 666-81, and "The *New England Courant*: Voice of Anglicanism," *American Journalism* 8 (1991): 108-41. Sheila McIntyre, "'I Heare it so Variously Reported': News-Letters, Newspapers, and the Ministerial Network in New England, 1670-1730," unpublished paper presented at the American Journalism Historians Association annual conference, London, Ontario, October 1996, points out that news in New England passed through the ministerial network and was disseminated by them in the form of public letters. This practice, McIntyre says, continued in John Campbell's *Boston News-Letter*. The ministerial network no doubt provided a religious tint to news.

[7]David A. Copeland, "'A Receipt Against the PLAGUE': Medical Reporting in Colonial America," *American Journalism* 11 (1994): 219-41.

while others did not understand the gospel message.

With numerous religious groups migrating to different regions of America, no two American colonies possessed the same religious makeup. Because the immigrants were from England, they tended to establish state-supported churches in most colonies, and the established religion tended to change from region to region. Few colonies offered their citizens free worship, and when they did, it was often done as a means of survival.[8]

Religious toleration slowly became an accepted concept in eighteenth-century America. Its development may not be directly attributable to newspapers, but they offered proponents of toleration an open forum for discussion. Still, toleration developed within a religious system that differed in each region of colonial America. Puritanism was the religion of New England, and its congregational form of worship became the essential element of society and government. The other form of religion of the colonial period that carried with it political power was that of the Anglican church, the principal religion of the Southern colonies that were founded under royal charters. Between the Puritanism of New England and the Anglicanism of the South — and existing in those regions as well — were Quakers, Baptists, Presbyterians, Methodists, Catholics, and various Reformed Protestant groups from Germany and the Netherlands. Anglicanism and Puritanism became competitors for power in colonial America, but all of the colonies in eighteenth-century America became royal colonies, and the charters given to groups such as the Quakers — and even Puritans — were terminated.

Even though royal charters changed the political setup of religion in colonial America, two other events may have done more to affect religion in society. First, Enlightenment thought created an atmosphere in which religious discussion became a part of everyday life.[9] These theological arguments were carried on in public meeting places, in tracts, and in newspapers. Second, revival changed the face of religion. The Great Awakening of the 1730s and 1740s created an explosion of religious publication, a news topic in newspapers, and did more to alter the face of religion in America than did any royal charter.[10] Central to the revival and to news surrounding it was an English itinerant preacher named George Whitefield. Controversial in America from 1739 until his death in 1770, he created what the historian Edwin Gausted called a phenomenon from which "none escaped its influence or avoided its controversy."[11] According to the historian Sydney Ahlstrom, Whitefield changed the standing order of American religion. He renewed religion in the colonies and caused religious schism.[12]

Because the Great Awakening produced a change in the religious power structure, colonials no longer found their lives arranged in a well-understood political

---

[8]As an example, Maryland was established by George Calvert as a refuge for Roman Catholics. The colony passed "An Act Concerning Religion" in 1649 calling for religious liberty as a way to encourage Catholic immigration. By 1654, however, Protestant immigrants to Maryland, who also accepted the offer of settlement, had banned free worship, an action aimed directly at Roman Catholics.

[9]See Henry F. May, *The Enlightenment in America* (Oxford and New York: Oxford University Press, 1976). Most Enlightenment thought in America was grounded in a belief in the existence of God with the belief that man's reason was sufficient for understanding all other aspects of life.

[10]Copeland, *Colonial American Newspapers*, 218.

[11]Edwin S. Gausted, *The Great Awakening in New England* (New York: Harper and Brothers, 1957), 42.

[12]Sydney E. Ahlstrom, *A Religious History of the American People* (New Haven and London: Yale University Press, 1972), 287.

and religious hierarchy.[13] The Great Awakening caused religious splits, and combined with the changes caused by royal charters, the power of certain religious groups waned. While religious revival may have been important to eighteenth-century America, it was not nearly as important as the changes it produced in the structure of society. Denominations divided; new ones began. Ministers, who had possessed considerable power in society in the seventeenth century and first third of the eighteenth, lost power. It was in this climate that colonial printers produced newspapers. How the religious climate of colonial America affected those news sheets is our topic of discussion.

## NEWSPAPERS AND RELIGION

Just as Benjamin Harris opened *Publick Occurrences* with references to religion, John Campbell's *Boston News-Letter* embarked on its run as America's first continually printed newspaper with a front-page story of potential political upheaval wrapped tightly with religious overtones. The April 24, 1704, *News-Letter* informed readers of a plot to overthrow Queen Anne, but the plot's basis was as much religious as political. The article claimed the French backed the plan to remove Anne, but England's Protestant religion was at the root of the plot. The news report stated that the best way to overthrow England was "to ruine the Protestant Interest" of the nation. The news of the Popish plot carried over to the back of Campbell's two-page newspaper where it was joined by a paragraph that stated, "the Rd. Mr. Pemberton Preach'd an Excellent Sermon on 1 Thes. 4.11. And do your own business: Exhorting all Ranks & Degrees of Persons to do their own work, in order to a REFORMATION."[14] The news of the sermon was placed in the paper by order of the governor.

The way in which the news of how the Pretender, James III, planned to take the throne from his half-sister, is an example of the way in which religion influenced news presentation and how religion could become the news. When the Pretender plot news is viewed in tandem with the insertion of the news of the sermon, the reader is afforded a basic glimpse into religious news that appeared in America's colonial newspapers. The relationship between news and religion fluctuated during the colonial period, but it never disappeared and was not always simple to understand. News of sermons preached, however, was fairly straightforward, and we begin with news of sermons, hymns, and other documents that affirm the religiosity of colonial Americans.

## BASIC RELIGIOUS NEWS

Colonial Americans were a religious people with estimates of as many as 60 per cent of them attending religious services regularly. But this percentage may be misleading because families worshipped at home, and the Bible was the one book almost every colonial possessed. When colonials were able to purchase books, commentaries and books on religion were their first choice.[15] Learning to

[13]Harry S. Stout, *The New England Soul: Preaching and Religious Culture in Colonial New England* (New York and Oxford: Oxford University Press, 1986), 185; Bonomi, *Under the Cope of Heaven*, 6.

[14]*Boston News-Letter*, 24 April 1704, 1 and 2.

[15]See Patricia U. Bonomi and Peter R. Eisenstadt, "Church Adherence in the Eighteenth Century British American Colonies," *William and Mary Quarterly* 39 (1982): 245-86; Mark A. Noll, et al, eds., *Christianity*

read in eighteenth-century America was, according to a 1735 story in the *American Weekly Mercury*, aimed primarily toward assuring that all children would be able to understand the Bible,[16] and more than 60 per cent of all printing jobs in the colonies by 1742 were for religious publications.[17] Similarly, colleges were begun in America to train ministers.[18] In light of these facts, it is not surprising that religion affected the news of colonial America or that colonials inserted into their newspapers their religious activities.

Activities that reflected daily religious practices and beliefs such as baptisms, ordinations, obituaries, sermons, hymns, scripture, prayer, denominational meetings, and religious commentary were placed in newspapers at the request of individuals, congregations, and colonial governments. Even murders and executions often reflected society's basic religious beliefs.

The *Boston Gazette* from its inception in 1719 through 1770 published weekly the number of baptisms in Boston and often provided yearly summaries. Notification that a minister had been ordained reflected the significance of ministers and the role of religion in communities. News of ordinations, while in newspapers throughout the colonies, was most prominent in Boston.[19]

Obituaries, too, could reflect the religiosity of society. While newspapers in the 1770s often simply listed the deaths and births of a community together, papers for most of the period provided more than a listing of those who had died, especially for prominent citizens. Often, obituaries included lines such as "a blameless Christian Life and Conversation,"[20] or a "flaming Devotion in his Prayers."[21] When Mary Saltonstall died in January 1730, her obituary stated "She was above all, adorn'd with exemplary Piety, which not only appear'd in her very reverent Behaviour in the Church of GOD, but in every mention of His sacred Name on any occasion, or whenever her Conversation turn'd on Religious Subjects."[22]

When sermons, hymns, scripture, or prayers were inserted into newspapers, they often reflected the turmoil present in the lives of people, which is exactly what a hymn-turned-prayer did when it appeared in October 1775 as the colonies braced for war with England, the motherland for most colonists:

> Teach me to feel another's woe:
> To hide the fault I see;

---

*in America* (Grand Rapids: William B. Eerdmans, 1983), 61; Oscar Theodore Barck, Jr., and Hugh Talmage Lefler, *Colonial America* (New York: Macmillan, 1958), 379; and Richard Beale Davis, *A Colonial Southern Bookshelf: Readings in the Eighteenth Century* (Athens: University of Georgia Press, 1979), 75-90.

[16]*American Weekly Mercury* (Philadelphia), 7 January 1734-35, 1.

[17]Copeland, *Colonial American Newspapers*, 218.

[18]David D. Hall, "Religion and Society: Problems and Reconsiderations," in *Colonial British America: Essays in the New History of the Early Modern Period*, eds. Jack P. Greene and J. R. Pole (Baltimore and London: Johns Hopkins University Press, 1984), 322.

[19]See, for example, *Boston News-Letter*, 18 November 1706, 4; 26 April 1708, 2; 1 December 1712, 2; 14 November 1720, 2; 15 January 1730, 2; *Boston Gazette*, 2 November 1730, 2; 5 February 1745, 2, 7 August 1750, 2; 11 February 1755, 3, 11 February 1765, 2; 3 September 1770, 3; *Boston Evening-Post*, 10 November 1735, 2; 19 May 1740, 2; 28 October 1745, 2; 11 February 1760, 3; 7 October 1765, 3; and *Boston Weekly Post-Boy*, 17 December 1735, 4; 19 May 1740, 2; 13 August 1750, 2; 13 October 1760, 3; 22 April 1765, 1; 6 August 1770, 3; 2 January 1775, 3.

[20]*Boston Evening-Post*, 1 October 1750, 2.

[21]*Boston News-Letter*, 11 January 1720, 2.

[22]*New-England Weekly Journal* (Boston), 26 January 1730, 2.

That mercy I to others show,
That mercy show to me.[23]

Following the capitulation of Canada in 1760 during the French and Indian War, a hymn announced that God "didst march through the Land in indignation, thou didst thresh the Heathen in thine anger. Thou wentest forth for the salvation of thy People."[24] God was, according to this and other hymns, an active part of the lives of the people.

Sermons, hymns, scripture, and prayers inserted into newspapers also provided a way for congregations to share important events, reinforce biblical beliefs, and chastise people for what was deemed sinful activity, such as a breech of the Sabbath, prostitution, sodomy, and adultery.[25] In each case, the newspaper report reflected a community's people turning their everyday religious beliefs into news or applying their religious standards to criminal activity.

Applying religious beliefs to criminal activity was especially apparent in news stories of murder. Murder was a direct violation of God's commandment, "Thou shalt not kill," and required the appropriate biblical response of "an eye for a eye." But before any kind of punishment could take place, according to newspaper accounts, the guilty needed to repent, reflecting society's conviction that even immoral and corrupt lives should end — not separated from God — but in harmony with the Creator. One Maryland man who had been sentenced to death, for example, confessed all of his past sins and then urged all of those in attendance to avoid the sins and passions that had led him to the gallows.[26]

Colonists' basic religious beliefs were reflected in newspapers in other ways, most notably in government decrees. Laws that affected religion were more likely to be passed in the first third of the century, but government decrees with religious connotations occurred throughout the colonial period. Laws in some colonies, for example, outlined the method for a church to select a minister.[27] Massachusetts even decreed mandatory church attendance in 1730.[28] In Connecticut, even as late as 1775, laws made it a crime to work on Sunday.[29]

One of the most common governmental decrees that reflected the religiosity of colonials was the call for a day of fasting and prayer. Governments throughout America issued calls for such days for any number of reasons, good weather and growing seasons, aid in war, or deliverance from disease.[30] In Massachusetts, the governor set aside a day for "both Ministers and People to Praise the Name of the LORD, for His Indulgences towards us another Year,"[31] while North Car-

---

[23]*Story & Humphrey's Pennsylvania Mercury; and the Universal Advertiser* (Philadelphia), 20 October 1775, 1.

[24]*Boston Evening-Post*, 15 December 1760, 3.

[25]*American Weekly Mercury* (Philadelphia), 28 May 1730, 3; and *Virginia Gazette* (Williamsburg, Dixon and Hunter), 23 December 1775, 4; *Pennsylvania Journal, or Weekly Advertiser* (Philadelphia), 19 September 1745, 3; ibid., 18 October 1750, 2; *Boston Evening-Post*, 22 April 1765, 3; *American Weekly Mercury* (Philadelphia), 8 October 1730, 3; and *South-Carolina Gazette* (Charleston) 29 March 1740, 3; *New-England Weekly Journal* (Boston), 4 August 1735, 1.

[26]*Maryland Gazette* (Annapolis), 17 May 1745, 4.

[27]*Boston Evening-Post*, 1 December 1735, 2.

[28]*American Weekly Mercury* (Philadelphia), 22 October 1730, 1.

[29]*Connecticut Journal, and New-Haven Post-Post*, 25 January 1775, 4.

[30]*Boston News-Letter*, 4 April 1720, 2; *Maryland Gazette* (Annapolis), 6 February 1755, 3; *South-Carolina Gazette* (Charleston), 12 April 1760, 1.

[31]*New-England Weekly Journal* (Boston), 2 November 1730, 1.

olina asked all citizens to participate in "a day of solemn FAST, PRAYER, AND HUMILIATION before Almighty God" after the colony learned of the shots fired at Lexington and Concord.[32]

Newspaper commentary also addressed ways in which society, writers feared, was losing its religious foundation. A *Boston Weekly News-Letter* writer saw the increase in the number of taverns in the port town as the creation of "Nurseries of Vice and Debauchery [that] directly lead to the Ruin of Society."[33] Similarly, another Boston writer, looking at life in the growing city, pondered, "Where is that love of God's House and Respect to his holy Day! Is not the Sabbath most grosly prophan'd in Defiance of the Authority of Heaven, and the wholesome Laws of this Province?"[34]

Through newspapers, one sees that colonial life and law often centered around religious beliefs and practices. Newspapers inserted these pieces of information, not out of obligation, but because they were part of everyday life, and colonists enjoyed reading about local occurrences.[35] But one may also observe another of religion's connections with news. Just as residents commented upon the state of life in Boston as it was perceived to be in juxtaposition with religious beliefs and religiously based colonial law, religion could also influence the interpretation of news and did just that throughout the colonial period.

## RELIGION'S INFLUENCE ON NEWS

Because religion was a part of nearly every colonial's life and almost every religious group viewed its understanding of God through its own theological lens, news interpretation was often colored by the religion of printers, correspondents, or writers to newspapers.

Religion's effect on news interpretation was especially evident in news of political events that involved the potential for Catholic-Protestant confrontations. Here, theological interpretation — and no doubt the historical relation between the two groups from the 1500s forward — influenced the news in America.

During most of the colonial period, North America was controlled primarily by two European nations, England and France. The two began fighting over control of the continent almost immediately with English occupation of French Quebec in 1629, slightly more than twenty years after both countries established New-World settlements. Colonists of the two powers continued to fight during the seventeenth century, and in 1689, the first of four declared wars between England and France, King Williams War, began. Newspapers covered each of these confrontations, the French and Indian War from 1754-1763 being extensively covered. While the news of each never overlooked political aspects and ramifications, the implied danger that French Catholicism represented to English Protestants often influenced how war news was presented.

The mention of Catholicism almost always evoked fear. For that reason, news of Catholic — and synonymously French — activity generally incited

---

[32]*Cape Fear Mercury* (Wilmington, N.C.), 28 July 1775, 2.

[33]*Boston Weekly News-Letter*, 5 July 1750, 2.

[34]*Boston Gazette, or Weekly Journal*, 14 August 1750, 1.

[35]Copeland, *Colonial American Newspapers*, 271, 273; and Julie Hedgepeth Williams, "A Romance with Local Happenings: Colonial Americans and Their Newspapers," paper presented at the American Journalism Historians Association annual conference, London, Ontario, October 1996.

people to act. Just as the *Boston News-Letter* had warned readers of a potential takeover of England by France in 1704 during Queen Anne's War and that a French victory would mean the downfall of Protestantism,[36] Philadelphia's *American Weekly Mercury* in 1725 did the same but expounded the fear factor. News of another attempt to place a French-backed Catholic "pretender" on the throne ran in the paper, but this time, printer Andrew Bradford also ran a story of describing what happened to Protestants when Catholic-backed forces captured Protestant territory. Bradford's report told of the way that Protestants in Poland were brought into the center of the city of Thorn. There, they had their hands chopped off. Following that, the Protestants, the "implacable Enemies of Papists," were drawn and quartered and left about to help subdue other Protestants who might consider further fighting.[37]

The fear of what a French Catholic takeover of England or America would mean surfaced again during King George's War, 1744-1748. The colony of New York passed laws to stop all Catholics from preaching in the colony, unless they could swear allegiance to the English government. The act considered Catholic activity as "traiterous Conspiracies."[38] By the time of the French and Indian War, accounts in newspapers often warned that the French were not fighting so much to take North American colonies away from the English, but to use warfare as a way to rid the colonies of Protestants. "[T]hey believe it their DUTY to cut our Throats," one writer to the *Maryland Gazette* warned.[39]

With the French surrender of Canada in 1760, news accounts reported that "Heaven appeared for us.... And thanks to HIM, who has subdued our cruel, proud and insulting Enemies," thus halting a French Catholic takeover of America.[40] News accounts were saying that God's divine intervention had taken place, another way in which religious belief influenced colonial news.

Many colonials observed the activities around them and credited those events to divine intervention, God's providence. This is exactly what colonial governments expected when they issued calls for days of fasting and prayer. God's providence became one way to explain the events of the world and another way in which the religious beliefs of colonial America affected news. News that was providentially driven was almost always news that directly affected those reading it. When, for example, God subdued the French Catholics in the reduction of Canada, the event may have occurred hundreds of miles from Boston, Philadelphia, or Charleston, but it had direct implications upon the citizens of each of those cities and on those in between.

When God's providence influenced the interpretation of news, it could be for good or bad. Giving God credit for the defeat of France, or noting that a successful growing season was "a Merciful Providence" of God[41] indicated religion's positive influence on news interpretation. Usually, God's intervention was used to explain negative news.

When, for example, Parliament raised colonial taxes in 1770, one writer in

---

[36]*Boston News-Letter*, 24 April 1704, 1.

[37]*American Weekly Mercury* (Philadelphia), 1 April 1725, 2; and 22 April 1725, 1.

[38]*Boston Evening-Post*, 4 March 1745, 2.

[39]*Maryland Gazette* (Annapolis), 31 July 1755, 2 (emphasis included).

[40]*Boston Gazette, and Country Journal*, 22 September 1760, 3; and *New-Hampshire Gazette* (Portsmouth), 26 September 1760, 2. The *Gazette* omitted the second half of the quote.

[41]*Publick Occurrences*, 25 September 1690, 1.

Boston explained the increase and other burdensome laws by saying, "God is angry with the inhabitants of this land, for the sin of oppression, especially in matters of religion."[42] When large numbers of women began having miscarriages in Boston, the news was explained as God invoking his wrath upon people who had lost contact with Him.[43] But by far the greatest way in which religion influenced news in terms of explaining it through divine providence came in the interpretation of natural disaster.

In the 1750s, a series of earthquakes shook America, Europe, and the Middle East. Newspapers called the American earthquakes "warnings which God in his mercy affords to a sinful people"[44] and natural occurrences "to awaken us to a more strict Observance" of the Sabbath.[45] Boston experienced a series of temblors in 1755, leading one correspondent to remark, "[It] cannot be suppos'd, that such terrible Events, as the laying Waste large & populous Cities, which has been frequently occasion'd by *Earthquakes*, should happen, without his special Influence and Direction."[46]

While God may have provided the ultimate in religious influence and direction on news interpretation, printers, too, allowed their own religious beliefs to influence how and what news appeared in their newspapers. Printers' religious views played a role in beginning and in what was printed in *Publick Occurrences*, the *Boston News-Letter*, and the *New England Courant*.[47] And a printer's religious views could affect presentation of news for years, which is exactly what happened with Boston printer Thomas Fleet.

Fleet began working in Boston as a printer in 1712, having fled England after angering Anglican leaders.[48] His newspaper career did not start until 1733 when he took over the *Weekly Rehearsal*, but he never lost his dislike of ministers. That dislike colored his news presentation, especially when information about George Whitefield was the topic.

Whitefield's itinerant preaching first came to Boston in 1740, and Fleet's disdain of the 25-year-old Anglican found its way into his *Boston Evening-Post* after a Whitefield preaching event turned tragic. Crowds filled the meeting church past capacity. When a board in the balcony snapped, people panicked, supposing that the balcony was about to fall. In the ensuing stampede for the doors, two women and a servant boy were crushed to death. Whitefield never demonstrated any remorse for the deaths, at least not in any Boston newspaper or in his published journal. Instead, he declared, "God was pleased to give me presence of mind; so that I gave notice I would immediately preach upon the common. The weather was wet, but many thousands followed into the field."[49]

---

[42]*Massachusetts Spy* (Boston), 23 October 1770, 2.

[43]*New-England Courant* (Boston), 3 July 1725, 2.

[44]*Boston Gazette, or Weekly Journal*, 22 May 1750, 1.

[45]*Boston Gazette, or Country Journal*, 1 December 1755, 1.

[46]Ibid., 24 November 1755, 1 (emphasis included).

[47]For a discussion of how religious views affected the beginnings of these newspapers, see Chapter 3. See, also, Wm. David Sloan, "A Silence in Massachusetts: John Campbell and the *Boston News-Letter*," paper presented at the American Journalism Historians Association annual conference, Lawrence, Kansas, 1992; Sloan, "Chaos, Polemics, and America's First Newspaper"; Sloan, "The *New-England Courant*: Voice of Anglicanism..."; and Sloan and Williams, *The Early American Press, 1690-1783*, 10-7.

[48]Isaiah Thomas, *The History of Printing in America* (1810; reprint, New York: Weathervane Books, 1970), 94.

[49]George Whitefield, *Journals, 1737-1741*, with an introduction by William V. Davis (Gainesville, Fla.:

Fleet reacted to the event by appending an editorial comment to news that Whitefield was leaving Boston. The printer said, "The Town is in a hopeful Way of being restor'd to its former State of Order, Peace and Industry."[50] Other printers, such as the *Boston Weekly Post-Boy's* Ellis Huske, reacted to Fleet's comment, and Fleet stated in his October 2, 1740, newspaper that he did not mean to slander Whitefield. But there can be little doubt that belittling Whitefield was exactly what he meant to do.

When Whitefield returned to Boston in 1745 on his second colonial preaching tour, Fleet led a concerted effort to keep him from preaching in any Boston pulpit. In one article, he intimated that Whitefield was an accomplice to criminal activity for getting a Topsail, Massachusetts, man to break into the Old-South Meetinghouse so that Whitefield might use the building for a service.[51] Before the Old-South incident, Fleet published pieces accusing Whitefield of not being "a true Christian" and of being "the great Instrument of causing the Divisions and Separations which have disturbed and rent in Pieces so many of the Churches of this Land."[52] In another case, a writer to the *Evening-Post* chastised Fleet for being so biased against Whitefield. Fleet, in an acerbic tone that one can almost hear as one reads his response, asked forgiveness and said, "I was so busy about Mr. Whitefield's Vindication ... and now honestly declare, that I would as soon print for him, as for any Man in this Province."[53]

While Fleet's dislike for Whitefield and ministers may have clouded his news presentation in the 1740s, it completely changed his slant on news in 1754. The colonies were quickly becoming engaged in a war for survival against the French and their Indian allies. At the same time, Whitefield returned for another series of revivals. While most newspapers only mentioned him and his preaching in passing and devoted all available news space to news of French and Indian encroachments, Fleet did the opposite. For nearly two months, beginning on September 23, the *Boston Evening-Post* railed against Whitefield to the exclusion of the fighting. The November 4 paper called him "an abandon'd Sinner" who had personally committed "Violations of the holy Laws of God."[54]

With Fleet, then, religion influenced the way news was presented and what news appeared. Whitefield was the catalyst for Fleet, but he was more. With Whitefield, religion became news in America.

*RELIGION BECOMES NEWS*

On Whitefield's coming to preach in America in 1739-1740, *Massachusetts Spy* printer-turned-historian Isaiah Thomas said, "[H]e became the common topic of conversation from Georgia to New Hampshire. All the newspapers were filled with paragraphs of information respecting him, or with pieces of animated disputation pro or con."[55] In fact, Whitefield's first preaching tour helped change colonial newspapers. With Whitefield, printers now had an individual in whom

---

Scholars' Facsimiles & Reprints, 1969), 462.

[50]*Boston Evening-Post*, 29 September 1740, 2.

[51]Ibid., 8 April 1745, 2.

[52]Ibid., 11 March 1745, 1, 2.

[53]Ibid., 21 January 1745, 1.

[54]Ibid., 4 November 1754, 1.

[55]Thomas, *The History of Printing in America*, 568.

almost all Americans were interested. Carrying his message from one end of the colonies to the other during seven preaching tours, Whitefield became the first celebrity for the media to follow, and it is estimated that before his death, most Americans had the opportunity to hear him preach at least once.[56]

Because most Americans were interested in Whitefield, he made religion a topic of news, not just a way to interpret news. Even though American newspapers had run sermons, baptisms, scripture, and the like for more than three decades before his arrival, those pieces of news were not the same as the news surrounding Whitefield. There was no controversy in listing baptisms in Boston, nor was there any concern about a colonial government asking God's help through a call for a day of fasting and prayer to God. Whitefield made news because it was almost impossible to be impartial when it came to his activities. People either applauded them or denounced them because what Whitefield did affected society. For that reason, he and his preaching tours became one of the first stories with intercolonial ramifications, and newspapers afforded space to news about Whitefield as they had to no other issue before.[57]

Whitefield's powerful voice, which allowed him to preach to thousands at one time, was as much an item of news as the controversy that surrounded his preaching. Papers said 8,000 heard him in Charleston;[58] 15,000, in New York;[59] and 23,000, in Boston.[60] The numbers led to accusations that he padded the attendance accounts to further his own image in the colonies and in England,[61] but Benjamin Franklin estimated that a crowd of thirty thousand could have heard an open-air Whitefield sermon.[62]

His sermons became news because he often discussed items or adopted religious positions that were sensitive to the convictions of colonials. When, for example, he refused to use the Anglican liturgy in a Charleston church, he riled the local clergy.[63] He also referred to Archbishop John Tillotson — after whom many American Anglican ministers patterned their preaching and theological positions — as a know-nothing of Christianity, knowing "no more Christianity than Mahomet."[64] The two events helped hasten Whitefield's departure from Charleston and led to his being banned from Anglican pulpits in Philadelphia.[65]

His preaching, coupled with other changes the Great Awakening brought on, created more news about religion in 1745. Religious groups throughout the colonies began to divide, and Whitefield was blamed for the division and reli-

---

[56]Harry S. Stout, *The Divine Dramatist: George Whitefield and the Rise of Modern Evangelism* (Grand Rapids: William B. Eerdmans, 1991), xiii-xiv.

[57]Two events, Whitefield's first preaching tour and the English and Spanish confrontation known as the War of Jenkin's Ear, occurred at approximately the same time. The two gave printers events that had the potential to affect all Americans, and both served to change the way in which news was presented in colonial America. For further discussion, see Charles E. *Clark, The Public Prints: The Newspaper in Anglo-American Culture, 1665-1740* (New York and Oxford: Oxford University Press, 1994), 261-3; and Copeland, *Colonial American Newspapers*, 217-8, 269.

[58]*Pennsylvania Gazette* (Philadelphia), 17 April 1740, 3.

[59]Ibid., 23 October 1740, 2.

[60]*New-England Weekly Journal* (Boston), 14 October 1740, 2.

[61]*Pennsylvania Gazette* (Philadelphia), 1 May 1740, 1.

[62]Benjamin Franklin, *Autobiography of Benjamin Franklin*, eds. J. A. Leo Lemay and P. M. Zall (Knoxville: University of Tennessee Press, 1981), 107.

[63]*South-Carolina Gazette* (Charleston), 21 August 1740, 3.

[64]*Pennsylvania Gazette* (Philadelphia), 10 April 1740, 1; and *New-York Gazette*, 19 May 1740, 1.

[65]Whitefield, *Journals*, 404.

gious disharmony. "Mr. Whitefield has been the great Instrument of causing the Divisions and Separations which have disturbed and rent in Pieces so many of the Churches of this Land," one writer declared.[66] These separations created yet another topic that made religion news, the new denomination.

New denominations were often held up for ridicule in newspapers. Presbyterians[67] and Quakers[68] became news when they attempted to establish churches. Baptists in the 1770s turned religion into news when they instituted calls for legislation for religious liberty throughout the colonies.[69] But, perhaps no better example exists of the way new religious groups could become news than the way newspaper stories portrayed Methodists from the 1740s forward.

There are several reasons that Methodism may have come under such strong attack and became a news topic. First, Methodism was a direct assault upon the Church of England, which one Methodist referred to as "the Scarlet Whore" of Revelation.[70] Second, Methodism's founders, John and Charles Wesley, had religious ties to George Whitefield, the trio having come to Georgia on a mission trip in the late 1730s. Since Whitefield was news, anyone associated with him, especially if they were perceived as attacking the prescribed church of the crown, might be considered news, too. Third, Methodism's formation coincided with the Great Awakening. As has been seen, this religious upheaval sparked newspaper stories about religion. The combination of these three factors made information about Methodists news in America.

Methodists were blamed for any number of events. They were accused of ruining the wool trade,[71] plotting to overthrow the South Carolina government,[72] and killing and maiming people because of their beliefs.[73] John Wesley was stoned after one of his followers caused those deaths.[74] One of the best ways that were discovered to attack Methodists came in the form of derision. News about Methodists often portrayed them as buffoons and anyone who converted to Methodism as insane.[75] One story in the *Maryland Gazette* reported how foolish Methodists could be. At one meeting, when it came time to pass the collection plate, a highwayman — who had been listening outside — stepped into the meeting room and passed his hat up and down the rows. The foolish followers of Methodism, the article stated, filled the hat full of money, never knowing it was a robber passing the hat until he left with the evening's collection.[76]

Even though newspaper accounts may have derisively discussed Methodists and other groups, the growing number of denominations in America created yet another topic of news about religion, news of religious liberty. Benjamin Franklin published a call for religious liberty in 1730[77] as did John Boydell in

---

[66]*Boston Evening-Post*, 11 March 1745, 1.

[67]See, for example, *Boston News-Letter*, 25 August 1701, 2; *New-England Courant* (Boston), 10 July 1725, 2; and *American Weekly Mercury* (Philadelphia), 22 July 1725, 3.

[68]See *Boston Evening-Post*, 15 December 1735, 3.

[69]See *Pennsylvania Chronicle, and Universal Advertiser* (Philadelphia), 19 March 1770, 1.

[70]*Boston Evening-Post*, 10 November 1740, 2.

[71]*New-York Weekly Journal*, 31 March 1740, 4.

[72]*South-Carolina Gazette* (Charleston), 13 May 1745, 2.

[73]*Maryland Gazette* (Annapolis), 22 August 1750, 3.

[74]*Boston Weekly News-Letter*, 6 September 1750, 2.

[75]See, for example, *Virginia Gazette* (Williamsburg, Rind), 8 March 1770, 2.

[76]*Maryland Gazette* (Annapolis), 31 January 1765, 1.

[77]*Pennsylvania Gazette* (Philadelphia), 30 July 1730, 2.

1735.[78] In New York in 1755 — despite the fact that the colony was fighting for survival against the French and Indians — the issue of religious liberty became a news topic for a five-month period as the colony sought to establish a publicly funded college with religious control. Printer Hugh Gaine wrote, "It is evident that Religion of whatever kind, can have no other Connection with the affairs of civil Society, than as it has a natural Tendancy to refine, and improve the Morals of its Members."[79]

Even though the concept of religious toleration had been news in America in different situations and colonies for forty years, it was not until the 1770s that the thrust for religious freedom reached its zenith. The concept of religious liberty was tied to the growing calls for political independence. When a Connecticut writer in Rhode Island's *Providence  Gazette* referred to how his colony could "take by force" people's property "to support a religion or worship they do not choose,"[80] readers could connect mentally this oppressive practice with the 1765 Stamp Act, the 1765 Quartering Act, the 1767 Townshend Acts, the 1768 British occupation of Boston, and the 1770 Boston Massacre.

Baptists pushed most strongly for religious toleration in the 1770s. Led by men such as Isaac Backus, they called for a tax boycott against support of state churches in Massachusetts.[81] Newspapers in other colonies picked up the stories, and support for Baptist calls for religious liberty began appearing. "I am sorry that ever any denomination of christians," a writer to the *Pennsylvania Chronicle* said following reports of Baptist activity for religious liberty in Massachusetts, "have even been deprived of this privilege."[82]

While religious liberty made news in colonial newspapers, it did not make toleration a universally accepted practice. The news of calls for toleration juxtaposed with news that derided Methodists. What one can see, however, is the way in which religious issues and figures became the topic of news in America. Neither war nor political controversy could erase religion as a topic of news.

## RELIGION, SOCIETY, AND NEWSPAPERS INTERTWINED

The relationship between religion and colonial newspapers is representative of the way in which religion and society entwined. Religion played a part in the lives of almost all eighteenth-century Americans, so, logically, it played a part in the news of the period as well. One cannot determine to what extent religious views affected religious interpretation of news, but one can observe how often religion made its way into newspapers. When, for example, colonials wanted to know about religious events, documents, and figures, they requested that sermons or hymns be inserted into newspapers. Sermons and hymns, along with baptisms, scripture, ordinations, and religious commentary, appeared regularly in newspapers, especially through 1745. After 1745, these types of news insertions or notices diminished to a certain extent, but they never disappeared.

Newspapers supplemented straight religious news items with religious inter-

---

[78]Religious liberty was a subject for the *Boston  Gazette* for numerous editions in 1735. See 17 February 1735, 2; 30 June 1735, 1; 11 August 1735, 1; 25 August 1735, 1; and 15 September 1735, 1.

[79]*New-York  Mercury*, 12 May 1755, 1.

[80]*Providence Gazette; and Country Journal*, 13 October 1770, 2.

[81]Ibid., 11 August 1770, 3.

[82]*Pennsylvania  Chronicle* (Philadelphia), 19 March 1770, 1.

pretation of events. When cures to diseases were discovered and then explained in newspapers, for example, God's part in securing the remedy was often discussed.[83] But religious interpretation of news could be based on animosity as much as on God's providence, and a printer's individual bias toward or against religion could affect the presentation of news, as the life of Boston printer Thomas Fleet demonstrates.

Religion finally became a primary news subject in colonial America. The catalyst was George Whitefield, although other aspects of religion such as the Catholic-Protestant dislike that accompanied news of English and French relations existed prior to his corning to America. He made news with his preaching and the way in which he and religious revivalism affected society. His work fed into other topics of religion for newspapers, principally the news of denominations and religious liberty. Even though his greatest influences upon newspapers took place from 1740-1745, newspapers never ignored him when he visited America. When he died of an asthma attack in New England in 1770, American newspapers lost their first celebrity. Papers estimated that 15,000 or more attended his funeral,[84] and other news reports compared him in greatness and importance with the Apostles.[85]

The relationship between religion and America's colonial newspapers should not be underestimated. Newspapers carried religious news, along with news that was understood through religious interpretation, throughout the eighteenth century. So when 1775 dawned with revolution on the horizon, it was only natural that printers should greet the year with a poem that outlined the relationship that so many colonials viewed as the relationship between themselves and God and consequently their nation and God:

TO Thee, great GOD, thro' whose indulgent care,
We view the dawning of another year,
Our annual song, inflam'd with love, shall rise,
Grateful as incense, curling to the skies.
STILL, may thy guardian Providence protect,
Sweeten our days, and all our paths direct:
Inspir'd by firm Religion's sacred Pow'r,
May noble acts illumine ev'ry hour:
So when life fades, to heav'n our souls shall wing,
Those blooming Regions of immortal Spring.[86]

---

[83]See, for example, *New-England Weekly Journal* (Boston), 1 January 1740, 3.

[84]*Connecticut Journal, and New-Haven Post-Boy*, 26 October 1770, 2.

[85]*Boston Evening-Post*, 8 October 1770, 3.

[86]*Essex Journal and Merrimack Packet: Or, the Massachusetts and New-Hampshire General Advertiser* (Newburyport, Mass.), 4 January 1775, 4.

5

# The Evangelical Origins of Mass
# Media in America / *1815-1835*
by David Paul Nord

IN THE EARLY SPRING OF 1815, the Rev. William Dickey of Salem, Kentucky, made his way down to the little wharf at the confluence of the Ohio and Cumberland rivers to pick up a package that had arrived for him by riverboat. The package was a bundle of religious tracts, sent by the Rev. Samuel Mills, who was then touring the West as an agent of the Massachusetts Missionary Society. They were the first religious tracts Dickey had ever seen. "I read them eagerly," he wrote to Mills, "and was glad to have it in my power, to give away a present, so suitable, and so acceptable, to many a destitute family. I directed those who received them, to read them over and over, and then hand them to their neighbours. Be assured, Sir, they have excited considerable interest among all classes. Religious Tracts have been much desired by us, ever since we heard of Societies of this kind. That so many numbers, and 6,000 of each, should be printed for gratuitous distribution, astonishes our people. They say, *It is the Lord's doing, and marvellous in our eyes.*"[1]

The Rev. Dickey's parishioners were understandably astonished, for what they were witnessing, even there in the wilderness of western Kentucky, was the first stirrings of something new in America: mass media. It wasn't really the Lord's doing, however; in this case, it was the very human work of the New England Tract Society. The New England group was one of dozens of tract and Bible societies that had sprouted up in the decade between 1805 and 1815. These groups gradually coalesced into two large national organizations: the American Bible Society (1816) and the American Tract Society (1825). The work of the Bible and tract societies of the early republic did not bring about the millennium of Christ, as their founders had hoped. The importance of these so-

---

[1]Letter from Dickey to Mills, printed in Samuel J. Mills and Daniel Smith, *Report of a Missionary Tour through that Part of the United States which Lies West of the Allegany Mountains* (Andover, Mass.: Flagg and Gould, 1815), 53. This volume has been reprinted in *To Win the West: Missionary Viewpoints, 1814-1815* (New York: Arno Press, 1972).

cieties in American history may lie elsewhere, for they helped to lay the foundation for mass media in America through their pioneering work in mass printing and mass distribution of the written word.

## THE POPULARIZATION OF PRINT

Historians have long been interested in the revolution in popular reading habits in the United States during the first half of the nineteenth century. Students of the book trade have pointed to the rise of the popular American novel, especially the works of James Fenimore Cooper after 1821, as a kind of take-off stage in the popularization of print.[2] Historians of journalism have seen a similar critical threshold for the newspaper industry in the development of the popular "penny press" after 1833.[3] Scholars have long debated the sources of this transformation, and a rather long list of "causes" has been assembled. Most of these can be classified as technological (improved printing, papermaking, and transportation), economic (improved business organization, growth of consumer manufactures and advertising, and population movements), or political (democratization of government and growth of public schooling).

In this essay, I propose to add the classification "evangelical." Perhaps more than anything else, the missionary impulse — first in purely religious crusades and then in more secular reform movements — lay at the foundation of the popularization of print in the nineteenth century. Though the growth of popular fiction and newspaper journalism in the early nineteenth century certainly had a profound and lasting impact on the popularization of print, it seems that it was the evangelical Christian publicists in the Bible and tract societies who first dreamed the dream of a genuinely mass medium — that is, they proposed to deliver the same printed messages to everyone in America. To this end, these organizations helped to develop, in the very earliest stages, the modern printing and distribution techniques associated with the reading revolution in the nineteenth century. Of course, the successes of the Bible and tract societies were not as extravagant as their dreams. But the results of their efforts were remarkable nonetheless. By 1830 in some sections of the country — long before the success of the penny press or the dime novel or the cheap magazine — they had nearly achieved their goal of delivering their message to everyone.

## THE MISSIONARY IMPULSE

It was the will to print, not the way to print, that first led American evangelicals into the business of mass media. By the 1820s, the Bible and tract societies would emerge as leaders in both printing technology and the organization of na-

---

[2]A standard account of this literary transformation is Henry Walcott Boynton, *Annals of American Bookselling, 1638-1850* (New York: Wiley, 1932), 138-40. See also Hellmut Lehmann-Haupt, Lawrence C. Wroth, and Rollo G. Silver, *The Book in America* (2nd. ed.; New York: R.R. Bowker, 1952), part III; and Richard Altick, *The English Common Reader* (Chicago: University of Chicago Press, 1957). An excellent recent overview is David D. Hall, "The Uses of Literacy in New England, 1600-1850," in *Printing and Society in Early America*, ed. William L. Joyce, David D. Hall, Richard D. Brown, and John B. Hench (Worcester, Mass.: American Antiquarian Society, 1983).

[3]See, for example, Edwin Emery and Michael Emery, *The Press and America* (4th ed.; Englewood Cliffs, N.J.: Prentice-Hall, 1978), chapter 10; and Michael Schudson, *Discovering the News* (New York: Basic Books, 1978), chapter 1.

tional distribution networks. But such was not the case at the beginning, in the first decade of the nineteenth century. The first efforts at organized evangelism through print in America were based upon long standard printing technology and traditional styles of local organization. It was the intensity of the missionary impulse that was new.

For many pious Christians, especially those with Federalist and pro-British political leanings, the turn of the eighteenth century was a time of grim foreboding. For them, the French Revolution had displayed vividly the excesses of both democracy and religious infidelity. Now, with the election of 1800, Jefferson, the arch democrat and infidel himself, was in power; and the political fortunes of the traditional Standing Order were bleak. It was a double burden for the conservative Christian Federalist. Not only was orthodox religion apparently under assault, but American government, both national and local, seemed increasingly disinclined to intervene on the side of traditional civil and ecclesiastical authority. With political power slipping from their grasp, many prominent Federalists and evangelical Christians turned to private voluntary associations and corporations to conduct the work of religious and moral regeneration.[4]

One such displaced Federalist was Elias Boudinot, friend of Washington, former president of the Continental Congress, leader of the Hamilton forces in the House of Representatives in the 1790s, and prominent Presbyterian layman. In 1801, out of power and seemingly out of step with the times, the sixty-year-old founding father published his first book, *The Age of Revelation*, a fundamentalist denunciation of Thomas Paine's *Age of Reason* and the whole spirit of the French Enlightenment. In the preface of the book, Boudinot wrote how shocked and dismayed he had been to learn "that thousands of copies of the *Age of Reason* had been sold at public auction, in this city (Philadelphia), at a cent and a half each, whereby children, servants, and the lowest people, had been tempted to purchase, for the novelty of buying a book at so low a rate; my attention was excited to find out what fund could afford so heavy an expense, for so unworthy an object."[5] Boudinot resolved to dedicate much of his remaining life and fortune to building a counter fund and counter organization for what he considered a more worthy object. His labors led to the formation of the New Jersey Bible Society in 1809 and the American Bible Society in 1816.[6]

The Rev. Jedidiah Morse of Massachusetts was another orthodox Christian Federalist who shared Boudinot's fears of the rising tide of democracy and irreligion. Bred in the traditional doctrines of New England Congregationalism, Morse believed that government should be conducted by men of wisdom and virtue, its object to enforce morality and right religion. However, with the traditional institutions of social order — church and state — now falling into the hands of Unitarians and Republicans, Morse urged the orthodox of New England to re-group and to organize private associations to carry on the work of Christ's

[4]On the movement of the old Standing Order into private institutions, see Peter D. Hall, *The Organization of American Culture, 1700-1900: Private Institutions, Elites, and the Origins of American Nationality* (New York: New York University Press, 1982), chapter 5.

[5]Elias Boudinot, *The Age of Revelation* (Philadelphia: Asbury Dickins, 1801), xx. See also George Adams Boyd, *Elias Boudinot: Patriot and Statesman, 1740-1821* (Princeton, N.J.: Princeton University Press, 1952), chapter 25; and Jane J. Boudinot, *The Life, Public Services, Addresses and Letters of Elias Boudinot*, 2 vols. (Boston and New York: Houghton Mifflin, 1896).

[6]Henry Otis Dwight, *The Centennial History of the American Bible Society* (New York: Macmillan, 1916), chapter 3. See also Boyd, *Elias Boudinot*, 257-60.

church on earth. For his part, Morse helped to organize the Massachusetts Society for the Promoting of Christian Knowledge in 1803 and, in 1814, the New England Tract Society, a precursor to the American Tract Society of 1825. "Too long have good men stood still, in criminal supineness or silent despondence," Morse wrote, "while a flood of licentiousness has been sweeping away the institutions of Christianity, and the landmarks of our fathers."[7]

Boudinot and Morse were prominent founders of what grew to be the national Bible and tract societies, but their beliefs and their notions of how those beliefs should be put into practice were typical of many religious men in the early nineteenth century.[8] Despite their denominational differences, they were quite similar in their fundamental religious, social, and political values. They were staunch conservatives, believers in tradition, deference, and hierarchy. In a sense, they were seventeenth-century men, mis-born into the eighteenth century, trying to come to terms with the nineteenth. On the one hand, they looked to the past. They rejected the secular rationalism of the eighteenth-century enlightenment, while longing for the ordered religious communitarianism of early America. They feared the rise of republicanism and liberal Christianity, while mourning the decline of Federalism and Calvinism. On the other hand, they looked to the future. They embraced the Hamiltonian program of new industrialism and economic development and the very modern world of large-scale private organization.

Very quickly, the dual commitment of such men to traditional values yet modern means would produce what might be called the industrialization of evangelism in America. At first, however, despite the will to evangelize, the available organizational and technological means were as old-fashioned as the religious ends.

Denominationalism was one force that slowed the growth of organized evangelism, but an even more salient characteristic of these first Bible and tract societies in the United States was localism. The first important American tract society was founded in New Haven in 1807; the first Bible society at Philadelphia in 1808. Within six years, more than one hundred Bible societies and dozens of tract societies were organized. The Philadelphia society was the largest, as well as the first, of the Bible societies. Its founders had contemplated building a national organization, but decided such an effort would simply be impossible at that time. Instead, they and the other local societies went their own way, with little communication or coordination among them.[9]

The denominationalism and especially the localism of the local Bible and tract societies was a great annoyance to missionaries such as Samuel Mills.

---

[7]*Proceedings of the First Ten Years of the American Tract Society, Instituted at Boston, 1814* (Boston: American Tract Society, 1824), 9. This volume has been reprinted in *The American Tract Society Documents, 1824-1925* (New York: Arno Press, 1972). See also James K. Morse, *Jedidiah Morse: A Champion of New England Orthodoxy* (New York: Columbia University Press, 1939); and Harvey G. Neufeldt, "The American Tract Society, 1825-1865: An Examination of Its Religious, Economic, Social, and Political Ideas" (unpublished Ph.D. dissertation, Michigan State University, 1971).

[8]The most detailed overviews of the missionary impulse of this era remain Clifford S. Griffin, *Their Brothers' Keepers: Moral Stewardship in the United States, 1800-1865* (New Brunswick, N.J.: Rutgers University Press, 1960); and Charles I. Foster, *An Errand of Mercy: The Evangelical United Front, 1790-1837* (Chapel Hill: University of North Carolina Press, 1960). See also Ronald G. Walters, *American Reformers, 1815-1860* (New York: Hill and Wang, 1978), chapter 1.

[9]*First Ten Years of the American Tract Society*, 198; Dwight, *Centennial History*, 7-9.

When Mills was preparing for this missionary tour of the West in 1814-15, he found that he had to solicit aid from a dozen or more local societies to collect enough Bibles and tracts to make the trip worthwhile. In his final report, he complained that the local societies cannot even meet the needs of their areas, much less the rapidly growing needs of the West. "It is a foul blot on our national character," he wrote. "Christian America must arise and wipe it away. — The existing Societies are not able to do it. They want union; — they want cooperation; — they want resources. If a National Institution cannot be formed, application ought to be made to the British and Foreign Bible Society for aid."[10]

It is not surprising that Mills should talk of British aid, for the British connection was the one major organizational link that transcended the localism of the American societies. Neither the legacy of the Revolutionary War nor the War of 1812, even while in progress, dimmed the enthusiasm of these Federalist evangelicals for the mother country. In fact, all of the American societies were to some extent dependent offspring of the great British societies. The Religious Tract Society, founded in London in 1799, was the source of nearly all of the tracts that were reprinted and circulated by the early tract societies in America. The British and Foreign Bible Society, founded in 1804, provided direct assistance to most of the new American Bible societies in the form of cash contributions or donations of Bibles and New Testaments.[11] One of the first acts of the organizers of a new American Society was usually to seek aid from abroad. As in colonial times, trans-Atlantic links could be stronger than links among the scattered communities of America, in spite of the widely shared and growing enthusiasm throughout America for the missionary cause.

In addition to providing material assistance, the British societies inspired the Americans with their vision of what religious mass media should be. Their plan was to achieve unity and to avoid denominational conflict by seeking the common denominator. The British and Foreign Bible Society agreed to publish the standard version of the Protestant Bible only "without note or comment."[12] The tracts printed by the Religious Tract Society in London and reprinted in America were usually brief homilies on the most widely acceptable of conservative Christian doctrines, or were simple narratives of conversion experiences. They were inexpensive pamphlets, about six inches by three and three-quarter inches in size, usually about four to twelve pages in length, and perhaps adorned with a simple woodcut on the cover. One of the most popular tracts on either side of the Atlantic in the early nineteenth century, for example, was "The Swearer's Prayer," a little homespun story of a man who came to realize that when he carelessly used God's name in vain he was actually calling for his own damnation.[13] According to the British plan, which the Americans adopted almost ver-

---

[10]Mills and Smith, *Report of a Missionary Tour*, 5-9, 47.

[11]William Jones, *The Jubilee Memorial of the Religious Tract Society* (London: Religious Tract Society, 1850), 612-3; William Canton, *A History of the British and Foreign Bible Society*, Vol. I (London: John Murray, 1904), 241-8. See also Frank Thistlewaite, *The Anglo-American Connection in the Early Nineteenth Century* (Philadelphia: University of Pennsylvania Press, 1959).

[12]"Laws and Regulations of the British and Foreign Bible Society," reprinted in Canton, *History of the British and Foreign Bible Society*, Vol. I, 18-9. See also John Owen, *The History of the Origin and First Ten Years of the British and Foreign Bible Society*, 2 vols. (London: L.B. Seeley, 1816).

[13]"Address to Christians on the Distribution of Religious Tracts," in *Proceedings of the First Twenty Years of the Religious Tract Society* (London: Religious Tract Society, 1820); American Tract Society, *Sev-*

batim, a good tract should be "pure truth," "plain," "striking," "entertaining," and "full of ideas." Simplicity was the key: nothing complex; nothing controversial.[14]

With the British model for inspiration, the problem for the local American societies was never lack of vision; the problem was lack of money and lack of capacity for mass printing and mass distribution. The history of the first ten years of the New England Tract Society, before its merger into the new American Tract Society in 1825, offers a case in point. The society was organized in 1814 by Jedidiah Morse and several other conservative Congregationalists, mainly associated with the Andover Theological Seminary. Their aim was expansive from the beginning: to build an organization, modeled after the Religious Tract Society of England, that would serve as a national coordinator and publisher for local societies throughout the United States.[15] To help organize this wider work, the society encouraged the formation of auxiliary societies and regional tract depositories, hired a traveling agent in 1819, and began publishing a magazine in 1824 to communicate with the branch societies.[16]

By 1821, the directors of the society had conceived of a grand plan for at least 100 well-stocked tract depositories, each serving twenty local societies, and altogether circulating six million tracts per year. Even such a mammoth effort as this, the directors declared, would be only a first step toward the ultimate goal of supplying every family in the country with a complete set of tracts.[17]

In fact, the New England Tract Society never came close to this goal. With its roots in rural Andover, the society developed few ties to the publishing and business worlds of Boston, much less to those of other major cities. The society contracted with a number of printers to do its work. It had no central printing location. In 1816, the society published 378,000 tracts, and over the next eight years the annual output was rarely more than 400,000. Each new tract was usually issued in an edition of 6,000, and then reprinted from time to time as demand warranted. In the years before 1824, the society's annual expenditures for paper and printing only once exceeded $5,000, not a large printing business even in that era. Even so, the society ran a debt every year except one between 1814 and 1824, and in the same period received only about $8,500 in outright donations.[18]

The Bible societies were equally determined to spread the word to every village, yet they found it equally difficult to do so. Many of the larger American

---

*enth Annual Report* (New York, 1832), 12-3. The American Tract Society (New York) will hereafter be referred to as ATS. On the success of "The Swearer's Prayer" see ATS, *Second Annual Report* (1827), 25; and ATS, *Third Annual Report* (1828), 11.

[14]Jones, *Jubilee Memorial*, chapter 3; "An Address to Christians Recommending the Distribution of Religious Tracts," in *First Ten Years of the American Tract Society*, 18-20.

[15]*First Ten Years of the American Tract Society*, 9. See also Elizabeth Twaddell, "The American Tract Society, 1814-1860," *Church History* 15 (June, 1946): 116-32.

[16]This section is based upon the New England Tract Society's annual reports, 1815-1824, which were reprinted by the society in 1824 in *First Ten Years of the American Tract Society*. The New England society changed its name to American Tract Society in 1823, two years before the founding of the New York-based American Tract Society in 1825.

[17]*First Ten Years of the American Tract Society*, 82-3.

[18]These figures are from the annual reports of the New England Society and a summary table in ibid., 178 and passim. Compare to general U.S. statistics on the value of printing work in Tench Coxe, ed., *A Statement of the Arts and Manufactures of the United States of America for the Year 1810* (Philadelphia: A. Cornman, Jr., 1814).

printers produced Bibles and New Testaments, but these were almost invariably in editions too small or too expensive to meet the demands perceived by Bible society organizers. Samuel Mills found in 1814 that even the oldest and wealthiest of the groups, the Philadelphia Bible Society, could make only a small donation of volumes for his missionary trip to the West.[19]

Eventually, the will to print drove the organizers of the Bible and tract societies to adopt better ways to reach the best end. In both Bible and tract work, the process was similar. One step was to seek and to promote new printing technology that would be more efficient for mass publication. In the 1810s and '20s, this meant stereotyping, steam-powered printing, and machine papermaking; and the Bible and tract societies were pioneer developers of all three. Another step was to put aside denominational differences and to build a genuine national organization for systematic distribution. A third step was to raise money. All three of these steps, it seems, carried the evangelical publicists inexorably to one place: New York.

*"THE FULL POWER OF THE PRESS"*

New York in the 1810s and '20s was engaged in a great commercial rivalry with Philadelphia and Boston, and it was winning. By 1821, some 23 per cent of the nation's imports came through New York. By 1831, the proportion was 50 per cent, and there was no longer any doubt that New York was to be the great commercial metropolis of the New World. In the single year of 1825, the year the Erie Canal opened, 500 new mercantile businesses opened their doors in the city.[20]

One New York firm that opened its doors that year was the newly organized American Tract Society. The founders of the Tract Society chose New York for the same reasons that other businesses did. New York was the leader in technology, transportation, and money. These were the worldly ingredients needed to turn God's divine will and man's pious plans into reality. As the new secretary of the society remarked, a publishing house in New York could print and distribute tracts "at so cheap a rate and in such quantities as to meet the demands of the nation.... The concentration of tract work in New York was what God designed."[21]

The first reason for locating in New York was technological. New York City after 1810 was the incubator of several new innovations in printing that would prove highly useful for Bible and tract publishing. The most important of these was stereotyping.

In stereotype printing, a facsimile of a whole page of type is produced by making a mold from a page composed of movable type and then casting a solid

---

[19]Mills and Smith, *Report of a Missionary Tour*, 47; Dwight, *Centennial History*, 14-7. See also Margaret T. Hills, *The English Bible in America: A Bibliography of Editions of the Bible and the New Testament Published in America 1777-1957* (New York: American Bible Society and New York Public Library, 1961), part I.

[20]Robert G. Albion, *The Rise of the New York Port* (New York: Scribners, 1939), 10, 13-4; Charles King, *Progress of the City of New York during the Last Fifty Years* (New York: D. Appleton, 1852), 74-5. See also Edward K. Spann, *The New Metropolis: New York City, 1840-1857* (New York: Columbia University Press, 1981), chapter 1.

[21]Helen C. Knight, *Memorial of the Rev. William A. Hallock, D.D., First Secretary of the American Tract Society* (New York: American Tract Society, 1882), 33-5.

metal "plate" in that mold. The stereotype plate can then be used in a regular printing press, in place of a page of movable type. Stereotyping was especially valuable for mass printing, mainly because the printer did not have to keep his capital locked up in standing type during a long press run. Once a plate of a page was cast, the movable types could be redistributed and immediately used again. With a complete set of plates for a work, the printer had the flexibility to produce as many copies and as many editions, as frequently or infrequently as he liked, without the expense of either keeping type standing or resetting it. Because producing the plates was itself a considerable investment of capital and labor, however, the savings of stereotyping grew large only on big jobs. Thus, not surprisingly, the first works stereotyped were standard, steady sellers — such as Bibles.[22]

The general idea of stereotyping was already old at the beginning of the nineteenth century, but the process did not become practical or economical until after 1802, when Lord Stanhope, the inventor of the Stanhope printing press, perfected the plaster-of-Paris molding technique in England.[23] By 1808, both Cambridge and Oxford university presses were printing with stereotype plates, and one of their best customers was the British and Foreign Bible Society.[24] The "secret" of stereotyping was brought to America in 1811 or 1812 by three or four type founders who had learned the process from Stanhope or his associates in England. The first book stereotyped in America was a catechism produced by John Watts in 1813. About the same time, one or two others, notably David and George Bruce, began work in stereotype founding. Significantly, all of the early pioneers of stereotyping in America worked in New York City.[25]

As in England, the first big customers of the stereotypers were the Bible societies. The Philadelphia Bible Society published a Bible in 1812 with plates imported from England, which were paid for largely by the British and Foreign Bible Society. This was probably the first stereotyped book printed in the United States. In 1816, the New York Bible Society began to publish its own Bibles from plates cast by Elihu White in New York. Stereotyping required a sizable initial investment, and the local New York society could not act alone. It needed the support, in the form of capital and the promise of future orders, of other local societies around the country.[26] Not surprisingly, the New York soci-

---

[22]For a general history of stereotyping, see George A. Kubler, *A New History of Stereotyping* (New York: Little & Ives, 1941); and George A. Kubler, *Historical Treatises, Abstracts, and Papers on Stereotyping* (New York: Brooklyn Eagle Press, 1936). Two very early pamphlets on the process have recently been reprinted. See Charles Brightly, *The Method of Founding Stereotype*, and Thomas Hodgson, *An Essay on the Origin and Progress of Stereotype Printing* (New York: Garland, 1982). Brightly's pamphlet was originally published in 1809; Hodgson's in 1822. This reprint volume has a useful introduction by Michael L. Turner.

[23]George A. Kubler, *The Era of Charles Mahon, Third Earl of Stanhope, Stereotyper, 1750-1825* (New York: Brooklyn Eagle Press, 1938); and John Bidwell, "Joshua Gilpin and Lord Stanhope's Improvements in Printing," *Papers of the Bibliographical Society of America* 76 (Second Quarter, 1982): 143-58.

[24]M.H. Black, "The Printed Bible," in *The Cambridge History of the Bible*, Vol. 3, ed. by S.L. Greenslade (Cambridge: Cambridge University Press, 1963), 466-7.

[25]Harry B. Weiss, "Type Founders, Copperplate Printers, Stereotypers in Early New York City," *Bulletin of the New York Public Library* 55 (October, 1951): 480-2; Kubler, *New History of Stereotyping*, 147-53. See also Harry B. Weiss, "The Number of Persons and Firms Connected with the Graphic Arts in New York City, 1633-1820," *Bulletin of the New York Public Library* 50 (October, 1946): 775-86.

[26]Hills, *English Bible*, 37, 46; E.B. O'Callaghan, *A List of Editions of the Holy Scriptures and Parts thereof Printed in America previous to 1860* (Albany: Munsell and Rowland, 1861), 110, 135. This pioneer work of bibliography was reprinted by Gale Research of Detroit in 1966.

ety in 1815 became one of the first of the major local societies to join with Elias Boudinot's New Jersey group in efforts to form a national association.[27] It was no mere coincidence that the adoption of stereotype printing and the movement toward a national organization based in New York occurred at the same time.

After the American Bible Society was founded in May of 1816, the Board of Managers of the new society determined that their "first exertions ought to be directed toward the procurement of well-executed stereotype plates."[28] Almost immediately, the three stereotypers then operating in New York began to compete for the business of the American Bible Society. In August, the board required sealed bids from all three, and awarded its first contract for three sets of plates to D. & G. Bruce for $4,000. Meanwhile, the New York Bible Society voted to turn over its plates to the new national society.[29] By the end of its first year, the American Bible Society had printed about 10,000 Bibles and was on its way to acquiring the capability of large-scale production. By the end of its third year, the society owned eight sets of plates for the whole Bible and two for the New Testament and was printing more than 70,000 volumes annually on eight hand presses in constant use. The acquisition of stereotype plates would remain a major item in Bible Society budgets, and the society would remain a major supporter of the handful of firms that dominated the stereotype founding business in New York.[30] By moving quickly into the new technology of stereotypography, the American Bible Society was able to become a leading American book publisher and printer by 1820, with a proportionally smaller investment than a traditional movable type printing firm.

The tract societies were somewhat slower than the Bible societies to move into stereotype printing, doubtless because the process would not have been as quickly valuable for small tracts as for Bibles. But with the constant demand for new editions of the same tracts, the tract societies also began to think about economies of scale in printing. And in 1823, the New England Tract Society began the costly process of stereotyping its tracts. The directors felt that this was a crucial part of their plan to build a genuinely national publishing operation.[31] In that same year, the New England society even changed its name to the American Tract Society, to proclaim its national commitment. But the capital investment for stereotype plates was considerable, and the society's expenditures shot up 131 per cent in 1823-24, while its tract production increased by only 64 per cent. The society's debt continued to mount as well.[32]

By early 1825, despite the misgivings of some of the conservative New England leadership, the American Tract Society was ready to merge with other ma-

---

[27]"Resolutions of the New York Bible Society," quoted in Dwight, *Centennial History*, 18-9. See also David J. Fant, *The Bible in New York: The Romance of Scripture Distribution in a World Metropolis from 1809 to 1948* (New York: American Bible Society, 1948).

[28]American Bible Society, *First Annual Report* (New York, 1817), 10. See also American Bible Society, *Minutes of the Board of Managers*, July 3, 1816, in American Bible Society archives, New York. American Bible Society hereafter will be referred to as ABS.

[29]ABS, *Minutes of the Board of Managers*, August 7, 1816, and August 17, 1816. See also Eric M. North, "The Production and Supply of Scriptures, Part I, 1816-1820," *ABS Historical Essay #18* (typescript), 1-2. Copy in the library of the ABS, New York.

[30]ABS, *First Annual Report* (1817), 11; ABS, *Third Annual Report* (1819), 10-1. See also North, "The Production and Supply of Scriptures, Part II, 1821-1830," *ABS Historical Essay #18* (typescript). Copy in the library of the ABS.

[31]*First Ten Years of the American Tract Society*, 128.

[32]Summary table, in ibid., 178.

jor local societies and to move its publishing operations to New York. In announcing the new, consolidated American Tract Society, formed in 1825 and based in New York, the founders declared that the centralization of stereotype printing was "a powerful argument in favor of union." "Tracts are now exceedingly cheap," they said, "but the Committee are greatly deceived if the formation of the American Tract Society does not render them cheaper than they are now."[33]

With the organization of the American Tract Society in New York, stereotyping became a major effort. Not only did the Boston and New York local societies turn over their plates to the national organization, but the new group also contracted for its own stereotyping, so that by the end of its first year the society had stereotyped 155 tracts (some 2,000 pages).[34] Moreover, in planning for a new headquarters building, the American Tract Society executive committee provided for the society's own stereotype foundry in the basement. With this kind of enthusiasm for the new technology of printing, it is little wonder that the executive committee spoke in its first annual report of the Christian obligation to use the "mighty engine" of print just as God himself had used the written word to reveal himself to man.[35]

Stereotyping was probably the most important, but was not the only, technological innovation in printing that the Bible and tract societies helped to bring into practical service in America. The societies were also two of the first publishing houses in America to install steam-powered presses. Of course, power presses are not absolutely necessary for mass printing; many hand presses will also do the job. And the Bible Society had at least twenty hand presses at work constantly by the mid-1820s. But the faster a single press can work, the more efficiently it can employ labor and the capital tied up in stereotype plates. Cheaper labor could also be hired to operate power presses (girls instead of men and boys, for example), a kind of efficiency not always greeted with sanguinity by the skilled artisans of the printing trade. But for the owners of capital, efficiency is efficiency; and from the beginning, the managers of both societies actively encouraged innovations and improvements in the printing press itself.[36]

Most significantly, both societies were early adopters of Daniel Treadwell's steam-powered bed-and-platen press, the first generally successful powered printing press to be built in America. Treadwell, a Bostonian, had studied steam-powered printing in England during a visit in 1820. The most famous English power press at that time was the cylinder press developed by Friedrich Koenig and first put into service on *The Times* of London in 1814. The Koenig press was extremely fast, but it also was expensive to install, was hard on type, and was not suited to fine-quality work. In America, where newspapers were highly localized and individual newspaper circulations were small, it was the book pub-

[33]*Address of the Executive Committee of the American Tract Society to the Christian Public* (New York: D. Fanshaw, 1825), 12. This pamphlet is reprinted in *American Tract Society Documents*. On costs of production, see Tables 1 and 2.

[34]ATS, *First Annual Report* (1826), 11-2, 15.

[35]Ibid., 18, 22. See also *Address of the Executive Committee*.

[36]Discussions of printing costs and techniques are common in the minutes of the ABS Standing Committee in the late 1810s and 1820s. The Standing Committee was a committee of five members of the Board of Managers appointed in the society's first year to conduct daily business between monthly board meetings. See also Hills, "Production and Supply of Scriptures," 6-10.

lishers who pioneered in power printing. And for them, in the 1820s, the cylinder press was unsuitable. What Treadwell did was to design and build in 1822 a press that stood, technologically, between the traditional hand press and the new cylinder steam press. In Treadwell's design, much of the work was still done by hand, and the pressure was applied downward by a platen. But there was no bar to pull. The platen was moved by steam, water, or horsepower; and the speed of the work was much faster than on a hand press. The Treadwell press, later much improved by Isaac and Seth Adams and others, remained the standard machine in much of the publishing industry for more than fifty years.[37]

The managers of the American Bible Society learned of Treadwell's experiments as early as 1822 or 1823 and were immediately interested. They contacted him in 1823 and began negotiations that would eventually lead to the installation of sixteen Treadwell presses by 1829. All of these presses, incidentally, were probably built by Robert Hoe of New York, under a franchise arrangement with Treadwell.[38] The firm R. Hoe & Company, then in its infancy, grew to be the leading manufacturer of printing presses in nineteenth-century America. The American Tract Society almost immediately after its founding in 1825 began to move to steam-power printing, installing its first Treadwell press in 1826, the first in New York. Nine more were soon added to the Tract Society's printing plant.[39]

At both the Tract Society and the Bible Society, the introduction of mechanical power was managed by Daniel Fanshaw, who was chief printer for each of the two societies at different times in the 1820s. Fanshaw was the leading entrepreneur of the steam-powered bed-and-platen press in New York City. He held exclusive rights to use the Treadwell press in New York, and he was an avid enthusiast of power printing. In the late 1820s, he was constantly seeking loans and mortgaging his property to finance more steam presses, and he was constantly nagging manufacturers such as R. Hoe for faster delivery. Fanshaw was also an expert in the use of stereotype plates, having worked for D. & G. Bruce before signing on with the Bible Society about 1817. Fanshaw seems to have been more of a developer than an inventor, though he is sometimes listed as a claimant to the title of the first steam-powered printer in America. Indeed, except for some experimental work by Jonas Booth in the early 1820s, Fanshaw's rows of Treadwell presses at the American Tract Society were the first of a very long line of power presses in the publishing houses of the city of New York.[40]

---

[37]James Moran, *Printing Presses: History and Development from the Fifteenth Century to Modern Times* (Berkeley and Los Angeles: University of California Press, 1973), 113-6; Robert Hoe, *A Short History of The Printing Press* (New York: Robert Hoe, 1902), 10-1. On the Koenig cylinder press, see Moran, *Printing Presses*, chapter 7. Jonas Booth is sometimes credited with introducing the power press in America, also about 1822. But he produced very few machines. See Moran, *Printing Presses*, 114.

[38]Daniel Treadwell letter to ABS, September 20, 1823, in ABS archives; ABS, *Minutes of the Standing Committee*, January 27, 1827, in ABS archives; *Address of the Board of Managers of the American Bible Society to the Friends of the Bible of Every Religious Denomination...*(New York: J. Seymour, 1829), 13; *An Abstract of the American Bible Society, Containing An Account of Its Principles and Operations* (New York: Daniel Fanshaw, 1830), 12. See also Hills, "Production and Supply of Scriptures," 11-5.

[39]*American Tract Magazine* 1 (April, 1826): 275; "Daniel Fanshaw," in *American Dictionary of Printing and Bookmaking*, reprint edition of 1894 original (New York: Lenox Hill, 1970), 184.

[40]Moran, *Printing Presses*, 114; *American Dictionary of Printing and Bookmaking*, 184; North, "Production and Supply of Scriptures," 41-4. See also Lawrence Thompson, "The Printing and Publishing Activities of the American Tract Society from 1825 to 1850," *Papers of the Bibliographical Society of America* 35 (Second Quarter, 1941): 81-114.

In addition to its early promotion of stereotyping and power-printing, the Bible Society was also a pioneer supporter of machine papermaking in the United States. Before 1800, papermaking was a slow, costly handicraft. A skilled workman made each sheet of paper separately on a screen frame dipped by hand through a vat of water and macerated cloth fibers. The first successful papermaking machine was developed by Nicholas-Louis Robert in France in the late 1790s. Robert's machine, which was later taken over by the Fourdrinier brothers of London, used an "endless wire cloth" (screen belt), in place of the hand-held frame, to produce an endless web of paper, without the need of skilled workmen. And it did the work, as Robert said in his patent application, at "infinite less expense,"[41] Though Robert exaggerated the cost savings of his machine somewhat, his process, under the name Fourdrinier, did revolutionize the papermaking process, allowing for enormously increased production, while gradually cutting the price of paper by about 60 per cent over the first half of the nineteenth century.[42]

The first papermaking machine in America, somewhat different from a Fourdrinier, was developed by Thomas Gilpin of Delaware and put into service in 1817. Gilpin's product immediately sparked the interest of newspaper and book publishers, and the first American book to be printed on American machine-made paper appeared in 1820, published by Mathew Carey of Philadelphia. In the late 1820s, several Fourdrinier machines (the style of machine that proved most successful) were imported from England and France. Then in 1829, George Spafford and James Phelps began to build their own improved Fourdrinier machines in South Windham, Connecticut. The buyer of the first Fourdrinier papermaking machine to be built in America was Amos H. Hubbard, who had been operating a hand-made paper mill at Norwich, Connecticut.[43] Hubbard was a chief paper supplier to the American Bible Society.

In its earliest years, the Bible Society preferred paper imported from France and Southern Europe and tried aggressively to have Congress exempt its imports from the 30 per cent duty imposed by the tariff of 1816.[44] The society also tirelessly shopped around among domestic papermakers in the 1810s and early 1820s. By the end of the 1820s, the society had developed major contracts with three or four manufacturers, including most prominently Amos Hubbard.[45] Hubbard not only supplied paper to the Bible Society, he enthusiastically supported its work. He was an active member of the very active Norwich auxiliary, and in August of 1829 — just three months after the installation of his new Fourdrinier machine — he became a Life Member of the national society, making his dona-

---

[41]Robert quoted in Dard Hunter, *Papermaking: The History and Technique of an Ancient Craft* (2nd ed.; New York: Knopf, 1947), 344, 346. See also Robert H. Clapperton, *The Papermaking Machine: Its Invention, Evolution, and Development* (New York and Oxford: Pergamon Press, 1968).

[42]On prices, see Donald C. Coleman, *The British Paper Industry, 1495-1860* (Oxford: Clarendon Press, 1958), 202-4; and Lyman H. Weeks, *A History of Paper Manufacturing in the United States, 1690-1916* (New York: Lockwood Trade Journal Co., 1916), 195, 223-4.

[43]Hunter, *Papermaking*, 351-6; and David C. Smith, *History of Papermaking in the United States, 1691-1969* (New York: Lockwood Publishing, 1970), 32.

[44]"Memorial to Congress" draft, ABS, *Minutes of the Board of Managers*, January 1, 1817, and May 7, 1818; ABS, *Second Annual Report* (1818), 21. See also North, "Production and Supply of Scriptures," 24-32.

[45]Hills, "Production and Supply of Scriptures," 47.

tion in reams of paper rather than money.[46]

The Bible Society was almost certainly Hubbard's chief customer, perhaps his only customer, in the first few years after he automated his mill. He worked closely with Daniel Fanshaw, the society's printer, to rapidly expand Bible production in 1829 and 1830. Fanshaw had a few complaints from time to time, but in general the Bible Society was pleased with the quality and the price of Hubbard's machine-made paper. And Hubbard by 1830 was a true believer in the process. "I find that the Paper-makers generally do not feel very cordial towards me because I sell paper so cheap," he wrote. "One man remarked that it would oblige him to stop his Mill."[47]

By the late 1820s, the managers of both the Bible and the Tract societies felt that they had developed the technical expertise — in stereotyping, printing, and paper manufacturing — to make the whole nation their audience. In 1827, the year after they had moved to steam printing, the officers of the Tract Society announced confidently that they could place at least one tract into the hands of every American in a single year. "Twelve millions of inhabitants are indeed a great many, but twelve millions of tracts can be printed and printed in one year, with no essential sacrifice to the community ... this *can be done*." Modern religious tract work, they said, "brings the art of stereotyping, and the full power of the press, of which every body has spoken, but the extent of which perhaps no one has ever duly estimated, to bear, in all the perfection of their energy, upon the moral welfare of our country."[48]

The leaders of the Bible Society were equally confident. In 1829, society secretary James Milnor declared that the printing plant had the capacity to produce a Bible for every family in the land — between 500,000 and 600,000 annually. "It is apparent," he told the annual meeting in May of 1829, "that there can be printed and bound, and issued from this Depository, during the ensuing two years, and for every succeeding period, all the Bibles and Testaments that public exigency in its most extended requisition can call for at our hands."[49]

*"SYSTEMATIC ORGANIZATION"*

The capacity of the print shop, however, was not the sole measure of success for mass media; this the leaders of both societies well understood. The nation must be systematically organized, and large sums of money must be raised. To this end, the societies' founders resolved, first, to set aside denominational and doctrinal differences and, second, to build unified, centralized national organizations.

Both societies were built upon the hope that the missionary impulse would prove stronger than denominationalism. And to some extent this turned out to be true, though both societies, especially the Tract Society, were supported mainly by the traditionally conservative church bodies. Following the British example, unity was achieved by seeking the lowest common denominator. For

---

[46]Ibid., 47-8; ABS, *Fourteenth Annual Report* (1830), 23; and ABS, *Fifteenth Annual Report* (1831), 24.

[47]Letters from Hubbard to the ABS, August 8, 1830, August 11, 1830, September 4, 1830, and September 11, 1830, in ABS archives.

[48]ATS, *Second Annual Report* (1827), 23.

[49]Milnor, quoted in Hills, "Production and Supply of Scriptures," 18. See also *Address of the Board of Managers.*

the Bible Society, this meant that the Bible would be published "without note or comment." The founders could agree on little else beyond the centrality of the Bible; but for the society's purpose, this was enough.[50] Similarly, the Tract Society resolved to publish only those tracts that would not offend any of the participating denominations. "The different denominations composing the Publishing Committee, come to their work with the solemn and honest stipulation to be each the protector of his own peculiarities," declared the Executive Committee in 1825; "and in this labour of mercy to publish and distribute such Tracts only, as shall inculcate those great doctrines in which they all harmonize."[51] For the American Tract Society, broad agreement on "a few great facts" was always a prime organizational consideration.[52]

The next step beyond interdenominational cooperation was the building of a genuine national organization. To this end, both societies organized elaborate systems of local auxiliary societies and branch distributors. In the same report in which it proclaimed its ability to print twelve million tracts a year, the Tract Society entreated its members: "Let the Society itself be roused to proper effort; let Branches and Auxiliaries be formed in our large cities and towns, in the capital of every State, and the chief town of every County, and Auxiliaries be formed in every parish and neighborhood, throughout the land." The Rev. Milnor, an officer of both societies, put the matter succinctly: "The machinery of a mill may be mechanically perfect in all its parts, but not a wheel will move without the impetus of water. And so those stereotype plates, giving so much facility to the art of printing, and those power-presses, multiplying with such unexampled rapidity impressions of the sacred pages, to produce their expected results, must be put in motion, and to put them in motion, pecuniary means must be supplied, and for these means, the occupants of these plates and presses must be dependent on their Auxiliaries."[53]

Both societies labored throughout the 1820s to establish national networks of branches and auxiliaries for raising funds and for distributing their products. The Bible Society increased its network of local auxiliaries from 207 in 1820 to 645 by 1829. The Tract Society had formally recognized 713 branches and auxiliaries by 1829.[54] Many of the newer societies were located in the West and in the new South, where the evangelicals felt the need for religious missionary work was most pressing.

Though the auxiliaries of both societies were increasingly far flung, the centers of operations remained in New York; and each society in the 1820s gradually centralized and systematized the power of the New York organization.

New York was chosen, not only because of its growing leadership in printing technology, but also because of its growing dominance as the nation's communications center in the new age of canals, steamboats, and ocean packets. "If the

---

[50]*Constitution of the American Bible Society* (New York: G.F. Hopkins, 1816). The ABS Constitution is reprinted in most of the society's annual reports. See also Dwight, *Centennial History*, 21-5.

[51]*Address of the Executive Committee*, 9. See also, "Constitution of the American Tract Society," in each annual report.

[52]ATS, *First Annual Report* (1826), 9-10, 36; ATS, *Eighth Annual Report* (1833), 5.

[53]ATS, *Second Annual Report* (1827), 23; Milnor, quoted in Hills, "Production and Supply of Scriptures," 18.

[54]ABS, *Fourth Annual Report* (1820), 16; ABS, Thirteenth Annual Report (1829), 7; and ATS, *Fourth Annual Report* (1829), 57.

signs of the times call for a National Institution," the organizers of the American Tract Society declared, "where might we look for the seat of its operations, unless where there are greater facilities of ingress and egress, and more extended, constant, and direct intercommunications with foreign ports, and every part of our interior, than are to be found in any other locality in the nation? ... Merchants assemble here, and opportunities are constantly presented for sending Tracts at a very small expense, and very frequently at no expense at all, to the remotest parts of the land, and of engaging the proper persons to use their influence in distributing them.... The City of New-York, eminently distinguished by its natural and local advantages, its accumulating population, and its increasing commercial prosperity and influence, seems destined, in the wisdom of Divine Providence, to become the centre of these extended operations."[55]

The Bible Society had already found the same opportunities in New York: "The constant intercourse maintained between a great metropolis, like New-York, with other ports, and with the interior of the country in every direction, supplies opportunities, at every season of the year, of conveying Bibles, with cheapness, security, and expedition, to the most distant places. And when to these propitious circumstances is added the comparative difference of expense in conducting an establishment on a large and on a contracted scale, in the purchase of materials, the cost of labor, and the superior execution of the work, the Managers feel warranted in the belief, that Bibles, issued from the general Depository of this Society, can be afforded at a much lower rate, in proportion to their quality, than from any other source."[56]

The watchword was "systematic organization," a phrase that appears frequently in both societies' literature. The centralization of all printing was the obvious first step. In its earliest years, the Bible Society experimented with branch printing, loaning a set of stereotype plates in 1816 to the Kentucky Bible Society at Lexington. But the managers soon abandoned this experiment and decided by 1823 that the best and cheapest work could be done only at the society's own house in New York.[57] By 1825, when the Tract Society was founded, it was already clear that centralized printing was preferable. The next step for both societies was to transform what tended to be scattered, autonomous local societies into auxiliaries subsidiary to a centralized, national organization.

To some extent, this transformation had to depend upon voluntary cooperation and persuasion. To build a cooperative, unified system of auxiliaries, both societies organized formal communication networks. The Tract Society continued the *American Tract Magazine*, begun by the New England Society in 1824, which was filled with correspondence from the various branches, as well as suggestions and guidelines from the national office. The Bible Society published a similar newsletter for auxiliaries called *Monthly Extracts*. Each issue carried the admonition: "It is recommended that these *Extracts* be read at the meetings of

---

[55]*Address of the Executive Committee*, 13. On the transportation/communication revolution, see George Rogers Taylor, *The Transportation Revolution* (New York: Rinehart, 1951); and Allan R. Pred, *Urban Growth and the Circulation of Information: The United States System of Cities, 1790-1840* (Cambridge, Mass.: Harvard University Press, 1973).

[56]ABS, *Fourth Annual Report* (1820), 8.

[57]ABS, *First Annual Report* (1817), 10, 21; ABS, *Second Annual Report* (1818), 10-1; ABS, *Minutes of the Board of Managers*, February 1, 1821, and February 6, 1823. See also Dwight, *Centennial History*, 49-50.

the Board of Directors of each Auxiliary and Branch Bible Society and Bible Association." The national offices also required regular reports from local societies, specified in detail how local societies should be organized and operated, and chastised those that didn't live up to their obligations.[58] Both national societies recognized that the auxiliaries were the key to systematic distribution, although the lingering localism of American institutions sometimes frustrated their drive toward centralized authority.[59]

Though largely dependent upon voluntary cooperation, each national office had some direct power to enforce its will. The structures of the organizations for example, vested administrative authority in the hands of small executive boards, which tended to be dominated year after year by the same small cliques of New Yorkers and New Englanders. The Constitution of the American Bible Society even specified that twenty-four of the thirty-six managers must reside in New York City or its vicinity. The constitutions of both societies also provided that auxiliaries must support the national organization financially in order to receive Bibles and tracts at discounted rates.[60] Though some of the stricter constitutional provisions were eventually relaxed, the national offices usually were able to use their centralized administrative power and control over the source of the product to turn the local societies to their point of view.

Another centralizing organizational technique was the employment of traveling agents hired directly by the national office. Bible and Tract society agents were a kind of cross between religious missionaries and traveling booksellers. They were hired, directed, and usually supported by the national office. The Bible Society's first agent, Richard D. Hall, began work in 1822, and in his first year's service he traveled 3,000 miles — preaching, chatting, exhorting, and organizing some thirty-five new auxiliaries. Hall's calling depended upon the improvements in transportation that were beginning to appear in America in that era, but he found that in 1822 the transportation revolution had not worked its wonders everywhere. He wrote from Wheeling, in the Ohio River valley: "I arrived at this place last Monday, and in consequence of so much unfavorable weather, and great fatigue in traveling, and intolerable roads, I am nearly outdone." The society, however, was very pleased with Hall's itinerancy; and by 1828 the American Bible Society had twelve agents in the field.[61]

The Tract Society also employed a dozen or more agents in the 1820s, especially in the sparsely populated regions of the Ohio and Mississippi valleys. Later the American Tract Society became famous for its extensive use of traveling missionary/salesmen — the so-called "colporteurs" of the mid-to-late nineteenth century.[62]

---

[58]*American Tract Magazine and Monthly Extracts*, passim. See also ATS, *First Annual Report* (1826), 12-3; ABS, *Eleventh Annual Report* (1827), 10-1, 96; ABS, *Sixth Annual Report* (1822), 82.

[59]ATS, *Fourth Annual Report* (1829), 17; ATS, *Seventh Annual Report* (1832), 18-9; ABS, *Fifth Annual Report* (1821), 28-9; *Abstract of the American Bible Society*, 26-7. See also Dwight, *Centennial History*, 40-7.

[60]"Constitution of the American Tract Society" and *Constitution of the American Bible Society*. See also Neufeldt, "American Tract Society," 22-3.

[61]ABS, *Seventh Annual Report* (1823), 20-1, 73-4; ABS, *Twelfth Annual Report* (1828), 30-1. See also *Abstract of the American Bible Society*, 18-9, 38. On the similarity to booksellers' agents, see Boynton, *Annals of American Bookselling*, 131-6.

[62]ATS, *Fifth Annual Report* (1830), 35-7; *The American Colporteur System* (New York: American Tract Society, 1836); and *Instructions of the Executive Committee of the American Tract Society to Colporteurs*

*"THE BENEVOLENT EMPIRE"*

All of these innovations — technical and organizational — cost money, and money was a third reason for locating in New York. Of course, the bulk of receipts for both societies came in the form of payment for books and tracts. But both societies were always scrambling as well for outright donations. New York City may have been less pious than Boston, but those New Yorkers who were pious tended to have more money. Many, in fact, were themselves New Englanders by birth and faith, though nascent New Yorkers by business.[63] And at least some of these evangelical New York businessmen were in a position by the 1820s to endow Christian benevolence with financial clout. The American Bible Society, for example, was able easily and quickly to raise $22,500 in the early 1820s for a new building. Similarly, the Tract Society was drawn to New York in part because a handful of New York philanthropists pledged $25,000 to put up a building and get the new organization started.[64] In the 1820s, it seemed that New York was a place where men could afford to be benevolent.

Probably the most benevolent of all was Arthur Tappan, a native of Northampton, Massachusetts, who made a fortune in New York in the import trade. Tappan supported dozens of philanthropic and reform causes, ranging from pure missionary crusades to radical antislavery. From the beginning, one of his major interests was the work of the American Tract Society. He was one of four New Yorkers who underwrote the society's founding, and he financed the purchase of the society's first Treadwell steam presses in 1826. In all, he gave at least $20,000. He also served on the finance committee and, when needed, delivered tracts door to door. Tappan also gave the American Bible Society at least $5,000 in the late 1820s.[65] Arthur Tappan was perhaps unique in the breadth and depth of his munificence. Yet Tappan was part of a wealthy and growing sub-culture in New York that seemed to bring together, for a time at least, traditional piety and modern finance — to help produce what has come to be known as "the benevolent empire" of the 1820s and '30s.[66]

For both the American Bible Society and the American Tract Society, the 1820s were years of millennial optimism. And, indeed, real progress was made toward the goal of establishing genuine mass religious media in America. The Bible Society began the decade printing about 60,000 Bibles and New Testaments annually. In 1828, the society printers turned out 100,000 for the first time, and then more than 300,000 annually over the next two years. The society also was able to improve the quality of its work, while at the same time to re-

*and Agents* (New York: American Tract Society, 1868). These two pamphlets are reprinted in *American Tract Society Documents*.

[63]Hall, *Organization of American Culture*, chapter 5; Edward Pessen, *Riches, Class, and Power before the Civil War* (Lexington, Mass.: Heath, 1973).

[64]ABS, *Seventh Annual Report* (1823), 8; ATS, *First Annual Report* (1826), 18; ATS, *Twenty-Fifth Annual Report* (1850), 22-3. See also John M. Gibson, *Soldiers of the Word: The Story of the American Bible Society* (Philadelphia: Philosophical Library, 1958), 57-8. For a general account of philanthropy in New York see Kenneth D. Miller, *The People are the City: 150 Years of Social and Religious Concern in New York* (New York: Macmillan, 1962).

[65]Lewis Tappan, *The Life of Arthur Tappan* (New York: Hurd and Houghton, 1871), 74-5; Bertram Wyatt-Brown, *Lewis Tappan and the Evangelical War Against Slavery* (Cleveland: Press of Case Western Reserve University, 1969), chapter 3. *The Life of Arthur Tappan* has been reprinted by Greenwood Press, 1970.

[66]Walters, *American Reformers*, 33.

duce the price of the least expensive volumes. In 1820, the cheapest Bible sold for 60 cents, the cheapest New Testament for 22 cents. In 1828, the society began to issue a cloth-bound New Testament for 12 cents, and reduced the cheapest Bible to 50 cents.[67]

The Tract Society printed nearly 700,000 tracts in the first year after its founding in 1825 — slightly more than 8 million pages. In 1829, the society produced more than 7 million tracts — 61 million pages — as well as more than 100,000 *Christian Almanacs*, books, and other publications. The nominal price for tracts remained 1 cent per 10 pages throughout the decade, but the society gradually improved the quality of the product by adding illustrations and free covers.[68] These prices do not necessarily reflect the actual cost to the final consumer, of course. In the case of both Bibles and tracts, large numbers were purchased at cost by auxiliary societies, and then simply given away to the public free of charge.

This kind of production placed both societies, particularly the Bible Society, in the first rank of American publishers by the late 1820s — though not at the very top. The largest and most prosperous publisher of that era, the model for later large houses such as Harpers, was Carey & Lea of Philadelphia. In 1829, an especially good year, Carey & Lea counted receipts of $202,000, twice the Bible Society's receipts of $101,000. But it seems unlikely that Carey produced more volumes than the Bible Society. Carey & Lea still served a traditionally diversified market, with many titles issued in editions of a few hundred copies, often sold by subscription. In the 1820s, Carey had only begun to move into what would become a genuinely popular literature. Carey's best-selling author in the 1820s, for example, was James Fenimore Cooper, the most popular American author at the time. Cooper's novels were published by Carey in editions ranging from 1,000 to 6,500 copies (the latter for *The Red Rover* of 1828).[69] Such large editions portended the large-scale popular publication that would come in the 1830s, '40s, and '50s. But in the 1820s, no publisher could match the enormous editions turned out at the Bible Society's house in New York City. As early as 1827, in fact, the managers of the society reported, matter of factly, that "printing of Bibles and Testaments in this country has fallen, in a good measure, into the hands of the American Bible Society."[70]

Indeed, in 1829, with thousands of stereotype plates at hand, with rows of steam-powered presses in place, with endless webs of paper flowing from Hubbard's and others' Fourdrinier machines, and with hundreds of branches and auxiliaries ready and waiting, the American Bible Society and the American Tract Society each felt confident to make a momentous decision: They formally adopted explicit plans to supply everyone in the United States with Bibles and tracts.

---

[67]ABS, *Fourth Annual Report* (1820) through *Fourteenth Annual Report* (1830), passim. See also Table 1 and the tables in Dwight, *Centennial History*, 576-7.

[68]ATS, *First Annual Report* (1826) through *Fifth Annual Report* (1830), passim. See also Table 2 and the summary table in ATS, *Tenth Annual Report* (1835), 2.

[69]David Kaser, *Messrs. Carey & Lea of Philadelphia: A Study in the History of the Booktrade* (Philadelphia: University of Pennsylvania Press, 1957), 48, 50, 81. See also David Kaser, ed., *The Cost Book of Carey & Lea, 1825-1838* (Philadelphia: University of Pennsylvania Press, 1963), passim. The Carey of "Carey & Lea" was Henry, son of the great turn-of-the-century publisher/bookseller Mathew Carey.

[70]ABS, *Eleventh Annual Report* (1827), 8.

## "GENERAL SUPPLY"

At the annual meeting of the American Bible Society in May 1829, the Rev. James Milnor, speaking for the board of managers, proposed a resolution that the society supply a Bible to every family in the United States that needed one, and to do it within two years.[71] The resolution passed easily, for it was the culmination of years of study, debate, and planning within the society. To reach everyone had always been the ultimate goal, of course; but before 1829 some leaders of the society had felt that it would be unwise to bind the society to a specific short-range goal that would be impossible to achieve. Now it appeared that the impossible was possible, after all. In the 1820s, the technical basis for America's first mass media had been laid. The managers were clearly awed by the unprecedented nature of such a plan: "In the course of events that have marked the age in which we live, few of a more striking character have occurred than the measure adopted at the late anniversary of the American Bible Society.[72]

Success in this first "general supply," as they called it, depended upon systematic surveys and organized distributions at the level of the local auxiliaries. There seemed to be evidence by 1829 that these things could be done. Ten state organizations were already engaged in efforts to canvass and supply "destitute" families in their areas. That is, they had, or at least thought they had, the capability to knock on virtually every door in their state. Moreover, several of the larger state societies pledged to the general effort, not only cooperation in the distribution of Bibles, but financial support as well. The New Hampshire society pledged $12,000; Vermont pledged $10,000; Connecticut also $10,000; and so on. Wealthy individuals, including the usual New Yorkers, also offered aid. Arthur Tappan, for example, pledged $5,000 for the "general supply."[73] Though the auxiliaries had sometimes been an annoyance to the central authorities in New York, now the auxiliaries in all parts of the country appeared to be, not only aroused to service, but capable of "systematic organization" and "judicious and systematic division of labor."[74]

The "general supply" of every family in the country in two years turned out to be the sort of task the pessimists had feared: impossible. At the end of two years, in 1831, the managers had to admit that, while they had God on their side, nature seemed set against their efforts. Population growth and mobility, especially in the West, made surveys difficult and quickly outdated. An unusually severe winter in 1830-31 throughout the country made distributions at times wholly impossible. Yet the results were striking, nonetheless; and the managers were pleased and optimistic that the goal could still be reached. "The greater part of the work is already done," they declared in 1831, "and can soon be brought to a happy and triumphant conclusion." They estimated that the work was "substantially completed" in thirteen states and territories, mainly in the East; three-fourths completed in eight states and territories; one-half com-

---

[71]ABS, *Thirteenth Annual Report* (1829), vi. See also *Address of the Board of Managers* and *Abstract of the American Bible Society.*

[72]*Address of the Board of Managers,* 2. See also Dwight, *Centennial History,* 85-91; and Gibson, *Soldiers of the Word,* 62-7.

[73]ABS, *Twelfth Annual Report* (1828), 28; ABS, *Thirteenth Annual Report* (1829), 41-2; Dwight, *Centennial History,* 88; and Tappan, *Life of Arthur Tappan,* 75.

[74]*Abstract of the American Bible Society,* 26-7; Dwight, *Centennial History,* 88.

pleted in two; and less than one-half in four, all in the western South.[75] Altogether, the society distributed 480,766 Bibles and New Testaments during the two years of the "general supply." And over the three-year period, 1829-1831, the society's presses printed more than a million volumes.[76]

TABLE 1

Printing Production and Unit Production Costs,
American Bible Society, 1821-1831

| Year (ending in May) | No. Volumes printed | No. Bible Equivalents (BE) printed* | Paper cost per BE | Printing cost per BE |
|---|---|---|---|---|
| 1821 | 59,000 | 38,000 | 62 cents | 19.9 cents |
| 1822 | 36,625 | 22,200 | 42 cents | 18.9 cents |
| 1823 | 52,600 | 33,000 | 46 cents | 15.0 cents |
| 1824 | 77,225 | 47,213 | 22 cents | 14.0 cents |
| 1825 | 48,500 | 32,450 | 47 cents | 19,5 cents |
| 1826 | 81,000 | 48,275 | 35 cents | 16.0 cents |
| 1827 | 76,734 | 51,709 | 46 cents | 17.2 cents |
| 1828 | 118,250 | 81,150 | 34 cents | 13.5 cents |
| 1829 | 344,500 | 223,340 | 11 cents | 11.6 cents |
| 1830 | 307,250 | 254,948 | 24 cents | 12.2 cents |
| 1831 | 270,000 | 225,200 | 22 cents | 10.1 cents |

*"Bible Equivalent" is a standardized unit of measure. It is the production of the Bible Society (Bibles, New Testaments, and Gospels) expressed in terms of what that production would have been if only complete Bibles had been produced. For a fuller explanation of how and why this rather odd statistic was computed, see the Appendix.

Source: American Bible Society, *Annual Reports* (New York, 1821-1831).

Table 1 shows the striking increase in production at the American Bible Society in the late 1820s and early 1830s. The data also suggest that the introduction of modern technology quickly helped to lower costs significantly, as early as 1829, when the society installed steam-powered presses and began to use machine-made paper. The average cost for paper per Bible Equivalent in the eight years 1821 to 1828 was 41.8 cents. In the three years 1829 to 1831 the average cost was 19.0 cents, a decline of 55 per cent. Meanwhile, the cost of printing fell from an average of 16.8 cents per Bible Equivalent in 1821-1828 to 11.3 cents in 1829-1831, a decline of 33 per cent. (For a definition of the term "Bible Equivalent" and a description of how the cost figures reported in Table 1 were computed, see the Appendix.)

The grand vision of a "general supply" also possessed the leaders of the American Tract Society, and the first well-planned movement in that direction began in New York City, also in 1829. The New-York City Tract Society developed what came to be known as "The Systematic Monthly Distribution"

[75]ABS, *Fifteenth Annual Report* (1831), 3-4, 17-8, 47-8.
[76]See table in Dwight, *Centennial History*, 577; and see Table 1.

plan. The goal was simple: to place in the hands of every city resident at least one tract, the same tract, each month. The idea was the ideology of modern mass media: to have everyone reading and talking about the same thing at the same time. The plan involved a complicated network of ward committees and district distributors. Under the plan, the city's fourteen wards were divided into 500 districts, with about sixty families per district. Each ward had a committee and a chairman, and each district at least one door-to-door distributor. In March of 1829, when the project began, the society counted 28,771 family units in the city, and visited all of them. According to the society's report for the month, 28,383 families were willing to take a tract; only 388 declined.[77]

The whole process was meticulously organized, mainly by such evangelical businessmen as Arthur Tappan (in charge of Ward 5) and his brother Lewis (in charge of Ward 1). Each district distributor was provided with a printed card of instructions, forms for reporting back to the central committee, and, of course, the proper supply of the tract-of-the-month. The instructions were very explicit, describing precisely when and how the district canvass and distribution should be done.[78] By 1831, the New York society was delivering more than 5 million pages of tracts per year to the city's 36,000 families. In addition, some of the more aggressive distributors had begun systematic distribution at the city's wharves, markets, hospitals, and public institutions. By 1833, more than 700 distributors were regularly engaged in this "efficient effort."[79]

Other cities picked up on the New York plan. Some 200 New England towns, including Boston, had launched monthly distribution programs by 1831. Philadelphia, Baltimore, Charleston, and other large cities also had programs under way. Even some rural counties were wholly covered, including some sparsely populated areas of the West. The national office of the Tract Society publicized the New York plan heavily and pressed it upon its auxiliaries and branches everywhere. While not disparaging what they called "miscellaneous distributions," the society's executive committee argued that only systematic, organized efforts would lead to the great goal of reaching all.[80]

Like the Bible Society's "general supply" of 1829-31, the Tract Society's "Systematic Monthly Distribution" over the same period was ostensibly a failure. The executive committee admitted in 1831 that some 10 million Americans were still beyond the net of the society's legions of distributors. Yet, like their colleagues at the Bible Society, the Tract Society directors were optimistic of eventual success. Remarkably, 2 million to 3 million people were being reached by the monthly efforts, at least fairly regularly. In the years 1829 to 1831, the society's production of tracts never fell below 5 million annually. Counting all its publications, the American Tract Society annually printed at least five pages for every man, woman, and child in America.[81]

Table 2 shows the growth of tract production at the American Tract Society

---

[77]ATS, *Fourth Annual Report* (1829), 28-9. See also Charles I. Foster, "The Urban Missionary Movement, 1814-1837," *Pennsylvania Magazine of History and Biography* 75 (January 1951): 58-9.

[78]ATS, *Fourth Annual Report* (1829), 74-6; ATS, *Eighth Annual Report* (1833), 31-2; ATS, *Ninth Annual Report* (1834), 126-8. See also Wyatt-Brown, *Lewis Tappan*, 53.

[79]ATS, *Sixth Annual Report* (1831), 16; ATS, *Eighth Annual Report* (1833), 23.

[80]ATS, *Sixth Annual Report* (1831), 24-7.

[81]Ibid., 28; ATS, *Eighth Annual Report* (1833), 24-8. See also Table 2.

TABLE 2

Printing Production and Unit Production Costs,
New England Tract Society and American Tract Society, 1821-1831

| Society | Year (ending in May) | No. regular tracts printed* | No. pages printed, all pubs.# | Production cost per 10 pages+ |
|---|---|---|---|---|
| New | 1821 | 468,000 | 4,680,000 | 1.0 cents |
| England | 1822 | 255,500 | 2,555,000 | 1.0 cents |
| Tract | 1823 | 470,000 | 4,700,000 | 0.8 cents |
| Society | 1824 | 770,000 | 7,700,000 | 1.0 cents |
| American | 1827 | 3,117,100 | 44,545,100 | 0.59 cents |
| Tract | 1828 | 5,019,000 | 74,657,200 | 0.53 cents |
| Society | 1829 | 6,268,000 | 88,432,000 | 0.53 cents |
| | 1830 | 5,239,000 | 77,577,100 | 0.64 cents |
| | 1831 | 5,383,000 | 68,786,000 | 0.49 cents |

*"Regular tract" means the standard duodecimo English-language tract, which was the staple of the Tract Society. Foreign language tracts and children's tracts, printed in much smaller numbers, are not included here.

#The total page figures for the New England Tract Society years are estimates based on the simple fact that the average tract was around ten pages. The page figures for the American Tract Society years are less rough, but they also have some estimates embedded within them. See the Appendix.

+During the New England Tract Society years, production costs were reported in aggregated form: "Expenses for paper, printing, etc." During the American Tract Society years, costs were reported in more detail. I have tried to make these figures as comparable as possible, including for the years 1827 to 1831 expenditures for paper, printing, and binding.

Source: American Tract Society (New England), *Proceedings of the First Ten Years of the American Tract Society* (Boston, 1824); American Tract Society (New York), *Annual Reports* (New York, 1827-1831).

in the late 1820s and early 1830s. Compared to the Bible Society, however, the cost trend for the Tract Society is more difficult to follow. The data in Table 2 seem to show a significant difference in costs between the New England Tract Society before 1824 and the New-York-based American Tract Society after 1825. Because the national Tract Society after 1825 moved increasingly into fancier tracts, book publication, and other more expensive printing, it is difficult to trace cost changes over time. In general, the data seem to suggest that cost remained fairly steady, though the quality and diversity of the product was upgraded considerably. (For a discussion of some of the complexities of cost accounting, see the Appendix.)

In short, both societies pushed themselves and their machines to the limit in the years 1829 to 1831, the years of the first "general supply" and the first "systematic distributions." These peaks of production were not reached again until 1836, on the eve of the Panic of 1837. For both societies the period 1829-1831 was the time of realization that the creation of mass media was possible in America.

## THE WONDER OF MASS MEDIA

Spreading the word by cheap books and tracts was missionary work well suited to the American scene, in the view of the evangelical publicists of the 1820s. They described their work as part of a new American age of innovation, discovery, and progress. They spoke of religious tracts in the same terms that would later be applied to popular American journalism and fiction: "short," "interesting," "pungent," "striking," "entertaining," yet "unassuming" — just the thing for a young, busy, mobile population of sinners. Like the hawkers of factual "news" in the penny press of the 1830s and '40s, the tract promoters declared their inspirational conversion stories to be "authentic narratives." "Ours is a nation of freemen," the Tract Society declared, "accustomed to think and act for themselves; an enlightened, investigating, reading people." In addition, every man could be a missionary in America — he needed only an armful of tracts. And, finally, tract work was cheap. "Perhaps in no way can the message of the Gospel be conveyed to more individuals at less expense."[82]

"To more individuals at less expense" — this, of course, was a dictum that made sense for messages other than the message of the Gospel; and reformers and publicists of a more secular bent soon borrowed the methods of the Bible and tract societies. The 1830s, in fact, saw a great evangelical outpouring of reform enthusiasm and a great growth of voluntary association and associational publication. Popular commercial publishing — especially popular journalism — also burst into prominence and public favor in the 1830s. In nearly every area of publication, the printing industry in the major cities, especially New York, prospered; and innovations in power printing, stereotyping, and papermaking — pioneered by the Bible and Tract societies — combined to reduce the costs of all kinds of publications.[83]

Many secular associations would eventually adopt the printing, distribution, and organizational methods of the Bible and Tract societies. One of the first to do so was the American Anti-Slavery Society. The experience of the Anti-Slavery Society with mass media in the 1830s suggests that the pioneering work of the Bible and Tract societies would have far-reaching implications.

The American Anti-Slavery Society was a rather small collection of immediate abolitionists who had very little standing in the realms of political power or public opinion in 1833, the year the society was founded. But the Anti-Slavery Society did have leaders who had studied, in the Bible and Tract societies, the uses of the cheap printed word. These leaders included, perhaps most notably, Arthur and Lewis Tappan of New York City.[84]

With the organizational and financial support of the Tappan brothers, the Anti-Slavery Society launched in the 1830s its own systematic distribution of abolitionist materials, its own version of a "general supply." In 1835, the soci-

---

[82]ATS, *Third Annual Report* (1828), 21-2; "An Address to Christians Recommending the Distribution of Religious Tracts," in *First Ten Years of the American Tract Society*, 18-20.

[83]U.S., Department of Interior, *Eighth Census of the United States, 1860: Manufactures of the United States in 1860*, III: cxxvi-cxxix, cxxxvii-cxl. See also Walters, *American Reformers*, 5-6; and James L. Crouthamel, "The Newspaper Revolution in New York, 1830-1860," *New York History* 45 (April, 1964): 104-8.

[84]The work of the Tappans in the American Anti-Slavery Society is described in Wyatt-Brown, *Lewis Tappan*. See also Lawrence J. Friedman, *Gregarious Saints: Self and Community in American Abolitionism, 1830-1870* (Cambridge: Cambridge University Press, 1982), chapter 3.

ety flooded the mails with more than a million pieces of antislavery literature, sent free to people all over the country, including the South. The materials ranged from four new monthly journals and a children's newspaper, to woodcuts, handkerchiefs, and even chocolate wrappers. This "great postal campaign" has been called the first flowering of the printing revolution in America.[85] It was not. It was, in many ways, simply another campaign in the tract war that the Tappans and others had been waging for more than ten years.

The reaction to these abolitionist tracts and pamphlets, however, was decidedly different from the reaction to "The Swearer's Prayer," "The Dairyman's Daughter," or the pocket New Testament. The reaction was close to hysterical. Southern newspapers thundered; mobs gathered; legislatures assembled to ban the importation of "incendiary literature." One southerner, writing to an evangelical friend, captured the grim foreboding that seized the South: "When I think of the myriads ... of papers ... from the prolific press in New York ... diffusing at once delusion and bitterness in the North, and exasperation through the South; of our own impudence in offering rewards for Tappan..., of our lynchings and excessive irritability throughout this whole season of agitation, how is it possible to avoid fearing the worst?"[86] For many Americans, in the North as well as the South, the postal campaign was clear evidence that abolitionism was an enormously rich and powerful conspiracy, centered in New York, which was determined to destroy traditional local values and institutions. For them, this nationalization of organization and communication was a threat to the decentralized structure of American republicanism.[87]

In reality, the American Anti-Slavery Society was neither rich nor powerful. It only seemed so because printing, paper, and postage were increasingly cheap. Indeed, this campaign did signal a new order of things, and it did emanate from New York. But it was not a mammoth conspiracy. It was simply the way evangelism — whether religious or otherwise — would now be done in modern America.

On July 29, 1835, a band of men broke into the U.S. Post Office in Charleston, South Carolina, and carried off a number of mailbags that had arrived from New York City, stuffed with abolitionist tracts, magazines, and newspapers. The next night, amid hanging effigies of Arthur Tappan and other antislavery leaders, some 3,000 Charlestonians watched and cheered as the abolitionist literature was put to the torch.[88] Ironically, what shocked and horrified these Charleston men and women was the same thing that had pleased the Rev. William Dickey and his parishioners in Western Kentucky just twenty years before. It was the wonder of mass media.

Between 1815 and 1835, centralized, systematic mass publication had become part of the American way of doing things. The origin, I have argued in this chapter, was religious and evangelical. But this evangelical spirit was expansive and not easily contained. Perhaps on that July night in Charleston in 1835 the full implications of what it means to live in a mass media society first

---

[85]Leonard L. Richards, *"Gentlemen of Property and Standing": Anti-Abolition Mobs in Jacksonian America* (New York: Oxford University Press, 1970), 72-3. On the postal campaign in general, see Wyatt-Brown, *Lewis Tappan*, chapter 8.

[86]Quoted in Wyatt-Brown, *Lewis Tappan*, 160-71.

[87]Richards, "Gentlemen of Property and Standing," 55-62.

[88]Wyatt-Brown, *Lewis Tappan*, 149.

began to rise in the minds of Americans. But by 1835, a few bonfires were already very much too late.

*APPENDIX*

The Cost of Bible and Tract Production, 1821-1831

The annual reports of the American Bible Society and the American Tract Society include data on the output of the societies' printing shops and on expenditures for categories of items, including paper, printing, and binding. Estimates of the costs of production can be computed from these data. Unfortunately, these estimates must be quite rough for both societies, especially the Tract Society, because of problems inherent in the data. The problems are described in this appendix; the estimates are reported in Tables 1 and 2 in the text.

The chief problems are these:

(1) Unit of Production. The first problem in figuring average costs of production over time was to determine a standardized unit of production. Each society produced different products in different quantities at different times, yet only broad categories of expenditures were reported. For example, the Bible Society produced New Testaments and Gospels as well as complete Bibles; the Tract Society published books, almanacs, and magazines as well as tracts. But expenditures for printing, paper, etc., were not broken down by class of product. In order to compare different outputs and costs over time, I standardized the Bible Society's production in terms of "Bible Equivalents" and the Tract Society's production in terms of "pages." For the Bible Society, the total number of Bible Equivalents (BE) in a year equals the number of Bibles plus the number of New Testaments (NT) and Gospels (G) expressed as proportions of whole Bibles. That is, $BE = B + (NT \times 0.3) + (G \times 0.03)$. The weights 0.3 and 0.03 are based upon the normal size of standard King James New Testaments and Gospels compared to complete Bibles. I used the page as the unit of analysis for the Tract Society, because sometimes (not always, alas) the total number of pages printed was given in the annual reports. Sometimes, however, only the total number of pages of tracts was given; the number of copies of magazines and almanacs were given, but not the number of pages. In these cases, I estimated the number of pages in order to arrive at a total production figure for each year expressed in terms of total pages.

(2) Changes in Quality. Despite these efforts at standardization, one important factor could not be standardized: quality. This was probably the chief imponderable. Both societies claimed to have upgraded the quality of paper used over time, but I could not measure this. No volume figures on paper consumption were reported, and no unit cost figures — just total annual expenditures by category. The Tract Society certainly increased the quality of its products significantly over the 1820s, with woodcuts, engravings, and stiff paper covers as well as better paper. The Bible Society also claimed that its books in the late 1820s were superior in materials and workmanship compared to the early years. Both societies printed different products in different size formats as well, which I could not take into account.

(3) Meanings of Categories. For neither society is the exact meaning of an expenditure category altogether clear. The Tract Society seems to have included

the cost of stereotype plates under their "printing" category; the Bible Society did not. More important, it is not clear in what way and at what rate the capital cost of new printing presses was being amortized by the annual printing charges to the societies. These and other uncertainties make it difficult to say exactly what the per-unit cost of printing was, year by year. For example, the Tract Society was making heavy investments in stereotype plates in the late 1820s, which kept "printing" expenditures misleadingly high.

(4) Aggregation. The financial reports of the Bible Society before 1821 do not contain breakdowns of expenditures by the same categories (paper, printing, binding, etc.) as the reports for 1821 and after. The same is true of the Tract Society before 1827. In general, the Tract Society tended to aggregate more expenditures into fewer categories than did the Bible Society. Between 1832 and 1834, the Bible Society did not disaggregate Bibles and New Testaments. These and other little changes in record-keeping created difficulties in investigating trends over time. Problems of aggregation largely explain the choices of dates and categories in the tables.

(5) Carry-over of Bills and Supplies. Charges for printing, paper, and other services were sometimes carried over from one year to the next. Paper was sometimes stockpiled in one year and used in another. But there is no indication of when this was done. Thus, production figures and expenditures listed for a given year are not necessarily congruent. For this reason, it is dangerous to put much stock in single year-to-year fluctuations.

# 6

# The Origins of the Black Press
by Bernell E. Tripp

BY THE 1820S, THE BLACK POPULATION in the North was made up of free blacks and runaway slaves, all seeking a better way of life. Many had received a formal education, while others possessed only rudimentary reading and writing skills. However, all seemed eager to accept a black newspaper devoted to their particular needs, since few white editors were willing to allow them access to mainstream newspaper columns.

Into this climate the Rev. Samuel Cornish and John Russwurm, two black free men, introduced *Freedom's Journal* in 1827. Historians have speculated that the inception of *Freedom's Journal* was "the result of a meeting of Messrs. Russwurm, Cornish and others at the house of M. Bostin Crummell ... in New York, called to consider the attacks of ... a local paper published in New York City ... by an Afro-American-hating Jew, which made the vilest attacks on the Afro-Americans."[1]

The antagonist was Mordecai M. Noah of the *New York Enquirer*. After reading Noah's attacks, Cornish and Russwurm responded with letters to the editor of the *Enquirer* and were denied publication. Outraged at being denied a voice, the two pooled their resources and began publishing *Freedom's Journal*.[2]

During its short life, *Freedom's Journal* attempted to improve the conditions of the black race. It worked temperately against slavery, but — aimed at free black readers in the North, since southern slaves, even had they been able to read, would not have had access to newspapers — it emphasized the elevation of the race through such means as education, civil treatment of blacks, equal rights, job opportunities, morality, and self-improvement. Like editors and publishers of the black newspapers that followed, Cornish and Russwurm were already community and church leaders, and their newspaper reflected their sense of obli-

---

[1]Irving Garland Penn, *The Afro-American Press and Its Editors* (Springfield, Mass.: Wiley and Co., 1891), 27-8.

[2]See Bella Gross, "'Freedom's Journal' and the 'Rights of All,'" *Journal of Negro History* 17 (July 1932): 243; Lauren Kessler, *The Dissident Press: Alternative Journalism in American History* (Beverly Hills: Sage Publications, 1984), 28.

gation to temporal and spiritual improvement. Cornish, who also directed America's second black newspaper, the *Weekly Advocate* (later renamed the *Colored American*), declared that that paper's purpose was to "carry to him [every man] lessons of instruction on religion and morals, lessons on industry and economy — until our entire people are of one heart and of one mind, in all the means of their salvation, both temporal and spiritual."[3]

Neither Cornish nor Russwurm possessed any newspaper experience at the time they founded *Freedom's Journal*. Cornish was a Presbyterian minister born in Delaware and reared in Philadelphia and New York. He organized the first black Presbyterian Church on New Demeter Street in Manhattan after his graduation from the Free African School.[4] Russwurm, a half-black Jamaican, was a graduate of Bowdoin College, one of the first blacks to graduate from any college in the United States. Previously, he had planned to study medicine in Boston before emigrating to Haiti.[5] However, following graduation he moved to New York, where he met Cornish and other black leaders and agreed to the proposal of establishing a newspaper.

The *Journal* itself usually consisted of four pages numbered consecutively from issue to issue, which included four columns on 10-by-15 inch paper. The paper appeared weekly on Fridays and was priced at $3 per year, payable half yearly in advance, or $2.50 if paid in full.

The paper contained some original articles, as well as items "lifted" from other newspapers — a commonly accepted practice during the period. Usually only about two of the sixteen columns of reading material in each issue were devoted to current news. The remaining columns contained such items as personal profiles, moral lessons, poetry, and advertisements. Numerous black leaders contributed sermons, speeches, and articles on scientific, educational, and political topics. Biblical excerpts and religious parables provided inspiration. Domestic and foreign news items reported meetings of black citizens, crimes against slaves, slavery in other countries, ship sailings, and other miscellaneous occurrences.

Even though slavery was among the topics addressed in the columns of *Freedom's Journal*, it was not a primary concern. In an environment that was reluctant to support black progress, it is unlikely that the paper could afford to be too outspoken against slavery. Considering that the paper would probably never reach the slaves or free blacks of the South, Cornish and Russwurm concerned themselves primarily with the blacks in the North and the development of racial unity and progress.

The first issue of *Freedom's Journal*, complete with its slogan "Righteousness Exalteth a Nation," did not take a strong stand against slavery — a movement that had not taken hold in 1827. Two articles were indicative of the intent of the publication — one depicted the "Memoirs of Capt. Paul Cuffee," a successful black fisherman; and the other was a reprint of "People of Colour" (clipped from the *Christian Spectator*) which examined slavery as a legal institution. The first emphasized the progress of blacks, while the latter was more of

---

[3]"Proposals and plan of a Newspaper of Color," *Colored American*, 4 March 1837.

[4]Lerone Bennett, Jr., *Pioneers in Protest* (Chicago: Johnson Publishing Co., 1968), 60.

[5]John B. Russwurm to Col. John S. Russwurm, 9 January 1826, Original in Ms. Section, Tennessee State Library and Archives; copy in Bowdoin College Library.

an *appeal* to examine the issue of slavery, rather than a *demand* for action.

Slavery was only one of the subjects the *Journal* editors addressed. Cornish and Russwurm also concerned themselves with providing a forum for black protest, as well as promoting such things as striving to achieve financial success and strong moral character in order to gain acceptance by a white society.[6]

A good example of the *Journal* editors' commitment to fulfilling a variety of objectives was revealed in the paper's first editorial, "To Our Patrons," which served as a statement of purpose. The editorial read in part:

We wish to plead our cause. Too long have others spoken for us. Too long has the publick been deceived by misrepresentations, in things which concern us dearly, though in the estimation of some mere trifles; for though there are many in society who exercise towards us benevolent feelings; still (with sorrow we confess it) there are others who make it their business to enlarge upon the least trifle, which tends to the discredit of any person of colour; and pronounce anathemas and denounce our whole body for the misconduct of this guilty one. We are aware that there are many instances of vice among us, but we avow that it is because no one has taught its subjects to be virtuous; many instances of poverty, because no sufficient efforts accommodated to minds contracted by slavery, and deprived of early education have been made, to teach them how to husband their hard earnings, and to secure to themselves comfort.[7]

In short, the editors expressed the need for blacks to speak for themselves and to acquire a sense of dignity, while dispelling previous misrepresentations of the race based on the unconscionable actions a few individuals committed. The editors emphasized the necessity for teaching blacks the things of which slavery, poverty, and prejudice had deprived them.

Cornish and Russwurm also planned to address the problem of educating the black population — not only basic reading and writing, but training in certain labor skills. Education, they declared, was the basis for blacks' social development.

Education being an object of the highest importance to the welfare of society, we shall endeavor to present just and adequate views of it, and to urge upon our brethren the necessity and expediency of training their children, while young, to habits of industry, and thus forming them for becoming useful members of society.[8]

Not only did the *Journal* editors print articles and speeches on the merits of education, but Cornish occasionally published a list of African Free Schools that black and white abolitionists had founded. He also criticized the teaching facilities and the lack of qualifications of the teachers. The opportunities for acquiring an education were more favorable for blacks than whites, Cornish wrote, and free

---

[6]See also, for example, Kessler, *The Dissident Press*, 28.

[7]*Freedom's Journal*, 16 March 1827.

[8]Ibid.

blacks should raise their voices in protest.[9]

The issue some historians presume to be of the greatest significance, slavery, was not addressed as vehemently as education. In the original statement of purpose, the editors did not mention slavery until the latter part of the editorial. Cornish and Russwurm asserted that it was the duty of *Freedom's Journal* to "vindicate our brethren, when oppressed; and to lay the case before the publick." But as for vowing any specific action against slavery, the editors were vague in their intentions. They wrote:

> And while these important subjects shall occupy the columns of the FREE-DOM's JOURNAL, we would not be unmindful of our brethren who are still in the iron fetters of bondage. They are our kindred by all the times of nature; and though but little can be effected by us, still let our sympathies be poured forth, and our prayers in their behalf, ascend to Him who is able to succour them.[10]

These were not staunch words that indicated a devotion to abolishing slavery. However, the intensity of the editors' stand against slavery gradually strengthened. Theodore Wright, a young abolitionist who would later work alongside Cornish, pointed out *Freedom's Journal's* impact in an address to the Convention of the New York State Anti-Slavery Society in 1837. Blacks, he declared, noted indications that whites would adopt "coercive measures" to halt black advancement.

> Immediately after the insurrection in Virginia, under Nat Turner, we saw colonization spreading all over the land; and it was popular to say the people of color must be removed. The [white] press came out against us, and we trembled.... Ah, Mr. President, that was a dark and gloomy period. The united views and intentions of the people of color were made known, and the nation awoke as from slumber. The *Freedom's Journal*, edited by Rev. Sam'l Cornish, announced the facts of the case, our entire opposition. Sir, it came like a clap of thunder.[11]

Cornish mainly limited his attacks on slavery to the columns of his newspaper and an occasional sermon. His words were cautious and subtle. Scathing sarcasm, however, also served a purpose. This characteristic is illustrated in the following excerpt from an April 6, 1827, issue: "Blessings of Slavery! Mr. John Hamilton of Lanesborough County, Va., was murdered on the 9th ult. by his slaves. Seventeen of them have been committed to the county jail to await their trial."

Despite the article mentioned above, the paper was primarily concerned with conditions in the North. However, it did occasionally include rare reports from the South — such as the first known newspaper account of a lynching.[12] The in-

---

[9]*Freedom's Journal*, 1 June 1827.

[10]*Freedom's Journal*, 16 March 1827.

[11]Quoted in Carter Godwin Woodson, *Negro Orators and Their Orations* (New York: Russell and Russell, 1969).

[12]Charles W. Porter, "The Black Press in America Before Emancipation" (M.A. thesis, University of Alabama, Tuscaloosa, Ala., 1970), 10.

cident, which occurred on June 20, 1827, in Tuscaloosa, Alabama, appeared in the August 3 issue. The report not only included details of the crime, but emphasized that this was "the second negro who has been put to death, without Judge or Jury in that county."

Initially, Cornish edited *Freedom's Journal*, while Russwurm served as proprietor. Under Cornish's guidance, the paper flourished. Editorials were well written, and the articles provided much-needed information to aid black progress. He had always considered self-help to be an important part in the elevation and refinement of blacks. Therefore, he encouraged industriousness and diligence. In the columns of his second paper, the *Colored American*, he said that through work each "one for himself, must commence the improvement of his condition. It is not in mass, but in individual effort and character, that we are to move onward to a higher elevation."[13] However, certain criteria had to be met. Before blacks could take their rightful place in society, they had to make several crucial changes. First, they were to abandon former useless practices and "cultivate honesty, punctuality, propriety of conduct, and modesty and dignity of deportment." Second, they were to engage in "untiring habits of industry, the dint of perseverance." Third, money was not to be spent on improving outward appearance, but "for the purpose of elevating our character, and improving our condition." Finally, blacks were to cultivate their intellect through the "accumulation of knowledge, extensive and solid."[14] The *Colored American* also became part of a larger campaign to help channel black energies toward more productive undertakings. Cornish explained that lotteries were usually rigged in favor of the operators and were also illegal and poor investments. Time could be better spent reading, attending lectures, and improving the mind.[15]

Once Cornish left *Freedom's Journal* only six months after its founding, attacks on the American Colonization Society grew particularly vicious. It was this topic that might have caused the split between the two editors. The issue involved the question of whether blacks would ever be free and equal to whites in the United States. Those who believed this situation would never exist advocated a colony of free blacks, chosen either voluntarily or by force, living in Africa as part of their own society. Both editors had originally been opposed to colonization. Within the first six months of operation, Russwurm began to favor the idea of colonization, while Cornish remained opposed to it.

Under Cornish's editorship, *Freedom's Journal* printed several letters from black and white readers against colonization.[16] Cornish also stated his paper's position in reply to an editorial that appeared in the Georgetown *Columbian and District Advertiser*. In the June 8, 1827, issue, he wrote:

That we have made any effort, through this Journal, to prejudice the minds of our brethren against the [American Colonization] Society, or render them suspicious of its motives, we positively deny: but that we are opposed to colonization in PRINCIPLE, OBJECT, AND TENDENCY, we, as unhesitating-

---

[13]*Colored American*, 22 April 1837.

[14]*Colored American*, 6 May 1837.

[15]See *Colored American*, 23 February 1839; and 18 March 1837.

[16]See, for example, the letter by "A Free Colored Virginian," *Freedom's Journal*, 6 July 1827; or the letter by "Investigator," 7 September 1827.

ly affirm. We have never desired to conceal our sentiments.

Historians disagree as to the importance of this discord between Russwurm and Cornish in their eventual breakup.[17] On September 14, 1827, Cornish announced his resignation in a *Freedom's Journal* article that praised Russwurm and cited health and other interests as the reasons for his departure, with no mention of their differing opinions on colonization. Cornish could not have been totally disgruntled with Russwurm, since Cornish remained listed as the paper's "General Agent" throughout *Freedom's Journal*'s existence. The *Journal* also ran advertisements for Cornish and published notices of weddings he performed.

Whatever the reason, by mid-September of 1827 Cornish had resigned from his position and returned to the Presbyterian ministry, leaving Russwurm as sole editor of the paper. Attacks on the colonization society continued, but to a less severe degree than under Cornish. Russwurm began to allot more space to colonization issues, and on September 26 he also commenced printing the minutes of the society's meetings.

Ironically, it was more than a year later before Russwurm publicly declared his change of heart. Faced with the outcry that *Freedom's Journal* readers raised over the paper's policy change, Russwurm wrote a personal editorial titled "Our Vindication" in support of his change of philosophy. In it Russwurm accused his general readership of attempting to deny his rights of free expression. He explained his change of position, citing colonization as a more preferable alternative to a life in the United States where the issue of race blocked all avenues for advancement. According to Russwurm,

> [A black man] may possess wealth; he may be respected; he may be learned; still all united will avail him little; after all, he is considered a being of inferior order; and always will be, as no opportunity will ever be afforded him to cultivate or call into action the talents with which an All-wise Creator may have endowed him.[18]

Russwurm saw colonization as the only solution to slavery and inequality. His dream of a civilization where a black man could live without fear of being enslaved was evidenced by his commencement address at Bowdoin College. He lauded the tenacity of the Haitian people and their ability to triumph over slavery to form a government that was equitable for all citizens — an occurrence he could not envision in the United States.[19]

In a later editorial, Russwurm implored his readers not to condemn the paper on the assumption that *Freedom's Journal* approved of the forms of prejudices exercised against blacks. Of these prejudices, he concluded,

> They at present exist against us — and from the length of their existence —

---

[17]See Carter R. Bryan, "Negro Journalism in America Before Emancipation," *Journalism Monographs* 12 (September 1969): 9; Roland Wolseley, *The Black Press, U.S.A.* (Ames: Iowa State University Press, 1971), 18; and Lionel C. Barrow, Jr., "Our Own Cause: 'Freedom's Journal' and the Beginnings of the Black Press," *Journalism History* 4 (Winter 1977-78): 121.

[18]*Freedom's Journal*, 7 March 1829.

[19]John Browne Russwurm, "The Conditions and Prospects of Hayti," Commencement Address, Bowdoin College, 6 September 1826.

from the degraded light in which we have ever been held — we are bold in saying, that it will never be in our power to remove or overcome them.[20]

It is unknown whether Russwurm was forced to leave the paper because of his conversion to colonization or if his fervor for the cause led to his resignation. He soon gave up his position on the paper and moved to a colony in Liberia. He went on to become the superintendent of public schools and later the editor of the *Liberia Herald*. He concluded his editorial duties at *Freedom's Journal* with his March 28, 1829, column. In it, he declared that he was "not the least astonished, that we have been slandered by the villainous — that our name is [a] byword among the more ignorant, for what could we expect?" He also listed what he considered to have been the original objectives of *Freedom's Journal*, which included: "the dissemination of useful knowledge; the defence [sic] of our community; the necessity and advantages of education; and lately, the expediency of emigration to Liberia."

When Russwurm departed for Liberia, Cornish returned to *Freedom's Journal* as editor — changing the name to the *Rights of All*. However, the paper's purposes remained the same — to provide accurate representation of blacks; to promote the advantages of diligence and economy; to extol the virtues of good moral character; and to instill within the readers the importance of education in improving the circumstances of their day-to-day existence.[21]

Cornish himself served as an example to the black community. He had risen from extreme poverty to relatively prosperous respectability, and he maintained an intellectual commitment to the idea that the race would have to do likewise.[22] He believed that blacks' failure to prosper economically and to acquire the skills to do so was the result of a tendency to "grasp after flowers, and neglect solid and wholesome fruits."[23]

Cornish never lost the opportunity to instill in his readers the need for education. He believed that through education blacks could help abolish prejudice and advance through the social ranks. *Freedom's Journal* and *Rights of All* encouraged education for blacks by advertising private schools in New York City and elsewhere and by promoting interest in the city's African Free Schools, organized and run by the New York Manumission Society. When declining attendance hindered the African Free Schools, Cornish established visiting committees to urge parents to send their children to school. Meanwhile, a committee was also formed to sew for children who lacked sufficient clothing to attend classes. Progress of both committee groups was duly reported in *Freedom's Journal*.[24]

Upon his return to the paper, Cornish also wasted no time in renewing his attacks against the colonizationists. His June 12, 1829, editorial declared that the goal of returning the "sons of Africa" to her coasts was a trifling matter, and the important tasks were to educate blacks and encourage them to pursue agricultural and mechanical careers. The editorial added:

---

[20]*Freedom's Journal*, 14 March 1829.

[21]*Rights of All*, 29 May 1829.

[22]Jane H. Pease and William H. Pease, *They Who Would Be Free: Blacks' Search for Freedom, 1830-1861* (New York: Atheneum, 1974), 262.

[23]*Rights of All*, 18 September 1829.

That the interest of the christian public, in behalf of the coloured people of this country, has diminished, in proportion to their zeal, in behalf of the Liberian colony, is evident to every enlightened man of colour, and also to every unprejudiced white man, and it is not our duty to call back, or at least to call for a division of the public attention, the public effort, and the public prayers in behalf of our brethren in this country.[25]

His idea of an industrious black race coincided with the paper's original philosophy for improving the black way of life, which encouraged blacks to learn a trade and to channel it into economically productive undertakings. *Freedom's Journal* readers had always been warned to buy only necessities, to save against hard times, and to invest surplus income carefully.[26]

Another of Cornish's causes expressed in the pages of the *Rights of All* was promoting responsible voting practices by qualified blacks who did not exercise the privileges. Since many free states barred most free blacks from voting by using such techniques as qualification tests and intimidation, Cornish thought it the duty of those who qualified to participate in New York elections. Not only did he urge the people to vote, but he chastised the "State" for using qualification tests that applied only to blacks.[27]

After Russwurm's departure, Cornish had hoped to revive the paper's sagging circulation figures and restore it to its former place as a leader of the black community. Russwurm's change of position on the colonization issue had alienated many of the paper's former supporters, leading to a reduction in subscribers. Abolitionist David Walker, whose pamphlet aimed toward the black population was the first sustained written assault upon U.S. slavery and racism, was a strong supporter of Cornish and the *Rights of All*. He appealed to blacks for their "cordial co-operation in the circulation of 'The Rights of All,' among us. The utility of such a vehicle if rightly conducted, cannot be estimated.... I believe he [Cornish] is not seeking to fill his pockets with money, but has the welfare of his brethren truly at heart."[28]

Despite Cornish's continued emphasis on the need for a means of communication between black Americans, a lack of financial support by the latter part of 1829 forced him to give up his efforts. Starved for subscriptions despite efforts of stockholders and friends to save it, the *Rights of All* (formerly *Freedom's Journal*) ceased publication.

Although short-lived, the paper had served to incite blacks into action and then recorded the results. However, its motive was not to instigate concerted action against slavery. Items pertaining to slavery, such as the editorial appearing on October 17, 1828, were extremely rare. The justification for that editorial was probably the proximity of the episode it addressed. The wharf from which a boat loaded with slaves departed for North Carolina or Virginia for later reshipping to New Orleans was located in New York City.[29] Because of the location, Cornish

---

[24]See, for example, *Freedom's Journal*, 21 December 1827; 11 January 1828; and 1 February 1828.
[25]*Rights of All*, 12 June 1829.
[26]See, for example, *Freedom's Journal*, 30 May 1828.
[27]See *Rights of All*, 16 October 1829.
[28]David Walker, *Walker's Appeal, in Four Articles; Together with a Preamble, to the Colored Citizens of the World* (Boston: By the author, 1830).
[29]*Freedom's Journal*, 17 October 1828.

deemed the event significant and worthy of editorial comment. Previous articles on slavery-related issues had been on events farther away, but this incident brought the issue to the Northern free blacks' own backyard.

On the contrary, the editors themselves made bigger statements about antislavery than their newspaper. Russwurm's departure incurred the displeasure of many of his former friends. In 1831, his successful editorship at the *Liberia Herald* and his increased political activity in Africa sparked a series of letters from outraged former supporters in the United States. One letter to the editor of the *Liberator* from a writer designated only as "R." declared that Russwurm's "ingratitude" would never be obliterated from the minds of his followers. He accused Russwurm of subverting the "pledge he made to colored brethren" and leaving the country "to dwell in that land for which the temptor MONEY caused him to avow his preferment."[30] Another letter writer, "C.D.T., a Philadelphian," also attributed Russwurm's change of attitude toward colonization to monetary gain. The writer determined that Russwurm converted the paper into a tool of the colonization society after failing to gain enough subscribers to support it.[31]

Russwurm's support of colonization also reduced his popularity among leaders of the period. With the exception of black leader and fellow journalist Martin Robison Delany, who praised Russwurm as an exemplary scholar, businessman, and community leader,[32] black leaders of the nineteenth century never forgave Russwurm for his alleged defection. Believing that a return to Africa and a revival of the great empires of the Middle Ages were the only escape for the black man, Russwurm expressed these ideas frequently during the time prior to his resignation. Other things that angered blacks in the community, who often burned him in effigy, were Russwurm's acceptance of an offer to join the Maryland Colonization Society and his defense of black exclusion laws in Ohio — both of which encouraged the emigration back to Africa. By supporting these ideas in *Freedom's Journal*, he was accused of "selling out" to the enemies of the black people.[33]

Yet Delany saw Russwurm as a "gentleman of splendid talents" who "as his first public act, commenced the publication of a newspaper, for the elevation of colored Americans, called '*Freedom's Journal*.'"[34] In his book, *The Condition, Elevation, Emigration, and Destiny of the Colored People of the United States*, Delany failed to mention Cornish as a collaborator for the paper or the uproar that Russwurm's colonization beliefs caused.

During the nineteenth century, leaders, unlike Delany, were almost unanimous in their denunciation of Russwurm and praise for Cornish. Today, Cornish is virtually forgotten, while Russwurm is considered a noted black nationalist.[35]

While attitudes toward Russwurm became increasingly negative, Cornish

[30]*Liberator*, 16 April 1831.

[31]*Liberator*, 30 April 1831.

[32]Martin Robison Delany, *The Condition, Elevation, Emigration, and Destiny of the Colored People of the United States* (Philadelphia: By the author, 1852), 129.

[33]Bennett, *Pioneers in Protest*, 65.

[34]Delany, *The Condition, Elevation, Emigration, and Destiny of the Colored People of the United States*, 129.

[35]Bennett, *Pioneers in Protest*, 65.

continued to maintain a respected position in the black community. His sermons were of especial significance to abolitionist William Lloyd Garrison. In a letter to his future wife, Helen Benson, Garrison detailed his attendance at sermons by Cornish and the Rev. Peter Williams and how he had "taken by the hand many of my colored friends, who were overjoyed to see me. To-morrow evening I shall meet some of the leading colored gentlemen, in relation to future concerns of the *Liberator* [Garrison's abolitionist newspaper]."[36]

Cornish also collaborated closely with ministers Williams and Theodore Wright and abolitionist Arthur Tappan in organizing the New York City Anti-Slavery Society. However, Cornish and the others became the society's sharpest critics — objecting to the low priority given to expanding black rights and job opportunities and to the white organizers' patronizing paternalism.

Consequently, Cornish never terminated his battle for equal rights and a higher social status for blacks. He applied his original principles to the operation and purpose of his second newspaper, the *Colored American*. He also became an active member in the national Negro conventions, which were politically oriented gatherings of black leaders that stressed the importance of advancements in black rights.

The task the two men began with *Freedom's Journal* — to create a newspaper that would fulfill the needs of the black society in America — was taken up by many others, both black and white. Whatever they sought to accomplish, Cornish and Russwurm had no way of knowing that their journalistic endeavors would be imitated and would multiply, despite immense hardships. *Freedom's Journal* was the black response to a closed forum for expression in the conventional press, and it labored through a period of high illiteracy among blacks and low circulation figures. Freedom and civility toward blacks dominated the pages of the paper, but *Freedom's Journal* was the first stage of a crusade for a black newspaper that would suit the informational needs of a black community.

---

[36]William Lloyd Garrison to Helen Benson, ALS, April 1834, Villard Papers, Harvard College Library, Cambridge.

# 7

# Religious Newspapers
# and Antebellum Reform
by Carol Sue Humphrey

HISTORIANS HAVE LONG GIVEN CREDIT to the role of religious groups in the rise of reform efforts in the early nineteenth century. However, they seldom give credit to the role of the religious media in sparking many of these reform movements. Most of the concerns that sparked the reform efforts first found printed expression in religious newspapers and magazines. Success came in many of these reform movements only after they grew beyond organized religion, but the original ideas and many of the original personnel came out of the milieu of religious and denominational journalism.

Religious newspapers and magazines appeared in record numbers in the early nineteenth century. After 1800, Americans became profoundly convinced of the potential impact of the printed word to mobilize public opinion. For many, the role the press had played during the American Revolution provided clear proof. It had been reinforced during the early years of the republic by the rise and growing influence of political party organs that sought to influence the voting records of both politicians and ordinary citizens alike. In 1838, Grenville Mellen described the Age of Jackson as the period that witnessed the beginning of "an ERA OF PAPER, and the AGE OF PRINT."[1] Religious crusaders of all persuasions believed in this fact as much as anyone else, and they all sought to use print media to share their thoughts with the world. As previously shown in the work of David Nord, religious groups quickly turned to the newest technology, such as stereotype printing and steam-powered presses, in order to spread their message as far and wide as possible.[2] Many of these changes originally occurred in groups producing Bibles and religious tracts because they had more money

---

[1]Quoted in Nathan O. Hatch, "Elias Smith and the Rise of Religious Journalism," in *Printing and Society in Early America*, edited by William L. Joyce, *et al.* (Worcester, Mass.: American Antiquarian Society, 1983), 270.

[2]David Paul Nord, "The Evangelical Origins of Mass Media in America, 1815-1835," chapter 5 of this book.

for investing in new equipment. However, the technological advances also slowly permeated the journalism field, as producers of religious newspapers and magazines adopted these new methods in order to improve the spreading of their message because "a well conducted religious periodical is like a thousand preachers, flying in almost as many directions, by means of horses, mail stages, steam boats, rail road cars, ships, etc., etc., offering life and salvation to the sons of men in almost every clime."[3] For example, utopian reformer John Humphrey Noyes declared that, given the choice between continuing his communal experiment at Oneida, New York, or publishing his newspaper, he would choose his newspaper because of the greater potential impact that a periodical publication possessed.[4] And, by January 1840, the editor of the *Biblical Repository* could declare that "of all the reading of the people three-fourths is purely religious ... of all the issues of the press three-fourths are theological, ethical and devotional."[5] As stated by historian Nathan Hatch, the religious press "made it possible for Americans by the thousands to speak their mind in print."[6]

Most of the religious periodicals that appeared between 1800 and 1830 seemed to differ little from those produced by the secular press, at least on the surface. They mixed religious and worldly material together, hopefully in a manner that was more than just attaching "religious principles and aims" to the normal content of a newspaper or magazine.[7] The editors of the religious periodicals hoped that their publications would give not "merely religious intelligence, but [be] a *news* paper, complete in every department of general news, yet upon a religious, instead of a political or literary basis."[8] The earliest religious newspapers and magazines were generally nonsectarian because most editors realized that the needed audience would not be found in only one denomination, and also because many editors hoped their journals would serve as a community news organ. In 1800, *The New-York Missionary Magazine and Repository of Religious Intelligence* began publication. The first missionary magazine in the United States, its producers used its pages to report on the work of various missionary societies and revival efforts throughout the country. A similar publication, the *Connecticut Evangelical Magazine*, first appeared in Hartford the same year, while the *Massachusetts Missionary Magazine* began publication in Boston in 1803.[9] The first religious newspaper published in the United States was the *Herald of Gospel Liberty*, established in Portsmouth, New Hampshire, in 1808 by Elias Smith, a Baptist minister.[10] Seven years later, John W. Scott established the ecumenical *Religious Remembrancer* in Philadelphia, a paper that

---

[3]*Religious Telescope* (Circleville, Ohio), 27 November 1839.

[4]Hatch, "Elias Smith," 251.

[5]*Biblical Repository* (Andover, Mass.), January 1840.

[6]Hatch, "Elias Smith," 276.

[7]Albert Elijah Dunning, *Congregationalists in America* (New York: J. A. Hill, 1894), 477.

[8]*Presbyterian of the West* (Cincinnati, Ohio), 30 December 1858.

[9]Frank Luther Mott, *A History of American Magazines, 1741-1850* (Cambridge, Mass.: Belknap Press of the Harvard University Press, 1957), 133.

[10]The earliest religious publications in the United States were magazines. First was *Christian History*, founded by Thomas Prince in Boston on March 5, 1743. Several others appeared before 1800, but religious periodicals were rarities until several years into the nineteenth century. Henry S. Stroupe, *The Religious Press in the South Atlantic States, 1802-1865* (Durham, N.C.: Duke University Press, 1956), 3; Wesley Norton, *Religious Newspapers in the Old Northwest to 1861: A History, Bibliography, and Record of Opinion* (Athens: Ohio University Press, 1977), 3.

covered the work of several Protestant denominations. Both of these editors believed that religious publications would provide the means to overcome denominational differences and decrease, if not eliminate all together, the disagreements between the various factions within organized religion, and so they both sought to reach out to all Christian groups in the United States (at least to all Protestant groups). An exception to this generalization, and a precursor of what was to come in the near future, was the *Evangelical Recorder*, a Presbyterian journal published in Auburn, New York, from 1818 to 1821. Its editor, Dirck Lansing, regularly used the pages of his publication to spread Presbyterian doctrine.[11]

By the 1830s, Lansing's type of journalism had become the normal way of operating because religious publications had become common enough in the United States to be produced by both numerous denominations and individuals. Denominations increasingly turned to periodicals to not only preach the gospel in general but to spread their particular version of Christianity throughout the country. And many more Americans expressed their denominational loyalties by subscribing to the magazines supported by their church. In the 1830s, Samuel Wait declared the need for periodical publications in order to coordinate denominational activities: "One reason, and a most important one it is too, why there has been in times past so little *concern of action* among the Baptists in North Carolina, is to be found in the fact that we have had no proper medium of communication amongst us, by which we could conveniently become acquainted with each other."[12] Other contemporaries stated that the best support for denominational benevolent activities came in those areas in which the church's newspaper or magazine had the most subscribers. Records also indicate that the denominations that enjoyed the most success in increasing the numbers in their churches also had the greatest involvement in journalism.[13] For example, in New York, the *Methodist Magazine* appeared quarterly beginning in 1830, while in Baltimore, Maryland, the *United States Catholic Magazine* began publication in the 1840s. In North Carolina, the Baptist *Biblical Recorder* began its long history in 1835, a publication run that continues to the present day. By 1850, the census noted the publication of 191 religious periodicals in the United States, about half of which were newspapers.[14] In 1823, the *Methodist Magazine* declared that "a religious newspaper would have been a phenomenon not many years since, but now the groaning press throws them out in almost every direction."[15] David Benedict declared that, in 1800, no one seriously considered the publication of a religious newspaper, but by 1830 the press had become the major mechanism for uniting believers and spreading the message around the country.[16] Publications, particularly newspapers, expanded because "the power of the printed word [served] to reinforce the spoken word and to extend the message

[11]Neal L. Edgar, *A History and Bibliography of American Magazines, 1810-1820* (Metuchen, N. J.: Scarecrow Press, 1975), 63; Hatch, "Elias Smith," 269.

[12]Quoted in Henry S. Stroupe, "The Beginnings of Religious Journalism in North Carolina, 1823-1865," *North Carolina Historical Review* 30 (January 1953): 6.

[13]Stroupe, "Religious Journalism in North Carolina," 15.

[14]Hatch, "Elias Smith," 269; Stroupe, *Religious Press*, 10-1; Norton, *Religious Newspapers*, 3; Mott, *American Magazines, 1741-1850*, 370.

[15]*Methodist Magazine* (New York, N. Y.), January 1823.

[16]David Benedict, *Fifty Years Among the Baptists* (New York: n.p., 1860), 25.

beyond the local audience."[17] As argued by the *Christian Herald* in 1823, "Preaching of the gospel is a Divine institution — 'printing' is no less so.... They are kindred offices. The PULPIT AND THE PRESS are inseparably connected.... The Press, then, is to be regarded with a sacred veneration and supported with religious care. The press must be supported or the pulpit falls."[18]

The editors of these religious publications had seldom trained for the business of journalism. Almost all of them were clergymen who perceived a newspaper or magazine as a useful tool for carrying on their work of reaching out to people and improving society because it allowed them to expand their parish beyond the local area and into the larger world. When Henry Holcombe founded the *Georgia Analytical Repository* in Savannah in 1802, he hoped to help fight crime and sin by providing moral support to those striving against them. Because of desires like Holcombe's, religious editors were dedicated to their newspapers and magazines, but they also often found their publication a daunting task. Many found it impossible to publish the periodical and continue their other religious activities. In 1824, the *Religious Remembrancer* was absorbed by the *Christian Gazette and Youth's Herald* because John Scott, editor of the *Remembrancer*, could not produce the paper and maintain his other "ministerial engagements."[19] Furthermore, these clergymen editors were unfamiliar with the mechanics of the business, and many found it difficult to remain solvent. Many proprietors poured all their money into their publications in hopes of stabilizing them. However, this goal generally proved elusive. Prior to the 1840s, religious journals seldom were truly successful. One exception to this trend was the *Christian Journal and Advocate*, published in New York, which circulated to 26,000 homes in 1826 and had reached 30,000 by 1830.[20]

As noted above, many religious publications seemed little different from ones put out by the secular press. Much of the content came from other journals, which the editor received as exchanges. However, several distinctions become obvious upon a closer examination. One variation related to money. Most of the religious periodicals used their profits to support some sort of religious work. For example, the *Religious Remembrancer* sponsored missionary work, while the *Christian Gazette and Youth's Herald* provided aid to men in training for the gospel ministry.[21]

The primary impact of the religious media on nineteenth-century reform movements came through the discussion of the need for Americans to become more Christ-like in their daily lives. The message of all these religious outlets centered around the need for spiritual and moral regeneration in the United States. Early in the nineteenth century, pastor Lyman Beecher called for moral living on the part of Americans because of the depravity of mankind: "Our fathers were not fools; they were as far from it as modern philosophers are from

---

[17]Hatch, "Elias Smith," 271.

[18]Quoted in Nathan O. Hatch, *The Democratization of American Christianity* (New Haven, Conn.: Yale University Press, 1989), 142.

[19]*Christian Gazette and Youth's Herald* (Philadelphia, Pa.), January 1824.

[20]Norton, *Religious Newspapers*, 6, 15-7, 24-8; Stroupe, *Religious Press*, 3-4; Robert A. Rutland, *Newsmongers: Journalism in the Life of the Nation, 1690-1972*, (New York: Dial Press, 1973), 117; John C. Nerone, *The Culture of the Press in the Early Republic: Cincinnati, 1793-1848*, (New York: Garland Press, 1989), 197-8.

[21]Norton, *Religious Newspapers*, 33-4.

wisdom. Their fundamental maxim was that man is desperately wicked, and cannot be influenced for good membership in society without the influence of moral restraint. With great diligence, therefore, they availed themselves of the laws and institutions of revelation, as embodying the most correct instruction and the most powerful moral restraint...."[22] Other clergymen declared that organized religion "may be regarded as the great spiritual hospital of the world, where all kinds of moral diseases ... are cured."[23] Since "their God is the great Reformer of the Universe," reformers could call on this source of strength to lead the rest of the world to a better way of life.[24]

Concentrating at first on the spiritual health of the nation, moral and social issues became increasingly important subjects of discussion in religious periodicals in the early nineteenth century. Sparked by the revival movement known as the Second Great Awakening, many people hoped to spread salvation and morality throughout the nation. They turned to the use of newspapers and magazines, sources of information that Americans already read in large numbers.[25] Between the War of 1812 and the Age of Jackson in the 1830s, general newspaper circulation in the United States grew twice as fast as the population, and religious periodicals matched or exceeded this advance.[26] In Virginia, the Presbyterian Synod considered a newspaper as "indispensable" for communication with its membership.[27] According to one editor, the religious publication "surveys the word not with the eye of the politician, or the merchant, but condenses, arranges, and reports the events of the day, as connected with the religion of Jesus Christ."[28] Newspapers and magazines provided the agency for "the sanctification of the whole vastness and variety of American life."[29]

Newspapers and magazines could serve in this role because of their growing impact in a variety of areas throughout the United States. In 1832, Alexis de Tocqueville noted the important potential of newspapers in America, stating that a newspaper could drop "the same thought into a thousand minds at the same moment ... without distracting [men] from [their] private affairs."[30] As early as 1816, one religious publisher, perceiving the same possibility, emphasized the potential impact of his newspaper and other publications like it in referring to "the benefits which it is probable will result to the community from the weekly promulgation of such a great variety of information, which must necessarily be communicated, through a medium so convenient and cheap, to the public."[31] In 1825, David Roper, in proposing a new religious periodical in Richmond, Virginia, expressed a similar idea. "The press," he wrote, "is now generally admitted to be one of the most efficient instruments of supporting any cause to which

[22]Quoted in John R. Bodo, *The Protestant Clergy and Public Issues, 1812-1848* (Philadelphia, Pa.: Porcupine Press, 1954), 153.

[23]*Methodist Correspondent* (Zanesville, Ohio), 20 December 1834.

[24]*Oberlin* (Ohio) *Evangelist*, 30 July 1851, 5 January 1853.

[25]Stroupe, "Religious Journalism in North Carolina," 1; Norton, *Religious Newspapers*, 1-2; Stroupe, *Religious Press*, 5.

[26]Hatch, "Elias Smith," 270.

[27]Stroupe, *Religious Press*, 8.

[28]*Northwestern Advocate* (Chicago, Ill.), 24 August 1853.

[29]Norton, *Religious Newspapers*, 2.

[30]Alexis de Tocqueville, *Democracy in America*, trans. Henry Reeve, 2 vols. (New York: Alfred A. Knopf, 1946), 2: 111.

[31]*Religious Remembrancer* (Philadelphia, Pa.), 17 February 1816.

it may be enlisted.... A thirst for newspaper reading prevails among all ranks of society throughout our country, and therefore opens an easy medium of access to many whose reading is almost exclusively confined to these fugitive productions."[32] Thirty years later, a Texas minister declared that "the periodical press is the body, life, and spirit of the nineteenth century."[33]

The awareness on the part of religious editors as to the potential impact of their publications produced another variance between the religious and the secular journals. This difference related to content and issues of importance to the editors. One editor stated that his paper would "embrace every subject relative to the Redeemer's Kingdom."[34] For most editors, the list of relevant subjects was a long one. Throughout the nineteenth century, religious editors used the pages of their publications to tell their readers not only how to get their spiritual lives in order, but also how they ought to behave in all circumstances. Religious newspapers and magazines sought to advertise and support the work of tract and Bible societies and Sabbath schools, as well as less clearly religious reform efforts such as helping orphans, establishing an institution for the deaf, eliminating or restricting smoking and drinking, closing theaters, and furthering the work of the American Colonization Society.[35] For example, in 1826, the New York *Religious Chronicle* praised the work of several Christian benevolent societies, which "aim[ed] at nothing more or less than the greatest good of our country.... With what gratitude then should every Christian and every patriot regard these noble institutions which work together in diffusing the light of the gospel. This is not the benevolence which exhausts itself in sighs and tears and sentiments.... But it is the benevolence of action."[36]

In pushing "the benevolence of action," Christian editors urged readers to get involved in a variety of reforms that stretched far beyond the obvious areas of witnessing to the lost and helping the poor and needy. In pushing such efforts, the religious press helped set the agenda for reform that came to dominate the thinking of many Americans in the first half of the nineteenth century. Early efforts centered around areas that could be tied to spiritual concerns fairly easily. Religious newspapers regularly carried announcements of the formation of institutions designed to educate Americans about faith and religion, such as tract societies or Sunday Schools.[37] Once the organization were formed, the press continued to report on their efforts, perceiving their activities as the "doings of the Lord," as the editor of the *Monthly Visitant* described them.[38]

When looking beyond the work of obviously religious organizations, many editors criticized behaviors or activities that they considered sinful. As early as 1805, the *Virginia Religious Magazine* attacked one of the favorite pastimes of the tidewater gentry, horse racing, because it encouraged gambling, fighting, and

---

[32] Prospectus for *The Christian Journal* (Richmond, Va.) published in the *Family Visitor* (Richmond, Va.), 8 October 1825.

[33] *The Texas Baptist* (Anderson), 27 September 1856.

[34] Plan for *Christian Herald*, printed in *Religious Remembrancer*, 17 February 1816.

[35] *Religious Remembrancer*, 13 January, 25 November, 30 December 1815, 17 February, 25 May 1816, 4 January 1817; *Christian Gazette and Youth's Herald*, 15 May, 31 July 1824; Stroupe, *Religious Press*, 5-7; John M. Havas, "Commerce and Calvinism: The *Journal of Commerce*, 1827-1865," *Journalism Quarterly* 38 (Winter 1961): 84.

[36] *Religious Chronicle* (New York, N. Y.), 13 May 1826.

[37] See, for example, *Religious Remembrancer*, 30 December 1815, 17 February and 25 May 1816.

[38] *Monthly Visitant; Or, Something Old* (Alexandria, Va.), July 1816.

lewd and inappropriate behavior in both the participants and the spectators.[39] In 1824, the *Christian Gazette and Youth's Herald* attacked a variety of problem activities. It spoke out against the breaking of the Sabbath in criticizing people who went from Philadelphia, Pennsylvania, to Camden, New Jersey, on Sunday. The running of a regular boat schedule between these two towns on this day of the week "offer[ed] easy avenues to sin to unprincipled careless multitudes." Clearly, "the day of the Lord is turned into [S]atan's carnival; do any doubt this?"[40] The same year, the same newspaper led a fight against dancing because such activity did not set a good example for non-believers to see: "It is inexpedient.... We have no example that Paul, or any of the apostles, ever danced. — There is not the least reason to believe that any of them ever did, after they were converted to the Christian faith. If their example is to be followed, it is clearly evident that Christians ought not to dance. The apostles left all, and followed Christ; Christians should follow their example."[41] This journal also declared that many of the problems of the urban poor in New York could be traced to the lack of Bibles in the homes of these families.[42] Other editors spoke out against the use of tobacco as a sin: "The habit of chewing, smoking, or snuffing tobacco, is not only disgusting, but it is absolutely sinful. Sinful, because it injures the health of the consumers, and is an altogether useless expenditure of time and money."[43]

The desire for spiritual change quickly led to a perceived need for moral reform, which found interpretation through a host of efforts designed to purify American society from all of its shortcomings. Many religious leaders and journalists advocated the development of free compulsory education as the primary method for achieving this goal. They believed that public schools offered an easily accessible means to teach moral virtues to an entire generation of citizens.[44]

Religious publications carried numerous reports of efforts to help the less fortunate. Those unable to care for themselves, such as orphans or the deaf and dumb, received attention throughout the country from such reformers.[45] In reporting the first-year successes of the Philadelphia Orphan Society, the *Religious Remembrancer* praised the organizers for their efforts: "they cannot fail to receive it with hearts deeply impressed with gratitude to God, and with lively emotions of pleasure, in being selected his instruments for purposes so honourable to themselves and so useful to those for whose benefit their Institution has been designed."[46] Religious reformers also sought to help those caught in the problems created by industrialism and urban growth, particularly the poverty-stricken immigrants who had recently moved to the United States. Programs such as shelters for poor women and children, inexpensive places to get food and shelter, and societies to help young people adjust to city life without losing their religious

---

[39]*Virginia Religious Magazine* (Lexington), October 1805.

[40]*Christian Gazette and Youth's Herald*, 14 August 1824.

[41]Ibid., 7 February 1824.

[42]Ibid., 20 March 1824.

[43]*Cincinnati* (Ohio) *Journal*, 12 November 1830.

[44]Wesley Norton, "Religious Newspapers on the American Frontier," *Journal of the West* 19 (April 1980): 19.

[45]See, for example, *Religious Remembrancer*, 25 November 1815; *Christian Gazette and Youth's Herald*, 31 July 1824.

[46]*Religious Remembrancer*, 13 January 1815.

faith began to appear in cities throughout the United States. Along with the desire to help came the hope of converting these people to Protestantism and middle-class values, but most Americans perceived these elements as essential for success in the nineteenth century industrial world. Many programs that today are associated with government welfare services were originally begun by religious charitable organizations working to improve the quality of life in American society. Examples of these efforts include job placement services, camps for inner-city children, and improved housing.[47] All of these efforts were reported and praised in the pages of religious newspapers and magazines.

Along with these efforts to help immigrants cope with economic problems came a surprising call by some religious editors for their readers to be more tolerant. William Speer, a former missionary to China, co-edited *The Oriental*, or *Tung Ngai san-luk*, a weekly English/tri-weekly Chinese newspaper published in San Francisco. Speer used the pages of his publication to urge racial and ethnic harmony, particularly in regard to the numerous Chinese immigrants working in California.[48] Other religious editors from all parts of the country attacked prejudice in all its many forms as "silly," "heartless," "brainless," and a major cause of the depravity of mankind.[49]

Efforts to improve life in inner-city slum areas generally led religious advocates to attack "community sins" that they perceived to be unique to urban life. Probably leading the way in this category was prostitution. Reformers attacked prostitution as undermining the entire basis of society and sought to eliminate it completely. A leading reform newspaper in this area appeared in New York during the 1830s. John R. McDowall, a Princeton divinity student, came to New York to distribute religious tracts for the American Tract Society. Horrified by what he saw, McDowall sought the help of Lewis and Arthur Tappan to open a house of refuge for women who desired to escape the evils of prostitution. To publicize this effort to deal with this evil of urban life, McDowall founded a weekly newspaper. *McDowall's Journal* sought to expose the "palaces of the passions" and "dens of abortion" that served to lead so many people astray. For McDowall and most reformers of this period, prostitution and abortion were twin evils that went hand in hand and had to be stamped out simultaneously. McDowall declared that abortion was so widespread that "dead infants are frequently found; sometimes in privies, wells, sewers, ponds, docks, streets, [and] open fields." McDowall's paper and his reform effort dissolved in 1833, primarily because of criticism from people who believed that discussion of subjects such as prostitution and abortion constituted obscenity, but other crusaders continued to discuss the need to face these problems in American cities.[50]

Another area in which religious advocates and denominational journalists took the lead in urging change was the temperance crusade. Drinking had been

---

[47]Steven Mintz, *Moralists and Modernizers: America's Pre-Civil War Reformers* (Baltimore, Md.: Johns Hopkins University Press, 1995), 56-7.

[48]Clifford M. Drury, "Presbyterian Journalism on the Pacific Coast," *Pacific Historical Review* 9 (December 1940): 644-5.

[49]*Northwestern Christian Advocate* (Chicago, Ill.), 2 March 1853; *Christian Times* (Chicago, Ill.), 31 August 1853; *Watchman of the Valley* (Cincinnati, Ohio), 21 January, 1 July 1847; *Oberlin Evangelist*, 13 February 1839; *Michigan Christian Herald* (Detroit), 19 February 1852, 23 June 1853; *Cross and Journal* (Cincinnati, Ohio), 27 November 1846.

[50]Mintz, *Moralists and Modernizers*, 67-9.

first identified as a potential problem by Dr. Benjamin Rush in a 1784 pamphlet entitled *An Inquiry into the Effects of Spiritous Liquors on the Human Body and Mind*. In 1808, Lyman Beecher, a pastor in Long Island, New York, read this pamphlet. Having been deeply effected by its descriptions of the negative impact of alcohol, Beecher launched a crusade to fight excessive drinking. He urged others to join the fight, and Jeremiah Evarts of Massachusetts began to use the pages of his journal, the *Panoplist*, to urge all good people to be temperate in their drinking habits.[51] Religious reformers declared intemperance to be a threat to a person's salvation. In criticizing the drinking that would take place on Christmas Day in 1824, the editor of the *Christian Gazette and Youth's Herald* declared "these same men who are thus [im]periling their souls, would feel it as an indignity offered to them were their title to the name of Christian brought in question! — They would not be stigmatized as heathens, yet by their conduct, evince more than a heathenish enmity to the blessed Redeemer."[52] The *National Philanthropist*, the first national temperance magazine, appeared in 1826. In 1836, the American Temperance Union formed to organize and broaden such anti-alcohol efforts. One of their first actions was the establishment of the *Journal of the American Temperance Union*, edited by the Reverend John Marsh, who had previously edited a temperance paper in Pennsylvania.[53] Support for the temperance cause varied somewhat between different denominations and different journal editors, but personal experience often influenced the stand of a particular individual. The editor of the *Star in the West* in Cincinnati, Ohio, came out strongly in favor of government restriction of liquor after he was accosted in the street by three drunken men, one of whom pointed a gun at his head.[54] Editors who supported temperance also wavered between restrictions and total abstinence. Most of the denominational journals came to support the elimination of all alcohol long before the general temperance movement took that step. One religious editor described the issue this way: "(We) must go for total abstinence, from all intoxicating liquors as beverages. We do not believe that a wise and beneficent God ever created in man a necessity for a drink that is productive of such infinite mischief of the human race. Whatever our columns shall permit us to say on this subject, shall be said with TOTAL ABSTINENCE inscribed upon our BANNER."[55]

Pacifism and the desire by some to eliminate all warfare also sparked interest in the religious press. Organized peace societies had appeared in the United States prior to the War of 1812, but they experienced their greatest success in the 1820s and 1830s. Such reformers condemned "war as a violation of Christian ethics and a barbarous anachronism" and urged all nations to move towards "the abolition of war and the arbitration of international disputes."[56] In 1816, a group of men met in Boston to form the Peace Society. The editor of the *Religious Remembrancer* praised this action, declaring that "if there be any meaning in the song of the celestial messengers who announced the advent of Christ,

[51]Bodo, *Protestant Clergy and Public Issues*, 184.

[52]*Christian Gazette and Youth's Herald*, 25 December 1824.

[53]Mott, *American Magazines, 1741-1850*, 165; Clifford S. Griffin, *Their Brothers' Keeper: Moral Stewardship in the United States, 1800-1865* (New Brunswick, N. J.: Rutgers University Press, 1960), 72.

[54]*Star in the West* (Cincinnati, Ohio), 8 May 1830, 22 August 1840, 27 August 1854.

[55]*New Jersey Freeman* (Boonton, N. J.), 15 June 1844.

[56]Mintz, *Moralists and Modernizers*, 117.

doubtless a field is open for cultivation by such institutions extensive as that occupied by 'Bible societies'; and HE who has blessed the exertions of these benevolent agents, has also said, 'Blessed are the peace-makers, for they shall be called the children of God'."[57] The activities of the Peace Society received coverage in many religious newspapers such as the *Evangelical Recorder*, published in Auburn, New York, by Presbyterians.[58] By 1828, the officers of the Peace Society felt sure that success was imminent: "The thing is not impossible. *It depends on us.* An union of action among all the Christians and philanthropists of the day would surely accomplish it, so far as Christendom is concerned, provided the present favorable crisis be seized, and no war should break out to blast our prospects, before our principles come into general operations, for there is no moral difficulty which zeal and perseverance will not overcome — there is nothing that ought to be done which zeal and intelligence will not do."[59] This expected success proved elusive, but the reformers continued their efforts. In 1834, "Philanthropos" argued in the *Calumet* that war ultimately caused all types of sin, such as drinking, vice, the violation of the Sabbath, and the failure to spread the gospel around the world. The journal's editor agreed and urged all pacifists to continue the fight.[60] The Mexican War sparked further efforts on the part of pacifists, particularly since many of them tied this particular conflict to the expansion of slavery, another area of concern for religious reformers. An abolitionist editor in New Jersey, John Grimes, couched his desire for peace and the end to all war in religious language: "We shall go for PEACE, for MORAL Reform, and for the correction of every abuse forbidden by Christianity; for until this is accomplished, we do not believe that 'peace on earth and good will to men' will reign to bless the human race."[61] For Grimes, and many others who thought as he did, Christian and pacifist were synonymous terms: "Christianity is a religion of love. It requires us to love our enemies — forgive them that injure us — return good for evil. There is no war in all of this. Christianity *saves* life; war destroys it. Hereby we test all professing Christians: if they engage in war or countenance it, they cannot be Christians."[62]

Pacifistic tendencies took a somewhat unusual turn among some editors of religious journals, particularly on the American frontier. Although seldom opposed to war itself, they did take strong stands against needless violence. Many spoke out against dueling and prizefighting. In 1827, the editor of the *Western Monthly Review* stated bluntly that "most moral writers have seen in the duellist, not only an Atheist, a contemner of all hopes and fears beyond the grave, ... but a man destitute of true courage.... We number among our acquaintances many who have fallen in duels."[63] Thirty years later, editors in Texas described the southern gunman as having the same "remarkably narrow mind" as John Brown, being convinced that "one kind of killing was demanded by religion." The result would be easy to predict, for a gunman, being convinced that "another kind was required by chivalry," could expect to lose "his life upon some

---

[57]*Religious Remembrancer*, 17 February 1816.
[58]Edgar, *American Magazines*, 143.
[59]Quoted in Griffin, *Their Brothers' Keeper*, 113.
[60]Ibid.
[61]*New Jersey Freeman*, 15 June 1844.
[62]Ibid., 20 March 1850.
[63]*Western Monthly Review* (Cincinnati, Ohio), December 1827.

'field of honor,' the floor of a grocery, the side-walk, or the dueling-ground."[64] Some editors even discouraged the open carrying of firearms because it encouraged conflicts. One New Jersey editor attacked dueling because it was inhumane and fostered aristocratic tendencies among its participants. This journalist went on further to condemn Henry Clay because "he has participated in five duels, and now, *refuses to say whether he will fight any more* or not."[65] Prizefighting had been a sport of sorts for many years, but it reached a new height of brutality in the 1840s, particularly in the large urban areas of the East Coast. Several religious editors attacked these bouts as savage and barbaric, describing the participants as the "bullies of the ring."[66]

Most religious editors did not oppose the use of the death penalty, but they discouraged public executions because it hardened the onlookers to violence rather than serving the hoped-for reformative purpose of making people afraid to commit criminal acts. In 1837, the editor of the *Western Christian Advocate* in Cincinnati described the public execution of a murderer who confessed just prior to his death that he became a criminal because of "disregard of parental authority, Sabbath breaking, intemperance, theft, robbery and murder." Such a public confession was possibly good for the soul of the convict, but "public executions [were] a great evil" because they did not deter people from committing crimes.[67] Another editor from the Northwest denounced capital punishment as well: "We deem it a practice unworthy a Christian people, being productive of no good, but an abundance of evil. It cannot repair the injury done, nor reform the offender, neither is it a salutary means of deterring others from the commission of the same offense."[68]

Probably the area of reform that received the most discussion in the press in the early nineteenth century was the issue of slavery, and the religious press did not differ from this emphasis. The development of antislavery sentiment in the Western world provides one of the most striking examples of a drastic change in moral values in history. As late as the 1750s, no American churches officially condemned slavery. A century later, the United States remained one of a very small number of countries to still recognize the legality of slavery. Yet many Americans had turned strongly against it. Some of the credit for this change of heart can be given to a growing number of newspaper and magazine producers who took public stands against the institution of slavery. As early as the Revolutionary era, some newspaper editors had criticized the existence of slavery in America, fearing that its presence endangered the future of the new nation.

Leading the way in criticizing slavery in the nineteenth century were several independent Quaker publishers who established clearly antislavery periodicals. Leading this group of publications was Elisha Bates's *Philanthropist*, which appeared in Cincinnati from 1818 to 1822. Also included were Charles Osborn's *Manumission Intelligencer* and Elijah Embree's *Emancipator*, both published in Jonesboro, Tennessee, in 1819 and 1820. In 1821, the most famous of these Quaker publications, Benjamin Lundy's *Genius of Universal Emancipation*,

---

[64]*Texas Christian Advocate* (Galveston), 13 April, 4 and 11 May, 1 June, 1858, 23 February 1860.
[65]*New Jersey Freeman*, 15 June, 25 July, 8 September 1844, 18 July 1848.
[66]*Michigan Christian Herald*, 4 November 1858.
[67]*Western Christian Advocate*, 13 January 1837. Although after the antebellum period, see also *Texas Christian Advocate*, 23 February 1866; *Evangel* (San Francisco, Calif.), 7 March 1861.
[68]*Star in the West*, 23 January 1836.

first appeared in Mount Pleasant, Ohio. Lundy had gotten his start in antislavery journalism writing for the *Philanthropist*.[69]

By this time, however, editors of traditional religious publications were also taking stands against what they had come to see as a sinful institution and their readers increasingly joined them in this opposition. Most of the criticisms of slavery in the religious periodicals differed from the concerns expressed in the secular press because they emphasized the immorality of the South's "peculiar institution" rather than the political or legal arguments that could be raised against it.[70] One letter to the editor of the *Religious Remembrancer* in 1816 declared: "Christians, ought not something to be done? Christians, 'by the mercies of God, I beseech you,' awake, and from your guilty country, wipe off the stain of slavery, — avert the wrath of God. Christians, by all that is sacred, by all that is dear — by all that is dreadful — I conjure you, purge your nation. One million and a half of coloured inhabitants in the United States — ignorant, and compelled to remain ignorant — immersed in sin and in misery — such is the sad picture before you."[71]

Such rhetoric became more common among denominational editors in the North, where slavery was becoming increasingly suspect. Southern religious editors, under pressure because of the important social and economic role that slavery played in the South, soon decided to avoid the issue whenever possible. Reflective of this development was a growing regional identity, expressed by many of the religious journals by the inclusion of *Southern* in their titles. As capably stated by editor Amasa Converse of Virginia, slavery was "a political subject, on which, in our view, the judicatories of the church have no right to interfere — and cannot interfere without doing great injury."[72] Five years later, a Charleston paper criticized antislavery advocates for their "pseudo-religious phrenzy called abolitionism."[73]

North of the Mason-Dixon line, however, antislavery opinions dominated in the religious media, particularly in the denominational magazines after 1820.[74] In that year, the Missouri Compromise produced much comment in the Northern religious press. Editors of two Ohio religious publications, the *Weekly Recorder* and the *Philanthropist*, both criticized the Compromise because it allowed slavery to grow, a development that would further entrench the institution in American society. The *Recorder* emphatically declared that slavery "should be arrested, and means should be adopted for its speedy and gradual abolition — for its utter extinction."[75]

Editors increasingly reported about the evils of slavery, "that blackest and most heinous" of sins,[76] and the growing opposition to it. An account of a slave

---

[69]Mintz, *Moralists and Modernizers*, 119; Mott, *American Magazines, 1741-1850*, 162. During its publication run, Lundy's paper appeared in Mount Pleasant, Ohio, and Greenville, Tennessee, before finally settling in Baltimore, Maryland. John Tebbel and Mary Ellen Zuckerman, *The Magazine in America, 1741-1990* (New York: Oxford University Press, 1991), 14-5.

[70]Edgar, *American Magazines*, 61.

[71]*Religious Remembrancer*, 26 October 1816.

[72]*Southern Religious Telegraph* (Richmond, Va.), 9 January 1839.

[73]*Southern Religious Advocate* (Charleston, S. C.), 22 November 1844.

[74]Edgar, *American Magazines*, 61-2.

[75]*Weekly Recorder* (Chillicothe, Ohio), 23 December 1819, 9 February 1820; *Philanthropist* (Mount Pleasant, Ohio), 23 August 1820.

[76]*Ohio Observer* (Cleveland), 5 September 1833.

auction in Baltimore clearly reflected these concerns: "... it is but justice to them [a large crowd] to state, that they manifested a strong indignation to the transaction, but it was done in pursuance of the laws of the State, and under the authority of the court, and what could they do? Such are the fruits of slavery, and the 'tree is known by its fruit'."[77] Most religious editors came to their stance against slavery for moral reasons rather than political or economic concerns. The continued existence of slavery was an affront to God and his plans for humanity. Men must "learn to regard slavery as not merely the denial of rights conferred in original creation, but as an outrage on the nature which the Son of God was pleased to make the temple of His divinity."[78] Slavery constituted the worst of evils that just had to be eradicated: "Slavery has been, and ever will continue to be the curse of every land in which it has been tolerated. Exempting as it does the white population from labor, enterprise of every species is palsied, and even the labor of learning requires too great a sacrifice of ease and of habits of idleness. It blights, indeed, every thing which falls within the pale of its influence — [it] is a pestilence whose bane no precaution or providence can avoid."[79]

Such an emphasis on the impact of slavery on the work of the dominant white society produced a fairly conservative view towards the end of slavery on the part of most religious editors. By and large, the denominational publications that opposed slavery supported colonization, believing that it was best for everyone if the freed slaves did not remain within the United States.[80] For example, the editor of the *Christian Gazette and Youth's Herald* strongly supported the efforts of the American Colonization Society, praising its work for "demonstrating the importance and the practicability of its objects."[81] Many denominational editors agreed, believing that the efforts at colonization would bring civilization and Christianity to Africa: "this will constitute the germ of civilization of the numerous inhabitants of that great portion of the earth, which has long remained in the darkness of ignorance and the shadow; and an effectual mean of hastening the happy period, when Ethiopia, emerging from the barbarism of degraded human nature, shall 'stretch forth her hands to God,' and worship Jehovah-Jesus as the almighty deliverer of the posterity of Ham, from the captivity of Satan and the slavery of their lusts."[82] Some antislavery advocates, while not strongly in favor of colonization, supported it anyway because it was a step towards the destruction of slavery in the United States. Samuel Mills of Princeton Seminary declared in 1817 that colonization would "ultimately be the means of exterminating slavery in our country." Asa Cummings, an antislavery clergyman from Maine and later the editor of the abolitionist *Christian Mirror*, supported colonization at first because it would "hasten the abolition of slavery," or at least "do something to mitigate the many injuries we have done them."[83]

Thus, most denominational journalists opposed slavery but did not favor radical activity to bring about its demise. Strong opposition to slavery appeared in the publications of the Congregational and Methodist churches in New York,

---

[77]*The Philadelphian* (Philadelphia, Pa.), 26 May 1826.
[78]*The Watchman and Reflector* (Boston, Mass.), 26 March 1857.
[79]*Columbian Reporter* (Taunton, Mass.), 15 October 1823.
[80]Norton, *Religious Newspapers*, 112.
[81]*Christian Gazette and Youth's Herald*, 15 May 1824.
[82]*Religious Remembrancer*, 4 January 1817.
[83]Both quotations from Bodo, *Protestant Clergy and Public Issues*, 128-9.

but neither group spawned support for revolutionary actions in order to produce its end.[84] Those religious reformers who believed that the organized churches in the United States had not taken a strong enough stand in opposition to slavery found themselves in the minority. Most of them generally left denominational journalism and took their ideas and expertise into the abolitionist camp. Elizur Wright, Jr., had started as an employee of the American Tract Society. After his conversion to abolitionism, he wrote regularly for the antislavery press. The Reverend Joshua Leavitt, previously the editor of the New York *Evangelist*, a Congregational paper that had advocated abolitionism, took over the reins of Arthur Tappan's New York *Emancipator* in 1837.[85] Leavitt began his journalistic career shortly after completing seminary, when he served as the editor of the *Seaman's Friend*, an evangelical periodical for sailors. He later served as managing editor for the *Independent*, a Congregational paper published in New York beginning in 1848. This journal reflected the antislavery opinions of Leavitt, who soon went a step further from religious journalism and helped form the Free Soil party to oppose the extension of slavery into the western territories.[86]

Elijah P. Lovejoy was the most famous of these religious reformers who shifted his career to abolitionism. Lovejoy, a Presbyterian clergyman, published a fairly typical and conventional denominational newspaper, the *Observer*. Lovejoy occasionally attacked slavery in the pages of his newspaper, but his criticisms paled next to the more radical jeremiads appearing in New England and other states along the East Coast. However, many of his readers perceived Lovejoy as a radical abolitionist. Originally publishing his paper in St. Louis, Lovejoy moved it to Alton, Illinois, across the Mississippi River from St. Louis, when threatened for his stance against slavery. On three occasions, a mob destroyed his press and attacked his house, but Lovejoy persevered and continued to publish his paper. When the mob came on November 7, 1837, to destroy the press for the fourth time, they set fire to the warehouse where it was stored. When Lovejoy ran out to escape the fire, he was shot and killed.[87] Lovejoy's death produced reactions of horror by many of his fellow denominational editors. The editor of the *Ohio Observer* in Cleveland cried that "the deed of horror, so long and unblushingly threatened, is done. The voice of blood, and the cry of justice, ... call us to awake to the signs of the times."[88]

Lovejoy receives much praise for his martyrdom in the cause of freedom of the press, but few historians comment on his Presbyterian background and that his death can also be praised as martyrdom for religious freedom as well. For Lovejoy, slavery constituted a sin that threatened the nation: "God has not slumbered nor has his Justice been an indifferent spectator of the scene.... In due time they [the souls of dead slaves] will descend in awful curses upon this land, unless averted by the speedy repentance of us all."[89] To publish in opposition to

---

[84]Tebbel and Zuckerman, *Magazine in America*, 17.

[85]Ronald G. Walters, *The Antislavery Appeal: American Abolitionism after 1830* (Baltimore, Md.: The Johns Hopkins University Press, 1976), 39.

[86]James Brewer Stewart, *Holy Warriors: The Abolitionists and American Slavery* (New York: Hill and Wang, 1976), 37; Frank Luther Mott, *A History of American Magazines, 1850-1865* (Cambridge, Mass.: The Belknap Press of Harvard University Press, 1957), 369.

[87]Mintz, *Moralists and Modernizers*, 130; Norton, *Religious Newspapers*, 113.

[88]*Ohio Observer* (Cleveland), 23 November 1837.

[89]*St. Louis* (Missouri) *Observer*, 16 April 1835.

slavery constituted part of his public statements about his religious convictions. Lovejoy, and others, did not believe his right to voice his religious beliefs could be legally restrained. Lovejoy gave his life in defense of both of these aspects of the First Amendment.

Such radical stances proved rare among all abolitionists, but they were particularly unusual among the religious journalists who came to oppose slavery. Lovejoy's death served to reinforce among many religious journals the need for restraint in efforts to deal with slavery. Joining the ranks of the radical abolitionists was not a common practice among denominational journalists. The religious press did not make its major contribution to the fight against slavery by leading the way in taking a strong stand against it. Rather, the religious press led the way by providing the ideas and the language that permeated the abolitionist litany. Religious newspapers and magazines, both denominational and independent, began describing slavery as a national sin before it became a national issue with the Missouri Compromise in 1820. Most editors in these circles agreed with their fellow worker, John Scott, when he used the pages of his newspaper in 1816 to urge Americans to "purge your nation" by getting rid of "the stain of slavery."[90] Two decades later, in 1835, the most famous abolitionist editor, William Lloyd Garrison, talked of slavery as "A SIN AGAINST GOD which exposes us to his tremendous judgments, and which ought to be immediately repented of and forsaken."[91] And, by the 1840s, this attitude had percolated down to a more local level among many Northerners, as indicated by John Grimes, a little-known abolitionist editor, who emphasized the evils of slavery in the first issue of his newspaper, the *New Jersey Freeman*: "We believe that slavery has been consuming the vitals of our nation, morally, politically, and religiously, therefore, we shall not labor *to purify slavery, to remedy its defects or correct its abuses, but to abolish it*. Believing that God created all men free and equal, we shall yield to no compromise, but seek the *total & unconditional annihilation of the system itself*."[92]

Religion, as expressed through periodical publications, both denominational and independent, provided the context in which abolitionism and other nineteenth century reform efforts were originally able to make their cries for change heard. The American public more clearly understood the radical reformers because they used language that originally had been used in the religious publications that appeared throughout the United States prior to the Civil War. Sometimes the speakers were even the same people who had earlier used their journals to call Americans to repentance of their sins in order to carry out God's will on earth. Although most of the nineteenth-century reformers did not reach their ultimate goals of complete triumph, what success they did experience owes much to their predecessors and fellow workers among the religious newspapers and magazines of antebellum America.

---

[90]*Religious Remembrancer*, 26 October 1816.
[91]*Liberator* (Boston, Mass.), 15 August 1835.
[92]*New Jersey Freeman*, 15 June 1844.

# 8

# The Mass Media and Revivalism in the Gilded Age
by Bruce J. Evensen

BEGINNING IN BROOKLYN during the fall of 1875 and continuing in Philadelphia, New York, Chicago, and Boston in the year and a half that followed there is a remarkable similarity in the front pages of the big city Gilded Age press. Each would attempt to outdo the other in column inch after column inch of coverage of the famous evangelist D.L. Moody, who had come to these cities to proclaim the good news of Jesus Christ. In the twenty-five years that followed, he preached to an estimated 100 million souls on both sides of the Atlantic and was able to reach many more than that when one considers the outreach of press reports. When he died at the dawn of a new century, he was arguably the best known and most admired American of the Victorian era, a celebrity born through the marriage of mass media and mass evangelism.

Moody's meetings were so widely attended that special tabernacles had to be built to contain the crowds that came. No municipal hall could hold them all. An attendance of 12,000, 16,000 and 20,000 pushed late nineteenth-century sound systems and Moody's larynx to the maximum. The eagerness to be present assured record-setting circulations in those newspapers covering the civic spectacle. Their daily stenographic accounts sold separately as collectors' editions when weeks and months of crusade-making had run their course.

Today, it may be difficult to understand what all the excitement was about. Contemporary evangelists need sex scandals to tease today's tabloid readers. Moody knew a hostile and, at times, indifferent press all too well. But through painstaking trial and error he created a sophisticated media strategy that became a central tool in his evangelistic work. He developed it in his 1873-1875 revival work in Great Britain. It was during this crusade that the English-speaking world discovered Moody and elevated him from a little known and lightly regarded Chicago layman to the best known and most widely quoted preacher in the Anglo-American world. This chapter is an analysis of the coalitions and alliances Moody built, the uses he made of the mass media, and the uses the media made of him during the rise of religious celebrity and civic spectacle in the Gilded Age.

When little known Chicago evangelist D.L. Moody and singer Ira Sankey arrived in Liverpool on June 17, 1873, the local press considered it less significant than the story of a ship's captain who had been fined for assaulting a steward "over pastry improperly cooked."[1] When he left the same city two years and two months later after preaching all over England, Scotland, and Ireland, Moody was celebrated as God's man for the Gilded Age, an evangelist whose success in sheer numbers seemed to swamp the outpouring of religious conversion that had marked the Reformation.[2] He won the adulation through record crowds and huge numbers of new converts, and these results came, at least in part, through his capacities as event organizer, in which mastery of the mass media was a significant component. His mission with the mass media was to reach readers unable to hear his preaching in person and to create a climate of opinion that would encourage "a great anxiety to be present."[3] His unprecedented abilities at consensus building and advance work included using friends in the religious press to announce his coming campaigns while advertising those meetings in the daily press "next to the truss ads if necessary." In city after city he labored with local committees of laymen and ministers who legitimized the ecumenicalism of his movement. When the curious came, the press was among them.

Moody reserved front row center seats to further their reporting of the spectacle, issued press releases to promote his evangelistic work, met with reporters to encourage continued positive framing of his revival work and publicly and privately acknowledged his debt to the press in the successful promotion and publicizing of "God's work."

Revivalist literature of Moody's day emphasized the sovereignty of God in bringing spiritual awakening while it deprecated man's meager ability to do much more than watch and wait. Moody emphasized, as Charles Finney had before him, what man must do to bring about revival. Since God was always interested in reviving His people, it was man's responsibility to "bring the mind into such a state that it is fitted to receive the word of God." That meant "breaking up the fallow ground" so that it might be "suited to receive grain." One "promoted" a revival by "taking advantage of man's excitability." The revivalist's duty was to "awaken men to a sense of guilt and danger" until "the tide rises so high as to sweep away the opposing obstacles." In Finney's and Moody's view "many have waited pointlessly on God's sovereignty," not realizing that "every event is brought about by means." What was needed in revival was "the wise use of constituted means" and among the most important means, from Moody's point of view, was the careful cultivation of the press.[4]

---

[1]*Liverpool Telegraph and Shipping News*, 18 June 1873, 3.

[2]*Dublin Daily Express*, 31 October 1874, 3; *Belfast Morning News*, 14 September 1874, 2; *Edinburgh Daily Review*, 8 December 1873, 3 and 5 January 1874, 2; *Newcastle Daily Chronicle*, 28 October 1873, 4; *Sheffield Post*, 9 January 1875, 7.

[3]*Dublin Daily Express*, 31 October 1874, 3; *Belfast Morning News*, 14 September 1874 2; *Sheffield Post*, 9 January 1875, 7.

[4]For D.L. Moody's insistence that "men go out and work" to bring about revival, see "Sermon Notes. Revival," in D.L. Moody Papers, Dolben Library, Northfield, Mass., and "Sermon Notes. Revival," D.L. Moody Papers, Moody Bible Institute, Chicago, Ill. (The "Moody Bible Institute" hereafter will be referred to as "MBI.") See also, William R. Moody, *The Life of Dwight L. Moody* (New York: Fleming H. Revell, 1900), chapter 42, "His Belief and Practice," 494-501. For Charles Finney's view on the importance of human

Mass communication historians have paid surprisingly little attention to the treatment in the secular press of religion in general and revival in particular. Although the religious press has its chroniclers, only recently have historians begun examining the cultural and social significance of religious reporting in the daily press. Historians of religious revivals have long signaled the importance of press coverage in gathering a constituency and legitimizing the activities of evangelists. And that was a connection Moody well understood. It is reflected in his decision to introduce himself and co-worker Ira Sankey, a singer, to British newspapers.[5] The press release briefly recounted Moody's birth in East Northfield, Massachusetts on 3 February 1837, the early death of his father, his life as a Boston shoe salesman, and his subsequent religious work in Chicago. He answered to the name "Crazy Moody" for his tendency to burst into the offices of Chicago's newspapers, insisting they publicize his work among the orphans and destitute of the city.[6]

His experiments in the power of publicity included his works of charity during the Civil War and the Great Chicago Fire of 1871. The need to rebuild his Chicago church and invigorate the work of the Young Men's Christian Association sent him overseas where he met evangelical leaders, who would figure prominently in the success of his 1873-1875 campaign. He visited the London office of R.C. Morgan, editor and publisher of a leading evangelical weekly, and met Lord Shaftesbury, a man known for his support of evangelical causes. He asked Harry Moorhouse, Britain's powerful "Boy Preacher," to "come to Chicago and preach for me."[7] When he returned home, he experimented with techniques and texts learned from Moorhouse.

Moody launched a public campaign to attract investors in a rebuilding project that would include, for its time, the largest lending library in the city. The effort solidified his relations with city philanthropists like John V. Farwell, George Armour, the meatpacking king, and Cyrus McCormick, of reaper fame, and strengthened his ties with Joseph Medill and the Chicago media establishment. He published his own paper, *Heavenly Tidings*, which widely publicized the use of all available means to promote Christian work in the city following

---

agency in promoting revivals, see Charles G. Finney, *Lectures on Revivals of Religion* (Oberlin: E.J. Goodrich, 1868), 920 and 35-47. Also, Charles G. Finney, *Memoirs of Charles G. Finney* (New York: A.S. Barnes, 1876), 24-41, and his discussion of revivals in Boston in 1856-1858, on 411-47. For a summary on the role of human agency in "winning souls" see Henry C. Fish, *Handbook of Revivals: For the Use of Winners of Souls* (Boston: James H. Earle, 1874), particularly chapter one, "What Is a Revival?," 11-24; and chapter 10, "Revival Means and Methods," 254-81.

[5]The British press borrowed heavily from Moody's self-representation. The account in the *London Daily News*, 10 March 1875, 3, is typical of the summaries that preceded Moody's arrival in cities scheduled for his crusade work.

[6]Moody's early days as a Chicago evangelist and his relations with the press are reported by veteran city newsman Frederick Francis Cook in *Bygone Days in Chicago: Recollections of the "Garden City" of the Sixties* (Chicago: A.C. Clurg, 1910), 305-11. Moody's letters home to his mother reflect a youthful determination to "have faith in my Lord. I know he will do thing rite. [sic] That is what I have to comfort me." See letter from D.L. Moody to Betsey Holton Moody, 13 October 1856, *Letters of D.L. Moody*, Volume 1 (Chicago, Ill.: Moody Bible Institute). As late as 1857, Moody seemed torn between making money and serving God. He wrote his brother George on March 17 that he had lent out $100 at 17 per cent interest. He commented, "I tell you hear is the place to make the money. I can make more hear in one weake then I could in Boston in a monnth [sic]."

[7]Accounts of Moody's preparations in Britain for his later revival work are found in George E. Morgan, *R.C. Morgan. His Life and Times* (London: Pickering & Inglis, 1908) 169-71; W. Moody, *The Life of Dwight L. Moody*, 131-43; and J.C. Pollock, *Moody: A Biographical Portrait of the Pacesetter in Modern Mass Evangelism* (Grand Rapids: Zondervan, 1963), 64-9.

its fiery ordeal. The effort furthered Moody's reputation as "an up and comer" who "gets things done" and finally freed him to go into crusade work on a full-time basis.[8]

*OFF TO A FALSE START*

Moody's eagerness to "be out of the business of begging" rushed his arrival in Britain and helped to get him off to a false start. He had told the *Chicago Tribune* that he was going to Europe "not to sightsee but to preach." But his announced crusade path — York, Manchester, Liverpool, Birmingham, Sheffield, Leeds, Bristol, Scotland and Ireland[9] — had one problem. No one in those cities had been alerted to his coming. He had hoped that a London vicar and a Newcastle merchant might coordinate his early meetings, but when he arrived in Liverpool on June 17, 1873, he learned both men had recently died. Moorhouse agreed to take Sankey into his home, while Moody went to London. There he persuaded Morgan to run an ad in *The Christian* asking "any friends who desire his help" to write him in care of the Y.M.C.A. in York.[10]

Morgan sent the ad to several hundred pastors in the north of England and Scotland, leading Moody to hope "invitations will be coming in from all over the country."[11] He hastily poured over a map of York and decided to canvas the town with posters promising "a memorable evening" of evangelistic services to all those attending. Fewer than fifty did, and they sat so far away Sankey could barely hear them sing. The following noon-day prayer meeting in a small upper room of the Y.M.C.A. — reached through a long, dark passageway — drew only six.[12] Moody intensified his poster and advertising campaign, and met with pastors and the press, to improve his numbers. Glowing accounts of his meetings appeared in Morgan's weekly, giving the crusade national visibility.[13] His decision to bring a singer made his early meetings a curiosity. Tradesmen, washerwomen, railwaymen, and a few soldiers from local barracks began attending. The York press thought the event worth a column inch or two.[14] Morgan's weekly praised Moody's meetings for being "pregnant with blessing," while it

---

[8]See Moody's fundraising letters to Cyrus H. McCormick, dated 15 April 1868; 24 November 1871; 24 February 1873 and 1 May 1873. McCormick financed Moody's plan to put up racks of Christian literature in passenger depots and hotels throughout the city and to train a staff to visit these locations three times weekly. In the first ten months of the program's operation two million pages of literature were distributed. McCormick liked the fact that Moody had arranged shipment of the tracts from Dublin at one sixth the cost of American tracts. See also, William T. Hutchinson, *Cyrus Hall McCormick. Harvest, 1856-1884* (New York: D. Appleton, 1935), 301-5. McCormick's ties as stockholder to the recently established *Chicago Daily News* furthered Moody's positive press from that paper. For Moody's generally warm relations with the city's dominant paper, the *Chicago Tribune*, see *Chicago Tribune*, 10 January 1867, 2; 11 January 1867, 4; 8 January 1869, 2; 12 January 1869, 4; 24 June 1870, 1; and 27 June 1870, 1. Also, *Chicago Evening Journal*, 11 January 1870, 4 and 8 June 1870, 1.

[9]*Chicago Tribune*, 25 May 1873, 9.

[10]Ira D. Sankey, *My Life and the Story of the Gospel Hymns* (Philadelphia: Sunday School Times, 1906), 42-4; *The Christian*, 26 June 1873, 17.

[11]Letter from D.L. Moody to John Farwell, dated 30 June 1873. Moody Papers, Box 8, Folder 95, Yale Divinity School Library. (Archival material from the Moody Paper collection at Yale University will be referred to in subsequent notes as the "Moody Papers/Yale.")

[12]Letter from Bennett to William Moody, dated 12 March 1900; diary entries of 20 June and 23 June 1873 by Emma C. Moody, Box 14, Folder 2, Moody Papers/Yale.

[13]*The Christian*, 10 July 1873, 28.

[14]*York Herald*, 28 June 1873, 7.

avoided crowd estimates.[15] Moody competed unsuccessfully with grouse shooting prospects in the Yorkshire moors for newspaper space. His meetings failed to
eclipse the perceived newsworthiness of a twenty-inch snake that was found
wrapped around the ankle of a celebrant at St. James Church who otherwise sat
happily asleep.[16]

Both at York and then Sunderland, Moody continued to feel his way. He
built on his alliances, listened to friends, and interrogated reporters and newspaper editors, when they gave him the time, to understand better what he was up
against. Moorhouse and Morgan accompanied Moody to Sunderland, hoping to
strengthen his showing in the northern shipbuilding town. Moorhouse's meeting got Moody off to a good start; and the endorsement of Arthur Rees, a seaman turned popular preacher, helped Moody win a hearing in the nonconformist
press, which welcomed his independence from the Church of England.[17]

Morgan, writing under the pen name "Omega," was doing all he could to
puff Moody in the pages of *The Christian*. A long profile introduced him to
Britain's evangelical readership. He was a "beloved brother" who "had left
home for the sole purpose of saving souls." He and Sankey "nobly depended
upon the Lord for the supply of all their temporal wants" and were sworn enemies of the forces of evil who held captive "the seething and lawless masses" of
the city. Morgan commended this "blessed work" to the "earnest attention of
God's saints everywhere."[18] Morgan's plea, however, fell on deaf ears within
Sunderland's pastoral community. Local rectors largely boycotted Moody's
meetings, arguing his success in the city might cut down on their collections.
Even members of the local Y.M.C.A. were reluctant to be seen publicly with
Moody for fear of alienating the local churches.[19] The Sunderland press attacked
his "presentational style of stray Americanisms" in what little attention they
gave him.[20] Moody and Sankey took to the streets leading marchers in songs of
praise as a way of "advertising our meetings" and in the hope that "outsiders
would be swept up in the exhortation."[21] But the local press stood mute, and
opposing churches failed to support the spectacle. When Moody escaped Sunderland three weeks into the campaign, he wearily remarked, "God save me from
the devil and ministers."

*THE BREAKTHROUGH*

Moody observed that a common problem at York and Sunderland had been lack
of support from evangelical assemblies in those cities. Without local legitimacy
the press remained skeptical, or even worse, indifferent. In agreeing to go to
Newcastle, a coal seaport, he received critical support from Richard Hoyle, a lay-

---

[15]*The Christian*, 17 July 1873, 8.

[16]*York Herald*, 28 June 1873, 5 and 7 and 5 July 1873, 8 and 11; *Yorkshire Chronicle*, 28 June 1873,
4 and 12 July 1873, 5.

[17]Emma Moody's diary entries of 30 July 30 and 31 July 1873, Box 14, Folder 2, Moody Papers/Yale;
Sankey, *My Life and the Story of the Gospel Hymns*, 48-9.

[18]*The Christian*, 7 August 1873, 11.

[19] Emma Moody's diary entry of 25 August 1873, Box 14, Folder 2, Moody Papers/Yale; W. Moody,
*Life of Dwight L. Moody*, 164-5.

[20]*Sunderland Times*, 2 August 1873, 2; *Sunderland and Durham County Herald*, 25 July 1873, 5 and
1 August 1873, 7.

[21]*The Christian*, 19 February 1874, 8.

man, and David Lowe, the city's leading Presbyterian pastor. William Skerry, Newcastle's most prominent Baptist, was a convert to Moody's cause after reading of his work in Morgan's newspaper. Through Skerry, Moody met Joseph Cowen, a Liberal member of Parliament and widely respected publisher of the *Newcastle Chronicle*, whose support proved critical to Moody's success.[22]

The strength of Newcastle's opposition to the State Church played to Moody's advantage. A petition by more than 400 clergymen in the Church of England to establish confession as a sacrament of the church struck many inside and outside the church as a repudiation of the Reformation and a symbol of how far the church had slipped from a previous position of honor in British society. Cowen's *Newcastle Courant* put it bluntly when it urged the Archbishop to "save the life of the church by cutting this cancer out."[23] Cowen's clarion call found support from future Moody benefactor, the Earl of Shaftsbury, who urged "believers everywhere to stand to the last" in resisting the corruption of spiritual devotion and religious worship in Britain.[24]

Moody helped mobilize this sentiment around him when he called for an all-day meeting in Newcastle on September 10. The unprecedented action was a risk. If it failed to generate large numbers, the campaign might easily stall out and suffocate for lack of public airing in the press. If it succeeded it would likely solidify his growing base in the North and might easily galvanize Nonconformist elements across the border in Scotland. Morgan gave Moody's dramatic gesture unprecedented coverage, four full pages in *The Christian*. Moody made the better known Skerry and Moorhouse partners in the all day event, drew Rev. William Moreley Punshun up from London to strengthen participation of area Methodists, and involved lay leaders from Bristol and Yarrow to strengthen his claim these meetings "are to be open and free, a celebration of what the Lord is doing in our midst." Cowen's account of the meeting emphasizes how audiences "were caught up in the spirit and intention of these words" resulting in "a holy and pleasing exercise." As the campaign deepened, he noted that "in ordinary circumstances it is difficult to fill chapels on Sundays," but Moody's meetings were "filled to overflowing" each night. People sit for hours "and like it."[25]

For seven consecutive weeks, Cowen and the *Newcastle Daily Chronicle* devoted increasing, daily coverage to Moody's campaign. The paper praised his ability to bring denominations together. "Almost impassable barriers seem to be disappearing," the paper observed. Moody's proclamation of "no new gospel," but "the eternal truths of the old one" created common ground for the region's many ministers. The Church of England might remain aloof, but that only magnified Moody's growing reputation among evangelicals. One thousand celebrants a night testified to the certainty "something extraordinary is happen-

---

[22]W. Moody, *The Life of Dwight L. Moody*, 165-6; Sankey, *My Life and the Story of the Gospel Hymns*, 57-8; *The Christian*, 18 September 1873, 5; Morgan, *R.C. Morgan. His Life and Times*, 174-5; *Newcastle Daily Chronicle*, 25 August 1873, 4 and 29 August 1873, 4.

[23]*Newcastle Courant*, 5 September 1873, 3.

[24]*The Christian*, 26 June 1873, 16; Morgan, *R.C. Morgan. His Life and Times*, 175-7; W. Moody, *The Life of Dwight L. Moody*, 154-5; Henry Varley, Jr., *Henry Varley's Life Story* (London: Alfred Holness, 1887), 103-21; McLoughlin, *Revivals, Awakenings, and Reform*, 183-4; *Zion's Herald* (Boston), 31 July 1873, 244; Pollock, *Moody: A Biographical Portrait...*, 109-11; H. W. Clark, *A History of English Nonconformity*, Vol. 2 (London: Chapman and Hall, 1913), 17-27.

[25]*The Christian*, 18 September 1873, 5-8; *Newcastle Daily Chronicle*, 11 September 1873, 3; 13 September 1873, 3; and 18 September 1873, 4; W. Moody, *The Life of Dwight L. Moody*, 149-50.

ing." Moody's meetings were moved to a larger hall, and tickets were required to "control the crowds unable to gain attendance."[26] That announcement intensified interest in the meetings even further. Some were "disgusted" by the democratizing effects of Moody's meetings. But critics only made his many defenders more passionate. Their attitude was captured in Cowen's claim that Moody was a "businessman" who conducted his meetings as a businessman ought.[27] Morgan ran 10,000 extra copies of *The Christian* to further Moody's message, and at Moody's suggestion area ministers and churches raised enough money to send a three-month subscription of *The Christian* to every one of the 40,000 ministers in the United Kingdom.[28]

Newcastle became the pattern of Moody's successful crusades in Scotland, Ireland, and the south of England. At each crusade site he received the commitment of evangelical pastors to participate in his meetings and to get their congregations to come. The curious followed. The secular press, seeing a good story, was not far behind. Cowen's stories were reprinted in Carlisle, Moody's next stop. Friendly stories in Carlisle found their way to Edinburgh, where he went after that. And so the pattern continued in the eighteen months that remained of his time in Britain. Morgan's publicity machine gave Moody a nationwide following. Soon some clergy in the Established Church joined in. For the secular press, that made the meetings an even better story.

*MOODY'S MARKETING STRATEGY*

Moody's success in Newcastle foreshadowed a marketing strategy that served well in Carlisle, Edinburgh, Glasgow, and the cities that would follow. Advertisements, signed by sympathetic ministers in each successive city promised "a blessing of unusual magnitude" for those attending Moody's crusades.[29] These ministers were in conspicuous attendance at Moody's meetings, where he urged converts and anxious inquirers to affiliate with friendly churches.[30] Press accounts of his success in Carlisle were republished in cities next on his schedule.[31] This meant that capacity crowds and full pews could be organized prior to his coming. In Carlisle, additional churches had to be opened to handle the overflow. The press reported that clergy not affiliated with the state church had begun "flocking" to Moody's cause "with one northern town after another catching the spirit of the enthusiasm."[32] Emma Moody began tracking her husband's success in the local press and sending the clippings home.[33] Her husband did

---

[26]*Newcastle Daily Chronicle*, 18 September 1873, 4; 20 September 1873, 4; 24 September 1873, 4; 4 October 1873, 4; and 11 October 1873, 3.

[27]Ibid., 28 October 1873, 4, 5 November 1873, 3; and 13 November 1873, 3; *The Christian*, 23 October 1873, 8 and 30 October 1873, 4.

[28]W. Moody, *The Life of Dwight L. Moody*, 150-1; *The Christian*, 27 November 1873, 4; Bernard A. Weisberger, *They Gathered at the River: The Story of the Great Revivalists and Their Impact upon Religion in America* (Boston: Little, Brown, 1958), 84-5.

[29]*Carlisle Daily Journal*, 18 November 1873, 3 and 19 November 1873, 2.

[30]Ibid., 20 November 1873, 2 and 21 November 1873, 4.

[31]For example, the *Carlisle Daily Journal*, 19 November 1873, at page three republished accounts of Moody's success in Newcastle. *The Daily Review* of Edinburgh reported news of Moody's work in Carlisle. The pattern was followed in the cities that followed.

[32]*Carlisle Daily Journal*, 20 November 1873, 2; 21 November 1873, 4: and 22 November 1873, 2.

[33]Letter from Emma Moody to her mother, dated 5 November 1873, Box 8, Folder 95. Moody Papers/Yale.

the same, encouraging prayer partners on both sides of the Atlantic to continue supporting his work.[34] The six-week build up to Moody's meetings in Edinburgh emphasized prayer and publicity. Moody stayed at the home of William G. Blaikie, a professor of apologetics at New College, who shared Moody's passion for prayer and publicity. Blaikie touted him to evangelical readers through his widely circulated *Sunday Magazine*, while facilitating Moody's contacts with local clergy and the press. The organization the two men helped to fashion proved to be a powerful tool in creating conditions that promoted success.[35]

"A spirit of excitement and expectation has been built up in many," *The Daily Review* of Edinburgh reported. "The desire to see and hear Moody becomes more and more widespread and earnest."[36] The press reported that many who were seen waiting for him read reports of his campaign in the Edinburgh press.[37] Even some reporters fell prey to the excitement. One of them, W. Robertson Nicoll, editor of *The British Weekly*, made his own profession of faith following a Moody meeting, finding its impact "difficult to ignore."[38] Sankey's own accounts of the crusades received nationwide circulation through *The Christian*.[39] Letters were printed from those who testified "Christ has come to Edinburgh."[40] The press, in turn, embraced the language of Moody's organizing committee and reported Edinburgh's "awakening" was a democratic movement. "If we're going to live in heaven together," he was quoted as saying, "why shouldn't we be united here."[41] *The Daily Review* reiterated that logic when it editorialized that he had united the nation's churches in a frontal assault against "spiritual slothfulness" and for "the revival of the spiritually dead."[42]

Moody's sense of the dramatic generated extensive coverage in Edinburgh's most widely read dailies. A "Week of Prayer" was launched through an urgent appeal to Scotland's 2,600 pastors.[43] When Margaret Lindsay, a teenaged convert at Moody's meetings, was critically injured in a train wreck following a watchnight service, the press made much of her determination to sing the words of her favorite hymn, "The Gate Ajar for Me," until her death two days later. Edinburgh's ticket committee found itself "unable utterly to meet the demand" with Moody's meetings "packed to the fainting point."[44] Nor was Moody any

---

[34]Letter from D.L. Moody to James H. Cole, dated 8 November 1873, Box 8, Folder 95, Moody Papers/Yale.

[35]William G. Blaikie, *For the Work of the Ministry* (London: Strahan & Co., 1873), 16-29; *Sunday Magazine* (Edinburgh), 1 February 1874, 5; Weisberger, *They Gathered at the River*, 191-2; Emma Moody's diary entry, 22 November 1873, Box 14, Folder 2, Moody Papers/Yale; Pollock, *Moody: A Biographical Portrait...*, 115; George Adam Smith, *The Life of Henry Drummond* (New York: Doubleday and McClure, 1898), 58-61; Henry Drummond, "Mr. Moody: Some Impressions and Facts," *McClure's Magazine*, December 1894, 59-60.

[36]*The Daily Review* (Edinburgh), 15 December 1873, 2.

[37]*Narrative*, 25, citing *The British Evangelist* of 13 January 1874.

[38]W. Moody, *The Life of Dwight L. Moody*, 205-6. See also, Donald Carswell, *Brother Scots* (New York: Harcourt, Brace, 1928), and Nicoll's introduction to Henry Drummond, *The Ideal Life: Addresses Hereto Unpublished* (New York: Dodd & Mead, 1897).

[39]*The Christian*, 4 December 1873, 11.

[40]*The Daily Review* (Edinburgh), 10 December 1873, 7.

[41]*The Christian*, 11 December 1873, 6.

[42]Ibid., 29 January 1874, 5, citing *The Daily Review* (Edinburgh) editorial of earlier in the week.

[43]*The Daily Review* (of Edinburgh), 3 January 1874, 2; 5 January 1874, 2; B January 1874, 3; and 7 January 1874, 3; *Edinburgh Courant*, 12 January 1874, 4; *Edinburgh Evening News*, 13 January 1874, 2.

[44]*Edinburgh Courant*, 18 December 1873, 2; *The Daily Review* (of Edinburgh), 19 December 1873, 2.

longer able to pray over individual requests at his meetings. Instead, prayers were offered in behalf of fourteen brothers for their unsaved sisters, eighteen sisters for their worldly brothers, those "fallen under the influence of drink, the covetous, the cruel, the doubter, the sick, the lame, and the halt."[45] Daily, the press reported answers to prayer, of "whole families coming to Christ." The demand for tickets to Moody's meetings became so intense that campaign organizers had to finally rent the six thousand seat Corn Exchange, which quickly became filled to over flowing each night."[46]

Moody reached his greatest success in Glasgow during the winter and spring of 1874. There, he was praised for recreating the religious fervor of the Reformation and for outdoing George Whitefield in the number of souls saved. Syndicated press reports meant that all Scotland was getting "into the spirit of hope" and "earnestly desired Moody" with Glasgow's 70,000 young men between the ages of 15 and 25 particularly targeted. Those who could not gain entrance to Moody's meetings were reported listening eagerly outside for "sounds of praise inside." Sometimes the temptation became too much and they crashed through the auditorium's doors. The press was reporting Moody's Scottish tour as "a spreading fire, an unusual day of the Lord's power." Communities receiving the news sent widely publicized petitions to Moody pleading with him to come to their cities.[47] At prayer meetings, he thanked God for reporters who had "communicated throughout Scotland" the power they had witnessed and he "besought Providence to put into their hearts the faithful chronicling of how Scotland had been blessed."[48] He shared letters from desperate readers overjoyed by accounts of his campaign that they had read in the press. He observed there was no way of estimating "how much good these reports are doing" and reiterated the importance of an advertising strategy that combined posters, handbills, and the daily press to saturate the city with news of the campaign street by street and house by house.[49] He endorsed a plan to subsidize "communicating the glad tidings of the Lord's work" by placing copies of *The Christian* in every Scottish home.[50] His coordinating committee made certain the word went out that a spiritual revival was sweeping Scotland. Placards of *The Christian* placed in the lobbies of more than 8,000 Scottish churches advertised that fact.[51]

Moody's influence over media accounts was not total. Glasgow's establishment paper, the *Herald*, castigated city clergy for falling for "Yankee tomfooleries," while decrying Moody's "theatricality" and "this new star system" in evangelism."[52] The *Herald's* accounts of the money Moody was supposedly

[45] *Edinburgh Evening News* (of Edinburgh), 22 December 1873, 3.

[46] *The Daily Review* (of Edinburgh), 23 December 1873, 2; *The Christian*, 8 January 1874, 5; Emma Moody diary entry, 1 January 1874, Box 14, Folder 2, Moody Papers/Yale; "Recollections of 1874," 8, by Mrs. Peter MacKinnon, of Campbeltown, Scotland, Archives and Manuscripts, Moody Papers/Yale, Group 28, Series I, Box 5; *Edinburgh Courant*, 5 January 1874, 4; *Glasgow News*, 10 February 1874, 4.

[47] *The Christian*, 26 February 1874, 3; 5 March 1874, 3; and 2 April 1874, 6.

[48] *Glasgow Herald*, 2 January 1874, 3 and 5 January 1874, 4; *The Daily Review* (of Edinburgh), 6 January 1874, 3 and 9 January 1874, 3; *North Briton Advertiser*, 13 January 1874, 3; *Portobello Advertiser*, 15 January 1874, 3.

[49] *Glasgow News*, 14 March 1874, 4; *The Christian*, 19 March 1874, 7.

[50] *The Christian*, 26 March 1874, 7.

[51] *London Daily Mail*, 21 February 1874, 5 and 6; *Glasgow Christian News*, 28 February 1874, 3; *The Christian*, 5 March 1874, 3; *Glasgow Daily Mail*, 16 March 1874, 4; *Androssan and Saltcoats Herald*, 23 May 1874, 3; *Dundee Weekly News*, 6 June 1874, 1.

[52] *Glasgow Herald*, 26 March 1874, 7; 4 April 1874, 6, and 14 April 1874, 3; Alastair Phillips, *Glasgow*

making in selling hymnals disturbed him greatly.

Friendly papers gave great play to his denial that he "was in it for the money," and Moody read that denial at his Glasgow crusade.[53] He had John Farwell launch a letter-writing campaign from Chicago to prove the point. A testimonial, signed by thirty-five prominent ministers and business leaders, received wide play in the Scottish press and undergirded the momentum of Moody's campaign.[54] He emerged from the crisis unscathed. His private quarters were awash in private letters "reaching chairs and shelves in every corner." When a Scottish newspaper published a biography of Moody, it quickly sold out and another press run was needed. One disaffected cleric was clearly puzzled. He thought "there is no proportion between Moody's abilities and his results."[55] What the analysis missed was Moody's capacities as an organizer and publicist who built coalitions that helped rally the masses to his cause.

Testimonies daily attested to the power of publicity in sustaining the momentum of Moody's meetings.[56] Salvation as civic spectacle legitimized personal conversion, particularly for the doubter seeking certainty. The magnitude of the meetings created an incentive for churchmen to forget their differences and for many in the daily press to suspend their skepticism. Something appeared to be happening. And whether the source of the spectacle was one part spiritual and one part secular, who was there to say? Critics might carp that not men's plans but God alone brought revival, but the reality was Moody's meetings in sheer size had taken on a curiosity as well as a weight of their own. No one in Glasgow had ever seen anything like it. The desire grew to get in on it. To those opposed to his careful cultivation of the press in publicizing revival work he suggested "new means must be found to spread the gospel" and "there is no more effective way of doing so" than the print press.[57] To ministers who rebuked the role of the press in filling auditoriums, Moody remarked that it was better than "preaching to empty pews."[58] He did not hesitate to privately and publicly thank reporters for helping him to reach those who would otherwise have been unreached.[59] In letters home he cited the circulation of the British press that had been friendly to the progress of his crusades and acknowledged their central role in "helping to stir the dry bones of the United Kingdom."[60]

---

*Herald,   1783-1983* (Glasgow: Richard Drew, 1983), 7-9 and 78-89; *Glasgow News,* 3 March 1874, 3 and 10 March 1874, 3; *The Christian,* 5 March 1874, 5.

[53]An account of the flap over the money Moody was making appears in the *London Daily Mail* and is reprinted in the *Glasgow News,* 21 February 1874, 5 and 6.

[54]*The Christian,* 7 May 1874, 6; letter from D.L. Moody to John V. Farwell, dated 7 May 1874, Moody's Letters, Volume 1, 1854-1879, Moody Papers, MBI; *Narrative of Messrs. Moody and Sankey's Labors in Great Britain and Ireland* (New York: Anson D.F. Randolph, 1875), 45-9.

[55]Diary entries of Emma Moody for 1 January 1874, 12 July 1874 and 13 July 1874, Box 14, Folder 2, Moody Papers/Yale. Also, "Recollections of 1874" by Mrs. Peter MacKinnon of Campeltown, Scotland, pp. 1-5; Archives and Manuscripts, Moody Papers/Yale, Group 28, Series I, Box 5. Moody's correspondence with *The Northy British Daily Mail* over establishing a Christian orphanage in Glasgow, is retained in Box 8, Folder 95 of the Moody Papers/Yale. See also, *The Daily Review* (of Edinburgh), 8 December 1873, 3; 10 December 1873, 7; 22 December 1873, 3; and 2 January 1874, 2; Pollock, *Moody: A Biographical Portrait...,* 127.

[56]"Recollections of 1874," by Mrs. Peter MacKinnon, 10-12, Archives and Manuscripts, Group 28, Series I, Box 5, Moody Papers/Yale.

[57]*Glasgow Christian News,* 28 March 1874, 3 and 18 April 1874, 5; *The Christian,* 26 March 1874, 7.

[58]For Moody's defense of his use of the press, see W. Moody, *The Life of Dwight L. Moody,* 423-34.

[59]*The Globe* (of London), 19 March 1875, 3; *The Daily Telegraph* (London), 13 July 1875, 3.

[60]See Moody's letter to Farwell, dated 14 November 1874; Moody Letters, Volume 1, Moody Papers,

## MOODY AS SUPERSTAR

By the time Moody left Scotland for Ireland on September 4, 1874, he was well on his way to becoming a Christian superstar whose exploits would be chronicled in the publishing world on both sides of the Atlantic. A narrative of his "marvelous work" in Edinburgh was being prepared by Partridge and Company days after he departed the city. More than a dozen book-length accounts of his Great Britain campaign would follow within three years. Various forms of his sermons began appearing in print. Some were edited by Henry Drummond. Others were published by companies unabashedly out to make a fast dollar off a suddenly hot prospect.[61] Moody publicist John MacPherson, who had written accounts of the Edinburgh awakening for *The Christian* and other publications, says Moody's new notoriety seemed to "disarm" his critics in the press and obligated "every newspaper" to cover his coming.[62] But that celebrity created new risks for Moody. He wondered how he could follow up his success in Scotland.[63] He considered a campaign in London, where his work had been heavily reported in the daily press, but decided divisions among the churches too great an obstacle.[64] His reluctant switch to Ireland gave his organizing committee less time to advertise and unify local congregations. This made him vulnerable to press criticism. When one congregant noisily interrupted a September 7 meeting in Belfast charging that Moody "had no business being in the pulpit," the protester was arrested. The local press had a field day. The man's fine struck editorial writers as a "small price to pay for telling our American guests off."[65]

Moody used his early difficulties in Ireland in a publicized campaign to rally all England to his side and to prepare the way for his London crusade. His open letter published in *The Christian* and sympathetic secular dailies appealed for nationwide noontime prayer to help him save Irish sinners.[66] His publicity proclaimed Ireland had "sat so long in the shadow of death" that his current campaign would prove whether God's work or the Devil's would be done.[67] In an open letter published in friendly papers Moody associated the awakening in Belfast with the Ulster revival of 1859. He moved his meetings outdoors, and as was the case in Edinburgh and Glasgow, the curious and incredulous came, padding the civic spectacle, and raising crowd estimates to ten, twenty, and thirty thousand depending on who was doing the estimating. He made headlines

---

MBI.

[61] See letter from Henry Drummond to Mrs. Peter MacKinnon, dated 30 June 1875, Box 8, Folder 96, Moody Papers/Yale. See also the publisher's preface in M. Laird Simons, *Holding the Fort: Comprising Sermons and Addresses at the Great Revival Meetings Conducted by Moody and Sankey* (Philadelphia: Porter & Coates, 1877), 2, which freely admits neither Moody nor Sankey was "consulted upon the subject" of publication and would therefore have no "pecuniary interest in the publication of this work."

[62] John MacPherson, *Revival and Revival-Work: A Record of the Labours of D.L. Moody and Ira D. Sankey* (London: Morgan and Scott, 1876), 43-4.

[63] "Recollections of 1874," by Mrs. Peter MacKinnon, 65-6, Archives and Manuscripts, Moody Papers/Yale.

[64] W. Moody, *The Life of Dwight L. Moody*, 207.

[65] *Belfast Morning News*, 8 September 1874, 2; *Belfast News-Letter*, 8 September 1874, 2.

[66] *The Christian*, 17 September 1874, 3 and 24 September 1874, 3. See also, *The Morning Post* (of London), 22 September 1874, 5. For background on *The Morning Post*, see Wilfred Hindle, *The Morning Post, 1772-1937* (London: George Routledge & Sons, 1937), ch. 11, "Palmerston's Paper, 1849-1867," ch. 12, "Algernon Borthwick," and ch. 13, "High Tory, 1867-1914."

[67] *The Christian*, 17 September 1874, 17-8.

when he said he would like to see crowds surpassing 100,000. Although attendance never approached that level, he seemed satisfied his Irish crusade was finally on track.[68] Dublin sustained the impression that his appeal had grown beyond evangelical Protestants. Some Irish papers might write him off as "a
preacher of the roaring type," but most followed the lead of the *Nation*, a leading
Catholic paper, which approved of his non-sectarian stand. The "deadly danger"
of the age was secularism, not Moody. Irish Catholics, the *Nation* observed,
preferred their Protestants "deeply imbued with religious feeling" rather than
"tinged with rationalism," and Moody's meetings seemed to genuinely offer
that.[69]

*THE ROAD TO LONDON*

Between December 1874 and mid-March 1875, Moody's entourage, which now
included a personal secretary to answer all the fan letters he was receiving, put
its organizational acumen to work in Manchester, Sheffield, Birmingham and
Liverpool as final preparations were underway for his four-month campaign in
the heart of London. These comings and goings were carefully chronicled in the
religious and secular press, along with heart-wrenching testimonies of those who
"met their saviour" at a Moody meeting.[70] His every move made good reading,
and for every newspaper that remained unimpressed, there were three others anxious to get in on a good story. Where he met opposition, he was able to turn it
to his advantage. In Sheffield, as had been the pattern elsewhere, he welcomed
clergy from the Church of England, as well as the opposing Ecumenical Union-
ists to join in his pre-crusade planning. Just as the Sheffield campaign was set to
open, the press publicized the reluctant withdrawal of a Church of England clergyman from the 21-member executive committee that was planning Moody's
visit. The resignation was treated in the local press as another instance of the established church's resistance to a revival movement not under its authority. Further investigation showed the clergyman was "threatened with ecclesiastical
prosecution" by a local incumbent the press saw as "an opponent of revival."[71]
The local press seized on this "lamentable" incident to excoriate the partisanship of the church and to embrace the ecumenicalism of Moody. "Crowds of eager, anxious people" were reported to be packing the city's largest hall "await-
ing Moody's message."[72] He did not disappoint. His "wonderfully simple and
winning style" struck the Sheffield press as overdue antidote to the pretenses of
the state church. "Ministers standing in pulpits," the press observed, could
never "get at the masses" as Moody had.[73]

Two thousand ministers and Christians workers met on February 5, 1875, at
London's Freemason's Hall to plan Moody's meetings in that city and to gen-

---

[68]Ibid., 24 September 1874, 6-8 and 1 October 1874, 8; *Belfast Weekly Telegraph*, 24 September 1874,
3; *The Witness*, 8 October 1874, 2; *Ulster Weekly News* (of Belfast), 24 September 1874, 2.

[69]*Dublin Nation*, 24 October 1874, 1.

[70]*The Witness*, 26 November 1874, 12; *Birmingham Daily Mail*, 18 January 1875, 2.

[71]*Sheffield Post*, 2 January 1875, 4; *Sheffield Daily Telegraph*, 4 January 1875, 4.

[72]*Sheffield Post*, 9 January 1875, 7; *Sheffield Daily Telegraph*, 10 January 1875, 1; *Sheffield and
Rotherham Independent*, 16 January 1875, 4.

[73]*Sheffield Evening Telegraph*, 16 January 1875, 4; *Sheffield Christian Messenger*, 16 January 1875, 3;
*Sheffield Post*, 16 January 1875, 7.

erate publicity for those meetings. Now such sessions became stories, too. Among those present were "well known Christian men of means," who could be expected to underwrite much of the $170,000 cost in evangelizing London.[74] The city would be divided into quarters with a house to house handbill campaign designed to reach "every square, street and lane" of the city and its suburbs. Volunteers canvassed he city block by block and left leaflets that Moody had written, urging the anxious to be present at his citywide crusade and to follow it in the daily press. Team members kept logs of all contacts and turned them in to their supervisors. The result was a highly publicized attack on the "one million Londoners indifferent to public worship," who now became targets of "the most gigantic religious undertaking of its kind in the world."[75]

*CELEBRITY STATUS*

The machinery of mass evangelism that Moody brought to London inevitably situated its leader at the center of the civic spectacle. "Pulpit photographs" appeared in the local press profiling his "history, character, the secret of his power, and the nature of his influence."[76] The London campaign was widely seen as "a masterpiece of administrative care and skill." A "great sea of humanity" engulfed Agricultural Hall, where Moody began his London crusade on 9 March 1875. Among them were hundreds of ministers and well known laymen from every participating denomination. "Titled gentlemen" did not find it unseemly to join them. Reporters covering the spectacle found "no screw loose anywhere."[77]

More than two and a half million people saw Moody speak during his 285 meetings in London. The press now kept count. Even his detractors admitted the stoutly built American "with the strange sounding twang" was "no ordinary ranter." Educated listeners might have no use for his massacre of the English language, *The Morning Post* noted, but nightly crowds of 21,000 didn't seem to mind.[78] "The appearance of the vast throngs was, in itself, a sight worth going many miles to see," newspapers reported. And his continuing capacity to attract capacity crowds made some see in him "another Spurgeon,"[79] a man "with an obvious desire to do good,"[80] someone whose "genuine gifts" would likely do the city "much good."[81] Even the oppositional *Vanity Fair* conceded that the "greatest multitudes gathered in this generation" nightly came to Moody's meetings demonstrating "there is in mankind a strong desire and yearning for something more than a mere material existence." His methods of marketing religion were of "universal application," it reported, and "he is not afraid of

---

[74]*The Christian*, 3 December 1874, 6; *Liverpool Mail*, 13 February 1875, 13 and 20 February 1875, 6; *London Daily News*, 8 March 1875, 2; *The Daily Telegraph* (London), 25 June 1875, 5; *The Record*, 10 March 1875, 1.

[75]The publicity work of Moody's coordinating committee for London is outlined in Box 8, Folder 96, Moody Papers/Yale. Aspects of the campaign are also summarized by the London correspondent of the *North British Daily Mail and the London Christian World* in the days leading up to the crusade.

[76]*Birmingham Daily Mail*, 18 January 1875, 2.

[77]*The Daily Telegraph* (London), 10 March 1875, 5; *The Times* (London), 10 March 1875, 3; *London Morning Post*, 10 March 1875, 6; *The Record*, 12 March 1875, 3.

[78]*London Morning Post*, 10 March 1875, 6 and 12 March 1875, 3.

[79]*The Record* (London), 17 March 1875, 2.

[80]*London Globe*, 19 March 1875, 2.

[81]*The Spectator* (London), 19 March 1875, 6.

them."[82]

Moody's meetings in Agricultural Hall, scene of cattle and horse shows, gave a whiff of his marketing approach. Here no high church was to be found. Instead, one met a simple man who offered a simple message to the masses. Queen Victoria, for one, declined to grace such proceedings. She had no doubt Moody was "sincere" but did wonder whether "this sensational style of excitement can last."[83] The comment came as figurines of Moody and Sankey were hawked on London street corners and doggerels were sung to their praises. "The rich and the poor," one rhyme went, "the good and the bad, have gone mad over Moody and Sankey."[84] Moody's printed sermons became big sellers at London's best book stores.[85] The 150,000 who weekly attended his meetings became instant customers for more news about Moody.[86]

As Moody prepared in mid-summer to close his campaign in Britain and return to the United States, the *Christian Standard* lamented that "we do not have a thousand preachers in our land such as Mr. Moody."[87] His final act in London was to thank the reporters who had "muted" his failures, while broadly disseminating his successes to an unsaved readership.[88] On the eve of his departure from Liverpool, he urged the 700 pastors who had gathered to see him off to embrace whatever means were available in reaching the masses for Christ.[89] For Moody that meant using the daily press as an instrument in mass mobilization with techniques he would continue to hone in a series of record-shattering crusades in Brooklyn, Philadelphia, New York, Chicago, and Boston.

*THE BRIGHT LAMP*

Salvation in the context of civic spectacle would become the pattern of Moody's ministry and many of the evangelists who would follow him. Moody's meetings were a businessman's Bible camp for believers and those anxious over the condition of their souls.

And what the machinery of big city evangelism now sacrificed in spontaneity, it gained in predictability. Organization and careful marketing might not assure success, but it certainly didn't hinder the work of evangelism either. Moody would always link the power of publicity to the preeminence of prayer.

---

[82]*Vanity Fair*, 3 April 1875, 3.

[83]Letter from Queen Victoria to the Countess of Gainsborough, dated 27 April 1875, cited in W. Moody, *The Life of Dwight L. Moody*, 212-3. Also, *London Daily News*, 16 March 1875, 6; *The Daily Telegraph* (of London), 12 March 1875, 2; *Vanity Fair*, 10 April 1875, 3; *Presbyterian Messenger*, July 1937, 14.

[84]The popular impact of Moody and Sankey is chronicled in the Moody Papers/Yale, Box 8, Folder 96. The doggerel is first cited in an undated issue of *The British Weekly* found in those papers. Figurines of Moody and Sankey manufactured during the London campaign can still be found in the Moody Papers at MBI. The two men look distinguished but accessible to their working class fans. Further recollections of Moody's appeal to London's commoners are found in D.L. Moody Centenary Addresses given in Westminster Chapel in London on 5 February 1937, by John A. Hutton, editor of *The British Weekly*, and G. Campbell Morgan of Westminster Chapel. The remarks can be found in Moody Papers/Yale, Box 16, Folder 19. See also, Edward Shillito, "Moody in England," *The Christian Century*, 17 February 1937, 217-8.

[85]A typical collection of these can be found in Rufus W. Clark, *The Work of God in Great Britain: Under Messrs. Moody and Sankey, 1873 to 1875; with Biographical Sketches*, 375-430.

[86]A good summary of this recognition is found in Hedley Morrish, "The Coming Moody Centenary," *The British Weekly*, 21 January 1937, 391. See also, "The Moody Centenary," *Advance*, 1 February 1937, 65.

[87]*Christian Standard* (of London), 25 June 1875, 3.

[88]*London Daily News*, 12 July 1875, 2; *The Daily Telegraph* (of London), 23 July 1875 3.

[89]*London Daily Chronicle*, 14 July 1874, 4.

His contribution to the science of evangelism was the introduction of civic spectacle as a means of rationalizing the process by which unbelievers could be made to believe. Even Moody seemed surprised at the magnitude of his success. He had "never met so many infidels" as he had in the largest cities of the British Isles. But that was because his operation had never quite so successful in drawing the unchurched and backslidden to him.

Moody's Great Britain campaign of 1873-1875 demonstrated that God's purposes and man's plans could now create conditions that let whole communities in on a public extravaganza larger than anyone had ever seen. The growth of Gilded Age mass media made that possible. Moody, as a practical man, found this marriage of secular means and spiritual purposes was not without its personal consequences. Celebrity was the unexpected price he paid for being among the first to understand the power of the press in reaching the realm of the unreached with the gospel message. Revivalists might continue to claim that quickening a slumbering spirit was God's job, not man's, but after Moody they could no longer dispute that modern crusade work required mass media and organization and lots of it to arrest the attention of indifferent communities. Moody knew sleepers would awake when God got on the front page. A review of his first moments through his final days in Britain demonstrates an emerging understanding of the role of organization and a media plan in awakening communities to the claims of Christ. His embrace of "the bright lamp" of a few friends in the evangelical press paved the way for fame if not fortune. Sermons and hymnbooks sold in the millions and financed the quarter-century work of evangelism to come.

Everywhere the pattern evolved in Britain would be repeated and, when possible, improved upon. Organization and advertising built early interest that prayer, the work of a united church, and the power of publicity helped to sustain. For Moody the use of every available means in bringing men and women to the truth of the gospel necessarily meant reaching them through the mass media, and it was during his early work in evangelism that this understanding emerged and was first developed. The Gilded Age press played an important role in creating civic spectacles that greatly aided Moody's efforts to bring men and women to repentance.

*9*

# Religion and Western Newspapers /
## *1860-1990*
### by Kyle Huckins

AMARILLO, TEXAS, IN 1895 WAS IN A HURRY. The Panhandle town's dry, dusty streets, which ran rivers of mud in a sudden storm, were busy with cattlemen moving out animals, wagons pulling newcomers from the Fort Worth & Denver City Railroad depot, and journalists from the youthful *Amarillo News* hustling stories for its pages.

Those Saturday-edition stories often were the talk of the town Sunday morning. "The young man does not go to church because he does not find there what he wants," one such piece proclaimed. "There is too much theology and too little practical help.... Too much threshing over old straw and too little breadstuff for the moral life."[1] This was a life meant for doing, not evangelizing, an existence dominated by the flat earth and the men who worked it, not the words and images of books and pastors.

Amarillo three generations later was still flat earth, still busy, but the industriousness of its citizens and their news editors had decidedly changed. In the 1960s, the city had nearly 130,000 inhabitants, a robust economy of oil and agriculture, rapid church growth,[2] and an *Amarillo Globe-News* unafraid to let employees publicly proclaim the Gospel. Wes Izzard, its editor and publisher, eulogized Cal Farley, head of an area Christian ranch for wayward boys, with praise and verses from the Book of Matthew. He wrote:

> Just as I am persuaded that the Founding Fathers of this country were brought together by Divine intervention, so am I persuaded that it was no accident that Cal came to Amarillo when he did.... When he found a hungry boy, he fed him; a thirsty boy, he bought him a Coke. If a boy was homeless, he took him in.... What was it the Master said about such a man as this?

---

[1] *Amarillo* (Tex.) *News*, 16 March 1895, 3.

[2] Personal communication with Clay Price, Statistics Division of the Baptist General Convention of Texas, December, 1996, and membership records from same.

"Inasmuch as ye have done it to one of the least of these my bretheren, ye have done it unto me."[3]

This change in the minds and copy of West Texas newspaper editors did not come overnight, nor did it come solely in the land bounded by Fort Worth on the east and El Paso on the west. The Plains and Southwest passed through five identifiable cycles of the depiction of religious movements and use of religious imagery, evolving from outright scorn for the devout to approval of spirituality.

The "Frontier Period," approximately 1860-1890, saw traditional doctrines mocked as Western papers, seeking to reflect local views, would only talk positively of religion in the context of church expansion showing evidence of civilizing influences. During "Politicization," 1890-1910, the region's newspapers recognized the West's growing political influence and argued for an incorporation of it into religious institutions. In the "Boomtown Era," about 1910-1929, editors aided the developing affluence of the oil and agriculture industries by utilizing religious imagery, but not doctrines, in news stories. Preachers quoted in news items or penning columns usually subscribed to a "gospel of prosperity," linking spiritual and worldly success.

The "Religious Revival Period" of the Depression and World War II witnessed a dramatic shift in religious depiction, as Plains and Southwest papers encouraged spirituality with directness and specificity. Finally, the "Modern Era," extending from 1945 to the present, has seen an expansion of religious coverage on news pages, even while overt religious imagery is compartmentalized into columns, editorials, and special departments.

*THE FRONTIER PERIOD, 1860-1890*

Editors in the American West, from the earliest frontier newspapers, "rarely varied much from the norms of their communities."[4] These writers, while iconoclastic, sarcastic, and independent, represented the ideologies of their communities rather than creating them.[5] Examining the spiritual genesis of the region, then, may provide insight into why the West's religion coverage evolved differently from that in other areas of the country.

The desire to freely believe in and practice religious doctrine and ideals was a primary motivation of those establishing the first permanent white settlements in New England. The centrality of religion extended to the dissemination of news, which evolved from reprinted sermons to the first American newspapers in the late seventeenth century. Well into the eighteenth century, many of these publications included long articles and commentaries with religious themes, secondarily addressing "secular" topics of the day.

Settlers of the South replicated the pattern, although most did not come for specifically religious reasons. Early South Carolina newspapers talked directly of

---

[3]Quoted in Louis Hendricks, *No Rules or Guidelines* (Tascosa, Tex.: Boys Ranch, 1981), 141.

[4]William H. Lyon, *The Pioneer Editor in Missouri, 1808-1860* (Columbia, Mo.: University of Missouri Press, 1965), 164.

[5]Robert L. Housman, "The End of Frontier Journalism in Montana," *Journalism Quarterly* 12 (1935): 133-45.

Christian doctrine;[6] the first editor-publishers of Alabama have been described as "public-spirited men, leaders in their communities.... They framed and interpreted the backwoods laws, saved the pioneers' souls, and taught their children."[7] Even if not Christian ministers themselves (though several were), most maintained a reverence for the ordained in their writings. For example, the *Raleigh* (N.C.) *Observer*, in a lengthy 1811 article, referred to preachers as "public labourers with zeal and fortitude" who, through their prayers, caused God to "pour out His spirit in a very wonderful manner, so that thousands" were saved.[8]

The West was not, however, won by the relatively like-minded and doctrined, as in the South, with the exception of the Mormon-dominated northern Rocky Mountains. The settlers came in waves, their wagons and prairie schooners navigating the grasslands and deserts. The Spanish, Orientals, and Central and Northern Europeans, upon landing, constructed ports of call after their own unique melting pots.

Their rural cosmopolitanism often filled the vacuum caused by the lack of organized government and churches. Farmers crowded out of Illinois, Indiana, and other Northern states wanted to go deep into the virgin land, while fortune-seekers wanted freedom to make deals with minimal oversight. Still others wanted the "elbow room" of the great open range.[9] These peoples and their reasonings, diverse as they were, held in common a dislike of formal institutions and controls.

Prior to the end of Indian troubles in the 1870s, it was not unusual for areas to go two or more years without a visit from a traveling preacher. Without the constant reminder of Providence, it seemed to fade in importance. Settlement preceded belief, and, frequently, where belief preceded settlement, there were problems.

West of San Antonio, several early missions had been abandoned, and mid- to late-nineteenth century newcomers wanted the assurance of the U.S. Army more than that of the Christian church. In that country lies San Angelo, an isolated spot of green at the confluence of four West Texas rivers. It owes its existence to Fort Concho, founded in 1867 among the hostile Comanche and Apache, rather than the short-lived Franciscan mission established there in the 1630s. The city's first major religious figure was the "Fighting Parson," whose sermons sometimes used pistol-whippings in addition to the Bible's nuances.[10] Thus, San Angelo grew up without a great enthusiasm for strict religious tradition. The *Concho Times*, its first newspaper, debuted April 24, 1880, with "A Quaker Printer's Proverbs" on the back of its folded sheets. "Never send an article for publication without giving the editor thy name," it read, "for thy name

---

[6]Julie Hedgepeth Williams, "The Media and the Personification of Society," in *The Significance of the Media in American History*, eds. James D. Startt and Wm. David Sloan (Northport, Ala.: Vision Press, 1994), 45-64.

[7]Quoted in Robert Ellison, "Newspaper Publishing in Frontier Alabama," *Journalism Quarterly* 23 (1946): 297.

[8]*Raleigh* (N.C.) *Observer*, 21 March 1811, 4.

[9]Joe B. Frantz, *Aspects of the American West* (College Station, Tex.: Texas A&M University Press, 1976).

[10]Federal Writers' Project, *Texas: A Guide to the Lone Star State* (New York: Hastings House, 1940), 472-3.

oftentimes secures publication for worthless articles."[11] The disrespect for an established, "East Coast" sect was apparent.

The ministry in general was a target of the frontier printer-journalist. Jokes were mainstays of the news pages, often filling in when out-of-town sources faltered. Since Western society saw the preacher as less "productive" than farmers, ranchers, or businesspeople, he became a natural butt of the humor.[12] The *Texas Panhandle* of Mobeetie, the first town in the Panhandle, enjoyed relating the tale of a preacher who set up a sound reflector so he could be better heard by his flock. Unfortunately, he could also hear the sheep, and "it was anything but pleasant to preach and listen to criticism on the sermon at the same time."[13]

There were defenders of religion among the first publishers of the West. The *Sioux Falls City Democrat*, the first newspaper in Dakota Territory, devoted its opening page to "Thanksgiving," a prayer to the "Father."[14] The paper failed in 1862, a victim of Indian depredations. Subsequent publications were notably less devotional; the territory's second paper, the *Yancton Weekly Dakotan*, early on amused itself with the tale of a "Hard Shell Baptist" whose supposed call to the ministry came courtesy of a donkey's clopping hooves.[15] An editorial made a brief salute to "the Genius of Religion" but carried the admonition "Come to Dakota!" eight times in the preceding five sentences.[16]

Churches did have a use in the Western frontier newspaper. They were evidence of progress, of the region assuming a rightful status in the eyes of the civilized world. Whether Methodist, Baptist, Episcopalian, Presbyterian, or of another denomination, they served the editors' commitment to boosterism.

To editors, this positive side of religion could help offset some of the distressing signs of societal backsliding. An 1884 edition of the *Lone Star* in El Paso carried a curt mention of how five cowboys attempted to paint its town red with firearms for brushes, firing guns into houses. A local man shot one of the marauders in the back of the head, likely killing him. In the column opposite the report of mayhem, an equally large item extended a "cordial invitation" to "strangers and citizens" wishing to go to services of the local Baptist church.[17]

The desire to claim churches in efforts to bring a prosperous image to a hometown sometimes led to schizophrenic reporting. Nestled away among the goats and bleaching sunlight in a remote section of New Mexico Territory, the *Mesilla Valley Independent* alternately boosted the establishment of church buildings and proclaimed heresy from its pages. Noting the graciousness of a pastor's residence and applauding the construction of a Catholic church, a convent, and an Episcopal chapel, it then launched into an attack on the authority of Scripture. It said:

Christ not only wasted his time, but also fell into bad company when he

---

[11]*Concho Times* (San Angelo, Tex.), 24 April 1880, 4.

[12]Shine Phillips, *Big Spring: The Casual Biography of a Prairie Town* (New York: Prentice-Hall, 1942), *passim.*

[13]*Texas Panhandle* (Mobeetie, Tex.), 28 March 1889, 1.

[14]*The Democrat* (Sioux Falls, Dakota Territory), 26 August 1859, 1.

[15]*Yancton* (Dakota Territory) *Weekly Dakotan*, 6 June 1861, 4.

[16]Ibid., 2.

[17]*Lone Star* (El Paso, Tex.), 4 October 1884, 3.

took to disputing with lawyers and doctors. The admission that he kept such company settles the divinity question, and casts a grave doubt over the whole narrative.[18]

Pioneer Plains and Southwest editors seemed most interested in promoting a general morality leading to an environment conducive to growth. They were willing to take on gambling and abortion, especially when they were problems outside their own areas,[19] and vigorously condemned crime and violence. What they did not want were Bible verses and the "substance" of religion.

The Western frontier journalist was an independent, a term with spiritual as well as political connotations. In a day when overt affiliations of newspapers were common in both spheres of human endeavor, the region's outlets stood out in their avoidance of opinion on substantial matters.[20] This distinction was likely both a practical endeavor, helping the editor retain subscribers of differing persuasions, as well as a reflection of the general populace, just as openness to Mormonism prevailed in the northern Rockies that Latter-Day Saints settled.[21]

The Rev. Daugherty, a Methodist, was the first preacher in Odessa, Texas, and very nearly its last. He "believed in peppering his discourses with plenty of hellfire," remembered Mrs. Ada Carter Johnson, an early resident of Odessa and one of its first newspaper publishers, who continued:

If the frontier religion had been put into words at all, it would have been summed up like this: The Big Boss is broadminded enough to understand how a feller feels and to know that no disrespect of Him is intended by the local ways of life.[22]

Johnson's statement clearly reflects a sympathy with the local attitude against organized religion. Such newspaper editors sought to aid development, dispel notions of religion as a serious solution for hardships, and seemed to serve a normative function in encouraging work rather than intellectual or spiritual pursuits.

## POLITICIZATION, 1890-1910

These journalists came along as the Western states gained population and power in the last decade of the nineteenth century and first decade of the twentieth. The Dakotas, Montana, Wyoming, and Oklahoma all achieved statehood, and New Mexico and Arizona readied themselves for admission. These areas more than doubled their population during those two decades, while older states in the region continued to grow. Large numbers of immigrants and businesspeople

---

[18]*Mesilla Valley Independent* (New Mexico Territory), 21 July 1877, 3.

[19]For example, *Lone Star*, 17 May 1884, 1. In a story on a festival in Monterrey, Mexico, the reporter opined, "The god of gambling sits enthroned on all such occasions. The effect is generally demoralizing on the common people."

[20]Robert L. Housman, "The Beginnings of Journalism in Frontier Montana," *Frontier and Midland* 15 (1935): 1-10.

[21]See *Deseret News* (Salt Lake City, Utah Territory), 15 July 1893 and *passim*; (Boise) *Idaho Tri-Weekly*, 17 March 1887 and *passim*.

[22]Velma Barrett and Hazel Oliver, *Odessa — City of Dreams!* (San Antonio, Tex.: Naylor, 1952), 5-6.

flocked to the West Texas countryside, filling in the once-quiet stretches. Odessa, Midland, Lubbock, and Amarillo grew rapidly, more than quadrupling population from 1900 to 1910.

With the construction of the Fort Worth & Denver and Santa Fe rail lines through the Texas Panhandle, Amarillo became the nation's largest rural cattle shipping point in the 1890s. Fifteen miles to the south, the founding of Canyon City (now Canyon) allowed immediate shipping of the herds of famed cattleman Charles Goodnight from his JA ranch.[23]

As populations grew and the business environment stabilized, newspaper editors were able to take stronger positions on political and spiritual matters. Surprisingly, this was not toward pushing religion out of politics, but rather in favor of confronting the "fact" that the pulpit was political by its very nature. Even the great evangelist Dwight L. Moody could not escape the populist barbs of the 1895 *Amarillo News*. It declared:

> Moody's ten-day engagement in Dallas with the Devil was merely a feint, which hardly drew His Majesty's attention from his every-day affairs. As usual, with the preachers, he prudently fired at long range; and his shots fell wide of the mark. He never dared assault the enemy's stronghold — behind the monopolistic laws of the country.[24]

Newspapers across the Plains joined the *Amarillo News* in stirring the controversial pot of religion and politics. William Allen White, the much-noted editor of the *Emporia* (Kan.) *Weekly Gazette*, also found the issues of populism and spirituality important, albeit from a completely different direction. "When a great political party begins to whine.... The wrath of God and man is against it ... the allied forces of Populism and Democracy on a platform, which, at its best, is but a whine."[25]

Increasing competition between papers, now numbering two, three, or four in a relatively small-sized Western city, made it possible for editors to enter into local opinion.[26] They emerged from behind their "independent" status of old to become personalities, sometimes political, sometimes personal. Their sharp-tongued language was frequently earthy, displaying tolerance of mistakes made in the line of hard, frontier-style work.

Quanah, atop the fertile soil of the Red River country of northwest Texas, was heady in 1898 with the railroads' arrival and its winning the county seat from a rival city.[27] A poem in the *Quanah Tribune-Chief* Christmastime editions that year explained "Why the Editor Swore," telling how he had a cold, the "devil" yelled for copy, and he "earnestly swore" while at his post. It rhymed: "But the angels who took it to heaven/Recorded this verdict there/The jury finds in the present case/'Twas a justifiable swear."[28]

One of Western journalism's most famous personalities of the era was Ed

---

[23]Pauline and R.L. Robertson, *Panhandle Pilgrimage* (Amarillo, Tex.: Paramount, 1976), 304-14.

[24]*Amarillo News*, 16 March 1895, 6.

[25]*Emporia* (Kan.) *Weekly Gazette*, 20 August 1896, 1.

[26]Tommy Thompson, *North of Palo Duro* (Canyon, Tex.: Staked Plains Press, 1984).

[27]Walter P. Webb, ed., *The Handbook of Texas* (Fort Worth, Tex.: Marvin Evans, 1952), 422-3.

[28]*Quanah* (Tex.) *Tribune-Chief*, 1 December 1898, 2.

Howe, the "Sage of Potato Hill." He had something to say about almost everything, his writings ranging from marital relations to politics to the foibles of little boys.[29] By the first decade of the new century, he was an old-timer, one of a
number of frontier newspapermen holding on to small-town empires.[30] He loved
newspapering, walking for miles to track down news. Whether it was a bumper
wheat crop or a wedding, he knew about it, and used his pages to let others
know. While successful as an entrepreneur and journalist, he had one unrelenting
hatred: preachers. "That people should have advanced so marvelously in everything else, as they have done, and carried along with them a doctrine they know
to be untrue, is a fact I have marveled at all my life. Never have I known a sincere religious man or woman," his son Gene recalled him lecturing. In a biographical profile that he wrote of his father, Gene called him "wretchedly unhappy."[31]

Some speculated that Ed's father, a severe, circuit-riding Methodist preacher,
turned him away from the altar; others thought he just enjoyed his vitriol.[32] His
lighter-hearted jabs at life ("Families with babies and without babies are sorry
for each other") and strong stand for the entrepreneurial community kept him in
business. Howe, as his Western contemporaries, did not indulge in the era's
Pulitzer-style sensationalism. "He insisted that sentimentalism and emotional-
ism and Socialism were menaces to progress and better living, and that religion
was the embodiment of the three of these," son Gene wrote.[33]

The attitude in older circles still was that religion didn't result in any fields
plowed or money made. However, a new generation of Westerners found profit
in spirituality, using religious imagery to promote commerce.

The first decade of the twentieth century saw the greatest growth spurt in the
history of the Texas town of San Angelo, as it tripled its population. The city's
grassy slopes became a railroad supply center, and raising sheep and goats began
to supplement the cattle trade on many ranches.[34] San Angelo's burgeoning
downtown district held an increasingly diverse array of businesses, with watch-
makers, department stores, and jewelers buying ads in the city's *Press* alongside
the land companies and windmill construction outfits. Images of spirituality
were part of the enterprises' pitch, perhaps a variation on the theme of church-as-
prosperity. "Honesty is preached from every pulpit," wrote a 1901 *Press* editori-
alist, "and the business world will not countenance anything but honesty."[35]

This honesty apparently did not extend to blacks, as that year's December 20
*Press* included "A Darkey's Prayer," in which a black man went into a field to
pray for angels to come, and when they did, he hid under his bed. The "darkey"
stammered, "I ain't got no wings to fly wid, en I'se too heavy to tote!"[36]

---

[29]Etta Lynch, *The Tactless Texan: Biography of Gene A. Howe* (Canyon, Tex.: Staked Plains Press, 1976), 12-3.

[30]Douglas C. McMurtrie, "The Beginnings of the Press in South Dakota," *Journalism Quarterly* 10 (1933): 125-33.

[31]Gene Howe, "My Father Was the Most Wretchedly Unhappy Person I Ever Knew," *Saturday Evening Post*, 25 October 1941.

[32]Lynch, *The Tactless Texan*, 7.

[33]Howe, "My Father Was the Most Wretchedly Unhappy Person I Ever Knew," 405.

[34]T.R. Fahrenbach, *Lone Star* (Dallas, Tex.: American Legacy Press, 1988).

[35]*San Angelo* (Tex.) *Press*, 22 November 1901, 2.

[36]Ibid., 20 December 1901, 3.

Plains and Southwest reporters and writers also had long distrusted Native American spirituality. Their stories seemed to assume the Indians' lack of worldly power translated to failing spiritual power, eventually internalized by some tribes through the prevailing culture and its messages. The *Quanah Tribune-Chief* carried Geronimo's views of an Indian uprising in Minnesota. He had said:

What can a few poor Indians do in a fight? They are making a great mistake and are fools. For years I fought the white men.... I thought that the Great Spirit would be with us, and that after we killed the white men, the buffalo, deer, and antelope would come back.... After I fought and lost ... I knew that the race of Indians was run. They are not the people that the Great Spirit loves, for if they were, he would protect them.[37]

Resistance to the prosperity theme came from the just-planted conservation movement, which took on some of the trappings of religion as Theodore Roosevelt signed legislation creating the National Park System. The revelations of John Muir, fusing environmentalism, Christianity, and paganism, held a powerful attraction for some.[38] The *Nevada Socialist* proclaimed that "real Christians" would support its policies.[39] Socialists also turned up in Kansas (much to Howe's chagrin), making an *Appeal to Reason* in Girard. Dark powers dominated *Lucifer the Light-Bearer* at Valley Falls.[40]

The religion/business mix did, however, prevail and sometimes was a cynical one. *Topeka* (Kan.) *Daily Capital* publisher Frederick Popenoe allowed the Rev. Charles Sheldon to edit the paper for a week in a style thought appropriate to Jesus. Popenoe's move was aimed at publicity, not spirituality, as his press agents talked up the East.[41]

*THE BOOMTOWN ERA, 1910-1929*

Texas harbored efforts somewhat less insidious but just as lacking in altruism. Electra was a lonely railroad siding in the Red River ranch country until drillers hit oil near town in 1911, leading to the first Lone Star oil boom since Spindletop near Beaumont.[42] The *Electra News*, a small weekly, pushed strongly for exploration, often with language borrowed from religious experience. The front page of its April 4, 1912, paper carried a "prophecy" by local oilmen that the town's field was to become a major producer, transfiguring the back 40 into a wealthy crossroads. The editor included social pressure with the spiritual imagery. "Don't knock, just put up your money and boost. If you have no money to help with, do not use what brains the creator gave you to knock against the

---

[37]*Quanah Tribune-Chief*, 13 October 1898, 2.

[38]Eldon Ernst, "American Religious History from a Pacific Coast Perspective," in *Religion and Society in the American West*, eds. Carl Guarneri and David Alvarez (Lanham, Md.: University Press of America, 1987), 3-41.

[39]Jake Highton, *Nevada Newspaper Days* (Stockton, Calif.: Heritage West Books, 1990), 118.

[40]Robert F. Karolevitz, *Newspapering in the Old West* (Seattle, Wash.: Superior), 65-87.

[41]Nino LoBello, "When Christ was Editor in Kansas," *Media History Digest* 9 (1985): 2-5, 30-1.

[42]Federal Writers' Project, *Texas*, 485-6.

town you live in," he urged.[43]

The Electra paper's coverage of religion itself was not condemnatory but was often negative toward traditional viewpoints. A 1913 item detailed proceedings of the International Bible Students Association, which determined the words "hell" and "hellfire" should no longer be used in Bible translations. "Sheol" and "Hades" should instead be interpreted, they felt, as "tomb" or "grave." The article gave no opposing view.[44]

Just forty years removed from the "Great American Desert" before settlement, West Texas went to World War I still seeking to prove itself equal to the older cities and towns back east. The fertile soil of the Red River Valley and Texas Panhandle sent cotton and wheat to the war effort, while the Permian Basin and Trans-Pecos contributed cattle. Thousands of men volunteered for duty, and settlers of German heritage were suspect.

Plains and Southwest papers extended their use of religious imagery from the marketplace to the war effort, giving the conflict strong support laced with ecumenical Protestant lingo. The 1918 *Electra News* thanked God that "courage is so common" among the West Texans going to battle and urged citizens on the homefront to volunteer more than time to defeating the Kaiser. "The widow's mite answers the purpose when it is pledged by persons of small means, but such a pledge is a reflection upon those who can pledge more. This is no 5 and 10 cents war," the paper said.[45]

There may have been something of a postwar reaction against this upswing in religious language. Mrs. Ada Carter Johnson's *Odessa Herald* gave secular, but not doctrinal, backing to the Salvation Army and Young Men's Christian Association in their relief work. Four stories on the YMCA appeared on a single page of her 1919 *Herald*, but none mentioned its spiritual activism, or even that "Christian" was part of its name.[46]

Unlike other areas of the country, however, the trend toward objectivism did not continue in the increasingly affluent region in the 1920s. Mining and large-scale ranching brought riches to the Plains states and West Texas. The populations of the Lone Star's Panhandle and South Plains counties more than tripled between 1920 and 1930. Many new residents were attracted by the burgeoning oil business, the new interest in natural gas, and discovery of helium and other valuable resources beneath the dry soil west of Fort Worth. Borger, midway between Amarillo and the Oklahoma border, attracted 35,000 residents within ninety days after the Dixon Creek No. 2 oil well roared to life. More than 3,500 prostitutes plied the streets before Texas Rangers stepped in to restore order.

Business boosterism characterized religious coverage and use of religious imagery in Western newspapers throughout the decade, even as U.S. journalism as a whole became more questioning and critical of newsmakers.[47] Nevada papers heralded the decade's prosperity by calling for an increased emphasis on development; Montana's Anaconda Copper Company operated a chain of Big Sky dailies through this period, using images of the pulpit to pound its pro-consum-

---

[43]*Electra* (Tex.) *News*, 4 April 1912, 1, 9.

[44]Ibid., 6 June 1913, 6.

[45]Ibid., 2 August 1918, 4.

[46]*Odessa* (Tex.) *Herald*, 14 June 1919, 3.

[47]Curtis MacDougall, "Newspaper Hoaxes," *Journalism Quarterly* 12 (1935): 166-77.

er opponents.[48]

Back in Texas, boomtown Electra saw its wealth increase steadily, several million barrels of oil pouring from its wells each year, and population nearing 5,000. During the 1920s, the *Electra News* regularly published a column by radio evangelist E.V. Cole, a believer in the "gospel of success," a highly listenable message for many tuned to a powerful new medium.[49]

Cole preached to readers in early 1926 that spirituality was tangible and that "men of faith ... turning obstacles into stepping stones to success" gave evidence of it. Interestingly, local newsmen saw clergy as money-hungry, as the *News* warned locals when a minister pushed for donations. A column joked about how an evangelist "is the only salesman who can increase his business by bawling out his customers."[50]

The "Radio Reverend" melded progress and religion his way, while those friendly to the social gospel applied their own touches. In New Mexico, *Albuquerque Morning Journal* editor Carl Magee, son of a Methodist minister, crusaded for the small businessman against the trusts and big corporations, through uncited, though recognizable, Bible passages. He believed that man could lift himself up, his inherent goodness making for an ever-improving society. Magee could go only so far, however. He shot a judge who came after him for a critical article the editor had written.[51]

The theme of progress was a strong one, with old-fashioned religious ways seen not as threatening, but outdated. Coverage of the Scopes trial, the last-ditch fight of "old religion" versus new interpretations, showcased the completeness of the transition.

The *Plains Journal* of Lubbock, long a small cotton-producing town on the South Plains, neither supported nor opposed Clarence Darrow in his harsh criticism of creationism. Its writers did come to the aid of defendant John T. Scopes, the Tennessee teacher sued for his alleged instruction on evolution. "In all this milling of various forces, the bashful and slender Mr. Scopes has all but been obliterated," lamented "Save Me From My Helpers!" by Gene Cohn, who added:

> If ever there had been a doubt in his mind of man's kinship with lower animals, one week of New York City would have convinced him.... [Scopes said,] "You'll find that Dayton has no humidity, no mosquitoes, a fine place for a vacation. Come along!"[52]

One of the most important moments for religious traditionalism in modern times had been reduced to a showman-style pitch for tourism, forsaking the inherent spiritual questions shaping so much of the century. Scopes, instead of answering for his culture-shaking decision, was congratulated for his hometown

---

[48]Richard Reutten, "Anaconda Journalism: The End of an Era," *Journalism Quarterly* 37 (1960): 3-12.

[49]Margaret Lamberts Bendroth, "Fundamentalism and the Media," in *Religion and Mass Media: Audiences and Adaptations*, ed. Daniel Stout and Judith Buddenbaum (London: Sage, 1996), 74-84.

[50]*Electra News*, 22 January 1926, 5, and 15 January 1926, 2.

[51]Benay Blend, "Carl Magee: A Muckraker Out of His Time," in *Journalism in the West* (special compendium) (Manhattan, Kan.: Sunflower University Press, 1980), 92-6.

[52]*Plains Journal* (Lubbock, Tex.), 5 July 1925, 3.

pride and promotion. This contrasted with coverage around the nation, which tended to focus on the scientific evidence offered in the case.[53]

*RELIGIOUS REVIVAL, 1929-1945*

West Texas' heady times of the 1920s ended within months of the stock market crash of October 1929. *Electra News* headlines told of how city taxes were going unpaid.[54] The *Amarillo Daily News* reported on the futile effort of the town's Mayor Thompson to eliminate all unemployment in the city within six months.[55] The Big Bend's *Alpine Avalanche* printed ads from the local school board urging citizens to pay their school taxes or face an end to local education.[56]

Worse than the industrial losses were the great dust clouds that enveloped the once-fertile farmland and ranches of the Plains. The plowing up of virgin grasslands in the World War I-era push for farm production had used up the fragile topsoil. The 1930s race to pay taxes on farms and ranches resulted in even more acreage plowed up and rendered worthless.

The desperation of the Great Depression, seeing the utter failure of man to control his destiny, seemed to make a significant change in the Western attitude toward public declaration of religious belief and its doctrines. For the first time, local newspapers provided to the devout not only tolerance, but encouragement.

In West Texas, the shift was dramatic both in society and its newspapers. The 1930 *Electra News* printed extensive articles about coming Baptist and Methodist revivals, giving scriptural references and doctrinal details.[57] The *Alpine Avalanche* cited Bible verses from Christian Science services and even allowed a local Baptist pastor to pointedly encourage church attendance. "There are some folks I know that need to get back and get busy in church and Sunday school work," the minister wrote. "Here's hoping I will see you next Sunday, with a smile as long as this preacher's face."[58]

The most abrupt turnaround of these newspapers may have been in Lubbock. From sympathy with Scopes five years before, its papers now backed not only capitalism but Christianity as well. The *Lubbock Daily Journal*, the successor to the *Plains Journal*, started carrying a "Thought for Today" from the Bible on its editorial pages. A late 1930 op/ed piece on gangster killings asserted the murders had their origins in a spiritual crisis showcased in the excesses of modern society. "You might come closer to it if you slipped into the Old Testament and said that the gangster was sent to punish us for our sins. He is, in fact, the product of our sins," it stated.[59]

As *Daily Journal* headlines talked of communists marching on the state capitol and drought aid for the South Plains, news reporters gave voice to religious

[53]Edward Caudill, "The Roots of Bias: An Empiricist Press and Coverage of the Scopes Trial," *Journalism Monographs* 114.

[54]*Electra News*, 6 February 1930, 1.

[55]*Amarillo* (Tex.) *Daily News*, 8 January 1931, 1, 13.

[56]*Alpine* (Tex.) *Avalanche*, 18 January 1935, 1.

[57]*Electra News*, 1930, *passim*.

[58]*Alpine Avalanche*, 22 March 1935, 2.

[59]*Lubbock* (Tex.) *Daily Journal*, 6 November 1930, 4.

critics of American life. W.D. Bradfield of the Methodist Episcopal Church assailed media opponents of prohibition, alleging that "wet" forces in the press were "muzzling" the voice of the people. A Thanksgiving proclamation by Lubbock Mayor J.J. Clements remarked that though his city was in the midst of strife, "on every hand, we have felt the influence of a divine power, instilling a feeling of security and faith."[60]

The *Borger Daily Herald*, a booster of the high and loose times of the oil boom little more than a decade previous, took a wide-ranging interest in religious matters, following up on the spiritual angle in secular news stories. Editions of spring 1938 described the importance of two rabbis approving surgery on a baby with cancerous growths in both eyes, opposing doctors who wanted to end the child's life.[61] A page-one story discussed how the Pope was saddened by Nazis covering Rome with swastikas instead of crucifixes on Holy Cross Day.[62] This came even as eastern editors complained bitterly about religionists.[63]

The sudden change in regard for religiosity may have been brought on by the realization of the end of a way of life. Rosaldo noted how evangelical Christianity can be a welcome alternative for those prohibited from exercising once-pleasurable or ritualistic behavior.[64] The end of frontier-style independence, buttressed by long-standing religious metaphor in societal communication, may have moved overt religious practice to a higher place in West Texas and Western society.

The shift also may have been in reaction to the once-severe treatment of spirituality. Gene Howe, in his devastating biography "My Father Was the Most Wretchedly Unhappy Man I Ever Knew," described how far the next generation of Western editors had come from the day of Ed Howe, the "Sage of Potato Hill" and militant foe of religion. Gene wrote:

> My womenfolks belong and I contribute to their church and other churches regularly. I'm ashamed that I haven't been to church more than I have. I go occasionally. The world needs more churches and more religious people; the breakdown of religion in other parts of the world hasn't helped civilizations. Ministers and church people generally, wherever I have been, have been most considerate of me.[65]

The extremism of frontier news editors' views of religion may have made the next generation inclined to give it a fairer trial. As publisher of the *Amarillo Globe-News*, Howe added a religion page, which carried strong support for organized religion, including details of conversions.[66]

The encouragement of religion and admiration for the religious during World War II transcended the war evangelism prevalent in World War I. The *Globe-*

---

[60]Ibid., 22 October 1930, 10, and 18 November 1930, 1.

[61]*Borger* (Tex.) *Herald*, 9 May 1938, 1.

[62]Ibid., 4 May 1938, 1.

[63]Stanley Walker, *City Editor* (New York: Frederick Stokes Co., 1934), 161.

[64]Ronato Rosaldo, *Culture & Truth: The Remaking of Social Analysis* (Boston: Beacon Press, 1993).

[65]Howe, "My Father Was the Most Wretchedly Unhappy Person I Ever Knew," 407.

[66]See, for example, *Amarillo Daily News*, 8 July 1944, 4.

*News* obituary for Dallas theologian and pastor George Truett included the beaming remarks of the Episcopal bishop of West Texas.[67] The motion picture *Going My Way*, about a pair of Catholic priests with humanitarian ideals, had "universal appeal" in portraying the "understanding and kindliness of the two," wrote the paper's entertainment reviewer.[68]

Interestingly, the region's papers seemed to resist reporting the war in spiritual terms. This may have been the result of the isolationism popular in much of the West, or a desire to portray Christian principles in as accurate a manner as possible. Aside from an occasional insinuation that the Germans were "godless," or thanking God for victory, the papers seemed reluctant to introduce deity into the conflict. This was not for lack of trying by the military; the *Sheppard Field Texacts*, reporting on events at a Wichita Falls installation, joined other Western base publications in linking war and religion.[69]

The trend in Plains and Southwest newspapers toward positive coverage of religion and the religious could be summed up by the backing of Boys Ranch by the *Amarillo Globe-News*. Cal Farley, a successful local businessman, started the non-profit effort in 1939 as a halfway house for boys who were runaways, orphans, or disruptive at home. Benefited by donations of land and money, Farley established the ranch as a private facility with a non-denominational, evangelical bent. The combination of religion with individual initiative and private funding reflected the evolving character of the region and its people. Howe and his reporters wrote numerous columns and news stories supportive of Boys Ranch, giving Farley the newspaper's "Man of the Year" award in 1952.

This type of coverage was wildly popular, reinforcing the notion that Howe had tapped into a mainstream view of religiosity developing in the region. Independent reader-interest surveys indicated the Amarillo paper had one of the highest ratings in the nation, surprising even New York industry officials.

*THE MODERN ERA, 1945-PRESENT*

Religion coverage across the U.S. had something of a renaissance during the 1940s and 1950s,[70] but reporters on the beat did not endorse spiritual movements. Rather, they devoted time either to local events or scientifically oriented looks at religionists.[71] This ran directly counter to the perceived aims of Plains and Southwest papers.

The revolution against traditional moral and religious values of the 1960s gained no visible backing among Western newspaper editors. Although religious imagery in news items had all but vanished by this time, part of a delayed trend toward objectivism, the region's typical daily carried several columns and departments devoted to bolstering a biblical view of society and personal relationships.

Texas' *Midland Reporter-Telegram* carried "The Mature Parent" by Mrs.

---

[67]*Amarillo Sunday News-Globe*, 9 July 1944, 4.

[68]Ibid., 16 July 1944, 11.

[69]*Sheppard Field Texacts* (Wichita Falls, Tex.), 1944, *passim*.

[70]Ray Erwin, "Religious News Now Makes Good Page 1 Copy," *Editor & Publisher*, 24 November 1951, 13, 52.

[71]Ray Erwin, "Christmas Stories Covered by Cornell," *Editor & Publisher*, 27 December 1958, 12.

Muriel Lawrence, whose martial status was noted in the column. In a 1968 answer to a mother who felt emotionally distant from her wayward daughter, Lawrence labeled the difficulties a spiritual problem, as the mother failed to move beyond selfish concern for her own relationships to those of all young lives with God.[72] A few pages away, a cartoon depicted two fishermen out on the water, their poles dangling over the side. One said to the other, "Out here, away from it all, the God-is-dead movement is dead, eh, Sam?"[73]

Several such features were shared across 1960s West Texas newspapers, evidence of the evolving religious character of the area. Both the *Reporter-Telegram* and the *Lubbock Avalanche-Journal* carried "The Country Parson," an "adult cartoon" centering on a white-haired preacher who ruminated about life in folksy, religiously-laced asides. Both papers ran Bible verses on the editorial page, with the *Avalanche-Journal* also publishing a weekly quiz on knowledge of the Word.[74]

The economic downturn of the early 1980s saw oil prices cut in half and livestock values in a downward spiral. Weak markets had a severe impact on the West, ending a mini-boom in the oil fields of Montana and the upper Plains states, and striking at the heart of the highly important agribusiness industry.

Both oil and agriculture historically have been vital to the West Texas economy. In the mid-1980s, the deepest days of the recession, Amarillo lost up to 2,000 members of its workforce each month, and Midland-Odessa's unemployment rate hit 20 per cent. The manager of one of West Texas' top oil machinery yards lamented that once "it was a dream to have a yard like this and equipment like this. Now it's a nightmare."[75]

In spite of the hardships, Western and West Texas newspapers continued their backing of religion. The *Lubbock Avalanche-Journal* printed a daily Christian prayer on its front page, and the *Midland Reporter-Telegram* quoted the Bible on the editorial page. Both gave boosts to spiritual causes and workers in their news.

"Dr. McClurg has never been one to pass up an opportunity, even if it means hard work," wrote Beth Pratt of missionary activities by a former Baptist university president in the Lubbock paper in 1983.[76] While Western newspapers printed non-traditional religious views, including guest columns supporting the ordination of women and news pieces detailing Catholic peace activism, editors were sure to reiterate their endorsement of traditional values. This came at the same time national newspapers assailed Jerry Falwell and religious conservatives.[77]

By the 1990s, the Plains and Southwest states' economies were rebounding, and the Phoenix and Wichita metropolitan areas, along with several West Texas cities, were known as strong centers for evangelical Christianity. Amarillo, Mid-

---

[72]Muriel Lawrence, "The Mature Parent," *Midland* (Tex.) *Reporter-Telegram*, 2 May 1968, 4D.

[73]*Midland Reporter-Telegram*, 2 May 1968, 3C.

[74]*Lubbock* (Tex.) *Avalanche-Journal* and *Midland Reporter-Telegram*, 1966, 1968, *passim*.

[75]H.G. Bissinger, *Friday Night Lights* (Reading, Mass.: Addison-Wesley, 1990), 229.

[76]Beth Pratt, "Dr. McClung to Serve as Interim Pastor of Belgian Church," *Lubbock Avalanche-Journal*, 16 October 1983, F29.

[77]Kyle Huckins, "Religion and Politics: The News Media Cover the Christian Conservative Movement," paper presented to the Southwest Symposium of the Southwest Education Council for Journalism and Mass Communication, November 1996.

land, Odessa, and Lubbock all supported large numbers of conservative and charismatic churches as well as active Christian Coalition chapters.[78]

The *Amarillo Daily News*, 100 years after the city's major paper had assailed Christian leader Dwight L. Moody, named a local volunteer its woman of the year based in large part on her spiritual activism and belief. Winfred Moore, longtime pastor of the First Baptist Church of Amarillo, had won the newspaper's "Man of the Year" award in 1977 and 1989.[79]

Respect for non-Christian religious traditions also prevailed in the 1990s, as the New Year's Day 1996 *Daily News* detailed the spirituality behind the buffalo. It stated:

> The Sioux and other tribes believe that buffalo embody their spiritual being, reminding them of how their lives were woven into the rhythms of nature. Tatanka was the giver of life, the provider of food, clothing, and spiritual inspiration.[80]

The day's editorial page quoted 2 Corinthians 5:17: "If anyone is in Christ, he is a new creation; old things have passed away; behold, all things have become new."[81] The passage's words illustrated the spiritual choice Westerners and their newspapers had made over the preceding century, moving from disdain for the substance of religion to open enthusiasm for its ways.

The religious conservatism of the Plains and Southwest is a relatively recent development, as shown by the region's newspapers. The changes in the use of religious imagery and depiction of the religious on Western news pages were tied to social and cultural factors over a span of five generations, dating from the first permanent white settlements. The echoes of these footsteps of spiritual progress can still be heard in the canyons, county roads, and churches of the American West.

---

[78]Bissinger, *Friday Night Lights*; personal communication, Alice Patterson, Texas field coordinator, Christian Coalition, November, 1996; personal communication, Price, Baptist General Convention of Texas.

[79]Beth Duke, "1995 Man and Woman of the Year," *Amarillo* (Tex.) *Daily News*, 1 January 1996, A1.

[80]Jeff Taylor, "Tribal Leader Pins His Future on a Bison Ranch," *Amarillo Daily News*, 1 January 1996, A3.

[81]*Amarillo Daily News*, January 1, 1996, A4.

# 10

# The Founding of *The Christian Science Monitor*
by Julie Hedgepeth Williams

S.S. MCCLURE BOASTED about his plan once too often.

He had been plotting a siege on Christian Science in *McClure's Magazine*, and until mid-1906 he had managed to keep the details quiet. McClure saw the mushrooming church as one of the horrors that muckrakers were called to correct. He touted his magazine as one that would benefit every Christian family,[1] and he intended to steer Christendom away from Christian Science, which he considered to be a dangerous cult. About the time Georgine Milmine began her research into Christian Science for the magazine, McClure spoke to his staff about their work in general. He said that *McClure's* was "performing a certain mission." God, he said, was "in our plans."[2]

As Miss Milmine was preparing her exposé, Christian Scientists were getting wind of the series. Two high-ranking church officials came to the *McClure's* offices to check out the rumor, but McClure brushed them off. His managing editor, Witter Bynner, gave them a sympathetic ear and claimed he was dissatisfied with Miss Milmine's work.[3]

But then S.S. McClure bragged in front of the wrong person. He told freelance journalist Martha S. Bensley about the coming attack on Christian Science and its founder, Mary Baker Eddy.

Miss Bensley's mother was a Christian Scientist.

Miss Bensley wrote to her:

---

[1]"Editorial Notes: Several Magazines in One," *McClure's Magazine* 8 (December, 1896): 192.

[2]S.S. McClure, speech, autumn 1904, quoted in Harold S. Wilson, *McClure's Magazine and the Muckrakers* (Princeton, N.J.: Princeton University Press, 1970), 285.

[3]Alfred Farlow to Christian Science Board of Directors, 18 May 1905, Archives and Library of The Mother Church, The First Church of Christ, Scientist, Boston, Massachusetts. All archival material from the Mother Church may also be found in Robert Peel's biography, *Mary Baker Eddy: The Years of Authority* (New York: Holt, Rinehart, and Winston, 1977).

Mr. McClure ... has been here a good deal lately; and among other things he has told me that McClure's Magazine is going to start a crusade against Christian Science. They have been at this for some two or three years and have collected as he put it "a whole trunkful of documents".... They are going to take up every phase and development of Christian Science and do what they can to ridicule and destroy it. This information is authentic. I heard it from Mr. McClure's own lips.[4]

After Miss Bensley's revelation, Christian Science officials no longer trusted Bynner's successor Will Irwin when he stated that McClure's "had no intention of publishing an exposé."[5] Scientists realized that a storm was breaking in the press. They hoped that it was a light shower and not a hurricane. And they prayed.

Prayer was a primary factor in McClure's distrust of Mary Baker Eddy and her Christian Science Church. Christian Scientists claimed to be duplicating, through prayer and without medical aid, the healing work of Jesus.[6] The ministry had made converts of many people healed of conditions ranging from tumors to alcoholism to severe injuries.[7] However, just as many people denounced Christian Science as sacrilege at best and fraud at worst. Duplicate Jesus' works? To many, it was unthinkable.

The storm that followed, carried out in the muckraking McClure's and the "yellow" newspaper the New York World, turned out to be full of mistakes, falsehoods, and self-contradictions. Reporters harassed the octogenarian Mrs. Eddy, and no matter what she did to tell her side of the story, they wrote the story as they imagined it should be. Ultimately, she founded The Christian Science Monitor to show her antagonists how journalism ought to be. It has remained a beacon of ethical reporting, in stark contrast to the attacks that necessitated it.

*GEORGINE MILMINE AND MCCLURE'S*

As S.S. McClure had told Miss Bensley, McClure's had been researching Christian Science for years. By December 1906 the first installment of fourteen by Georgine Milmine was ready to go to press. Although the series concentrated on the life of church founder Mary Baker Eddy, McClure's made no attempt to hide its contempt for Christian Science as a whole. In an editorial announcing the series, McClure's scoffed:

In fifteen minutes a clear-minded orthodox Christian could explain to a clear-minded pagan the essentials of his religion. It is different with Christian Science. Here understanding follows belief. To the normal, average mind, "Science and Health," [Mrs. Eddy's textbook of Christian Science] written as

---

[4]Enclosed in a letter of 10 July 1906, Augusta B. Bensley to John B. Willis, Mother Church Archives.

[5]Alfred Farlow to Christian Science Board of Directors, [15] July 1906, Mother Church Archives.

[6]Mary Baker Eddy, *Science and Health with Key to the Scriptures* (Boston: First Church of Christ, Scientist, 1906), xi.

[7]Testimony of Marguerite Jones, *Christian Science Journal* 3 (1886): 213; testimony of George M. Kochler, *Christian Science Journal* 17 (1899), 512-3; testimony of Arthur Brook, *Christian Science Journal* 22 (1905) 777-9.

it is in a cheaply symbolic style, seems hazy and obscure.[8]

Not only was *Science and Health* hazy and obscure, but so was its 86-year-old author. "[Mary Baker Eddy] has other traits, more subtle," the magazine said. "Above all ... there seems to reign a kind of megalomania — a thirst for great achievements and for great glory." *McClure's* suggested that Mrs. Eddy's "deepest motives must always remain a mystery." Despite its scorn for Mrs. Eddy and Christian Science, *McClure's* promised that the series would be fair. Miss Milmine had spent over two years of "close research" so that her stories were the most carefully documented series ever presented to American readers. "The result," *McClure's* bragged, "is probably as near absolute accuracy as history ever gets."[9]

The assertion of accuracy, given the magazine's first blunder, both amused and horrified people who knew Mrs. Eddy. The editorial included an autographed photograph of Mrs. Eddy. There was just one problem: the photograph was not of Mrs. Eddy at all. Instead it was a picture of one Sarah Chevaillier. Although church officials wrote to *McClure's* after seeing advance publicity on the series and warned editors of the error,[10] *McClure's* went ahead and published the photo with a disclaimer, aimed at discrediting church officials, "Other photographs taken in later years have been greatly retouched."[11]

Ignoring the mistake, Miss Milmine proceeded to set herself up as the arbiter of fact about Mrs. Eddy. "Beside the Eddy fact has developed the Eddy fable," she wrote, adding, "Allowance must always be made, in dealing with the early life of a great personage, for the dishonor of a prophet in his own country. That allowance has been made here."[12] Despite that promise, the series started with an unprovable speculation about Mrs. Eddy's hypnotic power over her students. Even though Mrs. Eddy expressly forbade the use of hypnotism by Christian Scientists,[13] Miss Milmine ascribed an unholy influence to Mary Baker Eddy's eyes. "Her most striking beauty was her big, gray eyes," Miss Milmine explained. "Deep-set and overhung by dark lashes, they had the gift of emotional expression.... All her life, those eyes have had such an effect upon their beholders that they may justly be called an important factor in her career."[14]

It was hard to believe that the young Mary Baker described by Miss Milmine could grow up to become the leader of even a ladies' garden club, much less a Christian denomination. Mary had been a sickly child and had not attended school consistently, keeping her behind her class and forcing her to be taught at

---

[8]"Editorial Announcement: Mary Baker G. Eddy: The Story of her Life, and the History of Christian Science," *McClure's Magazine* 28 (December, 1906): 211.

[9]Ibid., 215-216.

[10]The picture matches none of Mrs. Eddy taken at any time. Peel, *Mary Baker Eddy: The Years of Authority*, 270, identifies the picture as being of Mrs. Chevaillier and cites the church officials' letter.

[11]"Editorial Announcement," *McClure's Magazine* 28 (December, 1906): 212.

[12]Georgine Milmine, "Mary Baker G. Eddy: The Story of her Life, and the History of Christian Science," *McClure's Magazine* 28 (January, 1907): 227, 235. The profile ran through a series of articles published in *McClure's*. Further references will list the series as "Milmine, "Mary Baker G. Eddy," *McClure's*."

[13]Mary Baker Eddy, *Manual of the Mother Church, The First Church of Christ, Scientist, in Boston, Massachusetts* (Boston: First Church of Christ, Scientist, 1908), 53. The rule had been in effect prior to the final revision of the *Manual* in 1908.

[14]Milmine, "Mary Baker G. Eddy," *McClure's* 28 (January, 1907): 235.

home.[15] Miss Milmine twisted this fact to her advantage. "Her old schoolmates say that [Mary Baker] was indolent, constantly lolled in her seat, and spent much time scribbling on her slate. Apparently, she was incapable of concentrated or continuous thought," Miss Milmine wrote. Mary's character did not improve by the time she reached adulthood, according to *McClure's*. The magazine alleged that Mary, then Mrs. George Glover, abandoned her only son. Mrs. Eddy had already published a sorrowful account of her parting with her son, saying it was forced by her family because she was too ill to care for him, but *McClure's* boldly claimed that Mrs. Eddy's version was a lie.[16]

Although *McClure's* claimed to have only the facts, it was treading on shaky ground. Following the Chevaillier photograph blunder, the magazine carelessly moved the city of Wilmington, North Carolina, where George Glover died, into South Carolina.[17] *McClure's* took less than a page to give a summary sketch of Christian Science teachings,[18] while it gave some five pages to a similar sketch about the teachings of the late mental healer Phineas Quimby, whom it claimed was the true originator of Christian Science philosophy. Miss Milmine claimed that she had free use of Quimby's unpublished manuscripts to support that statement,[19] but the rival magazine *Human Life* quoted Quimby's son George as saying, "No one has seen [the manuscripts] and no one shall. I tell you they have all been after them, ... [including] these recent newspaper and magazine investigators. But I have never shown them."[20] Miss Milmine also said that Reverend James Wiggin had essentially written *Science and Health;* however, she also quoted Wiggin as saying that Christian Science was "ignorant" and "useless,"[21] an odd charge from the man who supposedly wrote the religion's textbook.

Nothing in the sect was sacred. Christian Scientists dated their denomination from 1866 when Mrs. Eddy, then Mrs. Daniel Patterson, recovered from a serious accident. As an article in the *Lynn* (Massachusetts) *Reporter* put it, "Mrs. Mary M. Patterson, of Swampscott, fell upon the ice near the corner of Market and Oxford Streets, on Thursday evening, and was severely injured." The newspaper reported that she was "insensible" as she was carried to a nearby home, where she "was kindly cared for during the night. Dr. Cushing, who was called, found her injuries to be internal, and of a very serious nature, inducing spasms and intense suffering. She was removed to her home in Swampscott yesterday af-

---

[15]Baker family writings frequently spoke of Mary's ill health. See, for instance, Martha Baker's writings of 18 July 1837 and 15 October 1837, and Abigail Baker's writing of 13 October 1837, now at The Longyear Historical Society and Mary Baker Eddy Museum, Brookline, Massachusetts. Eddy herself said that her father kept her out of school because "my brain was too large for my body." See Mary Baker Eddy, *Retrospection and Introspection*, 10, in *Prose Works other than Science and Health with Key to the Scriptures* (Boston: First Church of Christ, Scientist, 1925). *Prose Works* is comprised of a number of works, each numbered separately. Titles of the individual works will be listed separately, with a notation that they are part of *Prose Works*.

[16]Milmine, "Mary Baker G. Eddy," *McClure's* 28 (January, 1907): 237, 241-2.

[17]Ibid., 239.

[18]"Editorial Announcement," *McClure's* 28 (December, 1906): 213.

[19]Milmine, "Mary Baker G. Eddy," *McClure's* 28 (February, 1907): 340-7.

[20]Sibyl Wilbur O'Brien, *Human Life* (April, 1906), quoted in Sibyl Wilbur, *The Life of Mary Baker Eddy* (Boston: Christian Science Publishing Society, 1913), 103.

[21]Milmine, "Mary Baker G. Eddy," *McClure's* 19 (October, 1907): 695, 698.

ternoon, though in a very critical condition."[22] Mrs. Eddy later recalled what happened next. "On the third day thereafter, I called for my Bible.... As I read, the healing Truth dawned upon my sense; and the result was that I rose, dressed myself, and ever after was in better health than I had before enjoyed." The Bible passages had given her "a glimpse of the great fact that I have since tried to make plain to others, namely, Life in and of Spirit; this Life being the sole reality of existence."[23] Life and Spirit, she said, were God, present under all circumstances to heal any illness or injury.[24]

Miss Milmine was certain the story was fraudulent. "Several documents can be brought in refutation of this claim," she wrote. She referred to a letter that Mrs. Patterson penned to Julius Dresser, a student of Quimby's mental healing technique. The February 15, 1866, letter begged for Dresser's help. "The physician attending said I had taken the last step I ever should, but in two days I got out of bed *alone* and *will* walk; but yet, I confess I am frightened.... I am slowly failing," Mrs. Patterson wrote. Miss Milmine gloated that the letter "apparently disproves the miraculous account given above."[25]

The letter was already well-known. On March 7, 1883, Mrs. Eddy had told the *Boston Post* that she had appealed to Dresser in a moment of fear. After realizing she would have no support from Dresser,[26] she began seeking exactly why she had felt transformed in that moment with her Bible. Her search, she said, led her to discover the Science of Christianity, which she considered to be far more reliable than Quimby's personality-based healing.[27]

If Miss Milmine was aware of Mrs. Eddy's explanation to the *Post,* she was not impressed by it. Dr. Alvin Cushing himself, she found out, was eager to see Mrs. Eddy discredited. As he put it in a letter to Miss Milmine later, "My sons and others are very much stirred up that my name should appear in such a sacreligious [sic] affair as Christian Science."[28] He was happy to give Miss Milmine an affidavit. "I did not at any time declare, or believe, that there was no hope for Mrs. Patterson's recovery, or that she was in critical condition," the doctor wrote. He added that Mrs. Patterson did not "suggest, say, or pretend, or in any other way intimate" that she had recovered miraculously. "I have of course, no personal feeling in this matter," he said. "I regard [this affidavit] as a duty which I owe to posterity to make public this particular episode in the life of Mary Baker G. Eddy."[29] To *McClure's* readers who had no knowledge of the Lynn newspaper report or of the doctor's feelings about Christian Science, the affidavit was damning. Cushing himself was thrilled. He wrote Miss Milmine a letter of congratulation: "You are certainly showing the old lady up all right."[30]

As Miss Milmine's series progressed, she portrayed Mrs. Eddy's antagonists as heroes and her followers as stooges. Mrs. Eddy had divorced her second hus-

---

[22]*The Lynn Reporter* (Massachusetts), 3 February 1866.

[23]Mary Baker Eddy, *Miscellaneous Writings, 1883-1896,* 24, in *Prose Works.*

[24]Eddy, *Science and Health,* x, xi, 587.

[25]Milmine, "Mary Baker G. Eddy," *McClure's* 28 (March, 1907): 510-11.

[26]Julius Dresser to Mary Patterson, 2 March 1866, Mother Church Archives.

[27]Eddy, *Retrospection and Introspection,* 24-5, in *Prose Works.*

[28]Alvin Cushing to Georgine Milmine, 14 February 1907, Mother Church Archives.

[29]Milmine, "Mary Baker G. Eddy," *McClure's* 28 (March, 1907): 512-3.

[30]Alvin Cushing to Georgine Milmine, 14 February 1907, Mother Church Archives.

band, Daniel Patterson, for abandonment and adultery.[31] But Miss Milmine said that "Dr. Patterson seems to have been untiring in service, and to have placed his robust physical strength very manfully at the will of his invalid wife."[32] On the other hand, Mrs. Eddy's student and third husband, Asa Gilbert Eddy, was "a dull little man, docile and yielding." Even Asa Eddy's family was "shiftless," and Miss Milmine made fun of "his old-fashioned dress and singular manner of wearing his hair."[33] If Asa Eddy was dopey, his wife's followers were worse. "Her following was ... for the most part, made up of indifferent material — discontented women, and young men who had not succeeded in finding their place in the world," Miss Milmine wrote,[34] ignoring published statements by followers such as a sea captain, railway employees, and even former doctors.[35] *McClure's* described Mrs. Eddy's secretary Calvin Frye as being from a "slow" and "inarticulate" family.[36] Sounding a familiar theme, Miss Milmine repeated her belief that Mrs. Eddy was a fraud, hardly able to heal the sick as she preached.[37]

This healing, Miss Milmine knew, was the attraction of Christian Science, but she could not believe it was true. The only healing she quoted in full was that of a dog bitten by a rattlesnake. She thought it was funny and said so, titling it "One Amusing Incident."[38] Minimizing the abundant publishing of healings of the faithful, which appeared weekly and monthly in church periodicals,[39] Miss Milmine instead concentrated on sensational failures of Christian Science healers.[40]

The historical account that *McClure's* had promised became instead a theological attack. Mrs. Eddy and her followers reasoned that an all-loving, all-powerful God was in control of His creation and was always available, through prayer, to heal the sick without the use of drugs or medical procedures.[41] But Miss Milmine complained that Mrs. Eddy's students had no medical know-how. She growled that they "knew much less about physiology, anatomy, and hygiene than the average grammar-school boy knows to-day. They had not been taught how to tie an artery or to set a broken bone, how to take a patient's temperature or how to administer simple antidotes for poisons."[42] As to people who claimed to have been cured by Christian Science, Miss Milmine wrote off their healings as "alleged cures."[43] *Science and Health* also received a poor review. "Not one

---

[31]George Clark, court testimony later restated in an affidavit, 1 January 1907, Mother Church Archives.

[32]Milmine, "Mary Baker G. Eddy," *McClure's* 28 (April, 1907): 611.

[33]Ibid., *McClure's* 29 (May, 1907): 15.

[34]Ibid., *McClure's* 29 (August, 1907): 462.

[35]Joseph S. Eastaman, "The Travail of my Soul," *Christian Science Journal* 10 (1892): 68-72; testimony of Frank C. Prichard, *Christian Science Journal* 17 (1899): 661; testimony of Arthur Brook, *Christian Science Journal* 22 (1905): 777-79; testimony of Dr. A.M. Overman, *Christian Science Journal* 11 (1893): 136-7; *Chicago Inter-Ocean*, 17 January 1897, quoted in *Christian Science Journal* 14 (1897): 598-603; testimony of Dr. A.W. Paine, *Christian Science Journal* 17 (1899): 207-8.

[36]Milmine, "Mary Baker G. Eddy," *McClure's* 29 (September, 1907): 573.

[37]Ibid., *McClure's* 29 (May, 1907): 97.

[38]Ibid., *McClure's* 29 (October, 1907): 692.

[39]Ibid. See also, Milmine, *McClure's* 30 (February, 1908): 398-9.

[40]Milmine, "Mary Baker G. Eddy," *McClure's* 29 (October, 1907): 693-5.

[41]Eddy, *Science and Health*, 1-17.

[42]Milmine, "Mary Baker G. Eddy," *McClure's* 30 (February, 1908): 396.

[43]Ibid., *McClure's* 29 (October, 1907): 692.

page of her book is tinged with compassion.... It is not an exaggeration to say that 'Science and Health' is absolutely devoid of religious feeling," Miss Milmine commented.[44]

Theologians around the country had been calling Mrs. Eddy everything from exalted to insane, but Miss Milmine's lack of theological expertise was embarrassing. While explaining a shortcoming of Christian Science philosophy, Miss Milmine derided a statement made by Mrs. Eddy. Miss Milmine scoffed, quoting Mrs. Eddy: "'Ye shall know the Truth,' she said, 'and the Truth shall make you free.'"[45] Miss Milmine apparently did not recognize that the quotation that she faulted actually came from Jesus.[46]

*THE* WORLD *AND THE "NEXT FRIENDS"*

*McClure's* was not the only publication crusading against Christian Science. Joseph Pulitzer's yellow newspaper, the *New York World*, was also seeking destruction of the denomination. While Miss Milmine was putting the finishing touches on her research, two reporters from the *World* appeared at Mrs. Eddy's home in Concord, New Hampshire, and began asking if the 86-year-old church leader were still alive. The reporters insisted on meeting with Mrs. Eddy and having a neighbor identify her. Accordingly, the reporters, James Slaght and a Mr. Lithchild, met with Mrs. Eddy and her neighbor, and Lithchild even commented to church official Lewis Strang after it was over, "She is certainly a well-preserved woman for her years." Slaght, for his part, "gave me to understand that he was thoroughly satisfied as to the soundness of Mrs. Eddy's physical and mental condition," Strang wrote.[47]

Two weeks later, however, on October 28, 1906, the *World* bristled with a sensational story. "Mrs. Mary Baker G. Eddy Dying," the headlines proclaimed on page one. "Founder of Christian Science Suffering from Cancer and Nearing Her End." The paper said that Mrs. Eddy was being impersonated for the public by Mrs. Parmelia Leonard, a member of the staff at Mrs. Eddy's home, Pleasant View. Mrs. Eddy's secretary-footman, Calvin Frye, was in command of the Eddy household and fortune, the paper claimed.

Under those dramatic headlines, the newspaper published a letter from Mrs. Eddy to the *Boston Herald,* dated October 19. "Dear Sir: — " it read. "Another report that I am dead is widely circulated. I am in usual good health, and go out in my carriage every day." The accusations in October 28's *World* were spectacular. "This letter, published by a reputable newspaper ... is doubtless authentic. If the signature be genuine, Mrs. Eddy, founder and head of the Christian Science Church, has affixed her name to a falsehood," the *World* declared. "Reporters for the World have seen and spoken to Mrs. Eddy in her guarded home at Concord, N.H., within the last few days. She is very feeble and seem-

---

[44] Ibid., *McClure's* 31 (June, 1908): 186.

[45] Ibid., *McClure's* 28 (April, 1907): 333. Eddy cites the passage three times in her major works. In *Science and Health*, iii, she attributes the quotation to the Bible. In *Message to the Mother Church, Boston, Massachusetts, June, 1901*, 10, in *Prose Works*, and in *Miscellaneous Writings*, 241, in *Prose Works*, she cites the line with quotation marks, obviously assuming readers will understand the famous words to be those of Jesus.

[46] John 8:32.

[47] Lewis Strang to Cornell Wilson, memorandum, 27 October 1906, Mother Church Archives.

ingly in the shadow of death. She suffers from cancer, and a Boston cancer specialist visits her secretly every week." The *World* said that while Mrs. Leonard impersonated Mrs. Eddy for a carriage drive around Concord each day, "to move the real Mrs. Eddy from her bed would have meant almost certain death to the enfeebled woman." The *World* did not keep its feelings about Christian Science a secret. On page one it described the church as "Christian Science, so called," and referred to it as a cult.

If Strang wondered why Slaght and Lithchild had changed their minds about Mrs. Eddy's soundness, he did not have to wonder long. The *World* gave away its plans in that October 28 issue. "But now that the amazing facts have been made public the door so long barred by the footman-secretary may be opened. Legal action to ascertain the full truth is practically assured," the newspaper said.[48] The *World* was orchestrating a legal attack on Mrs. Eddy. For the moment, the nature of the coming litigation was unclear. But if the public were to be convinced that Mrs. Eddy was at death's door, then the Mrs. Eddy who appeared in public had to be proven a fake. Thus, *World* reporters began a campaign of harassment against the aged church leader. The newspaper bragged about a fact-gathering scheme carried out during one of Mrs. Eddy's carriage rides. The *World* said:

> In order to clearly see the face of the supposed Mrs. Eddy the two investigators reported to a simple strategy. One afoot stepped to the right hand window of the coach, the other in a carriage passed to the left. Down ducked the parasol [which the occupant was carrying] to the right, blocking the view on that side but leaving an unobstructed vision for the man in the carriage. The woman in the Eddy carriage was younger than the aged founder of Christian Science by many years.[49]

Despite the reporters' confidence, however, they still thought it necessary to bring in a John J. Hennessy to try a similar trick another day. "Hennessy took his stand on the designated corner on the afternoon of that day and waited," the *World* described. "Twenty minutes passed, and then the Eddy carriage made its appearance, its sleepy fat horses slowly jogging along guided by August Mann, with liveried [Calvin] Frye beside him in the role of the footman." This time the supposed impersonation did not involve a parasol; it involved an elaborate bell system. Frye, the newspaper said, would ring a bell hidden under his foot to alert the "bogus Mrs. Eddy" of any suspicious onlookers, and she, in turn, would pull down the curtains of the carriage. "But Frye saw no menace in the well-dressed young man standing at the State House corner, one foot raised on a convenient fire-plug, and both hands busy with a refractory shoestring," the newspaper said. "As the carriage slowly turned the corner, the open, uncurtained window was within six feet of Hennessy's keen eyes."

"I could not help smiling to save my life," Hennessy told the *World*. "The woman was Parmelia J. Leonard."[50]

---

[48]"Mrs. Mary Baker G. Eddy Dying: Footman and 'Dummy' Control Her," *The New York World*, 28 October 1906. Further references to the newspaper will list it as *"World."*

[49]"The Mrs. Eddy of the Carriage Not the Mrs. Eddy of the House," *World*, 28 October 1906.

[50]"Mrs. P.J. Leonard, of Brooklyn Identified in the Eddy Coach," *World*, 28 October 1906. Although

The assault continued the next day. The *World* published a sensational account of Asa Eddy's alleged attempt to hire a man to kill one of his wife's enemies,[51] a charge that even Miss Milmine later admitted was "highly improbable."[52] The *World* would probably have considered Miss Milmine a dupe of the church, for it said, "The facts, suppressed by the use of money and the power of the influence exerted everywhere by the cult, are here draged [sic] into the light for the first time."[53] The *World* did not attempt to interview Mrs. Eddy on any of the charges, since she was conveniently on her deathbed. However, the newspaper did give space to Parmelia Leonard's son Frank, who issued a statement denying the *World's* claim that his mother impersonated Mrs. Eddy.[54] Likewise, the paper printed Calvin Frye's denial of the *World's* "sensational report." Frye said:

[Mrs. Eddy] is not slowly dying from cancer, nor has she a cancer or any chronic or organic or functional disease. She has never been visited by a cancer specialist, nor do I or anybody else provide old school surgeons and physicians, dentists and the entire range of pharmacists for attendance upon Mrs. Eddy as stated by The World.

Frye also suggested a new reportorial trick. "Had the reporters of The World really desired to learn whether Mrs. Leonard impersonated Mrs. Eddy on Mrs. Eddy's drive," he commented, "it would have been a very simple matter for these reporters to have called at Pleasant View while Mrs. Eddy was driving and asked for Mrs. Leonard."[55]

In spite of these denials, the *World* continued to put forth its story as the only accurate one. The paper needed public support if it was to pull off the still-unexplained legal action. "In all the Christian Science churches copies of The World containing the facts of the fraudulent impersonation of the almost lifeless Mrs. Eddy by Parmelia J. Leonard ... were passed from hand to hand," the newspaper boasted. "Never in the history of the cult had its devotees been so stirred."[56]

The *World* next unwittingly crossed its own story of October 28 by running a description of hard-nosed newsmen who refused to believe Concord residents' assertions that the woman who drove through town each day in her carriage was, indeed, Mrs. Eddy. "It is impossible for an outsider standing on the street to make out the features of the female within the carriage," the article said, never bringing up the question of how Hennessy had therefore managed to make out her features earlier.[57]

Reporters swarmed into Concord to cover the supposed fraud. Mrs. Eddy de-

Leonard was from Brooklyn, she was at that time serving on the staff at the Eddy home. Peel, in *Mary Baker Eddy: The Years of Authority*, gives her first name as Pamelia instead of Parmelia.

[51]"Records Tell of Arrest of 'Dr.' Eddy and Accomplice Who Were Indicted on Evidence of Man Hired to Commit Crime — Mysterious Influence Caused Case to Be Dropped," *World*, 29 October 1906.

[52]Milmine, "Mary Baker G. Eddy," *McClure's* 29 (August, 1907): 455.

[53]"Records tell of Arrest," *World*, 29 October 1906.

[54]"Mrs. Leonard's Son Issues Statement," *World*, 29 October 1906.

[55]"Mrs. Eddy Invisible; Denials Galore," *World*, 29 October 1906.

[56]"Mrs. Eddy's Loyal Readers Strive to Refute Disclosures," *World*, 29 October 1906.

[57]" 'Mrs. Eddy Is Very Feeble and Looks 100 Years Old,' " *World*, 30 October 1906.

cided to grant an interview to some of them, with Sibyl Wilbur O'Brien of the *Boston Herald* to put forth the questions. The interview was brief, and Mrs. Eddy left the reporters to go on her carriage ride. The accounts by various newspapers were different. Apparently each reporter saw exactly what he or she expected to see. The *World*, of course, stated that those accounts that differed from its own opinion were wrong — even though *World* reporters were not invited to the interview. The *World* said that "one or two papers have printed reports describing the trembling, shrunken shape of the old woman as strong and erect, her quavering and pining voice as clear and deep and her tottering step as a free stride." It quoted reporter Viola Rodgers as saying that "Mrs. Eddy is an extraordinary woman at eight-six, ... with many remarkable traits of a still vigorous and active personality, [as] was plainly indicated by her presence and manner," and then hinted that Ms. Rodgers was being paid off by the church. The *World* noted that reporter Eleanor Ames saw things differently. She described Mrs. Eddy as "a physical wreck, tottering, pallid, like a vision from beyond the grave."[58]

Appalled, the *New York American* took the opportunity to scold the *World* in an editorial:

It would be interesting to know just exactly why The New York World thought it necessary to make a bitter and untruthful attack upon Mrs. Mary Baker G. Eddy....
It was an attack upon a woman.
It was an attack upon old age.
It was an attack upon religious belief.
... [I]t doesn't take very much manhood in a newspaper editor to realize that a woman of eight-six years of age is entitled to veneration from every man, especially when her life has been exemplary, AND WHEN SHE HAS DONE NO ONE ANY HARM.
We are glad that Mrs. Eddy's good health made it possible for her personally to refute the inexplicable, slanderous attack upon her.
And we trust that the New York World, as far as it is possible, will see fit to confine its attacks to MEN, and, if it must attack WOMEN, that it will at least exempt THOSE PAST FOURSCORE.[59]

While the *American* wondered why the *World* was mounting the attack, behind the scenes the *World* was pursuing the promised lawsuit in earnest. Reporter Slaght arrived in Lead, South Dakota, to visit Mrs. Eddy's somewhat estranged son, George Glover. Slaght brought a letter from former U.S. Senator William Chandler in which Chandler agreed to "act as counsel concerning questions in connection with Mrs. Mary Baker G. Eddy." The letter said that Mrs. Eddy "may be so nearly worn out in body and mind, as a confirmed invalid, that she is incapable of managing her business and property affairs."[60]

Before long, Glover and his daughter Mary came back East to visit Mrs.

---

[58]"Scientists To Ask Law To Open Mrs. Eddy's Home," *World*, 31 October 1906.

[59]"The World's Disgraceful Attack on Mrs. Eddy: It Combined a Good Many Unpleasant Features," *New York American*, 3 November 1906.

[60]"Relatives Sue to Wrest Mother Eddy's Fortune From Control of Clique," *World*, 2 March 1907.

Eddy. They gave the *World* a big story: "As we entered the bedroom at Pleasant View, in Concord, ... we saw my mother seated in an arm-chair at the extreme end of the room.... We were greatly shocked by the gauntness of my mother's face. It was furrowed and the skin was like parchment."[61] In another story the next day, Glover said that his mother "was a slave and a prisoner in her own home."[62]

The story of the January visit, however, did not break until March, when the *World* announced: "Relatives Sue To Wrest Mother Eddy's Fortune From Control Of Clique. Bill in Equity Filed at Concord by Only Son of the Founder of Christian Science, His Daughter and a Nephew ... Plaintiffs Declare Her Helpless in the Hands of Calvin Frye, Alfred Farlow and Other Leaders. Mrs. Eddy Herself Appears as Petitioner; Through Others."[63] The harassment had taken a sinister twist. If Mrs. Eddy's relatives gained control of her finances, they could effectively dismantle her church.[64] The *World* played innocent. It said that "this action is in no sense an attack upon Christian Science nor upon Mary Baker G. Eddy. On the contrary, Mrs. Eddy herself appears as the real petitioner, and the suit is brought by her relatives as 'next friends.'"[65]

Mrs. Eddy was anxious. Her life's work was in danger. She wrote to several trusted students and begged them to come to Pleasant View "to watch with me one or two weeks as the case may require. This hour is going to test Christian Scientists and the fate of our Cause and they must not be found wanting.... I see very clearly that the prosperity of our Cause hangs in the balance."[66] She had no interest in being a petitioner in the lawsuit and did not hesitate to make her feelings known. "It is over forty years that I have attended personally to my secular affairs, to my income, investments, deposits, expenditures, and to my employees," Mrs. Eddy wrote to Judge Robert N. Chamberlin of the Superior Court in Concord. "This suit was brought without my knowledge and is being carried on contrary to my wishes. I feel that it is not for my benefit in any way but for my injury, and I know it was not needed to protect my person or property."[67]

Reporter Leigh Mitchell Hodges of *The North American* newspaper confirmed Mrs. Eddy's feelings. He interviewed her at her home and came away convinced that she was alive, well, in control of her affairs, and uninterested in being a party to the lawsuit. Hodges asked what she thought would come of the "next friends'" lawsuit. "Why, good must come of it, of course," she answered. "Hard as it is to bear, it cannot but cause the truth to stand out more clearly in the end. It is not so much a personal attack on me as a conspiracy against Christian Science." Mrs. Eddy told Hodges:

---

[61]"Glover Says His Mother Talked of Murder Plot At Concord Interview," *World*, 2 March 1907.

[62]"Mrs. Eddy's Son Gives Reasons For Bringing Suit To Free Mother," *World*, 3 March 1907.

[63]*World* (headline in text), 2 March 1907.

[64]Calvin Hill, one of Eddy's associates, stated that had the "next friends" won the lawsuit, they would have obtained possession of Eddy's property as well as the copyright of *Science and Health*. See Hill, "Some Precious Memories of Mary Baker Eddy," compiled by Francis Thompson Hill, in *We Knew Mary Baker Eddy, Third Series* (Boston: Christian Science Publishing Society, 1953), 53-4.

[65]"Relatives Sue To Wrest Mother Eddy's Fortune From Control of Clique," *World*, 2 March 1907.

[66]Mary Baker Eddy to Calvin Hill, 24 March 1907, quoted in Calvin Hill, "Some Precious Memories of Mary Baker Eddy," compiled by Francis Thompson Hill, in *We Knew Mary Baker Eddy, Third Series*, 54.

[67]Mary Baker Eddy to Judge Robert N. Chamberlin, 16 May 1907, quoted in Norman Beasley, *The Cross and The Crown: The History of Christian Science* (New York: Duell, Sloan and Pearce, 1952), 431-3.

They say I am not able to take care of my affairs.... Ask any of those who here surround me whether or not I am the active head of this house. From roof to cellar I am mistress. I supervise everything that goes on within these walls. Outside them, on the place, everything is deferred to my decision. Ask any one who is in a position to know this!

Hodges added, "The vigor with which she endowed her words and the expression that accompanied them evidenced not only the possibility, but the extreme probability of her being this very thing."[68]

Mrs. Eddy went on to speak of the *World*. "Finally, as you know, it came out with the news that I was dead," she told Hodges. "I don't look it, do I? ... Newspapers should be edited with the same reverence for Truth, God, as is observed in the administration of the most serious affairs of life." Clearly she thought the *World* was not edited to those high standards.

The "next friends" case went to court in August. Although the lawsuit was ostensibly brought to assure that an elderly woman was not controlled against her will, the real target of the suit was her religious teaching. Chandler, in his opening speech, stated that Mrs. Eddy was insane because her theology was insane. He had drawn up a list of "delusions" that Mrs. Eddy was suffering from. "Mrs. Eddy's book, 'Science and Health,' alone is proof that she is suffering from ... systematized delusions and dementia," he stated. Chandler added that Mrs. Eddy's method of curing disease was insane, and that she was insane to link her system with Christianity. It was evident, he said, that Mrs. Eddy was senile.[69]

To disprove such assertions, Mrs. Eddy's counsel contacted a prominent psychiatrist,[70] Dr. Allan McLane Hamilton, and asked him to examine the aged leader in order to testify on her behalf. The amazed Hamilton replied, "Perhaps you do not know that I appeared recently in the Brush case and attacked Christian Science?" The counsel was well aware of that fact.[71] The fact that Hamilton was an antagonist to the religion made his word all the more authoritative in court.

Hamilton agreed to make an assessment. He visited Mrs. Eddy at her home on a hot summer afternoon. Although she seemed a little uncomfortable in the heat, Hamilton observed no symptoms of insanity or mental disease. "I found nothing the matter with her," he stated flatly. He found her completely competent to manage her own affairs. "She did not manifest any delusions, which she probably would have done had she been a paranoiac, as it has been asserted she was.... For a woman of her age I do not hesitate to say that she is physically and mentally phenomenal."[72]

Two days later, the court sent three experts of its own to examine Mrs. Eddy and determine her mental state. The three, Judge Edgar Aldrich, attorney Hosea

---

[68]"North American Interviews Mrs. Eddy; Tho' 86, Shows Vigor of Woman of 70." *The North American* (Philadelphia, Pa.), 14 July 1907.

[69]"Chandler Bares Mrs. Eddy's Fear Of Evil In Court," *World,* 14 August 1907.

[70]In that era, some psychiatrists were called "alienists," as were Hamilton and George Jelly, below.

[71]Report of Dr. Allan McLane Hamilton, "Examination of Mrs. Eddy at Pleasant View, Monday, August 12, 1907, 2 p.m.," reprinted in *Quarterly News of the Longyear Museum and Historical Society* 32, no. 4 (1995): 524.

[72]Ibid.

Parker, and psychiatrist Dr. George F. Jelly, went to Concord to question her. Lawyers for both sides accompanied them.[73] The experts were kind to the aged woman. "If you feel fatigued, we want to have you speak of it and let us know," Aldrich told her.

"Thank you," Mrs. Eddy replied. "I can work hours at my work, day and night, without the slightest fatigue when it is in the line of spiritual labor."

The three wanted to know about her finances. Aldrich posed a hypothetical question. "My life insurance is coming due pretty soon, and I want to make good use of it. What do you consider good investments?"

He was momentarily taken aback by her answer. "I do not put [my investments] into life insurance," Mrs. Eddy said. "God insures my life."

Aldrich was forced to revise his question and ask how she would invest $100,000. "I prefer government bonds," she said. "I have invested largely in government bonds, and I prefer bonds to stocks. I have not entered into stocks." She went on to say that she preferred investing in states. "I have books that give definitely the population of the states, and their money values, and I consult these, and when I see they are large enough in population and valuation to warrant an investment, I make it."

Aldrich was impressed. "Well, I should think that was pretty sound," he said.

The questioning went on for some time, and Mrs. Eddy wound up telling the three experts about her church and her personal history. As Benjamin Orange Flower reported it in the magazine *Arena*, Chandler left Pleasant View saying, "She is smarter than a steel trap."[74]

The next day in court, nothing was mentioned about Mrs. Eddy's financial situation. Instead attorneys for the "next friends" tried to persuade the court that Christian Scientists gave up reason for "an insane belief which persists and abides despite all evidence."[75]

Aldrich was on Mrs. Eddy's side by now. "Suppose in the course of two hundred years the Christian Scientists outnumbered all other denominations, and would be more than half the population of this country, and the government should be administered by them," he said. "Would you hold that it would be a wise administration of government if they passed laws which would declare all the rest as not believing as they do under insane delusions?"[76]

Less than a week later, Chandler withdrew from the "next friends'" case. Mrs. Eddy's counsel asked to have the trial completed in order to prove his client's worthiness, blaming the suit on "a great newspaper which had hired and paid eminent counsel to bring it."[77] In the *Arena*, Flower referred to the "suit brought by alleged 'next friends,' but really started by a certain New York newspaper, which has retained great counsel and paid the bills. It is based on false pretenses, and is unique in the history of legal procedure. We [question] whether

---

[73]Portions of the lawsuit transcript follow. The transcript is quoted in Beasley, *The Cross and The Crown: The History of Christian Science*, 440-68.

[74]Benjamin Orange Flower, "The Collapse of the Case Against the Founder of Christian Science," *The Arena* 38 (September, 1907): 320. Flower quoted the report from the Boston *American* newspaper.

[75]Quoted in Beasley, *The Cross and The Crown: The History of Christian Science*, 458.

[76]Ibid., 460.

[77]Ibid., 464.

it is brought in good faith."[78] It was no secret that the *World* was behind the "next friends."

Concluding the case, Chamberlin ruled that the "next friends" had to pay the court costs.[79] The suit had ended, but for Mary Baker Eddy, it was obvious that there was work to do.

*COUNTERPOINT:* THE CHRISTIAN SCIENCE MONITOR

Disturbed by the attacks in the press, Mary Baker Eddy took a step she had been contemplating for a long time. She was interested in the publication of news; her church periodicals had for many years carried secular news.[80] In 1896, she had published a statement that "a newspaper edited and published by the Christian Scientists has become a necessity." She said at the time:

> Looking over the newspapers of the day, one naturally reflects that it is dangerous to live, so loaded with disease seems the very air.... A periodical of our own will counteract to some extent this public nuisance; for through our paper, at the price at which we shall issue it, we shall be able to reach many homes with healing, purifying thought.[81]

However, her church periodicals had a denominational slant until the end of the "next friends" case.

As the attacks by *McClure's* and the *World* came to a head, a Boston newspaperman named John L. Wright wrote to Mrs. Eddy with an idea he had had for two years. He thought the church should consider "establishing a Scientific daily newspaper. It seems to me that such newspapers are greatly needed." The recent behavior of the press had sparked his letter. "The disappearance so largely of the more stable, sane, patriotic newspaper, the usurpation of the newspaper field in great centres by commercial and political monopolists, and the commercialization of the papers — their management mainly for dividends ... constitute, I believe, a great misfortune to the country," he wrote.[82]

Mrs. Eddy scribbled a note at the bottom of Wright's letter, although she never sent it to him. "Beloved Student," it read. "I have had this newspaper scheme in my thought for quite a while and herein send my name for our daily newspaper 'The Christian Science Monitor.'"[83] After toying with the idea for several more months, the 87-year-old Mrs. Eddy made the plan official to other church leaders in an August 8, 1908, communiqué. "Beloved Students: — " she wrote. "It is my request that you start a daily newspaper at once, and call it the Christian Science Monitor. The Cause demands that it be issued now." Ac-

---

[78]Flower, "The Collapse of the Case Against the Founder of Christian Science," *The Arena* 38 (September, 1907): 320.

[79]Beasley, *The Cross and The Crown: The History of Christian Science*, 469.

[80]See, for instance, *The Christian Science Weekly* (1 September 1898): 1-2. The *Weekly* was later renamed *Christian Science Sentinel*. A current events column continued in the *Sentinel* until mid-1906.

[81]Eddy, *Miscellaneous Writings,* 4 and 7, in *Prose Works.*

[82]John L. Wright to Mary Baker Eddy, 12 March 1908, Mother Church Archives.

[83]Mary Baker Eddy to John L. Wright, [12 March] 1908, Mother Church Archives. Erwin Canham, later an editor of *The Christian Science Monitor,* says the reply was never sent. See Canham, *Commitment to Freedom: The Story of The Christian Science Monitor* (Boston: Houghton Mifflin, 1958), 21.

cording to a prospectus statement, it would not be just a local paper. Rather, *The Christian Science Monitor* would cover the whole continent and be of interest abroad. It would not be denominational in flavor, but it would be "a strictly up-to-date newspaper, in which all the news of the day that should be printed will find a place." Most of all, it would "publish the real news of the world in a clean, wholesome manner, devoid of the sensational methods employed by so many newspapers." It would also represent "reform in journalism."[84] It was clear that Mrs. Eddy and her church had seen too much shoddy journalism in the recent attacks by the press. They planned to produce a model newspaper, one that would be a beacon of decent reporting.

By August 11, the church's board of directors had agreed to provide a building for the publication of the paper, and the church's publishing society had agreed to take on the duty of organizing and starting the *Monitor*.[85] By August 13, officials had called in two expert newsmen who determined that the newspaper would require two presses, costing $25,000 apiece; a building set on pilings; 90 to 100 employees; a $125,000 yearly payroll, and a subscription rate of $3.50 per year. The officials said confidently, "We should expect wide circulation on this continent."[86] Apparently, they thought the general public was as fed up with muckrakers and yellow journalists as they themselves were.

Work on the *Monitor* progressed at an incredible speed. Mrs. Eddy had given a deadline of approximately 100 days for founding the paper.[87] A sample copy of *The Christian Science Monitor* was produced on September 15, 1908, roughly a month after the instructions were given to start the paper.[88] On October 17, 1908, the denominational magazine *Christian Science Sentinel* let its readers in on the secret by issuing a call for Christian Scientists in the newspaper business to apply for positions at the upcoming *Monitor*.[89] By its next issue a week later, the *Sentinel* had to say, "It was not known that so large a number of Scientists were now engaged in newspaper work, and so many applications have been received that the invitation to apply is now discontinued."[90]

The *Monitor's* presses were nearly ready to roll. Mary Baker Eddy was about to launch a newspaper that would be an example to journalists everywhere. Referring to the *New York World*, she told one of her students, "Now we will show them what a good newspaper can do."[91]

The rebuke to the *World* and *McClure's* was gentler than their attacks had been, but it was clearly there in the first issue of the *Monitor*. Mrs. Eddy published a letter to the editor by Frank Bell, managing editor of Pennsylvania's

---

[84]Archibald McLellan, "The Christian Science Monitor," *Christian Science Sentinel* (17 October 1908): 130.

[85]Minutes, 11 August 1908 meeting of Christian Science Board of Directors and Trustees of the Publishing Society, quoted in Canham, *Commitment to Freedom: The Story of The Christian Science Monitor*, 25.

[86]Trustees of the Publishing Society and others to Mary Baker Eddy, 13 August 1908, Mother Church Archives.

[87]Daisette D.S. McKenzie to Paul S. Deland, 29 December 1948, quoted in Canham, *Commitment to Freedom: The Story of The Christian Science Monitor*, 24. McKenzie recalled the deadline as about three months.

[88]Mother Church Archives.

[89]"Notice," *Christian Science Sentinel* (17 October 1908): 129.

[90]"Notice," *Christian Science Sentinel* (24 October 1908): 151.

[91]Quoted by Stephen Gottschalk, *The Emergence of Christian Science in American Religious Life* (Berkeley: University of California Press, 1973), 273.

*Harrisburg Telegraph*, deriding sensationalistic reporting. He wrote, "As a newspaper man I thank you for The Christian Science Monitor in prospect, and I feel sure that such will be the sentiment of hundreds of newspaper workers all over the land when The Monitor in fact shall have demonstrated the feasibility of clean journalism." He went on to make a dramatic prediction about the importance of the *Monitor* in the future of newspapers. "A definition of 'monitor' is, 'One who advises,'" Bell wrote, "and I foresee that when this Christian Science Monitor shall have proved that there is such a thing as newspaper successes along non-sensational lines, there will follow a widespread readjustment of news policies, for which I am sure none will be more truly thankful than an army of honest, conscientious toilers in the ranks of newspaperdom."[92] The *Monitor* clearly intended to give legitimacy to journalists who preferred facts to sensation and innuendo. Mrs. Eddy seconded Bell's remarks in her editorial for the inaugural issue. "The gentleman, Mr. Frank Bell, has caught my thunder," she wrote. "The object of The Monitor is to injure no man, but to bless all mankind."[93] It was a far different statement than S.S. McClure's boast two years earlier that he would "ridicule and destroy."

The *Monitor* did just what it intended. It became and has remained a shining light of ethical journalism both in its American and international editions. Although the *Monitor* does not enjoy a huge circulation, it is a rare journalist who will not praise it as the best example of journalistic integrity and sound reporting.

To *McClure's* and the *New York World*, *The Christian Science Monitor* was an unexpected outcome of their campaigns against Christian Science. They had intended to crush the growing religion but instead found they were out of their realm. While muckrakers had effectively exposed the evils of big business, Miss Milmine and S.S. McClure blundered into a world of faith and conviction when they turned on religion. While the *World* had played general by driving the nation into the Spanish-American War, it found that the walls of religious belief would not crumble because the *World* willed it so. In the realm of ideas, it was impossible to say whose faith in God was right and whose was wrong.

Mary Baker Eddy apparently saw the errant crusaders much as Theodore Roosevelt had. He had called crusading journalists "muckrakers" after the character in John Bunyan's *Pilgrim's Progress* who failed to see the heavenly crown being offered because he never looked up from the muck.[94] As Mrs. Eddy apparently saw it, her journalistic antagonists were so blinded by the filth of their trade that they turned their back on a church that was doing just what they advocated: fighting for the common good, battling to restore the sick to health and the sinning to reform. The major difference was, of course, that Christian Science asked followers to do so by taking hold of the heavenly crown. Crusaders tried the more worldly avenues of publication, court challenges, and harassment.

Mrs. Eddy knew what she had to do. "A Christian Scientist reflects the

---

[92]Frank Bell to Mary Baker Eddy, 2 November 1908, in *The Christian Science Monitor* (Boston), 25 November 1908.

[93]Mary Baker Eddy, "Something in a Name," *The Christian Science Monitor*, 25 November 1908.

[94]Theodore Roosevelt, speech, 4 April 1906, quoted in Judson A. Grenier, "Muckraking and the Muckrakers: An Historical Definition," *Journalism Quarterly* 37 (1960): 553. See also John Bunyan, *The Pilgrim's Progress* (1678-1688; reprint, Oxford: The Clarendon Press, 1967), 199-200 in reprint edition.

sweet amenities of Love [God], in rebuking sin, in true brotherliness, charitableness, and forgiveness," she had written.[95] She therefore could not lash out in hatred against her attackers. In the Bible, Jesus commanded that anyone compelled to walk with his brother one mile should walk with him twain instead.[96] Very well. If she were compelled to walk a sensationalistic mile of turn-of-the-century journalism, she would take journalism down a better path for that second mile. She would rebuke the press' sins in a brotherly way by offering reform journalism a model for its own reform in *The Christian Science Monitor.* And, coincidentally, she would gracefully refute the charges that she was insane and on her deathbed by founding a daily newspaper in roughly one hundred days and then directing it until her death nearly two years later as she approached her ninetieth birthday.

In spite of the fact that crusading journalism was on top of the world in 1908, Frank Bell's prophecy in the opening issue of the *Monitor* proved true. The advent of the *Monitor* was followed in a few years by a great shift in American journalism. Although there was no provable connection between the *Monitor* and what eventually happened, sensationalistic crusades by muckrakers and yellow journalists shortly fell from popularity, and the *Monitor* became the world's most admired example of ethical journalism.

---

[95]Eddy, *Manual,* 40.
[96]Matthew 5:41.

# 11

# The Jewish Contribution
# to American Journalism
by Stephen J. Whitfield

THE SUBJECT OF THE RELATIONSHIPS OF JEWS to journalism is entangled in paradox. Their role in the press has long been an obsession of their enemies, and the vastly disproportionate power that Jews are alleged to wield through the media has long been a staple of the antisemitic imagination. The commitment to this version of bigotry has dwarfed the interest that scholars or Jews themselves have shown in this problem, and such disparity merits the slight correction and compensation that this essay offers.

This feature of Judeophobia is perhaps inaugurated in a significant way in the squalid and murky origins of *The Protocols of the Elders of Zion*, the most ubiquitous of antisemitic documents. This forgery had its basis in a chapter of the novel *Biarritz* (1868) by Hermann Gödsche, titled "In the Jewish Cemetery in Prague," which formed the contours of the "Rabbi's Speech" that exposed the methods of the conspiratorial ambition to dominate Christendom and indeed the planet. "If gold is the first power in this world," the rabbi informs his co-conspirators, "the second is undeniably the press.... Our people must become the editors of all daily newspapers in all countries. Our possession of gold, our skill in devising means of exploiting mercenary instincts, will make us the arbiters of public opinion and enable us to dominate the masses." With this influence, the rabbi fiendishly predicts: "We shall dictate to the world what it is to have faith in, what it is to honor, and what it is to curse.... Once we are absolute masters of the press, we will be able to transform ideas about honor, about virtue, about uprightness of character, we will be able to deal a blow against ... the family, and we will be able to achieve its disintegration.... We shall declare open war on everything that people respect and venerate."[1]

This passage from the precursor to the *Protocols* has been quoted at some

---

[1]Norman Cohn, *Warrant for Genocide: The Myth of the Jewish World Conspiracy and the Protocols of the Elders of Zion* (New York, 1967), 273.

length because it foreshadowed the conception of Jewish power in and through journalism that was to be repeated for over a century. It is commonly known that antisemitic fears were stirred by the Jewish involvement in finance; it is insufficiently realized how often this phobia was coupled with animus against the Jewish participation in journalism. As a locus of sinister or repellent Jewish influence, the newsroom was second only to the bourse. A little over a century ago, the historian Heinrich von Treitschke warned that "across our Eastern borders there pushes ... a troop of ambitious, trousers-selling youth, whose children and children's children will someday dominate Germany's exchanges and Germany's press." Nor was the Swiss historian Jacob Burckhardt immune from the impression that Jews exerted special impact upon the "venal" press.[2]

The final German example is extracted from *Mein Kampf*, whose preface explains the book's purpose as an account of the Nazi movement and of the political development of its Führer. The author does so "insofar as it may serve to destroy the foul legends about my person dished up in the Jewish press." Before even getting to the text itself, he reveals his paranoia and his rage — not by alluding to race, or to the dangers of pollution and infection, or to the stock market, or to religion. In his sole reference to Jews in the preface, the author of *Mein Kampf* mentions only "the Jewish press." The chapter retracing his steps in becoming an antisemite bristles with memories of the degenerate Jewish journalists who operated as liberals or as Marxists in *fin-de-siècle* Vienna. "For one Goethe," the inmate of Landsberg Prison concludes, "nature easily can foist on the world 10,000 of these scribblers who poison men's souls."[3]

In more muted form and with shifting emphases, this theme crosses the Atlantic as well. Henry Adams became the most impressive historian of the country that both his grandfather and great-grandfather had served as President. But on the subject of one immigrant group, Secretary of State John Hay remarked, Adams was "clean daft. The Jews are all the press, all the cabinets, all the gods and all weather. I was amazed to see so sensible a man so wild."[4] The most mischievous and important of American Judeophobes was probably the wealthiest citizen of the world's wealthiest country as well. More than anyone else, Henry Ford made the *Protocols* internationally famous. They punctuated the editorial policy of the weekly he owned, the *Dearborn Independent*. From 1920 until 1927 antisemitic columns ran in this newspaper, and the series titled "The International Jew" was later published in book form. The first in the series (May 22, 1920) set the tone. After observing the tentacles of Jewish financiers within the American economy, the editorial announced that "Jewish journalists are a large and powerful group here.... They absolutely control the circulation of publications throughout the country." Later in 1920 Ford's newspaper warned that from the northeastern section of the United States, "poisonous infections of revolutionary doctrine" were being "spread throughout the country upon the wings of 'liberal' publications subsidized by Jewish money."[5]

---

[2] Steven E. Aschheim, *Brothers and Strangers: The East European Jew in Germany and German Jewish Consciousness, 1800-1923* (Madison, 1982), 42-3, 68; George L. Mosse, *Germans and Jews: The Right, the Left, and the Search for a "Third Force" in Pre-Nazi Germany* (New York, 1970), 58.

[3] Adolf Hitler, *Mein Kampf* (Boston, 1943), vii, 57-9, 61.

[4] Hay quoted in John Higham, *Send These to Me: Jews and Other Immigrants in Urban America* (New York, 1975), 183.

[5] Cohn, *Warrant for Genocide*, 159; Morton Rosenstock, *Louis Marshall: Defender of Jewish Rights*

One ambition ascribed to Jews in journalism was to implicate the United States in war. This is a theme not readily found in German antisemitism, probably because the United States has been far less hospitable to militarism and also because the American tradition of isolationism was until fairly recently so tenacious. A little known example of this charge of war-mongering can be located in the writing of H. L. Mencken, an ornament of American letters who was the most inescapable journal of the 1920s. But during the First World War, Mencken's opposition to the conflict and to American intervention made him a beleaguered and rather subdued figure. He was no antisemite, and yet he was impelled to comment in 1922: "Fully four-fifths of all the foreign news that comes to the American newspapers comes through London, and most of the rest is supplied either by Englishmen or by Jews (often American-born) who maintain close relations with the English.... I was in Copenhagen and Basel in 1917," Mencken added, "and found both towns — each an important source of war news — full of Jews representing American journals as a sideline to more delicate and confidential work for the English department of press propaganda."[6] What is peculiar about this appraisal is its direct collision with the assessment of the British ambassador in Washington, Sir Cecil Spring-Rice, who wrote on November 13, 1914 that the American Jewish bankers of German ancestry were "toiling in a solid phalanx to compass our destruction. One by one they are getting hold of the principal New York papers ... and are bringing them over as much as they dare to the German side." Spring-Rice stressed the power of this lobby so adamantly that he may well have curtailed his own career. His government believed him enough to replace him in Washington with a prominent Jew, Lord Reading (Rufus Isaacs), possibly in the hope of placating the American press.[7]

An even more vigorous opponent of American intervention in the Great War than either Ford or Mencken was a Midwestern congressman, Charles A. Lindbergh, Sr.; and in the 1930s his son entered the political cockpit in order to keep the United States out of another European conflict. In a radio speech in Des Moines, Iowa, on September 11, 1941, Lindbergh identified "the three most important groups which have been pressing this country toward war ... the British, the Jewish and the Roosevelt administration." Speaking of the Jews, he warned: "Their greatest danger to this country lies in their large ownership and influence in our motion pictures, our press, our radio and our government." Although his own father's isolationism had been fueled by distrust of Eastern bankers and financiers, Colonel Lindbergh himself underscored Jewish control of what later came to be called the media. He also provided the helpful advice that, by pushing their case for military intervention against Germany, Jews would only encourage antisemitism.[8]

Bigotry that stressed the conspiratorial power of Jewry became inconsistent during the war against Nazism, disreputable after the Holocaust, remorselessly

(Detroit, 1965), 128-9, 130; Leo Ribuffo, "Henry Ford and The International Jew," *American Jewish History* 69 (June 1980): 444-6, 453, 461, 469-70.

[6]H. L. Mencken, *Prejudices: A Selection*, ed. James T. Farrell (New York, 1958), 107-8.

[7]Conor Cruise O'Brien, "Israel in Embryo," *New York Review of Books* 21 (March 15, 1984), 36.

[8]Selig Adler, *The Isolationist Impulse: Its Twentieth Century Reaction* (New York, 1961), 279.

sour after the triumph of a democratic Israel.[9] In the post-World War II era, such hostility found favor primarily in the Soviet bloc and in the Arab world — and among their allies. Let two illustrations suffice to indicate the persistence of this aspect of antisemitism. In 1956 public rallies of the Polish Communist party blamed the country's problems on "the press" and "the race" (the two words rhyme in Polish), neatly updating a familiar combination.[10] And in a 1980 speech before the UN's General Assembly, the Senegalese delegate who headed the Committee on the Exercise of the Unalienable Rights of the Palestinian People complained that news organizations "dominated by Jews" had neglected or distorted the Palestinian cause. The diplomat referred especially to the *New York Times*, the *Washington Post*, and the three American television networks.[11]

But an accusation that could echo from Eastern Europe to the East River has been picked up by almost no American voices. Almost. When Vice President Spiro Agnew blasted the liberal slant of the eastern "establishment" press-primarily television-in 1969 (in the same city as Lindbergh's speech of almost three decades earlier), it was the most vigorous, deliberate assault by a leading official on the press in American political history. Unlike Lindbergh, Agnew made no mention whatsoever of Jews. That did not prevent some of his more excitable supporters from drawing one conclusion from the vice president's condemnation of news organizations in which Jews happened to be prominent, and media figures as well as the American Jewish Committee noticed an increase in antisemitic hate mail. Even as Agnew protested that he was being unfairly smeared for having instigated this vitriolic attack, he told Barbara Walters on NBC's *Today Show* that a "Jewish cabal" exercised mastery of the American media, permitting "Zionist influences" to tilt policy unduly toward Israel. Agnew repeated this charge in published American interviews and even in his novel, *The Canfield Decision* (1976). Two ex-speechwriters for the vice president, William Safire and Victor Gold, denounced Agnew's remarks, which President Ford called "wrong, both substantially and morally."[12] A recent aspirant for Gerald Ford's former job, the Reverend Jesse Jackson, has also taken notice of Jewish influence on American banks and the media.[13]

And yet the paradox mentioned at the outset of this essay bears emphasis: the subject has captivated the adversaries of the Jews far more than it has either Jews themselves or independent scholars. In a biography of Mordecai Noah, the first significant journalist of Jewish origin in the New World, Professor Jonathan D. Sarna states categorically: "There is no history of Jews in American journalism."[14] The researcher is therefore required to begin with specialized monographs, such as biographical portraits of individuals appearing in encyclopedias and reference works. One journalist's book, Stephen D. Isaacs' *Jews and Ameri-*

---

[9]Leonard Dinnerstein, "Anti-Semitism Exposed and Attacked, 1945-1950," *American Jewish History* 71 (September 1981): 134-49.

[10]Zbigniew K. Brzezinski, *The Soviet Bloc: Unity and Conflict* (Cambridge, Mass., 1960), 249n.

[11]*New York Times*, December 16, 1980, 3; "UN Protocols," *New Republic*, 183 (December 27, 1980), 7.

[12]Stephen D. Isaacs, *Jews and American Politics* (Garden City, N.Y., 1974), 50-2; Stephen Birmingham, "Does a Zionist Conspiracy Control the Media?" *MORE* 6 (July-August 1976): 12, 16-7; Deirdre Whiteside, "Agnew: What's the Motive?" *MORE* 6 (July-August 1976): 17.

[13]"Jackson and the Jews," *New Republic*, 190 (March 19, 1984), 9.

[14]Jonathan D. Sarna, *Jacksonian Jew: The Two Worlds of Mordecai Noah* (New York, 1981), 164, n.16.

can Politics, does include a chapter speculating on the apparent over-representation of such journalists on the contemporary political landscape. But the topic is not treated in a historical — much less a general scholarly — way; nor is the overview on the subject of journalism in the Encyclopedia Judaica interpretive. It too is primarily biographical in orientation, tracking the careers and achievements of reporters, editors, and publishers in various countries — one of whom even became the prophet and father of the Zionist state. The only previous scholarly study on the role of Jews in American journalism highlights the critiques that have been rendered of the problematic nature of the press itself.[15] The rest is "no comment."

In breaking this silence, a scholar must weigh without apology the validity of the claim of Jewish over-representation in the media. An argument is not ipso facto false because it is repeated by African champions of the P.L.O., or by a disgraced vice president of the United States. The law of averages works in a fashion that allows for the possibility of even an antisemite being correct some of the time. But however exaggerated or unwarranted the beliefs of bigots may prove to be, the conspicuous attractiveness of journalism for many Jews merits analysis and explanation, within the context of modern Jewish experience. The raw statistics utterly belie the expectations envisioned in the Prague rabbi's speech of dominating the daily press. Nearly 1,800 daily newspapers are currently published in the United States. Jews own about fifty, or less than 3%, which is the proportion of Jews in the general American population.

Even when these particular newspapers' circulation is taken into account (8%), it is evident that newspaper publishing is hardly an awesome sign of Jewish entrepreneurship.[16] There are nearly 9,000 radio stations and more than 600 television network affiliates, but no data on the ethnic and religious identification of their owners appear to be extant. According to the only published figures on the percentage of Jews among American editors and reporters, the 3.3% so identified is only slightly above their proportion in the general population.[17]

The two most newsworthy American cities do, however, seem to be covered by a large fraction of journalists of Jewish birth. According to a 1976 study, a quarter of the Washington press corps was of Jewish background. A volume of Jewish economic history published a year earlier claims that "it has been estimated that ... 40% of ... [New York's] journalists are Jews." Marcus Arkin fails to disclose the basis of this estimate or even its source. But since New York is the media capital of the country, and not only the most populous concentration of Jews on the planet, the proportion of Jews in the general population is more relevant than their percentage in the city itself. Arkin's estimate is therefore almost certainly too high, perhaps much too high.[18]

The proportion of Jews among Washington and New York journalists is probably closer to that of post-World War I Germany than post-World War I

[15]Stephen J. Whitfield, "From Publick Occurrences to Pseudo-Events: Journalists and Their Critics," American Jewish History 72 (September 1982): 52-81.

[16]Kalman Seigel. "Journalism." Encyclopedia Judaica (Jerusalem, 1971), X, 307; Isaacs, Jews and American Politics, 49.

[17]John W. C. Johnstone, Edward J. Slawski, and William W. Bowman, The News People: A Sociological Portrait of American Journalists and Their Work (Urbana, Ill., 1976), ix, 9, 26, 198, 225.

[18]Stanley Rothman and S. Robert Lichter, Roots of Radicalism: Jews, Christians, and the New Left (New York, 1982), 97; Marcus Arkin, Aspects of Jewish Economic History (Philadelphia, 1975), 212-3.

Hungary. There were 740 editors in responsible positions in Prussia in 1925, of whom 41 (a little more than 10%) identified themselves as Jews. By a much more indulgent standard (which would include half-Jews, converts to Christianity, and Jews professing no faith whatsoever), 192 Jews toiled among the 3,475 editorial employees in Prussia that year. Hungary is a more striking case. According to official statistics, among 1,214 journalists in the country in 1910, 516 were Jews. In 1920, the number fell to 358 (36%) and was a little lower in 1930. Such figures, it need not be added, triggered the animosity of Hungary's antisemitic People's Party.[19]

Numbers of course do not correlate with influence, nor participation with impact; and the prestige of certain papers cannot be quantified. Here too analogies in European history can be found. In the Weimar Republic as earlier in the Second Reich, special distinction was conceded to the Jewish-owned *Frankfurter Zeitung* and the publishing houses of Ullstein and Mosse. And the Jewish editorial control of the *Berliner Tageblatt* and the *Vossische Zeitung* typified the Jewish presence across the spectrum of the liberal and leftist press, even though the conservative and right-wing press (dominated by the Hugenberg trust) enjoyed greater circulation. The most prestigious newspaper in Central Europe was undoubtedly Vienna's *Neue Freie Presse*, which Jews published and wrote *feuilletons* for. In the remoter provinces of Franz Josef's empire, some visiting cards contained the following boast below the engraved name of the bearer: "Subscribes to the *Neue Freie Presse*."[20]

In the United States, as Agnew's own partisan speech implied, some news organizations are more respected and important than others. According to one recent survey, the reporters whose beat is Washington, D. C. acknowledge that they are most influenced by: 1) television networks, 2) weekly newsmagazines, 3) the wire service, and 4) four newspapers — the *Washington Post*, the *New York Times*, the *Washington Star*, and the *Wall Street Journal*.[21]

With the exception of the wire services (the Associated Press and United Press International), these are institutions in which Jews have tended to congregate. A 1979 survey revealed that 27% of the employees of the *Times*, the *Post*, the *Wall Street Journal*, *Time*, *Newsweek*, *U. S. News and World Report*, the three networks, and the Public Broadcasting System were of Jewish origin. Fifty-eight per cent of the producers and editors at ABC were Jews.[22] They were conspicuous at the top. The Sulzberger family retains its ownership of the *New York Times*, whose executive editor is A. M. Rosenthal, associate editor is Jack Rosenthal, chief of the editorial page is Max Frankel, and metropolitan editor is Sydney Schanberg. Eugene Meyer had bought the *Washington Post* at an auction in 1933; and it was under the leadership of his daughter, Katherine Graham, raised as a Lutheran, and executive editor Benjamin C. Bradlee, a Brahmin, that the newspaper became the chief rival to the *Times*. For the *Post*'s Pulitzer Prize-

---

[19]*Encyclopedia Judaica*, X, 306; Jacob Rader Marcus, *The Rise and Destiny of the German Jew* (Cincinnati, Ohio, 1934), 97; Nathaniel Katzburg, *Hungary and the Jews, 1920-1943* (Ramat-Gan, Israel, 1981), 21, 30.

[20]Donald L. Niewyk, *The Jews in Weimar Germany* (Baton Rouge, La., 1980), 15; Amos Elon, *Herzl* (New York, 1975), 99.

[21]Stephen Hess, *The Washington Reporters* (Washington, D. C., 1981), 90.

[22]Rothman and Lichter, *Roots of Radicalism*, 97; Edward J. Epstein, *News from Nowhere: Television and the News* (New York, 1973), 222-3.

winning exposure of the Watergate scandal, the two most famous local reporters in history benefited from the support of editors Howard Simons, Harry Rosenfeld, and Barry Sussman. Warren Phillips was editor of the *Wall Street Journal*, whose current managing editor is Norman Pearlstine. Marvin Stone was editor of *U. S. News and World Report*, long the extended shadow of David Lawrence; it is now owned by Morton Zuckerman. Edward Kosner was editor of *Newsweek*. The managing editor of *Time* was Henry Anatole Grunwald, who began as the magazine's part-time copyboy. William Paley was chairman of the board of CBS, while Fred Friendly and Richard Salant were presidents of its news division. The Sarnoff family was long dominant at NBC, whose news division was headed by Richard Wald. Leonard Goldenson was president of ABC, while the executive producer of its evening news was Av Westin. The president of the Public Broadcasting System was Lawrence Grossman. The president of National Public Radio has been Frank Mankiewicz, the son of the co-scenarist of Hollywood's most brilliant film, a portrait of a press lord, *Citizen Kane* (1941).

Statistical measurement cannot convey the impact that Jews have exerted upon American journalism. How can the prestige of the *New York Times* be tabulated? In its authoritativeness as the newspaper of record, in its reputation for accuracy and comprehensiveness, the *Times* is in a class by itself. It has a news staff of 550 in New York alone, where its Times Square newsroom covers 1.3 acres. In communicating "all the news that's fit to print," 6 million trees are chopped down annually. The *Times* Sunday edition typically runs over 400 pages, printed in enough copies to paper over the island of Manhattan twice.[23] But what does it mean for its editors and reporters to realize that their words will be read and pondered in the White House and in the Kremlin, in City Hall, and in the libraries and archives of posterity?

Or how does the scholar measure the impact of Walter Lippmann (1889-1974)? He was probably the most admired American journalist of the twentieth century; and one reputable historian considered him "perhaps the most important [American] political thinker of the twentieth century" as well. Because Lippmann's approach to journalism was interpretative, he made little impression on the process of news gathering. But it was said in Washington during his prime that foreign governments formally accredited their ambassadors to the President and by private letter to Lippmann, who seemed to stride above the etiquette of diplomacy when it suited him. His regular pilgrimages to Europe were so rigorously arranged that, in 1961, Nikita Khrushchev's request to delay Lippmann's Soviet visit by a few days, due to an unanticipated political crisis, was turned down. The Russian dictator then rearranged his *own* plans so that he could meet the American journalist. (The resulting interviews earned Lippmann a second Pulitzer Prize.) Quantification of his stature can sometimes be attempted. When Lippmann spoke at the National Press Club to celebrate his seventieth birthday, more correspondents were in attendance than had come to hear Khrushchev speak in the same room a little earlier.[24]

Or how is the impact of Herbert Bayard Swope (1882-1958) to be assessed?

---

[23]"The Kingdom and the Cabbage," *Time* 110 (August 15, 1977), 73-4, 80.

[24]Introduction to Clinton Rossiter and James Lare, eds., *The Essential Lippmann: A Political Philosophy for Liberal Democracy* (New York, 1965), xi; William L. Rivers, *The Opinionmakers* (Boston, 1965), 59, 60; Ronald Steel, *Walter Lippmann and the American Century* (New York, 1980), 462-3, 526-7.

He won the first Pulitzer Prize for reporting (in 1917) and gained fame as the executive editor of the *New York World* in its heyday, the 1920s (when Lippmann ran the editorial page). He coined the term "op ed" page, a feature for which he was primarily responsible. From a Roosevelt campaign speech of 1932, Swope singled out the phrase "new deal," thus labeling not only an administration but also an era. When it was over, he coined the phrase "the cold war" (which Lippmann gave currency).[25] He instituted the newspaper practice of capitalizing the word "negro"; and under his direction the *World* won a Pulitzer Prize for a series exposing the Ku Klux Klan. Lord Northcliffe of the *London Daily Mail* considered Swope the finest reporter of his time, so that late in the 1920s, when the promising humorist James Thurber sat down in a speakeasy and was told only later that he had been in the company of Swope, he feigned astonishment. He'd been under the impression that Herbert Bayard Swope was a legend. Swope possessed so much *chutzpah*, RCA's David Sarnoff once remarked, "that if you wanted to meet God, he'd arrange it somehow." Maybe that was an exaggeration, but Swope did seem to know everyone else of importance, and never underestimated the value of wire-pulling — sometimes quite literally, as when Swope complained directly to Sarnoff when a friend's television set went on the blink. Swope was so famous that he became one of the first *Time* magazine cover subjects, so arrogant that he listed among his favorite books not only the Bible and the *World Almanac* but also any volume containing a reference to himself, so imperious that he could scoop other reporters by dressing exactly like a diplomat and getting a front row seat at the Versailles Peace Conference. The impression he made was so distinctive, effusive, and flamboyant that, after deluging a convalescent Ring Lardner with get-well messages, the humorist wired back: "CAN'T YOU SUGGEST ANY WAY TO END THIS CORRESPONDENCE AMICABLY STOP MY PERSONAL PHYSICIAN SAYS EXCITEMENT OF HEARING FROM YOU DAILY IS BAD FOR ME...." Swope's written legacy is surprisingly sparse and unenduring, but his hellzapoppin personality lifted him into the most formidable newsman of his age.[26]

Let one other biographical illustration suggest the elusiveness of measuring the Jewish role in American journalism. If Swope lived the myth of American journalism, Ben Hecht (1894-1964) not only partook of it but also, more than anyone else, created it. It is from him that Americans learned newspapermen were corrupt, cynical, wenching, dissolute, coarse, drunken rogues, insensitive to anyone's privacy, oblivious to puritanical codes — and therefore having more fun than anyone else. Born on the Lower East Side, Hecht began his professional career in Chicago at the age of sixteen. His first assignment, given to him by the publisher of the *Chicago Journal*, was to write obscene verses for a stag party. Over a decade of such intimacy with the vulgarities of his profession and the raunchiest features of city life gave him material for *1001 Afternoons in Chicago* (1922) and for later autobiographical novels like *Gaily, Gaily* (1963) and his spirited memoir, *A Child of the Century* (1954). But his greatest achievement as

---

[25]E. J. Kahn, Jr., *The World of Swope* (New York, 1965), 33, 133n, 182-4, 240-1, 260-3; Eric F. Goldman, *The Crucial Decade — and After: America, 1945-1960* (New York, 1960), 60.

[26]Kahn, *The World of Swope*, 7, 16, 26, 30-1, 41, 55n, 226-8, 360; Rosemarian V. Staudacher, "Herbert Bayard Swope," in Perry J. Ashley, ed., *American Newspaper Journalists, 1900-1925* (Detroit, 1984), 280-90.

a mythmaker was *The Front Page* (1928), in collaboration with Charles Mac-Arthur.[27] This piece of gallows humor has bobbed up in three Hollywood versions, the last directed by the Viennese *bon vivant*, Billy Wilder, who had learned in the pages of Karl Kraus' *Die Fackel*, among other forums, of the pertinence of journalism as a peephole into modern malaise.[28] Newspaper experiences were the capital that Hecht drew upon for writing fiction and films, and his recounting became the standard against which the vicissitudes of the profession came to be measured.

Since such examples could be multiplied, the limitations of space make it impossible (as newsboys used to scream) to "read all about it." It is therefore preferable to elucidate such impact rather than merely illustrate it.

One theory that should not be immediately discounted is that Jews are simply more talented than other peoples. Their gifts could flourish especially after the walls of medieval ghettoes tumbled, after the isolation of the *shtetlach* was punctured, as centuries of frustrated energies seemed to evaporate within a couple of generations. The belief in the superiority of the Jewish "race" was enunciated not only by Disraeli but also by nineteenth century writers less susceptible to romanticism. Nietzsche, for instance, acknowledged the Jews' "energy and higher intelligence, their accumulated capital of spirit and will, gathered from generation to generation through a long school of suffering." Thus Nietzsche explained their preponderance.[29] Mark Twain was impressed by the "marvelous fight in this world" that the Jew had made, "with his hands tied behind him." Even at the dusk of the nineteenth century, the Jew was "exhibiting no decadence, no infirmities of age, no weakening of his parts, no slowing of his energies, no dulling of his alert and aggressive mind."[30] Exceptional accomplishment was therefore the predicate of exceptional talent, and antisemitism the consequence of envy aroused by "racial" superiority.

But whatever tribute such testimony pays to Jewish self-esteem, it leaves unexplained why Jewish influence is more pronounced in some fields than others, why Jews gravitate toward some occupations rather than others. Even if all forms of ethnic and racial discrimination in the United States were to be miraculously obliterated, its occupational structure would probably not reveal a random distribution of minorities. Their experiences and values are hardly identical, and therefore their predispositions and interests can in the aggregate be expected to diverge. Neither talent nor intelligence can be summoned at random, to be enlisted and developed whenever a barrier of discrimination is battered down.

Even if there were some way of "proving" the superior mental endowment of the Jewish people, even if the application of its gifts could be sorted out, history would still have to be appealed to in accounting for the special responsiveness of many Jews to opportunities in liberal professions such as journalism. There has

---

[27]Ben Hecht, *A Child of the Century* (New York, 1955), 108, 112-3, 180-1, 364-5; Doug Fetherling, *The Five Lives of Ben Hecht* (Toronto, 1977), 18-41, 71-86.

[28]Kenneth Tynan, *Show People: Profiles in Entertainment* (New York, 1979), 116; Anthony Heilbut, *Exiled in Paradise: German Refugee Artists and Intellectuals in America from the 1930's to the Present* (New York, 1983), 254; Maurice Zolotow, *Billy Wilder in Hollywood* (New York, 1977), 273.

[29]Nietzsche quoted in Walter Kaufmann, *Nietzsche: Philosopher, Psychologist, Antichrist*, 3rd. ed. (Princeton, N. J., 1968), 289.

[30]Mark Twain, "Concerning the Jews," in *The Complete Essays of Mark Twain*, ed. Charles Neider (Garden City, N.Y., 1963), 249.

to be some sort of "fit" between skill and milieu, between potentiality and circumstance. That is why the *Encyclopedia Judaica* dates the Jewish contribution to European journalism at the beginning of Emancipation itself, conjecturing that a people already relatively urban and literate found itself "in the right place at the right time." Moreover, the encyclopedia asserts, the "gift of adaptability permitted the Jew to act as an intermediary, the link between the event and the reader, as the journalist has often been called." The press offered "brightness and novelty," an outlet for a people that felt little if any devotion to pre-modern tradition. Also pertinent here are the speculations of sociologist Arthur Ruppin that "city life forces people into intensive interaction, into an exchange of goods and ideas. It demands constant mental alertness.... The great mental agility of the Jews ... enabled them to have a quick grasp and orientation in all things...."[31]

Such comments get us closer to the truth, though they would appear to be more applicable to the nineteenth century than to the twentieth. They are more useful in explaining the initial attraction that journalism might have exerted on the newly emancipated, not why — if anything — the Jewish involvement has persisted without noticeable loss of intensity. By the twentieth century, especially long past its midpoint, the relative historical advantages that literacy and urbanity might have conferred should have become quite marginal. The conjectures of the encyclopedia and of Ruppin undoubtedly apply more directly to Europe than to the United States, which was post-Emancipation from its inception as an independent nation and has posed no official restrictions upon Jews.

This theory, like others, suffers from the disadvantage of blurring or ignoring the distinction between journalists themselves and their employers. With some important exceptions, Jews often achieved prominence on the business side before the expressive side. This distinction was put most cogently by A. J. Liebling, who realized early on that he "did not belong to a joyous, improvident professional group including me and [publisher] Roy Howard, but to a section of society including me and any floorwalker at Macy's. Mr. Howard, even though he asked to be called Roy, belonged in a section that included him and the gent who owned Macy's. This clarified my thinking about publishers, their common interests and motivations."[32] Liebling himself wrote primarily for *The New Yorker*, where there was publisher Raoul Fleischmann before there was editor William Shawn.

But the persuasiveness of the generalization depends in part on what one makes of Joseph Pulitzer (1847-1911), certainly among the most inventive and spectacular figures in *fin-de-siècle* journalism. The format and style of the two newspapers he owned, the *St. Louis Post-Dispatch* and the *New York World*, established the rules for layouts, features, and photography that newspapers in this century have largely been content to imitate. In the late nineteenth century, as American antisemitism was approaching its peak, Pulitzer bore the handicap of being considered a Jew, without enjoying the spiritual advantages that adherents of Judaism can cultivate. His father was part-Jewish, his mother was a Catholic, he himself was at least nominally an Episcopalian, and his children were not raised as Jews. In the haunted, afflicted years of his greatest wealth and fame,

---

[31] *Encyclopedia    Judaica*, X, 303-4; Ruppin quoted in Raphael Patai, *The Jewish Mind* (New York, 1977), 377-8.
[32] A. J. Liebling, *The Wayward Pressman* (Garden City, N.Y., 1947), 103-4.

Pulitzer employed a series of secretaries to read to him the news that his failing eyesight prohibited him from following. There is some grandeur in his insistence that his secretaries be capable of literate and sparkling conversation. There is none in the advice that the young men were given not to speak to the publisher on the topic of Jews.[33]

Adolph S. Ochs (1858-1935), who bought the *New York Times* in 1896, harbored his own sensitivities on the topic. But his identity as a Jew was not in doubt. He married the daughter of the most innovative of nineteenth century rabbis, Isaac Mayer Wise; and he and his descendants remained members of the flagship Reform synagogue, Temple Emanuel. "Religion is all that I stand for as a Jew," Ochs announced in 1925. "I know nothing else, no other definition for a Jew except religion." So constrained a classification exhibited a logic of its own. Faith was so private and minor a feature of family life that his descendants and relatives generally were informed that they were Jewish on the eve of their departure for boarding school. Having severed the bonds of peoplehood, the Sulzberger family through its foundation gave a pittance to Jewish philanthropies: $1,800 to the U.J.A. in 1973, $900 the year after the Yom Kippur War.[34]

But limiting Jewishness to religious belief did not keep the family that has owned the *Times* from realizing that others might be troubled by Jewish "clannishness" and cohesiveness, and therefore much effort was expended to limit the perception of the *Times* as a "Jewish" newspaper. If the business side preceded the expressive and editorial side, that was because it was undoubtedly a matter of *Times* policy. Under Ochs, Arthur Hays Sulzberger, and Orville Dryfoos, no Jew rose to the position of managing editor. That barrier was scaled by A. M. Rosenthal, but only after the chief foreign correspondent, Cyrus L. Sulzberger, kept him from covering a UN conference in 1948: "One Jew in Paris is enough." In 1952, when Daniel Schorr, then a *Times* stringer in the Low Countries, asked for a staff position, C. L. Sulzberger rebuffed him with the observation that "we have too many Jews in Europe.[35] It is commonly believed that Theodore Bernstein, the newspaper's authority on usage, the "technical genius" of the bullpen, could have risen to the post of managing editor had he been a Gentile. It is also widely assumed that *Times* policy once disguised the given names of Jews, so that bylines were given to A. (for Abraham) M. Rosenthal, A. (for Abraham) H. Raskin, *et al.* The current associate editor, Jacob Rosenthal, forced the *Times* to break its rule against informality; the masthead lists him, rather incongruously, as Jack Rosenthal.[36]

The history of American journalism cannot exclude Jews whose interest was not in deadlines or headlines but merely in the bottom line. Terms like "brightness and novelty," or bridging the gap "between the event and the reader," make little sense in evaluating the career of Samuel I. Newhouse (1895-1979). He took charge of his first newspaper, the *Bayonne Times*, at the age of

---

[33]W. A. Swanberg, *Pulitzer* (New York, 1967), 8, 33-9;42, 1361 377.

[34]Harrison E. Salisbury, *Without Fear or Favor: The New York Times and Its Times* (New York, 1980), 28-30; Gay Talese, *The Kingdom and the Power* (Cleveland, 1969), 59, 91-4, 168-9; Birmingham, "Does a Zionist Conspiracy Control the Media?" 14, 15.

[35]Salisbury, *Without Fear or Favor*, 28-9, 401; Isaacs, *Jews and American Politics*, 47-8.

[36]Talese, *The Kingdom and the Power*, 59, 60, 91-3, 109-16, 168; Salisbury, *Without Fear or Favor*, 403; Birmingham, "Does a Zionist Conspiracy Control the Media?" 15.

seventeen. By the time of his death, he owned thirty-one newspapers, seven magazines, six television stations, five radio stations, twenty cable-TV stations, and even a wire service. Only two other newspaper chains were larger; none was more profitable. But profit was all that mattered to Newhouse; no publisher was less interested in the editorial policies, which varied, of the newspapers he owned. He didn't bother reading his own products, preferring the *Times* instead. His credo was simple: "Only a newspaper which is a sound business operation can be a truly free, independent editorial enterprise." His sons now direct his empire.[37] Entrepreneurship having nothing to do with expressiveness has also characterized the careers of Moses Annenberg (1878-1942), the immigrant who founded Triangle Publications (the *Daily Racing Form, Philadelphia Inquirer, New York Morning Telegraph*), and his son, Walter, who founded *Seventeen* as well as the magazine with over 17 million readers, the second greatest circulation in the United States, *TV Guide*.[38] Dorothy Schiff, the former publisher of the *New York Post*, whose grandfather was the venerable communal leader and banker Jacob Schiff, undoubtedly spoke for her peers when she confirmed an axiom that, "once you reach a certain financial level, people don't think of you as anything but very rich." Unpredictable and frivolous, she ran the *Post* from 1939 till 1976 in a style akin to the last line in *Citizen Kane*: "I think it would be fun to run a newspaper!"[39] They belong to the history of American business, not the *Oxford Companion to American Literature*.

Other explanations for the Jewish predilection for journalism also merit scrutiny and criticism. In *Jews and American Politics*, Stephen Isaacs argues that the intellectual and verbal resourcefulness that Jews have historically cherished is rewarded in the mass media.[40] Since the deities and divinities that peoples worship are clues to their culture, it is no surprise that the Jewish God is something of an intellectual, since the rabbis believed that even He studies the Torah. By now Isaacs' explanation smacks of a commonplace — which does not mean that it is false, only that it is familiar. Truisms are often hard to separate from truths, and this one at least has the virtue of identifying the core of values that may be the matrix of a Jewish occupational proclivity as well as a contrast with other values stressed among Gentiles. If the Jewish encounter with modern society does differ from the experience of others, the explanation may well be connected to alternative beliefs.

But Isaacs' theory is also quite restricted. Almost no publishers or network executives have been intellectuals. The celebrated journalists who grew up ignorant of the Judaic religion and stress upon the Word would make a long list. Nor does the explanation incorporate those journalists whose success has been visual rather than verbal. The most prestigious award of the National Cartoonists Society, for example, is called the "Reuben," in honor of the first president of the society, Rube Goldberg. The most honored of political cartoonists is the

[37]Richard H. Meeker, *Newspaperman: S. I. Newhouse and the Business of News* (New Haven, 1983), 2-3, 23, 158, 165, 166; *Time*, 114 (September 10, 1979), 68.

[38]John E. Cooney, *The Annenbergs* (New York, 1982), 56, 66-7, 126, 160-1, 184-6, 380; A. James Reichley, "Moe's Boy Walter at the Court of St. James's," *Fortune* 81 (June 1970), 88, 90-3, 134, 136, 139.

[39]Dorothy Schiff quoted in Jeffrey Potter, *Men, Money and Magic: The Story of Dorothy Schiff* (New York, 1977), 123; Jack Newfield, *Bread and Roses Too* (New York, 1971), 237-44; Nora Ephron, *Scribble Scribble: Notes on the Media* (New York, 1979), 1-9.

[40]Isaacs, *Jews and American Politics*, 43-4.

*Washington Post's* Herbert Block ("Herblock"). Al Capp (*né* Caplin) created the Dogpatch of *Li'l Abner*, which was syndicated in 500 newspapers and has entered the mainstream of popular culture. Verbal resourcefulness had nothing to do with the photojournalism of Erich Salomon in Germany, Alfred Eisenstaedt in Germany and then with *Life* magazine, or Robert and Cornell Capa, Budapest-born brothers whose original name was Friedmann. Probably the most famous shot ever taken by an American photojournalist was Joe Rosenthal's depiction of four U. S. Marines raising the flag on Iwo Jima — an icon of heroism and patriotism. And in sports announcing one cannot ignore such figures as Mel Allen and Howard Cosell, or Nat Fleischer of *Ring* magazine, whose approach to subjects like the New York Yankees and Muhammad Ali bore little trace of Talmudic learning.

Stephen Isaacs also notes the Jewish representation in a field that, "like all forms of mass education, prizes the non-ethnicity of universalism" and especially the ideal of objectivity. Those opting for journalism as a career might therefore hope to be judged by their merit, not their religious or national origin.[41]

This generalization is partially valid, for the Jews attracted to it have usually been quite assimilated and deracinated, eager or anxious to blend into civil society. One of the most brilliant editors of the *Neue Freie Presse*, Theodor Herzl, was far down that road himself; and after he had been irrevocably stung by the spectacle of antisemitism, he dreamed of a mass conversion of Jews at St. Stephen's Cathedral.[42] Perhaps this is not too farfetched a context to discuss the star foreign correspondent of the *New York Daily Tribune* from 1852 till 1862, Karl Marx. His parents having converted, Marx was formally baptized as a Lutheran; and he grew up into an atheist. It is less well-known that the only occupation for which he was ever paid was journalism. When he edited the *Rheinische Zeitung*, Marx depended on Jewish businessmen in Cologne for support; but his greatest success was writing for the American newspaper edited by Horace Greeley. Marx submitted 350 articles that he himself wrote, plus another dozen in collaboration with F. Engels. The *Tribune's* managing editor, Charles A. Dana, once announced that Marx was "not only one of the most highly valued, but one of the best-paid contributors attached to the journal." The contributions ceased in 1862, however, when Greeley fired Dana, who had permitted antisemitic material to be published in the *Tribune*. Several articles infected with such material had been submitted by Marx.[43]

Perhaps the epitome of the "non-ethnicity of universalism" was Lippmann. In the more than 10 million printed words of wisdom and counsel that he imparted in his lifetime, Jews were almost never mentioned. He did write an analysis of antisemitism for the *American Hebrew* in 1922, blaming the excrescence of bigotry primarily on the vulgarity and ostentatiousness of nouveaux riches Jews themselves. Lippmann claimed that Jews were oversensitive on the subject of discrimination and urged them to uphold "the classic Greek virtue of moderation." No one was more anxious to suppress whatever bound him to ancestral custom and belief. He agreed that his *alma mater*, Harvard College, was correct

---

[41]Ibid., 45.

[42]Elon, *Herzl*, 114-7.

[43]David McLellan, *Karl Marx: His Life and Thought* (New York, 1973), 285-9; Lewis S. Feuer, *Marx and the Intellectuals: A Set of Post-Ideological Essays* (Garden City, N.Y., 1969), 38.

in imposing a limit on Jewish admissions. More than 15% of the student body, Lippmann suspected, would generate a *Kulturkampf*; and his own "sympathies are with the non-Jew[,] ... [whose] personal manners and physical habits are, I believe, distinctly superior to the prevailing manners of the Jew."[44] From 1933, no column by the most influential pundit of his time mentioned the persecution of Jews in the Third Reich, though two columns in 1938 did suggest that the "surplus" population of Europe should be sent to Africa — the very continent that the Zionists had tumultuously rejected four decades before. During the Holocaust Lippmann wrote nothing about the camps; afterwards he wrote nothing either. Though he never converted to any version of Christianity, Lippmann's efforts to obscure his own origins reached ludicrous proportions. For a book of tributes on his seventieth birthday, a boyhood friend realized that the sage would never speak to him again were the fact of Jewishness — a birth defect — mentioned. (It wasn't.) Ronald Steel's excellent biography records the nervousness that one friend experienced in playing Scrabble with Lippmann. She worried that the letters forming the word "Jew" might come up, perhaps upsetting the champion of disinterested reason, the Apollonian savant who wrote in 1915: "Man must be at peace with the sources of his life. If he is ashamed of them, if he is at war with them, they will haunt him forever. They will rob him of the basis of assurance, will leave him an interloper in the world."[45]

One final case of how fiercely such journalists tried to bleach out their origins is A. J. Liebling (1904-1963). A crack reporter at the *New York World* under the direction of Swope, he became the inventor of modern criticism of the press and was among the shrewdest monitors of its performance. Liebling bragged that he could "write better than anyone who could write faster, and faster than anyone who could write better." Both of Lippmann's wives were Gentiles; so were all three of Liebling's. Identifying with the Irish toughs among whom he was raised, attending Dartmouth when it was perhaps the most religiously restrictive of Ivy League colleges, Liebling became a war correspondent for *The New Yorker* and was more pained by the devastation that Nazi Germany was wreaking on France than on European Jewry. His third wife commented: "Even Hitler didn't make him an intensely self-conscious Jew." Liebling once declined to attend a literary salon on Manhattan's Upper West Side because "sheenies who are meanies will be there." He was an eccentric as well as a witty and facile craftsman who suffered the strangest of deaths, because he was a gourmand who became a glutton. Devouring the forbidden foods like lobsters, clams, and oysters, Liebling simply ate himself to death.[46]

There are of course exceptions to Isaacs' generalization; a few American journalists did not propel themselves furiously from their Jewish origins for the sake of a neutral or abstract universalism. Although Mordecai Noah (1785-1851) was

---

[44]Walter Lippmann, "Public Opinion and the American Jew," *American Hebrew* 110 (April 14, 1922), 575; Steel, *Walter Lippmann and the American Century*, 188-95.

[45]Anthony Lewis, "The Mysteries of Mr. Lippmann," *New York Review of Books* 27 (October 9, 1980), 5; Steel, *Walter Lippmann and the American Century*, 195-6, 330-3, 373-6, 446; David Halberstam, *The Powers That Be* (New York, 1979), 370; Carl Binger, "A Child of the Enlightenment," in Marquis Childs and James Reston, eds., *Walter Lippmann and His Times* (New York, 1959), 21-8; Walter Lippmann, *The Stakes of Diplomacy* (New York, 1915), 62-3; D. Steven Blum, *Walter Lippmann: Cosmopolitanism in the Century of Total War* (Ithaca, N. Y., 1984), 36-9, 43-4.

[46]Raymond Sokolov, *Wayward Reporter: The Life of A. J. Liebling* (New York, 1980), 1, 9, 14, 21, 25, 30, 42, 98-9, 135, 151-2, 232, 262-3, 305, 310.

a "restorationist" rather than a genuine forerunner of Zionism (before the term had been coined), he was an advocate of Jewish rights as well as a skillful, polemical journalist who helped usher in the form of mass communications associated with the liveliness and sensationalism of the penny press.[47] Ben Hecht, for whom a boat transporting refugees illegally to Palestine was named, was certainly the most fervent Jewish nationalist to emerge from American journalism. He became a leading champion of the Irgun, and an indignant critic of David Ben-Gurion. But his blazing opposition to Nazism and commitment to Jewish rights came after his newspaper career was essentially abandoned. Swope's support of the Jewish Telegraphic Agency, his presence at the creation of the Overseas News Agency, and his fundraising for the United Jewish Appeal also transpired after he had ceased working for the *World* or any other newspaper. He had nothing to do with the astonishing decision of his brother, Gerard, once the president of General Electric, to bequeath the bulk of his estate (nearly $8 million) to Haifa's Technion in 1957.[48] A younger example of comfort with Jewish identity is Martin Peretz, who edited the campus newspaper at Brandeis University and in 1974 became the editor-in-chief of *The New Republic* (which Lippmann had helped to found six decades earlier). Peretz has presumably been responsible for the considerable interest that the magazine has shown in the Middle East, primarily from a Labor Zionist perspective.[49]

If the rarity of such figures tends to corroborate Isaacs' point, an even more striking phenomenon invalidates it. For if objectivity and universalism are supposed to have made the profession so appealing, the influx of Jews to journals of opinion and to partisan organs would not be so large. Neutrality would hardly characterize *The New Republic* from Lippmann and Walter Weyl through Gilbert Harrison to Peretz, nor *The Nation* under Victor Navasky, nor *Dissent* under Irving Howe, Lewis Coser, and Michael Walzer, nor *The Progressive* under Morris Rubin, nor *Partisan Review* under Philip Rahv and William Phillips, nor *The New York Review of Books* under Robert Silvers and Barbara Epstein, nor *The Public Interest* under Daniel Bell, Irving Kristol, and Nathan Glazer. Norman Cousins, for three decades editor-in-chief of the *Saturday Review*, played an influential role in the genesis of the nuclear test ban treaty of 1963. Having already helped found SANE (Committee for a Sane Nuclear Policy), Cousins was asked by President Kennedy to organize a citizens' committee for a nuclear test ban treaty to press for senatorial ratification. Cousins contributed $400,000 of his own money in that effort, even selling the *Saturday Review* to do so — a triumph of political belief over journalistic professionalism. The Nixon administration's "enemies list," which was provided to the Senate's Watergate investigating committee in 1973, included CBS's Daniel Schorr ("a real media enemy") and Marvin Kalb; NBC's Sander Vanocur; and columnists Sydney Harris, Joseph Kraft, Max Lerner, and Frank Mankiewicz.[50]

The underground press that surfaced in the 1960s made no pretense of reach-

---

[47]Sarna, *Jacksonian Jew*, 152.

[48]Hecht, *Child of the Century*, 84, 482-586; Fetherling, *Five Lives of Ben Hecht*, 119-39; Kahn, *World of Swope*, 433-9.

[49]Robert Leiter, "Renaissance Man," *Present Tense* 11 (Winter 1984): 18-23; William A. Henry III, "Breaking the Liberal Pattern," *Time* 124 (October 1, 1984), 78.

[50]Fred W. Friendly, *The Good Guys, The Bad Guys and the First Amendment* (New York, 1976), 34; Donald Paneth, *The Encyclopedia of American Journalism* (New York, 1983), 511.

ing for the asymptote of objectivity. A short list of its luminaries would include Paul Krassner (*The Realist*), Marvin Garson (*The Berkeley Barb*), Jeff Shero (*Rat*), Allan Katzman (*East Village Other*), and Jesse Kornbluth and Marshall Bloom (Liberation News Service). Like other radical journalists, from the dawn of the twentieth century, their writing was a direct extension of their politics and indistinguishable from it (indeed often a substitute for political action). Consider Trotsky's remarkable refusal of Lenin's offer, immediately after the October Revolution of 1917, to head the new revolutionary government. Trotsky, whose nickname was *Pero* (the Pen), wanted to direct the press instead. Having come from New York earlier that year, where he had made his living as a journalist, Trotsky exhibited an understandable preference.[51]

Even the slightest nod in the direction of comparative history would sabotage Isaacs' stress on the attractiveness of objectivity. American newspapers have generally developed in the direction of defining themselves in terms of the gathering and dissemination of information, as quickly as possible, under the aegis of impartiality. But European newspapers, say, from the Congress of Vienna until the rise of Nazism operated according to other principles — pronouncing (and therefore forming) opinions, promoting a set of political and cultural attitudes. Such journalism was a forum for the *Weltanschauungen* of publishers, editors, and writers. And yet Jews flourished as fully in such an environment as have journalists of Jewish birth in the United States. It was not because of the allure of objectivity that Herzl won success as a *feuilletoniste* for the *Neue Freie Presse*, nor Léon Blum as a critic in the French socialist press, nor Arthur Koestler as a correspondent for the Ullstein house in Berlin.

Even within the context of American media, objectivity is not universally prized, quite apart from the growing suspicion that it may be impossible to attain. Lippmann and David Lawrence largely invented the syndicated column of opinion and interpretation. Its eminent practitioners today include David Broder, Joseph Kraft, Paul Greenberg, and Anthony Lewis. The career of William Safire suggests how misleading it would be to remove the study of journalism from cognate fields. Safire began as a public relations counselor (once called "press agent"), became a speechwriter for Richard Nixon in particular, then a lexicographer, a novelist, and primarily a columnist — honored with a Pulitzer Prize — for the *New York Times*, all without breaking stride. Swope saw no conflict between his role as an editor and his services as a publicity flack for Bernard Baruch.[52]

For in every vocation affecting public opinion and taste, Jews have achieved prominence. Edward L. Bernays, a nephew of Sigmund Freud, was one of the two pioneers of public relations. Albert Lasker played a comparably innovative role in advertising. Paul Lazarsfeld, who came to the United States from Vienna in 1935, was (among other accomplishments) a pivotal figure in marketing research. So was his pupil, Ernest Dichter,[53] who became a lay analyst in Vienna

---

[51]Robert S. Wistrich, *Trotsky: Fate of a Revolutionary* (London, 1979), 140.

[52]Victor S. Navasky, "Safire Appraised," *Esquire* 97 (January 1982), 44-50; Jordan A. Schwarz, *The Speculator: Bernard M. Baruch in Washington, 1917-1965* (Chapel Hill, N. C., 1981), 201-6.

[53]Edward L. Bernays, *Biography of an Idea: Memoirs of Public Relations Counsel: Edward L. Bernays* (New York, 1965), passim; Richard S. Tedlow, *Keeping the Corporate Image: Public Relations and Business 1900-1950* (Greenwich, Conn., 1979), 39-45, 91-7; John Gunther, *Taken at the Flood: The Story of Albert D. Lasker* (New York, 1960), 44-78, 146-73, 193-222, 244-56; Daniel J. Czitrom, *Media and the*

(with an office across the street from Freud) and later pioneered in motivational research (first for CBS). Samuel Lubell, Louis Harris, David Garth, and Daniel Yankelovich have been among the nation's leading pollsters. They are now an obligatory adjunct of politics as well as journalism, yet their vocation does not regard the standard of disinterested objectivity as always relevant to its purposes.

There is another possible explanation for the disproportionate impact that Jews have exerted in the American media. It is advanced tentatively, because it is at best only partly satisfactory, because it cannot cover all the cases or withstand all objections. No theory on this subject can. But it enjoys the advantage of taking into account the experience of other countries in the Diaspora, and applies especially well to the particularities of the American framework. The speculation allows one to acknowledge the historical singularity of the Jewish people without requiring for its theoretical validity the journalists' knowledge of or fidelity to Judaic tradition and values.

This thesis holds that the press has been a key instrument in the recognition that we inhabit one world — not one village or valley or province or nation. Journalism is not only a bridge between reader and event, as the *Encyclopedia Judaica* avers, but between people and people. And a certain dispersed and vulnerable minority might be especially sensitive to the recalcitrant problems posed by human diversity and plurality. Exile made the Jews aware that the world is larger than parochial and even national boundaries, and some Jews became hopeful that those borders might be transcended. Positioned as outsiders, they were vouchsafed the knowledge of relatives and other co-religionists abroad, were given at least a glimmering sense that there *was* an abroad, a life elsewhere. Jews were therefore responsive to cosmopolitanism, or trans-nationalism, a tendency to see the world as one.

Such a marginal situation and such an international spirit have commonly been appreciated by scholars explaining the Jewish penchant for trade, even though the Biblical Hebrews were not famous for their business acumen. In describing the comparatively large number of Jews working for American newspapers prior to the Civil War, Professor Sarna has observed that "journalism. ..permitted the kind of independence and mobility that Jews have often looked for in their occupations.... Commerce on a large or small scale," he added, "depends on information. Jewish merchants, travelers, peddlers and, of course, relatives served as 'reporters' long before the public press had any interest in printing the news." But other scholars have not extended or tested Sarna's claim that "Jews had the kind of cosmopolitan outlook that journalism demands.[54] Too little curiosity has been piqued by this explanation for the Jewish attraction to journalism.

The cosmopolitan character of mass communications can be verified biographically. The effort to reduce the gaps of time and distance was especially pronounced in the career of Israel Ben Josephat (1816-1899), a rabbi's son who was baptized in Berlin in 1844 and moved to London in 1851. He became best known for founding the news agency Reuters, for he eventually became Baron Paul Julius von Reuter. He began with pigeons, then cable, and then telegraph

---

*American Mind: From Morse to McLuhan* (Chapel Hill, N. C., 1982), 127-36; "Ernest Dichter," *Current Biography*, 1961 (New York, 1962), 130-2.

[54]Sarna, *Jacksonian Jew*, 5-6.

— just as he followed political reports with commercial news and then general news. Reuters thus became perhaps the leading international news agency.[55] The inventor of the press interview, the prime "pseudo-event," was Henri Blowitz-Opper (1825-1903). He was born in Bohemia, wrote for Parisian newspapers, and became a French citizen, but achieved widest recognition as a correspondent for *The Times* of London.[56]

It was not necessary, however, to be an immigrant to seize the possibilities of communicating to newly literate, increasingly enfranchised, and empowered masses. Joseph Moses Levy (1812-1888) owned and edited the *Sunday Times* for a year; but he is more important for having published, beginning in 1855, London's first penny morning newspaper, the *Daily Telegraph*. Levy simply cut the previous price in half. The *Daily Telegraph* was Liberal until 1879, after which it switched to the Conservatives. Levy's eldest son, Edward Levy-Lawson, succeeded him, making the paper livelier in its presentation of news and famous for its crusades.[57] Thus father and son played roughly the same roles in British journalism that were performed by two quite different figures in the United States. The American innovator of the penny press was not a Jew, but he was an immigrant: James Gordon Bennett, a Scotsman. An even more pivotal practitioner of mass journalism was Pulitzer, the immigrant from Hungary. The tableau of his final years — with teams of secretaries reading to Pulitzer his favorite German and French literary works in their original languages — is a sign of how cosmopolitan a figure he cut in American journalism.

Of course the American case is complicated by the obvious fact that it has been a nation of immigrants; and a thesis that is scientifically elegant would have to demonstrate that immigrant Jews, or immigrants generally, were represented in journalism more fully than in the American populace. Such validation cannot be accomplished, and impressionistic evidence will have to do.

For it is striking that Adolph Ochs of the *Times* and William Paley of CBS were the sons of immigrants; David Sarnoff of RCA/NBC was born in Russia. Lippmann had made many trips to Europe as a child and was attuned to advanced European thinkers like Bergson, Wallas, and Freud. Swope, Hecht, and Liebling were also the sons of immigrants; and Liebling's dying words could not be understood because they were delivered in French.[58] The closest American equivalent of the *feuilleton* was undoubtedly "Topics of the Times," whose anonymous but much-admired author was Simeon Strunsky, born in Russia. Even today, long after the era of mass migration of Jews is over, the editorial page of the *Times* is directed by Max Frankel, born in Germany. Abe Rosenthal was born in Canada to immigrants from Russia. Henry Anatole Grunwald, the chief of all Time, Inc. editorial enterprises, was born in Vienna. Luce himself, the co-inventor of the newsmagazine, was born in China to Presbyterian missionary parents; and the Calvinist sobriety and rectitude of the *Times'* James Reston may well have stemmed from his Scottish birthplace. Such biographical

---

[55]Graham Storey, *Reuters: The Story of a Century of News-Gathering* (New York, York, 1951), 3-31, 87; *Encyclopedia Judaica*, XIV, 111-2.

[56]*Encyclopedia Judaica*, IV, 1134-5; Ernst Kahn, "The *Frankfurter Zeitung*," *Lee Baeck Yearbook* (London, 1957), II, 229.

[57]*The Times* (London), *The History of The Times: The Tradition Established, 1841-1884* (London, 1939), 294-6; *Encyclopedia Judaica*, X, 1489-90.

[58]Sokolov, *Wayward Reporter*, 320.

data are suggestive.[59]

There is, however, no philosopher's stone that can transmute the unstable mixture of competing theories into the purity of a single explanation. Even though monocausality lacks credence, a stress upon the cosmopolitan sympathies of Jews would rectify scholarly neglect.

Complications will continue to bedevil the study of Jews in American journalism. Even though the subject cannot be studied in isolation, confined to the twelve-mile limit of the shores of the United States, it must also be fixed within the compass of a society in which an independent press has flourished and in which the talented, the ambitious, and the lucky could often be handsomely rewarded. Freedom of the press has occupied a central place in the democratic design; and even wayward pressmen could point out that their occupation is one of the few (along with the clergy, firearms production, and the liquor business) granted Constitutional protection. Jefferson committed the logical flaw of the excluded middle term when he expressed a preference for "newspapers without a government" over "a government without newspapers."[60] But his extravagant tribute to journalism was to echo for nearly two centuries of the republic, even though individual journalists have been hated and vilified, lost duels, and been beaten up and tarred and feathered and murdered. Their power has been respected even when it has not always been exalted. It failed to strike Americans as odd that one of the legendary lawmen of the Old West, "Bat" Masterson (1853-1921), ended up as an editor of the *New York Morning Telegraph*.[61] It was also natural for the comic book creators of Superman, Joe Shuster and Jerome Siegel, to provide the man of steel and righteousness with the earth-bound identity of a newspaper reporter, Clark Kent of the *Daily Planet*. Perhaps the most beloved of recent Presidents, John F. Kennedy, was first employed as a journalist (the only time he was off the public payroll). Had he lived long enough to retire from the White House, Kennedy had contemplated becoming a publisher. He too thought that it would be fun to run a newspaper, like Citizen Kane. (The eponymous film had as its working title *American*.[62]) Jews could succeed as journalists in part because journalists could succeed in America.

Finally, what will continue to render this topic enigmatic is the larger question of Jewish identity in modern times. Here is not the place to explore the definition of who a Jew is. But it is certainly fair to assert that *at most* only a segment of ethnic identity or religious heritage has ever been implicated in what journalists have done, and therefore the task of determining a distinctive Jewish contribution is complicated when so many Jews have blended so successfully into the structure of social organization. What they have achieved as individual journalists betrays only the most tenuous link to their sensibility as Jews, but that is why a study of their influence and motivations promises to shed further light on the elusive meaning of Jewish modernity in mass society. During a his-

---

[59]Halberstam, *The Powers That Be*, 549-51; Nathan Glazer, "The Immigrant Groups and American Culture," *Yale Review* 48 (Spring 1959), 395-7.

[60]Letter to Edward Carrington, January 16, 1787, in *The Portable Thomas Jefferson*, ed. Merrill D. Peterson (New York, 1975), 415.

[61]Paneth, *Encyclopedia of American Journalism*, 288.

[62]Pauline Kael, "Raising Kane," in Kael, Herman J. Mankiewicz, and Orson Welles, *The Citizen Kane Book* (Boston, 1971), 29, 57; Arthur M. Schlesinger, Jr., *A Thousand Days: John F. Kennedy in the White House* (Boston, 1965), 1017.

torical period when it is hardly a disability and indeed something of an asset to be a Jew in America, journalism is among the indices of full participation in the host society. The press badge is a certificate of "making it." Far from signifying a cabal or a conspiracy, the Jewish representation in the mass media demonstrates the hospitality of the American environment, the congruence of American values — and the benign challenge that is thereby posed to the singularity and survival of a tiny and ancient people.

# 12

# The Evangelical Origins of Muckraking
by Bruce J. Evensen

"OH, GOD, GIVE ME FAITH. Oh, God, lead me out of this valley of depression. Oh, God, I am fearful and downcast, help me today to do my work bravely. I try to do large things, too large for me; I am not willing to be simple, straightforward, humble. I am terrified to speak generalities, to judge men and women by appearances, not realizing that they too, are having a bitter struggle within themselves. I am tempted to attack, not to press forward with positive faith. Oh, God, take me out of this. Oh, God, let me see and feel thy constant presence, let me feel my connections with thee and through thee with all of my neighbors."

The prayer is that of Ray Stannard Baker, one of the most prominent of the muckrakers, and the meditation appears in a 1908 notebook, which was written at the height of muckraking agitation for a better America.[1] What makes the statement so illuminating is not its moral thrust, for historians have seen that impulse at work in the reformers' call to action. But what chroniclers have paid insufficient attention to is the vital struggle of faith that appears at the center of many of the muckrakers' personal lives and how this warfare became externalized in their writings.

This chapter analyzes the private and public writings of seven muckrakers in the context of the evangelical origins of this remarkable group of men and women. In doing so, the researcher is reminded of the dangers of over-simplification, of Lincoln Steffens' warning to Upton Sinclair on the occasion of Edmund Wilson's muckraking of the muckrakers more than fifty years ago. "The fact that he lumps us is a bad sign," Steffens wrote, suggesting they consider killing the critic and pleading self-defense.[2] Fearing a similar fate, this research will attempt to portray seven of these muckrakers as individuals, who shared a common context, which in turn produced a literature as rich and complex as the men and

---

[1] Ray Stannard Baker, Notebook "K" (1908), 131, Library of Congress.
[2] Ella Winter and Granville Hicks, The Letters of Lincoln Steffens, vol. 2 (New York: 1938), 928. Copy of letter from Steffens to Upton Sinclair, dated September 25, 1932.

women who made it.

A half century's research on the muckrakers has found no shortage of opinions on who they were and what they intended.[3] Historical interpretation of the muckrakers' work basically divided over the question of whether the muckrakers were "liberal social reformers" or "conservative advocates of middle-class values and interests." The debate arose in the post-World War II generation of historians who placed the muckrakers in the broader context of the debate then underway over "consensus" and "class conflict." The effect of the discussion was to diminish the role of the muckrakers as moral crusaders and to see them instead as self-interested defenders of the status quo.[4]

What these frames of reference have tended to overlook is what the muckrakers saw themselves as doing and the deeply personal struggle over faith that informed their work. Two historians, Richard Hofstadter and Harold Wilson, have argued the muckrakers were attempting to achieve an "unselfish consensus" based on "Protestant and Social Gospel norms."[5] But the Hofstadter hypothesis, later developed by Hays, Wiebe, and Mowry, saw this popular appeal as a pretext through which the muckrakers attempted to fend off changes brought by industrialization and immigration that threatened their social position.[6] Wilson similarly sees a sociological explanation behind muckraking agitation.[7] They were driven as well, he writes, by a morality of absolutes that confused the fragmentation stemming from immigration, the concentration of wealth, and the rise of the cities, with a deterioration in the old order familiar to them.

Wilson argues that this "morality of absolutes" stemmed from the muckrakers' abandonment of the faith of their fathers and their conversion to Social Darwinism. This transformation, he suggests, took place with "remarkable ease" and led to a "radical social Christianity" that was the synthesis of Darwinian determinism and the altruism of the Golden Rule. The muckrakers "swept divinity" and "inspiration" aside in "heralding a new social order" that was essen-

---

[3]See Harry H. Stein, "American Muckrakers and Muckraking: The 50-Year Scholarship" *Journalism Quarterly* 56 (1979), 9-17, for a summary of the literature. H.U. Faulkner, *The Quest for Social Justice, 1898-1914* (New York, 1931); C.C. Regier, *The Era of the Muckrakers* (Chapel Hill: 1932). and Louis Filler, *Crusaders for American Liberalism* (Yellow Springs: 1939). Compare to post-war works by Richard Hofstadter, *Age of Reform: From Bryan to F.D.R.* (New York: 1959); Eric Goldman, *Rendezvous with Destiny: A History of Modern American Reform* (New York: 1959); Henry P. May, *The End of American Innocence: A Study of the First Years of Our Time* (New York: 1959); Judson Grenier, "Muckraking and Muckrakers: An Historical Definition." *Journalism Quarterly* (1963); John E. Semonche, "Teddy Roosevelt's 'Muckrake Speech': A Reassessmen," *Mid-America* (April 1960); Stanley K. Schultz, "The Morality of Politics: The Muckraker's Vision of Democracy," *Journal of American History* (December 1965); John G. Cawelti, *Apostles of the Self-Made Man* (Chicago, 1965); Harold Wilson, *McClure's Magazine and the Muckrakers* (Princeton, 1970); Richard L. McCormick, 'The Discovery That Business Corrupts: A Reappraisal of the Origins of Progressivism," *American Historical Review* 86 (April 1981); Robert M. Crunden, *The Superfluous Men: Conservative Critics of American Culture, 1900-1945* (Austin, 1977) and *Ministers of Reform: The Progressive Achievement in American Civilization, 1889-1920* (New York, 1982); and Shiela Reaves, "How Radical Were the Muckrakers? Socialist Press Views, 1902-1906," *Journalism Quarterly* 61 (Winter 1984).

[4]See Wm. David Sloan, "American Muckrakers, 1901-1917: Defenders of Conservativism or Liberal Reformers?" 271-82 in Sloan, *Perspectives on Mass Communication History* (Hillsdale, N.J., 1991).

[5]Wilson, *McClure's Magazine and the Muckrakers*, 265-89; Hofstadter, *Age of Reform*, 173-212.

[6]Hofstadter, *Age of Reform*, 210. Samuel P. Hays, *Conservatism and the Gospel of Efficiency: The Progressive Conservation Movement, 1890-1920* (Cambridge, 1968); Robert H. Wiebe, *Businessmen and Reform: A Study of the Progressive Movement* (Cambridge, 1968). See also George E. Mowry, *The Era of Theodore Roosevelt, 1900-1912* (New York: 1958); John Breman, "Seven Progressives," *Business History Review* 35 (1961); and Gabriel Kolko, *The Triumph of Conservatism: A Reinterpretation of American History, 1910-1916* (New York: 1963).

[7]Wilson, *McClure's Magazine and the Muckrakers*, 285-9.

tially mechanistic. Human society led by a divine "force" was evolving progressively. The purpose of law and governments was to recognize this transformation and to develop policies and institutions to move matters along.[8]

An analysis of the diaries, notebooks, and private papers of several leading muckrakers casts doubt on whether they embraced Social Darwinism with "remarkable ease" and brings into perspective the inner conflicts that lay behind the public proclamation of their progressivism. The battle they waged was not so much that people should have faith but to describe what that faith should be in. For some muckrakers the higher criticism of Bible commentators had shaken the certainty of the old-time religion. Their challenge then became finding an absolute to substitute for a belief in the Bible as the inspired Word of God, something that could arouse a generation to right thinking and conduct. It is perhaps the final paradox of the progressive period that those who tried to teach others how to live were themselves forever searching for the same answers.

### S.S. MCCLURE: A PROGRESSIVE PILGRIM

The process of spiritual seeking and uncertainty is nowhere more apparent than in the life of Samuel Sidney McClure, the founder of the progenitor muckraking magazine. McClure remembered only three books from his Ulster home — a Bible, Foxe's *Book of Martyrs*, and *Pilgrim's Progress*. His Presbyterian parents, he writes in his autobiography, had been caught up in a revival that swept Northern Ireland in 1859. The experience had changed their lives by returning them to the "simple teachings of the early church." His father's death and his mother's poverty weighed heavily upon him when he arrived in Galesburg, Illinois, with fifteen cents in his pocket. At Knox College he would find a "purpose" for his life.[9]

"Forms wax old and perish," he wrote in his class notes. "Principles are eternal." Principles of "right and wrong" necessarily had their foundation in teaming up with God in the battle over His creation. "We see that we are engaged in a terrible conflict," he wrote, following his studies of the Apostle Paul, "not with flesh and blood, but with principalities and powers and the rulers of the darkness of this world." He was sure that "though strife be long, yet slowly and surely it will end with the glorious triumph of the right."[10]

There were two great facts of civilization as McClure saw it — the individual and the state. The latter existed solely for the former, even as the human soul existed only for God. God would equip the "sensitive, shrinking, quivering soul" to fight His battles for Him. For God had placed in the hearts of those who followed Him an "enthusiasm" for service. It was only through such service that one's self was brought into proper view. Individuality consisted of following "enthusiastically" the pathway of service God had for man.[11]

It was in June of 1893, the month the bottom dropped out of the Stock Market and the panic spread westward from Wall Street, that McClure published the

---

[8]Ibid., ch. 19.

[9]S.S. McClure, *My Autobiography* (New York: 1963), 8, 59 and 62.

[10]McClure mss. Writings, n.d., Knox College class papers. Lilly Library. Indiana University. Bloomington, Indiana.

[11]Ibid.

first number of his monthly magazine. Though it would be a decade before the publication would take on the appearance of a muckraking journal, McClure from the outset saw it as having a high purpose. In April of 1894 while in Paris searching for literary material for the magazine, he wrote his wife that he saw himself "playing for high stakes." He reported that he was in an "awful condition." He owed "heaps of money everywhere." He had not even paid his church dues. Yet he felt himself on the edge of a great breakthrough. The Lord had some "great work" for him to do.[12]

As McClure shifted around with various ideas to make the magazine more attractive, his wife warned him to be true to his high ideals and not sacrifice the magazine to commercial interests. McClure's statement of policy throughout this period remained high-minded. His May 1894 issue, which featured a piece by Henry Drummond on American evangelist Dwight L. Moody, told readers it was endeavoring to "reflect the moving spirit of this time" by setting forth the achievements of the "great men of the day" and the "human struggle for existence and development."[13]

It was not only McClure's wife, but his mother, Elizabeth, who expressed concern that the magazine be put to still higher purposes. In January 1895, she wrote him that her time on the earth was now "short." She therefore encouraged her son to publish only the work of men "sound in God's word." If her son wanted to bring "honor and glory to God" there was "only one way to do it." And that was "God's way." Her son needed to find "God's will." The magazine could be an instrument for that will, but she feared her son might miss this chance through lack of prayer and failure to "study God's will." Her greatest delight would be to have her son "if possible" follow the steps of his parents, so that whatever he did, he would do it "for God."[14]

By the end of the year, McClure could boast that circulation had risen from 45,000 to 80,000. Along with John S. Phillips, an old college classmate, now his chief editor, he promised "noble entertainment" and "worthy knowledge" in coming issues designed to "uplift, refresh and encourage all who read it."[15]

While it has been suggested that McClure turned to muckraking to boost circulation, his greatest gains in readership had taken place years earlier, thanks in large part to Ida Tarbell's series on Abraham Lincoln. The series had been promoted as "proceeding in an original way with the subject." Tarbell's writing, readers were promised, would be both "entertaining and carefully considered." It would rely on materials that had been gathered directly "from original sources," from people who had known Lincoln personally as well as from the President's own writings and correspondence.[16]

*McClure's Magazine* sold out in November and December of 1895, having shown a gain of 175,000 in circulation since the series started, while closing out the year with a readership of over 300,000. McClure wrote that his soul seemed finally "at rest." The "days of struggle" seemed over. He was now happy with

---

[12]McClure mss. Correspondence. Box 3. Folder 4. April 12, 1894. S.S. McClure to Hattie McClure.

[13]*McClure's Magazine*, May 1894, 89.

[14]McClure mss. Correspondence. Box 3. Folder 7. Elyatt (Elizabeth) Simpson to S.S. McClure. September 2, 1895.

[15]*McClure's Magazine*, December 1894, 3. Also, *McClure's Magazine*, July 1895, 16.

[16]*McClure's Magazine*, October 1895, 480.

his God.[17]

Tarbell's Lincoln portrait and the publicity surrounding the series idealized him as a perfect type while satisfying McClure's need to offer his readers a leader worthy of emulation. The piece celebrated Lincoln's pioneering origin and made much of the fact that he came from the stock of a "pioneering race of men and women." He had emerged from an ideal past where "lessons learned in early school out in the forest were grand and good." Everything around and about Lincoln "was just as it came from the hands of the Creator." It was "good" and it was "beautiful." It developed "both the head and the heart." It produced a remarkable President, who had celebrated democratic sacrifice at Gettysburg and the ideal of liberty when he emancipated the slaves. It was then, *McClure's* reported, that "God knew that he was good."[18]

McClure's Lincoln series was more than a circulation-building device. It was McClure's effort at constructing an ideal type, someone who had "striven with God" in the "glorious triumph of the right." When McClure returned to Knox College after his election to the board of trustees, he remarked that it had been thirty-eight years since Lincoln had last addressed a Galesburg audience. "What a legacy to our people," he commented, "was the memory of Lincoln." Soon the time would come when "no one living shall have seen Lincoln." That is why it was necessary to remind this and future generations what he stood for. Integrity, honor, and truthfulness had emanated from "his very soul." This generation needed heroes like that.[19]

Just after the Lincoln series, McClure wrote Phillips an excited letter. He reported "stumbling on" what would probably be "the most important publishing venture of our time." A long-awaited new translation of the Bible had just appeared. Its whole purpose had been to "re-discover the Bible, to make it really understandable." It would be an "indispensable book to all who believed in the Bible."[20] As originally conceived, the Bible series would run in twenty parts over four years.

Within weeks, McClure had booked passage to Palestine ostensibly to find background material for the series. His letters to his wife reveal the journey to have been a personal odyssey of faith. Passing through each of the seven gates of the Old City of Jerusalem, McClure marveled that "God was here as a man, and I can't get away from that." Days later he reported that he was "reading and re-reading the gospels." He never knew the Bible to be "so fascinating." He was now convinced as never before that "God approves of our work."[21]

The years leading up to *McClure's* muckraking were filled with this endless stream of hope balanced by periods of ambivalence and skepticism. His ceaseless efforts at entering into fellowship with men of like-minded faith finished only in

[17]McClure mss. Correspondence. Box 3. Folder 10. Letter from S.S. McClure to Hattie McClure. September 2, 1895.

[18]*McClure's Magazine*, January 1896, 206. Also, McClure mss. Correspondence. January 1896. Box 3, Folder 12.

[19]McClure mss. Writings, n.d. "The Greatness of Knox College" (1894).

[20]McClure mss. Correspondence. Box 3. Folder 12. Letter from S.S. McClure to John Phillips. February 10, 1896.

[21]McClure mss. Correspondence. Box 3. Folder 13. Letters from S.S. McClure to Harriet McClure. May 4, 10, 11, and 16, 1896. On the 16th he added, "I realize more and more the miracle of Christ's life. His words and deeds seem more and more wonderful."

frustration. "I attended a Salvation Army preaching service," he wrote his wife. "It was bad." Booth's great army kept shouting "that God was there and at work, though they didn't seem to really believe it. It made me sad."[22] Throughout what remained of the nineties, the magazine described its purpose as offering month to month "transcription" of the times, encouraging the upbuilding of the nation's "moral self-respect." McClure wrote that while his was not a "religious magazine," no "Christian family" should be without it. McClure advertised himself as offering the family something to live by and for.[23] At century's end, McClure wrote his wife how "aware" he had been of God's blessing. And she wrote him how convinced she was that there was yet "some special work" he would do to "help bring the world back to God."[24]

McClure was now poised at the beginning of his career as the country's greatest muckraking publisher. It was a period of acute financial and personal hardships that would ultimately lead to his surrender of the magazine and the dashing of his hopes to build through it a publishing empire. "The year 1902 has been the most prosperous in the history of *McClure's Magazine*," he told his readers, while writing his wife the magazine was "starved" for funds.[25] Muckraking had made no immediate impact in circulation patterns and was expensive to do properly. "I'm having my usual breakdown," he wrote his wife, in another of his talent hunts in Europe. Ida Tarbell, he later told his wife, would be her "mainstay" in the event of his death.[26]

McClure proved a very lively corpse. The next decade would see muckraking cause a minor sensation, and McClure for a short time rode its crest, dining with President Roosevelt and Alexander Graham Bell, while addressing large audiences on the dangers that lurked all around. In January 1904 he told the Twentieth Century Club in Brooklyn that nationwide those who broke the law conspired to put in office those "who let them." Machines existed in nearly every American city, and they operated to benefit some at the expense of others. Machine politics had left America "at the bottom of all civilized countries." Major corporations led in the "lawlessness." The people needed to rise and "protect" themselves. That was what *McClure's* was in business to help them to do.[27]

Years later he told the New York branch of the Y.M.C.A. the same thing. "The whole function of government," he observed, had been "to protect those who could not protect themselves." Beginning with Ida Tarbell's attack on the Standard Oil Trust, he told them, "we have fought for those unable to defend themselves."[28]

A generation later, as historians began to write their summaries of the Progressive period in American history and the magazine that had tirelessly pro-

---

[22]McClure mss. Box 3. Folder 15. Letter from S.S. McClure to Harriet McClure. August 9, 1896.

[23]*McClure's Magazine*, December 1896, p. 192, and October 1897, 1101.

[24]McClure mss. Box 3. Folder 21. The letters were exchanged on June 2, 1899.

[25]*McClure's Magazine*, October 1902. Also, McClure mss. Box 4. Folder 3. From S.S. McClure to Harriet McClure, April 24, 1902.

[26]McClure mss. Box 4. Folder 6. Undated. Letter from S.S. McClure to Harriet McClure. Also, Box 4. Folder 8. Letter from S.S. McClure to Harriet McClure. March 22, 1903.

[27]McClure mss. Box 4. Folder 12. Address to the Twentieth Century Club. Brooklyn, New York. January 30, 1904.

[28]McClure mss. Box 6. Folder 6. Address to members of the 57th Street branch of the Y.M.C.A. April 10, 1911.

moted its program, McClure wrote Tarbell that critics had gotten it all wrong. His "overwhelming passion" with the magazine had been to make it "as perfect as possible" by laying out a series of principles through which partial men could be made whole.[29]

## TARBELL'S "RELIGION"

McClure was to maintain a lifelong friendship with Ida Tarbell, the first of the muckrakers, and a woman whose spiritual sensibilities may have been the closest to his. Like McClure, Tarbell wrote extensively about the forces that formed her. She described herself as having been raised in a God-fearing Western Pennsylvania family, rigorous not only in its church attendance, but also in prayer meetings and revivals. She had received Christ at age eleven. The life of prayer that followed aroused "self-observation," and this took her to the literature of Darwin and Spencer.[30] After serving as preceptress at the Poland Union Seminary in Poland, Ohio, where she taught geology and botany, she went to France, and there continued both her studies and her spiritual search, which by the early nineties found her still attempting to reconcile her "need to feel and to know."[31]

On the eve of McClure's offer to join his staff, she remembered that she was "continuing [her] search for God in the great cathedrals of Europe." She later explained the impact this spiritual quest had on her muckraking career. It grew out of a childlike "conviction of divine goodness at work in the world." Despite the growing sense of life's injustice and ugliness she could not shake an "inward certainty" that the "central principle of things is beneficence." This "serene, stable self-assurance" had a "hold" on Tarbell. It remained even as she embraced Darwinian evolution and lost the sense that God had a "human outline."[32]

Tarbell expressed little patience with the fundamentalist-modernist argument then permeating the church. She thought herself "outside" that quarrel. One's works and character reflected "true spirituality." Christianity was simply the "best system" because it was based on the "brotherhood of man." Political institutions consistent with that divine purpose were good. Those that operated on the basis of a different set of ethics were dangerous.[33]

When she accepted McClure's offer and returned to America, she was immediately struck by the changes that had taken place during her several years' absence. What she most feared now, she wrote, was that "we were raising our standard of living at the expense of our standard of character." She was convinced that "personal human betterment" necessarily rested on a "sound moral basis" as well as a "personal search for the meaning of the mystery of God."[34]

Tarbell wrote that her personal search for answers to that mystery was at the center of her muckraking. It formed her notion of how a "decent and useful person" could be formed and later could learn to function in a social system antago-

---

[29]McClure ms. S.S. McClure to Ida Tarbell. October 1, 1937. See also McClure mss. Box 4. Folder 17. Letter from S.S. McClure to Harriet McClure. August 27, 1904.

[30]Ida M. Tarbell, *All in a Day's Work* (New York 1939), 15-6.

[31]Kathleen Brady, *Ida M. Tarbell* (New York, 1985), 31 and 61.

[32]Ida M. Tarbell, "My Religion," 1-2. Lawrence Lee Pelletier Library. Allegheny College. Meadville, Pennsylvania.

[33]Ibid., 3-7.

[34]Tarbell, *All in a Day's Work*, 407.

nistic to individual dignity. Her "History of the Standard Oil Company" serialized in *McClure's Magazine* was a revelation of the evil at work in human society. John D. Rockefeller employed "force and fraud, sly tricks and special privilege to get his way." His activities were only a symptom of a phenomenon that went deeper. Blackmail was becoming a "natural part" of business practice. The result, she found, was not only a "leech" on the public pocket, but the "contamination of commerce." Only the principles of Christian fair play, she argued, could transform business practice and make it a "fit pursuit for our young men."[35]

Biographers might charge that Tarbell's "greatest miscalculation" was that she relied on the Golden Rule too much and law not enough in bringing about change, but what they fail to appreciate fully is how Tarbell, McClure, and other muckrakers understood their primary role and the intensely spiritual environment in which that fervor arose. Tarbell was not indifferent to the need for legal reform; but like her fellow muckrakers, she understood the central importance moral regeneration and moral consensus played in creating a human community in which democratic institutions could be allowed to work. Amelioration of "human sufferings, inequalities, greed, ignorance," she wrote, did not come through law alone, but was as well a fundamental matter of the human heart.[36]

She saw her whole life as having been spent in a "striving in solitude and silence to enter into a fuller understanding of the divine." But that understanding, she insisted, was the only means by which the "moral diseases" — pride, greed, hypocrisy, cruelty, irreverence, and cowardliness — that so afflicted the age could be overcome. If the Bible gave men and women anything, it gave them a conception of how they ought to live. What is more, it showed them a way in which "the essential brotherhood of man" could be brought into being. She was convinced it came by bearing witness to an "inner light," a light that, if encouraged to develop, was alone capable of binding men to other men. Men would either "hunger and thirst after righteousness, mercy, meekness, and purity of heart," she wrote, or give way to the "poisonous" selfishness implicit in modern living. Her writing had been to call people to righteousness and to show them a means of how they might establish "right conduct" for themselves and their communities.[37]

*BAKER'S SPIRITUAL UNREST*

*McClure's* publication in January 1903 of the third installment of Tarbell's series on Standard Oil coincided with Lincoln Steffens' exposé on Minneapolis political practices and Ray Stannard Baker's attack on corrupt labor practices. The edition was billed as an analysis of the American "contempt" for law, and it was to do much in igniting Baker's forty-year fire for progressive causes. It was a journey that would take him from *McClure's* to the *American Chronicle*, to a career as the author of best-selling fiction, and finally as an aide to and biographer of Woodrow Wilson. The whole of this extraordinary progression was

---

[35]Ibid., 6, 27-9 and 407. Also Tarbell, *History of the Standard Oil Company* (New York, 1904), 268 and 287-9.

[36]Tarbell, "My Religion," 7-8. Also, Mary E. Tompkins, *Ida M. Tarbell* (New York, 1974). 158.

[37]Tarbell, "My Religion," 7-8.

punctuated by flashes of spiritual certainty and spiritual unrest and a life consciously led in service to God.

Baker began his autobiography by remembering that the Bible on which he had been brought up in St. Croix Falls, Wisconsin, had highlighted within it by his Presbyterian parents the phrase, "in the sweat of thy face thou shalt eat bread." Rigorous self-discipline became a life's commitment. "I read. I studied," he wrote. From an early age he felt, as Tarbell did, "the essential truth of the teachings of Christ."[38] His father, educated at Oberlin, helped matters along. Ray earned a silver dollar from his father for finishing *Pilgrim's Progress* while in grade school. He took his meals in a dining room beneath the motto "Thou God seest me."[39]

Perhaps no future muckraker had a firmer foundation laid in religious life than did Baker. Sunday in St. Croix Falls was a day entirely set apart. Sunday school and church in the morning were followed by a study of the scriptures in the afternoon, and, at six, an evening service. In addition, there were the weekly Thursday evening prayer meetings in which the Bakers took the leading role.[40]

"Plow deeply, till thoroughly," his father told him as he prepared to begin his career in journalism. "Scatter the seed with care and the harvest will be all you hoped for."[41]

Like other muckrakers, Baker for a lifetime fought a "spiritual unrest" as he attempted to reconcile his old familiar faith with the higher criticism then engulfing much of the church. Like Tarbell, he sought the silence of personal rumination, even sequestering himself in an Arizona desert for a time, to carry on his crisis privately in personal faith. "I was brought up a Presbyterian," he later observed, "but I liked being a Quaker best. When the talk began I was usually not so certain. I found myself descending from the high places." Darwin's theories of evolution and natural selection had put him "much at sea as to what I should believe." The serpent, he said of his mental confusion, "began to tempt me."[42] Baker traced his "literature of exposure" to his encounters with William T. Stead in Chicago.[43] The editor and evangelist's efforts to "clean up" that city mobilized Baker's "spirit of service" and put him on a muckraking path of "earnest endeavor." Baker's biographer sees the whole of that career as stemming from a moralism that was "deepseated, almost inexplicable, and which remained the basis of a lifetime of action."[44]

Baker's muckraking attack on the churches of his day along with his own private notebooks and papers give the clearest idea of how his personal "journey of faith" formed a framework for his public writing. His criticism of New York City's Trinity Church, one of the nation's wealthiest congregations, was broadened into a critique of the "malaise" that had fallen over the Christian commu-

---

[38]Ray Stannard Baker, *American Chronicle: The Autobiography of Ray Stannard Baker* (New York, 1945), 2 and 58.

[39]Robert C. Bannister, *Ray Stannard Baker. The Mind and Thought of a Progressive* (New Haven, 1966), 3, 12 and 13.

[40]Ibid., 14.

[41]Baker, *American Chronicle*, 17.

[42]Ibid., 57-8.

[43]William T. Stead, *If Christ Came to Chicago* (Chicago, 1894; Evansville, 1978). See also, Stead, *The Americanization of the World Or the Trend of the Twentieth Century* (New York, 1901; New York, 1902).

[44]Baker, *American Chronicle*, 30-2. Also, Bannister, *Ray Stannard Baker*, 14.

nity. The problem was that the churches "lacked a moral vision." They did not know what they believed. They knew nothing of "social justice" and as a consequence had "no message for the common man." Baker's visits to many of the leading churches convinced him that they had a "passion for efficiency" that they put to "no real purpose." The churches had come to appreciate the "crisis" they were in and were now trying to "get back to the people." They were throwing money at the problem of community relations when it was not money but "the human touch" that was required."[45]

Wilson has suggested that Baker and many of his fellow muckrakers became good Social Darwinists and "swept aside" the need for a personal, active faith. But Baker states explicitly in *The Spiritual Unrest* that the churches had a dual mission — both to the individual and the community. This recognition is reiterated throughout his notebooks, where he argues that "individual salvation" and "community salvation" are "complementary and reciprocal."[46]

Publicly, Baker held up the work of Walter Rauschenbusch as a theology which could lead to the church's acceptance of its "new social mission" which sought to "save man and his society." Baker's criticism of the old evangelism was that it had not been "selfless" enough. Rauschenbusch's message had been to show that sin not only affects an individual's relationship to God but also his relationship to others. Repentance required the turning away from sin not for the sake of oneself alone but for the sake of the community in which he lived. In this human community, Christ was the ultimate exemplar. His life alone had given the pattern upon which the church could hope to "magnify" itself. That pattern called for a church that "touched its neighbors" thereby strengthening the community's "fragility of faith."[47]

Baker's own efforts at church planting show how seriously he took the question of community worship in the moral upbuilding of his society. Here his "righteous indignation," as Tarbell had called it, could be put to work providing communicants a sense of shared values and mutual responsibility. How could men be their brother's keeper, he wondered, if they did not know that they were brothers? What the church now needed were "Elijahs" willing to "imitate the life of Christ." This required risks and "sacrifice."[48]

Baker saw Woodrow Wilson as an Elijah offering Americans a course of action rooted in communitarian responsibility. Baker wrote that he was bewildered by the "fixity" of the President's "immovable faith" while feeling at the same time a certain "envy." He saw in the "certainty" of Wilson's "rock-like faith" the "creative impulse" with which the new administration could defeat the powers of "bossism" and "venality," as well as the "wretched conditions which had become the American way of life."[49]

In one of his notebooks, Baker admitted to a certain lifelong agitation behind the creative energy of his work. He had never denied the "reality of spiritual things" or the "essential unity" of the "inner voice" available to all men. But

---

[45]Ray Stannard Baker, *The Spiritual Unrest* (New York, 1909), chs. 1 and 2, particularly 87-100.

[46]Ibid., 142 and 230. Also, Baker, Notebook "J," p. 116. Library of Congress.

[47]Baker, *The Spiritual Unrest*, 272-81.

[48]Baker, *American Chronicle*, 182-4. Also, Baker, Notebook "I," 104, and Notebook "L," 20.

[49]Ray Stannard Baker, *Woodrow Wilson and World Settlement*, vol. 1 (Gloucester, 1960), 1-2, 13-4 and 21. Also, Baker, *American Chronicle*, 60, 92-3 and 176-8.

what had that to do with Christ's personal call on his life, and the lives of others? It appeared that Christ "depended on us" for doing his work on the earth, he wrote. Christ had obtained a "unity with God" that Baker had desperately sought in his own life and that he had sought to make possible in the lives of others. A year before his death, he wrote that the effort had not been without its frustrations. "Each age," he supposed, "must worship its own thought of God." Baker remembered that as a boy, the "face" of God had ever been before him. As an adult, he feared, he would never see His face again. In old age, he saw God's handiwork everywhere about him.[50]

## LINCOLN STEFFENS AND THE MCNAMARA CASE

"I have been contending all my life," Lincoln Steffens wrote at the end of his autobiography, "and always with God." The man considered as pre-eminent of the muckraking writers, saw all the cities and states he had muckraked as being part of but a single story. "They had different names, dates and locations," he wrote, "but the essential facts were all described by Christ in the New Testament." Jesus had known the "worthlessness of the good people," Steffens was sure. Like Christ's, his had been a lifelong mission to save a world indifferent to life-giving instruction.[51]

A veteran newspaperman when he came to the *McClure's* group, Steffens crucified municipal government in "The Shame of the Cities" series. He reported how he had soured on the "best people" when he saw that "the law-abiding backbones of our society, in city after city, start out for moral reform, but turn back," when they saw it would cost them something. Christianity, he became convinced, provided the only possibility of real reform. It conveyed a faith, a hope, but more crucially a "vision" of how to act.[52]

As was the case with many of the muckrakers, Steffens came to his moral sensibility early in life. His conversion skipped a generation. Contemporaries described his grandfather, the Reverend Joseph Steffens, as a "bold defender of the faith once delivered to the saints." The parents of Lincoln Steffens, however, appear to have been nominal Christians who went to church out of "social habit." Nevertheless, Steffens took a liking to Sunday school and, under the moral instruction of a California neighbor, read the Bible seriously in his early and mid-teens, even planning a career in the ministry.[53]

Steffens' parents "followed his conversion patiently" as his intellect led him away from the institutional church. He was beginning to find that "even though the music was wet, the sermon was dry." Like Tarbell, he went to Europe, ostensibly to study, but not incidentally to find a more satisfactory basis for his faith. In Berlin, he attended a nondenominational American church and wrote home that he was becoming suspicious of "hot-house Christians." Those who had a "thoughtful comprehension of the full meaning and true spirit of Christ had come to the knowledge gradually and reasonably. The following year he wrote his father from Heidelberg that he had received a letter from his sister, Dot,

---

[50]Baker, Notebook VII, 149-53. Also, Notebook "L," 20. Also, Bannister, *Ray Stannard Baker*, 119.

[51]Joseph Lincoln Steffens, *Autobiography of Lincoln Steffens* (New York, 1931), 523-6.

[52]Ibid., 525.

[53]Ibid., 72. Also, Justin Kaplan, *Lincoln Steffens: A Biography* (New York 1974), 22.

asking about becoming a Catholic. He urged restraint. Dot was in greater danger of rejecting the divinity of Christ, he wrote his father, than turning to the Catholics.[54]

The day before he died, Steffens, writing a preface to a collection of his works, said he always understood himself to be a "teacher." In the days in which he had "breathed the news" he had in mind giving his readers life-saving instruction. Speaking for the historical record, he argued that Old Testament writers were the original muckrakers. The trouble was, in New Testament times, ministers had never taught the true message of Christ to the Christians.[55]

Muckraking, Steffens once observed, had not gone far enough in proposing solutions to the corruption of the nation's political system. The problem was not to replace "bad men" with "good men" but to work for fundamental economic reforms that would prevent the perpetuation of a government of privilege. Steffens chafed under McClure's admonition to "find the facts" and to leave the interpretations to others. His career at *McClure's* and *American Chronicle* was characterized by his continuing efforts to have his colleagues recognize what he saw as fundamental to any campaign of reform.[56]

In December of 1909, he wrote his mother that he was finally coming to terms with the "self-doubts" that had so long plagued his work. He was now working on the "biggest thing I've ever tackled." It would be a series of articles on the life of Jesus. "I want to tell Christians," he wrote her, "what their Christ said they should do." He admitted that while he could not "accept it all myself," he was prepared to show how Christ could "solve" the problems of the cities and their corrupt administrations. "I can't expect to convert the Christian Church to Christianity," he told her, "but I can show what would happen if they would but believe."[57]

The articles were never written, but Steffens' intentions are important in understanding his involvement in the McNamara case and its aftermath. The McNamara brothers had gone on trial in the fall of 1911 for the bombing of the Los Angeles *Times* building in which twenty-one people had been killed. Steffens appears to have intervened in the brothers' behalf in part because of his friendship with their attorney, Clarence Darrow, but also because he thought by doing so he could focus international attention on the causes of the bombing and his plan to prevent future episodes of similar violence.

Steffens succeeded in obtaining a confession from the brothers, in exchange, he thought, for a ruling that all charges be dropped against them. His real scheme had been to lay before the court and the assembled press his notion that the "application of the Golden Rule" was crucial to future labor-business relations, for without it, the country ran the risk of perishing in civil strife. But the deal fell apart, James McNamara receiving a sentence of life imprisonment and his brother John, who had headed the Structural Iron Workers, receiving a sen-

---

[54]Winter and Hicks, *The Letters of Lincoln Steffens*, 11. Copy of letter from Lincoln Steffens to Lou Steffens. August 25, 1889. Also Winter and Hicks, 49. Copy of letter from Lincoln Steffens to Joseph Steffens, July 18, 1890.

[55]Joseph Lincoln Steffens, *Lincoln Steffens Speaking* (New York, 1936), ix. Also, Steffens, *Autobiography*, 375.

[56]Steffens, *Autobiography*, 375.

[57]Winter and Hicks, *The Letters of Lincoln Steffens*, 234-5. Copy of letter from Lincoln Steffens to Mrs. Joseph Steffens, December 21, 1909.

tence of six to twelve years. Steffens bitterly blamed the outcry from the churches on the eve of sentencing as turning the trend in public opinion against him and spent the rest of his life seeking pardons for the McNamaras.[58]

Before the trial he had observed that his "drift toward Christianity" had been triggered by his "systematic search" for remedies to the problem of city management. He had studied socialism, anarchism, the single tax, and "from time to time" the Bible. He was "amazed" at the teachings of Jesus. They seemed "new" to him. Jesus saw and understood, he wrote, what Christians did not. He knew the "evils" of society, and he knew their "cure." What was needed was spiritual renewal of the individual, leading to the application of the Golden Rule to society.[59]

But the McNamara case had shown him he had misunderstood the enemy. Steffens' attack on the institutional church was far more severe than that of Baker and far more personal than that of his friend Upton Sinclair. The "Christian world" leaps on men when they are down, he sadly wrote. "We meant to have them forgiven," he said of the McNamaras, but "all the church wanted was their blood. It makes me sick." At the height of his disillusion, Steffens wrote his family, "I'm getting lots of letters from clergymen. They may be right. It is possible that Christianity will not work. I may have to admit it. If I must, I shall, you know."[60]

Steffens was now muckraked in the press under the title "Golden Rule Steffens." He retaliated by wearing a small gold cross from his watch chain, calling himself "the only Christian on earth." Even from his vantage point, many years after the experience, Steffens observed that Christianity could not be found in its churches. What they preached instead was "hate and disappointed revenge."[61]

Steffens' remaining years were spent courting Communism, finding it the only "true" Christianity, and in defending its "necessary" violence. His project on the life of Jesus remained unfinished, and an anticipated work on the life of Satan hardly was begun. He saw a consistency of outlook in the trail he had taken from muckraking to Marxism. "Religion" remained forever central to his thinking and work. "From religion my reason would never be emancipated," he observed late in life. "By it I was conformed to my generation and made to share its moral standards and ideals." Early assumptions concerning "good and evil," "virtue and vice" remained his mind's measure of all things and the framework for his entire endeavor.[62]

*THE MAN WITH THE "CHRIST COMPLEX"*

Shortly after the publication of Lincoln Steffens' "The Shame of the Cities," the

---

[58]There is an excellent summary of the impact of the McNamara case on Steffens in Russell M. Horton's *Lincoln Steffens* (New York, 1974), 86. See also Steffens, *Autobiography*, 670-5; and Winter and Hicks, *The Letters of Lincoln Steffens*, 286-8.

[59]Winter and Hicks, *The Letters of Lincoln Steffens*, 243. Copy of letter from Lincoln Steffens to William Kent, April 19, 1910.

[60]Winter and Hicks, *The Letters of Lincoln Steffens*, 243. Letter from Lincoln Steffens to Laura Steffens, November 191. Also, Winter and Hicks, 286. Letter from Lincoln Steffens to Lou and Allen Suggett, December 24, 1911.

[61]Steffens, *Autobiography*, 688. Also, Horton, 85.

[62]Kaplan, *Lincoln Steffens*, 118.

author received a visit in his office from Upton Sinclair. "What you report," Sinclair told him, "is enough to make a complete picture of the system, but you seem not to see it. Don't you see it? Don't you see what you are showing?"[63]

Over the years, the two men's programs for reform were perhaps more closely alike than any of the other muckrakers. While Sinclair stopped at socialism, Steffens went on to advocating communism as a means of solving the structural problems of capitalist society. Despite the divergence, the men maintained an active and respectful correspondence for more than thirty years. From the first they had shared a certain spiritual kinship. Still early in his career when Sinclair sent Steffens a copy of his *Cry for Justice*, Steffens understood it to be a "Bible for the faithful."[64]

Of the criticisms Sinclair suffered in his long career the one he received most gladly was the charge he suffered from a "Christ complex." "The world needs a Jesus," Sinclair reportedly answered without embarrassment, "more than it needs anything else."[65]

Like McClure, Tarbell, Baker, and Steffens, Sinclair lived into old age and left an autobiography to describe the impulses that formed his muckraking and led to the publication of *The Jungle*, his sensational indictment of the nation's meat-packing industry. Though he had always considered ancestors a "bore," Sinclair's relatives claimed royal descent from English roots and his great-grandfather was apparently Commodore Arthur Sinclair, who had fought in the first American naval battle after the Revolution as well as the War of 1812. In a biographical note, Sinclair would admit that a history of his ancestors read a little like "the history of the American Navy."[66]

By the time Sinclair was born in September of 1878, the family's fortunes had faded through the ravages of the Civil War and on "a sea of liquor." Sinclair's father came from a family in which four "gentlemen of the Old South" had turned drunks. His earliest memories were of his father going off as a whiskey salesman and coming home drunk. Sinclair remembered his boyhood homes as a succession of "sordid" rooming houses he shared with a status-seeking mother, who appeared determined to make him an Episcopal bishop. "I became a dreamer," he wrote. "When I was 17 I came to the conclusion that Providence must have some special purpose in keeping me in the world."[67]

It was an horrific world tied to his father's unending drinking cycles. Upton remembered the father's constant prayers seeking forgiveness, the father's ongoing promises that he would stay sober, and his heart-rending debacles. As an adolescent, Sinclair remembered fishing his father out of bars and hearing the old man say his salvation had been "lost," because he had "fallen again."[68]

Sinclair saw those early years through the eyes of faith, it making him in life, by his own admission, a hopeless idealist. By fifteen he was an "ardent little

---

[63]Steffens, *Autobiography*, 434-5.

[64]Upton Sinclair, *My Lifetime in Letters* (Columbia. Mo., 1960), 52. Copy of letter from Lincoln Steffens to Upton Sinclair, October 15, 1915.

[65]Steffens, *Autobiography*, 434-5.

[66]Upton Sinclair mss. Biographical Data Correspondence, 1814-1916. Box 1. Folder 1. Lilly Library. Indiana University. Bloomington, Indiana.

[67]Upton Sinclair, *Cup of Fury* (Great Neck 1956), 12 and 13. Also, Upton Sinclair, *The Autobiography of Upton Sinclair* (New York, 1962), 27.

[68]Sinclair, *Cup of Fury*, 20-1.

Episcopal boy" teaching Sunday school classes at the Church of the Holy
Communion in New York. He had gone to church every afternoon during Lent,
"not because I was told to," he later wrote, "but because I wanted to." He had
read his Bible "straight through," and while writing in his seventies remembered that "its language and imagery" had ever been "a part of me." The church
had given him a "moral earnestness" to the problems of human life that formed
the basis of his lifelong struggle for social justice.[69]

He had supported himself as a writer since the age of sixteen. In these early
years he wrote his mother that he would see to it that they never again lived in
vermin-infested rooming houses. He was making her a promise that he could
keep. He assured her, "Whether you believe it or not, God's in heaven, who
made this world." Sinclair wondered if He knew "what this life is all about any-
how." He hoped that there might be "a higher motive in this world than the
love of money" and "a higher end than getting it."[70]

Sinclair wrote dime novels for cheap magazines to help finance his schooling
at the City College of New York and Columbia University. It was there he began his lifelong "lover's quarrel" with the church, producing in 1918 *The Profits of Religion*. Whether muckraking the churches or the meat-packing industry,
Sinclair measured all men by his "impossibly high standards of honor, conti-
nence, honesty, Christianity and truthfulness." He observed, "We have a continent with a hundred million educated people, materially prosperous but spiritually starving. I would be willing to wager that if I announced I had a visit from
God last night and I communicated a new revelation from it, I could have a
temple, a university, and a million dollars within five years at the outside."[71]
Sinclair privately wrote that he felt he had been born "to reform." He told fellow
muckraker Edwin Markham, "I want to give every second of my time and of my
thought and every ounce of my energy to the worship of my God and to the ut-
tering of the unspeakable message that I know he has given me." His muckraking attack in *The Jungle* had been a part of that message. He "poured" into it all
the "tears and anguish and pain" that he had known in life. His *Cry for Justice*,
written in 1915, was an anthology of social protest, that could serve as a "Bible" for the "discouraged and wounded" in their struggle against the economic
institutions that oppressed them.[72]

One of those institutions, as he saw it, was the church. And while Sinclair
never abandoned his belief that organized religion was a bastion of "predatory,
capitalist interests," this opinion never led him to abandon his personal faith in
God, nor his certainty that Christ's teachings were the ultimate way to social
betterment. God had given him "a vision of a world without poverty and war,"
where "Cod's children" would not be destroyed. His career had been a cautious
labor to "make that vision real to my fellow men." It was a vision of a better
world, in which "courage, resolution and hope" animated the activities of men
in their behavior to other men. That was the only real hope for civic betterment.

---

[69]Ibid., 14-5.

[70]Sinclair mss. Box 1. Folder 5. Copy of letter from Upton Sinclair to Priscilla Sinclair.

[71]Sinclair mss. Box 1. Folder 2. "Little Known Facts About Well-Known People," an article by Dale
Carnegie. Also, Sinclair, *Autobiography*, 31; and Leon Harris, *Upton Sinclair: American Rebel* (New York,
1975), 11-4.

[72]Sinclair, *Autobiography*, 112. Also, Harris, 171; and Upton Sinclair, *The Cry for Justice: An Anthology of Social Protest* (New York 1915), 18.

Sinclair was sure God had put him on the earth to give this one message to his fellow man. That "work" had for a lifetime been his all-consuming passion.[73]

## THE MAN WITH THE HOE

"I have a deep interest in your social gospel," the muckraking poet Edwin Markham wrote Upton Sinclair in May of 1910, "but I think you push it a little too far into the front of the stage."[74]

Despite the admonishment, Markham shared the thrust of Sinclair's social criticism and agreed with Baker and William Allen White that God "required cooperation" in bringing about change in the relations between business and labor and that central to that teaming was the application of the Golden Rule. The publication of his "Man with the Hoe" in 1899 won him worldwide recognition as a fighter in behalf of the working man. The poem itself was heralded as the "battle-cry of the next thousand years."[75] It led to the publication in 1900 of a collection of Markham's poetry and a separate volume that included the famous poem and his commentary on it. Both were publications of the Doubleday and McClure Company and reflected the underlying assumptions of much of the muckraking press in its infancy.

Clearly, Markham saw himself in Millet's depiction of a worker "bowed by the weight of centuries" and leaning over his hoe with the "emptiness of ages in his face" and the "burden of the world" on his back. The youngest child of pioneering parents, Markham never knew his father and quarreled with his mother during "lonely years" of farm and ranch work in Lagoon Valley, California. He saw himself one of the "hoemanry" who worked under "hard and incorrigible conditions." The "smack of the soil" and the "whir of the forge" had ever been in his "blood." What the hoeman represented to Markham, and by extension to other muckrakers of like-minded faith, was a "type of industrial oppression" found in "all lands and labors." The hoeman was the "symbol of betrayed humanity, the toiler ground down through ages of oppression, through ages of social injustice." His stooped image became a rallying cry for abolishing the "awful degradation of man through endless, hopeless and joyless labor." [76]

It was not the mere poverty of the industrial worker that Markham deplored "but the impossibility of escape from its killing frost." The only solution lay in the recognition of "Christ's work of public and organic righteousness." It was through that work that He sought to save both man and society from themselves. Work was "good" only if it was done "in the passion of joy." Men and women had achieved political liberty, but now they must follow the example of Christ if they were to achieve "industrial freedom." That freedom would only come when "we realize that I am my brother's keeper." Out of that realization would come "cooperation," which Markham, and then White after him, would describe as the "logic of Christianity."[77]

---

[73]Sinclair, *Autobiography*, 55. Also, Sinclair, *Cup of Fury*, 16; and Harris, 168.

[74]Sinclair, *Letters*, 96. Letter from Edwin Markham to Upton Sinclair, May 26, 1910.

[75]Louis Filler, *The Unknown Edwin Markham* (Yellow Springs, Ohio, 1966), ch. 5. Also, William L. Stidger, *Edwin Markham* (New York, 1933), ch. 6.

[76]Edwin Markham, *The Man with the Hoe* (New York, 1900), 19 and 23.

[77]Ibid., 32, 37-9 and 45-7.

In the thirty-five year career as lecturer following the publication of "Man with the Hoe," Markham continued to call for moral regeneration as the fountainhead for greater social justice. What had been the "purpose of Christ," he asked, "if not the realization of fraternity." That was the "holiest of all words," the word that carried with it the "essence of the gospels" and the "fulfillment of all revelations."[78]

In forty years of writing, Markham never achieved the impact he had with his critique of industrial relations. His work on "Lincoln, the Man of the People," as well as his crusade against child labor in *The Children of Bondage*, continued his passionate call for social justice, while collections published through 1920, particularly "The Shoes of Happiness" and "The Gates of Paradise," reflected his continuing assertion that man needed to cooperate with a "divine strategy" if he hoped to live a better life.[79]

In a private notebook, Markham recorded that it was "injustice" that he had "detested most." Men must learn that the only solution to the problem was the "carrying of the Christ-purpose in the heart" or what he called the "inbrothering of men for the common good." He was sure that "in a generation" the application of just such a principle would "cure all our social sorrows." The church should join the writers of the day in pushing a "spirit of reform." He observed, "the saving of men's souls is very closely connected with the amelioration of their social and industrial conditions." The church in the new century needed more than anything else "a baptism of the Holy Spirit," which he believed was the same as saying, "Social Spirit."[80]

*A THEORY OF SPIRITUAL PROGRESS*

Nowhere does the social spirit find a greater champion than William Allen White, the sage of Emporia, Kansas, who first came to the McClure group in 1897 with the publication of his "Boyville" stories and who stayed on the national scene as a publicist for progressive causes for more than forty years. It was during his first trip to the East that he had lunch with Theodore Roosevelt at the Army and Navy club, quickly falling under "the Great Man's spell." What followed was a highly public twenty-year career that White understood as service to the "moral vision" the two men shared. This vision recognized that a "social evolution" was already underway and needed to be encouraged by national policymakers. White saw it as a "step-at-a-time process to secure for the working classes, better environment in playgrounds, schools, housing, wages and shop conditions." He reasoned that "after a generation or two of workers bred in the newer, cleaner environment, a new vision will come to the workers — a vision which will justly solve the inequalities of the capitalist system." Unlike Steffens and Sinclair, White remained convinced that "capital may be harnessed for the

[78]Ibid., 47.

[79]Edwin Markham, *Lincoln and Other Poems* (New York, 1901). Also, Edwin Markham, *The Shoes of Happiness and Other Poems* (Garden City, 1931; originally 1913); and Edwin Markham, *The Gates of Paradise and Other Poems* (Garden City, 1920).

[80]Edwin Markham Scrapbook. "The Markham Book." January 1894. Box 3455. Library of Congress. Washington, D.C. Also an article he wrote for the *New York Times*, appearing October 21, 1899, and an interview with the *San Francisco Bulletin*, appearing December 30, 1900, in Box 355.

common good as well as for private greed."[81]

How that "harnessing" would occur is best described in White's epistle, *A Theory of Spiritual Progress*, published in 1910. White wrote that although the world was hardly a "chocolate eclair" there could be no denying that life on the planet was "outward bound." The choice between life as an "eternal grind" and an "eternal journey" was lived in the context of a society where "the public sense of evildoing was widening." This was a good sign, because "cruelty becomes intolerable as men become aware that it exists." As the "sensibilities" of the common man grew, his capacity for "kindness" grew. His goodwill broadened. His fellow man benefited. People insisted on the passage of laws more closely approximating patterns of social justice. This was the core of White's theory of "spiritual progress."[82]

The theory visualized the working out of Darwinian evolution in societal terms based on the Golden Rule and the character of Jesus Christ. In 1914, White wrote that he believed the world was "growing better" because it was becoming "more and more capable of understanding the social and spiritual message of Jesus Christ." It seemed to him that society was coming to recognize what he had long seen — "that Christ is not only the living God, but the only true growing God in all the world."[83]

White's spiritual intensity appears to have come from his mother, even as his spiritual unrest appears to have been drawn from a conflict lived out between his parents.[84] White's mother had been an early convert to anti-slavery Republicanism, who had moved while a teenager with a Congregational family to Galesburg, Illinois. There she witnessed the Lincoln-Douglas debate, falling "platonically in love" for a lifetime with Lincoln. It took ten years of hard work to get her education at Knox College, where she sat under the teaching of Dr. Albert Hurd, the man whose daughter would marry White's sometime boss — S.S. McClure.[85]

White's father was a lifelong Democrat, interested in the political life of Kansas. For a time, he had even served as the mayor of a small town, Eldorado. He had little use for his wife's campaign to civilize their only child, by encouraging his church activities and by reading to him out of the Good Book at night. White idealized his schooling on the Kansas plains. "We sang gospel hymns every morning," he wrote, "and the teacher read a chapter in the Bible. There was no nonsense about that. For we were all little Protestants. She made us say the Lord's prayer after Bible reading, and then we were all started off right for the day. At noon we sang another gospel hymn and loved it."[86]

White's own conversion came during his college days. He called it the "night of the light." It left him with a sense that even if the higher criticism be

---

[81]William Allen White, *The Autobiography of William Allen White* (New York, 1946), 300. Also, William Allen White, Letterbook September 20, 1913. A letter from William Allen White to Fred D. Warren. Container B29, pt. 2. Library of Congress.

[82]William Allen White, *A Theory of Spiritual Progress* (Emporia, Kansas, 1910), 3. 13, 15, 24 and 36.

[83]William Allen White, Letterbook. June 3, 1914. A letter from William Allen White to Rev. Clifford Cole. Container B29, pt. 2.

[84]Sally Griffith, *Home Town News* (New York, 1988), ch. 1, particularly p. 28, and ch. 4, particularly 169-79..

[85]White, *Autobiography*, 67.

[86]Ibid., 38.

right, and much of the Bible a "myth," there was no getting around who Jesus Christ was. To White's mind, Jesus was the "greatest hero in history." Human happiness was achieved only to the degree people "made His philosophy a part of human institutions." Jesus had died to save the world by "demonstrating through His crucifixion and the symbol of his resurrection the indestructibility of truth."[87]

The essence of White's social gospel stemmed from his conviction that the simple application of the Golden Rule in human affairs would regenerate the social order. "I think the job of the church today," he wrote, "is to make a public opinion that will so revolutionize our industry, commerce, and political life that it will be possible for a man to live a generous, useful Christian life without hurt or harm to himself or his family."[88]

While he preached a message of spiritual reconciliation, White, like many of the publicists for progressivism, had a hard time reconciling the old familiar faith with the relativism of the new moral order. The churches were failed institutions. He had only gone to them as a lad, he snapped, to meet pretty girls, and had continued going as a father because he thought it might be good for his children. But a preacher's business was not "any more exalted" as a "calling" than was the work of the newspaperman. The purpose of both, he charged in *The Old Order Changeth*, was to recognize that in the "daily struggle for existence" God was nevertheless "fulfilling himself in the affairs of man." The growth of democratic institutions had been "God-inspired." The "upward direction" of social change had proved there was a "director."[89]

Theodore Roosevelt had been "God's man" because he had "kept the faith" while serving as a role model for how the twentieth-century man should act in his relations to other men. He had encouraged the development of the "hero" in every person and in so doing had demonstrated that the "kingdom of God is within us." The revolution from "kings to capitalism" had been but one step in an evolutionary process at work in the human community.[90] Now democracy was "seeking to control capital." Roosevelt had shown a way of "expanding people's vision" to what democracy was about. Democracy was the playing out of the "self-abnegation of the Christian life" and was the greatest movement "in all of our national life."[91]

*PROGRESSIVISM AND PESSIMISM*

White's pre-war assertion that the "worker for good will is paid in eternity" and that "righteousness exalted a nation" as the "divine spark" burned "in every soul" may have seemed like wearied rhetoric to the generation of the twenties. White continued to chronicle the great men and movements of his time, always

---

[87]Ibid., 108.

[88]John DeWitt McKee, *William Allen White: Maverick on Main Street* (Westport, Conn., 1975), 199-200.

[89]William Allen White, Letterbook. November 23, 1914. A letter from William Allen White to Eugene Bryan. Library of Congress.

[90]William Allen White, *The Old Order Changeth* (New York, 1910), 251 and 263.

[91]Walter Johnson, ed., *Selected Letters of William Allen White: 1899-1943* (New York 1947), 34 and 97. Also, White, *The Old Order Changeth*, 3-4 and 229-38. Also, McKee, *William Allen White: Maverick on Main Street*, 198-203.

reshaping them in his image of the past. "What a God-damned world this is!" he wrote Baker, following Harding's election. "Starvation on the one hand, and indifference on the other, pessimism rampant, faith quiescent, murder met with indifference, the lowered standard of civilization faced with universal complaisance, and the whole story so sad that nobody can tell it. If anyone had told me ten years ago that our country would be what it is today, and that the world would be what it is today, I should have questioned his reason.[92]

In 1925, White wrote *Some Cycles of Cathay*, a work that fairly summarized much of the thinking and many of the fears of that remarkable group of men and women who had fought with their pens for progressive purposes for more than a generation. He claimed that his belief in democratic growth under the influence of the Christian philosophy as expressed in the teachings of Christ and the Golden Rule remained unshakable. It alone provided a framework that dignified "individual humanity." That had been his message all along.[93]

White and his contemporaries remained convinced that there was a "moral purpose behind man's destiny." People still needed to learn that central fact. The cycle in which people now lived had sadly shown that "men will not take truth except through force and at a terrible cost." But eventually they must be made to see that the only hope for the human community lay in recognizing "the destiny God has given us." That destiny must continue to be made known to them by writers of the new generation. It was a destiny in which all people could progress "together" or not at all, for they could live "by faith" that would sustain a "larger vision" or they would succumb to the "chaos" around them.[94]

White's hope, and the hope of his fellow foot-soldiers, was that social justice would become a permanent part of economic and political institutions as people came to develop the "Christ" that was in them. This belief was a complex of many ideas, most central of which were the writers' own evangelical upbringings, the impact of Darwinian evolution and the higher criticism on that belief, and the lifelong struggle that then emerged to integrate their faith to the social problems their generation encountered. What makes their work all the more remarkable was that it sprang from the crucible of the writers' own spiritual and intellectual struggles, yet became translated into a social program designed to solve the fundamental injustices of their era.

The paradox of the progressive program the muckrakers espoused was that many of them wondered whether it could really be made to work. These men and women who earnestly tried to teach other men and women to be their brother's keeper remained lifelong pupils themselves. Their lives were experiments in man's personal struggle with God and his social relationship to other men.

---

[92]Johnson, *Selected Letters of William Allen White*, 213. Copy of letter from William Allen White to Ray Stannard Baker, December 8, 1920.

[93]William Allen White, *Some Cycles of Cathay* (Chapel Hill, 1925), preface and 123.

[94]Ibid., 23, 60 and 87-8.

# 13

# The Religious Roots of Sigma Delta Chi
by Judith M. Buddenbaum

ON THURSDAY, MAY 6, 1909, TEN YOUNG MEN dressed in their Sunday suits and wearing black and white pledge ribbons in their lapels marched into Meharry Hall on the campus of DePauw University and took their seats in a front pew just as the chapel speaker for the day began the invocation.[1]

The men were Gilbert B. Clippinger, Charles A. Fisher, William M. Glenn, Marion H. Hedges, Aldis Hutchens, Edward H. Lockwood, LeRoy H. Millikan, Eugene C. Pulliam, Paul Riddick, and Lawrence Sloan. Their brief demonstration announced to the university and to the world that they had founded Sigma Delta Chi, an honorary fraternity for members of the journalism profession.

In writing about professionalism, scholars generally depict a nationwide trend arising from the faith in science that began during the nineteenth century and continued into the twentieth. As part of this trend, some say journalists borrowed the values and methodology of the sciences as they banded together to improve their status in the face of poor working conditions, to quiet complaints about commercialism, sensationalism, and "yellow journalism," and later to deal with a growing suspicion that values and even facts are subjective.[2]

However, a study of the first two volumes of the *DePauw Daily* newspaper, later writings by the founders of Sigma Delta Chi, and other material related to Sigma Delta Chi located in the DePauw University Archives suggests this general account of the origins of professionalism is only a part of the explanation.

The founders of Sigma Delta Chi were concerned about status, but their concern was purely local, growing out of conditions on the DePauw campus. They appear to have assumed that journalists who did not engage in sensationalism had their rightly deserved status on other campuses and in the real world of professional newspaper work. Their desire to see Sigma Delta Chi become a nation-

---

[1]"Sigma Delta Chi Came Out," *DePauw Daily* (Greencastle, Ind.), 6 May 1909, 1.

[2]Edwin Emery and Michael Emery, *The Press and America*, 4th ed. (Engelwood Cliffs, N.J.: Prentice-Hall, 1978), 510-3; Clifford G. Christians, Quentin J. Schultze and Norman H. Sims. "Community, Epistemology and Mass Media Ethics," *Journalism History*, 5(1978): 38-41, 65-7; Michael Schudson, *Discovering the News* (New York: Basic Books, 1978), 152-4, 160.

wide fraternity was partly due to a school spirit that expected DePauw to be preeminent in all areas, but it was also partly the result of a determination to spread their own values to other journalists. Those values were grounded as firmly in the Methodist religion as in science and social science.

## THE ACADEMIC AND CULTURAL CLIMATE AT DEPAUW

In the first decade of the twentieth century, DePauw University, with an enrollment of approximately 500 men and women, was one of the three largest universities in Indiana.[3] It had a reputation for academic excellence and professional training, but it was also a Methodist school where the noted evangelist Billy Sunday could send his daughter without fear for her reputation or her faith.[4]

The only blot on the DePauw record came from campus politics that involved not only class elections and authorized student government activities, but also "class scraps," student demonstrations against faculty and administrators and their decisions, and sporadic episodes of vandalism.[5]

An anonymous student writing in the February 1906 *Bulletin* that Fisher, Hedges, Riddick, and Pulliam would have received as an orientation guide for prospective students reported: "Probably we have as much excitement and feeling about college politics as anywhere.... Three fraternities form one party, and a good many of the non-fraternity men and some sorority girls with them; while six fraternities, some of the non-fraternity men, and the rest of the sororities form the other."[6] This party factionalism touched all campus activities and was the cause of the birth and death of at least five student newspapers from 1893 to 1907. During this period the custom was for the student body president to name the newspaper editor who, in turn, would use his position to support the party, sometimes going so far as to exclude all mention of the rival faction. Publication of "bogues" — scandal sheets published by one faction to undermine the reputation of members of the rival party — were also common.[7]

No newspapers or "bogues" from this partisan era have been preserved in the DePauw Archives, but some idea of the state of DePauw journalism at the time can be found in the yearbooks. In the 1905 *Mirage*, the *DePauw Weekly* used its allotted space to complain:

One thing is needed badly. That is a permanent organization of some sort that will give the paper a sure foundation. A constitution expressly for the college organ is essential.... Student fights should not select those who are to have it in control. A more conservative method should be followed and only men of newspaper and journalistic inclination be editors of it.

Factionalism limits the influence of the paper to a noticeable degree, in that the staff does not feel perfectly free in certain instances to do what they should

---

[3]William Warren Sweet, *Indiana Asbury-DePauw University 1837-1937* (New York: Abingdon, 1937), 132.

[4]"Billy Sunday Picks DePauw," *DePauw Daily*, 13 April 1909, 1.

[5]Sweet, *Indiana Asbury....*, 170-7.

[6]"A Student's Description of Life at DePauw," *Bulletin*, Greencastle, Ind., DePauw University, New Series 3(1):24. February 1906.

[7]George B. Manhart, *DePauw Through the Years*, 2 vols. (Greencastle, Ind.: DePauw University, 1962), 1:258.

be allowed to do.[8]

Although the *Weekly* appeared sporadically for another year or so, publication apparently ceased during the 1906-07 school year.[9] The 1907 *Mirage* has no entry for a student newspaper.

This situation could not have pleased the student founders of Sigma Delta Chi. The same *Bulletin* that explained party politics to new students also reported, "the student body gives you the impression of being here for business."[10] By the fall of 1907 all of the founders except Glenn and Sloan were on campus, and for them "business" meant journalism. They had come to DePauw already committed to careers in journalism, and at DePauw they expected to receive both a classical education and practical preparation in their chosen field.[11]

In his inaugural address, DePauw President Edwin Holt Hughes promised an education that would combine a grounding in religion and the classics with opportunities to apply the lessons derived from that kind of study to practical situations;[12] the *Bulletin* extolled this blend of classical and "scientific" work:

Take these classic old halls, where perhaps your grandfather used to recite and then look over yonder to Minshall Laboratory, new and conspicuous for its up-to-dateness, and in these extremes you have typified the DePauw spirit.[13]

That blend of a classical education and practical experience existed for the future lawyers, doctors, ministers, scientists and teachers, but the journalism students found only the classics. In order to get the practice, they first had to make journalism respectable on the DePauw campus.

*THE QUEST FOR RESPECTABLE JOURNALISM*

During the fall of 1906, as the *DePauw Weekly's* problems with campus factionalism mounted, Fisher, Hedges, Hutchens, Lockwood, Mann, Millikan, Paul and Foster Riddick, and a handful of other students found a friend in Nathaniel Waring Barnes, professor of rhetoric and composition. Together they established the Press Club.

Beginning on January 15, 1907, the students and their advisors met monthly in fraternity houses or at Barnes' home for food, conversation about journalism, and criticism of the students' reporting efforts. In these meetings they discussed publishing a daily student newspaper. The idea was accepted, and planning began. During the summer of 1907 arrangements were made to use the *Greencastle Herald's* facilities to print the paper.[14]

[8]"DePauw Weekly," *Mirage* (Greencastle, Ind.: DePauw University, 1905), 105.

[9]Manhart, *DePauw....*, 258.

[10]"A Student's Description...," 24.

[11]William Meharry Glenn, *The Sigma Delta Chi Story* (Coral Gables, Fla.: Glade House, 1949), 63-72; Russ Pulliam, "Methodism Shaped Life View of Publisher Pulliam," *DePauw Alumnus*, July 1979, 34-5.

[12]Edwin Holt Hughes, "The Message of Christian Education," *Bulletin*, Greencastle, Ind., DePauw University, New Series 1(1): 14-32. February 1904.

[13]"Introduction," *Bulletin*, Greencastle, Ind., DePauw University. New Series 3(1):1. February 1906.

[14]"DePauw Daily," *Mirage* (Greencastle, Ind.: DePauw University, 1909), 190, 199; "Editorial," *DePauw Daily*, 29 May 1909, 2.

The first *DePauw Daily* rolled off the presses on Tuesday, October 1, 1907. With that issue the campaign to make journalism respectable on the DePauw campus began in earnest.

The lead article, filling the entire first column and part of the second column on page one, consisted of congratulatory "telegrams" to the paper. The messages may have been written by the *Daily* staff, but they did call attention to the new paper. They also described the kind of reporting the students hoped to do.[15] The "Society and Personal Mention" column on page four contained a quote from a Professor Kleinsmid saying "the *DePauw Daily* is a good thing and should be supported from the financial standpoint as well as the literary."[16] The page-two editorial explained the paper was being published on a trial basis because "[t]he management was met with the demand, 'Show us your paper and we will subscribe.'" The editorial called for at least 200 new subscribers unless "you desire to be classed as members of a second rate, unprogressive school...."[17]

During the remainder of the first week, the *Daily* carried letters of support from the *Indianapolis Star*, the *Indianapolis News*, and the *Indiana* [University] *Daily Student*,[18] as well as editorials describing the newspaper and calling for new subscribers to it.[19]

By Tuesday, October 8, funding was "secure," and the staff announced in an editorial that publication would continue for the entire school year. However, many students apparently were still unwilling to believe that this paper deserved their full support because the editorial went on to say:

... there is not a man on the staff who is receiving one cent of emolument or one hour of credit for his work. Every member of the staff has put his name down for two dollars and fifty cents, [the subscription price]....

This paper is as much yours as it is ours and you should have as much interest in it. Now besides the financial end, you can give strong support [by contributing news and essays].[20]

The congratulatory letters and the editorials describing newspaper policy and calling for contributions of news and opinions from readers were constant features of the campaign for respectability during the next two years,[21] but two events during the first month of publication quieted student mistrust of the newspaper by demonstrating the *Daily* was not a mouthpiece for any campus faction.

On October 11 the paper announced in a page one story that the newspaper would be reorganized with staff positions open to all students, including fresh-

---

[15]"Good Words of Cheer," *DePauw Daily*, 1 October 1907, 1. "Authors" of the telegrams include William R. Hearst, John D. Rockefeller, Tammany Hall, and King Alfonse of Spain.

[16]"Society and Personal Mention," *DePauw Daily*, 1 October 1907, 4.

[17]"Good Morning," *DePauw Daily*, 1 October 1907, 2.

[18]"Many Pretty Bouquets," *DePauw Daily*, 3 October 1907, 1.

[19]"Editorial," *DePauw Daily*, 3 October 1907, 2; Editorial," *DePauw Daily*, 4 October 1907, 1907, 2; "Aufwiedersehen," *DePauw Daily*, 5 October 1907, 2.

[20]"All's Well," *DePauw Daily*, 8 October 1907, 2.

[21]See, for example: "Paper Pleases Him," *DePauw Daily*, 26 November 1907, 2; "Trustees Like the Daily," *DePauw Daily*, 30 January 1908, 1; "Editorial," *DePauw Daily*, 3 March 1908, 2; "Why Country Editors Get Rich," *DePauw Daily*, 10 October 10 1908, 2; "Foster Clippinger Praises Daily," *DePauw Daily*, 4 February 1909, 1.

men, on a competitive basis. A constitution would also be adopted.[22]

The same day, Pulliam, a freshman, joined the staff as assistant business manager.[23] Two weeks later the *Daily* listed new members of the Press Club who would also be working on the newspaper.[24]

During October the paper also reported, without editorial comment, that the faculty declared Gilbert Clippinger's election as president of the sophomore class void because of voting irregularities[25] and that C.U. Crick was elected president in a subsequent election.[26]

Although the promised constitution with its guarantees that staff selections would be permanently separated from student politics did not appear until late February,[27] the handling of the Clippinger-Crick election and the staff reorganization won the confidence of the university community. From then on, the student journalists were free to devote the majority of their editorial attention to their concern for the status of DePauw journalists in relation to their peers on other campuses.

The campaign for status for journalism education began on December 3 with a *Daily* article announcing that the Press Club would "launch a movement" for a new journalism course.[28] It continued after Barnes was given faculty permission to teach such a course on a non-credit basis.[29] By quoting guest lecturers in stories about the Press Club and journalism class, the staff planted the ideas that journalism is a profession comparable to law, medicine, and the ministry,[30] that college training in journalism is necessary,[31] and that college-educated journalists are concerned about ethics,[32] use methods compatible with religious values,[33] and can "add a bit more to the world's knowledge,"[34] and be a "great force for good ... and a strong element in the development of [citizenship]."[35]

The attempt to make DePauw journalism the equivalent of what the staff assumed journalism to be on other campuses began with the first *Daily* editorial linking a call for subscribers to school pride,[36] and continued throughout the two year period with news stories and reports about journalism on other campuses,[37] and exchanges of editorials with the Indiana *Daily Student*,[38] *Purdue*

---

[22]"May Reorganize Staff," *DePauw Daily*, 11 October 1907, 1.

[23]Masthead, *DePauw Daily*, 11 October 1907, 2.

[24]"Berths for Three Men," *DePauw Daily*, 23 October 1907, 1.

[25]"New Elections Held," *DePauw Daily*, 19 October 1907, 1.

[26]"Crick Was Elected," *DePauw Daily*, 30 October 1907, 1.

[27]"EXTRA," *DePauw Daily*, 25 February 1908, 1.

[28]"Press Club Meeting," *DePauw Daily*, 3 December 1907, 1.

[29]"Course Allowed by Faculty Meeting," *DePauw Daily*, 11 December 1907, 1.

[30]"A Great Field," *DePauw Daily*, 24 October 1907, 1.

[31]"Work in New Field," *DePauw Daily*, 14 January 1908, 1; "Barnes-Managing Editor," *DePauw Daily*, 6 October 1908, 1.

[32]"Yellow Journalism," *DePauw Daily*, 17 April 1908, 1.

[33]"Meredith Nichols," *DePauw Daily*, 20 January 1909, 1.

[34]"Work in New Field," *DePauw Daily*, 14 January 1908, 1.

[35]"A Freshman," *DePauw Daily*, 15 January 1908, 2.

[36]"Editorial," *DePauw Daily*, 1 October 1907, 2.

[37]"Miami University," *DePauw Daily*, 15 January 1908, 1; "Journalism is Important," *DePauw Daily*, 9 January 9, 1909, 1; "Decline in Editorial Standards," *DePauw Daily*, 23 April 1909, 2; "Colonel Wilson," *DePauw Daily*, 22 May 1909, 1.

[38]"Decline in Editorial Standards," *DePauw Daily*, 23 April 1909, 2.

*Exponent*,[39] and *Indianapolis News*.[40] By the spring of 1909 the students had been, for the most part, successful in their campaign to make journalism respectable on the DePauw campus. The *Daily* had undergone two transfers of editorial control without any interference from campus politics[41] and had become an "institution."[42] But certain problems remained. The faculty still had not granted university credit to students taking the journalism course, and there were rumors the course itself would be discontinued.[43] There was also the matter of the status of DePauw journalism compared to the status of journalism at other schools. During this two-year period the DePauw Press Club was a member of the Indiana State Intercollegiate Association of Press Clubs along with Indiana and Purdue universities and Wabash, Hanover, and Earlham colleges. Indiana University was the leader in that organization,[44] but DePauw students were unaccustomed to accepting second-class status.

Although an honorary fraternity for the journalism profession was not necessary to secure the continued operation of the *DePauw Daily* and was not really necessary to provide student journalists with status equal to that of other interest groups on campus, the idea occurred to the journalism students that such a fraternity was a logical additional step in their campaign for respectability.[45]

Accounts differ as to whether the idea for the new fraternity belonged to Glenn and Sloan[46] or to Millikan, Hutchens, and Mann,[47] but the idea certainly grew out of the realization that such an organization would validate the status of journalism on the DePauw campus and would also secure DePauw's place among other schools by providing a platform for spreading the DePauw brand of respectable journalism.

*THE MARKS OF A RESPECTABLE JOURNALISM*

The earliest statement about the kind of journalism the students considered respectable and the kind they hoped to provide appeared in an editorial on October 12, 1907:

There are three paramount duties that should govern every newspaper in its attempt to produce something of value to the reading public. First it must give the news, second it must verify it where possible, and third it must present it to the readers in as good form as possible. If there is a failure in any

[39]"Editorial," *DePauw Daily*, 3 March 1908, 2.

[40]"Editorial," *DePauw Daily*, 6 December 1907, 2.

[41]"Daily Election Today," *DePauw Daily*, 25 April 1908, 1; "Ballots To Be Collected," *DePauw Daily*, 9 May 1908, 1; "Thirty," *DePauw Daily*, 12 May 1908, 2; "Try-outs," *DePauw Daily*, 27 March 1909, 1; "New Staff is Elected," *DePauw Daily*, 11 May 1909, 1.

[42]"Probation Period for New Staff," *DePauw Daily*, 11 May 1909, 2.

[43]"Press Club to Banquet," *DePauw Daily*, 12 May 1909, 3.

[44]"Press Club Members," *DePauw Daily*, 2 April 1908, 1; "Edward Lockwood of DePauw," *DePauw Daily*, 10 April 1908, 1; "Press Club to Meet at IU," *DePauw Daily*, 7 April 1909, 1; "Preparations for Meeting," *DePauw Daily*, 22 April 1909, 1; "Press Club Admits Hanover," *DePauw Daily*, 23 April 1909, 1; "Convention a Success," *DePauw Daily*, 8 May 1909, 1.

[45]Manhart, *DePauw...*, 142-4, 204, 273, and 274-82.

[46]Glenn, *The Sigma Delta Chi Story*, 17-32; Paul Riddick, "Letters," Sigma Delta Chi file, DePauw University Archives, DC 945. July 30, 1976, and August 13, 1976.

[47]Charles C. Clayton, *Fifty Years for Freedom* (Carbondale: Southern Illinois University Press, 1959), 7-11; Pulliam, "Methodism Shaped...," 34.

one of these three lines there is a falling away of subscriptions and a growing tone of dissatisfaction. Therefore, for this reason, if no other, the editors desire to please their readers.[48]

In practice, the definition of news became comprehensive coverage of all events and all shades of opinion on campus or related to campus activities. Good form became defined as journalism free from personal attacks and sensationalism. The desire to please readers was met both through comprehensive news coverage and through repeated requests for readers to contribute news tips, provide news releases, and express their concerns personally to the staff or publicly through letters to the editor.[49]

But those attributes were never intended to make the newspaper a mere conduit for other people's news and views. Rather, giving the news in "good form" and pleasing readers were methods designed to attract the readership that would allow the newspaper to separate itself from power groups. A respectable newspaper was seen as an independent voice in society and an independent force for good, as defined by the newspaper itself. A news article about the Press Club told how, through the work of club members, "'yellow' journalism is receiving its sentence, ... the days of the subsidized press [are] waning, ... the black-and-white muckrakers must give way to intelligent reformers."[50]

As an independent, reform voice, the *Daily* spoke out, even before its place on campus was assured, against an attempt by "underclassmen" and "certain fraternity leaders" to organize Ku Klux Klan activities.[51] It also criticized faculty members who "abuse their powers and privileges."[52] Later the *Daily* broke the long-standing school policy against student involvement in non-student political movements[53] with a call for students to support Taft in the 1908 election and to work on behalf of local temperance candidates and the referendum to make Putnam County, where DePauw University is located, a "dry" county.[54] The *Daily* also investigated an administration attempt to substitute a mandatory activity fee for the well-established custom under which each organization selected a business manager to raise any necessary funds[55] and expressed frequent concern that students develop sound moral values and exhibit proper behavior.[56] Each issue, beginning with the first, carried "Little Stories of Daily Living," which presented short sermons based on reports of happenings on the DePauw campus.

Although the *Daily's* opposition to partisanship, dislike for sensationalism, interest in public morals and behavior, and desire to be a public service are very similar to the press philosophy developed by other "progressive" voices of the

---

[48]"Two Toots," *DePauw Daily*, 12 October 1907, 2.

[49]"All's Well," *DePauw Daily*, 8 October 1907, 2; "Editorial," *DePauw Daily*, 24 September 1908, 2; "Editorial," *DePauw Daily*, 8 October 1908, 2; "Editorial," *DePauw Daily*, 8 December 1908, 2; "Editorial," *DePauw Daily*, 4 February 1909, 2.

[50]"Press Club to Meet," *DePauw Daily*, 10 April 1908, 1.

[51]"A Mystery," *DePauw Daily*, 5 October 1907, 1.

[52]Untitled item, *DePauw Daily*, 23 October 1907, 2.

[53]Manhart, *DePauw*..., 260-61.

[54]"Editorial," *DePauw Daily*, 24 October 1908, 2; See also Manhart, *DePauw*..., 261.

[55]"Business Managers Should Stay," *DePauw Daily*, 29 April 1909, 2.

[56]"Editorial," *DePauw Daily*, 4 October 1907, 2; "Food Fights in Dorm," *DePauw Daily*, 9 November 1907, 1; "Editorial," *DePauw Daily*, 1 November 1908, 1; "Editorial," and "Opinions," *DePauw Daily*, 12 December 1908, 2; "Editorial," and "Opinions," *DePauw Daily*, 4 February 1909, 2.

era,[57] the students' reporting style was somewhat different. A sense of fairness required them to report all events and cover at least two sides of most controversies, but it did not lead them to separate fact and opinion or to avoid marshaling arguments in news stories.[58] Instead of the summary lead followed by a piling up of facts in inverted-pyramid fashion espoused by "scientific" reporting, the students advocated and frequently used the rhetorical style of the pulpit.[59]

*JOURNALISM AND METHODISM*

The borrowing from the progressive movement and from the methodology of science and social science that occurred in the paper was really a borrowing filtered through the teachings of the Methodist Church. It was done for the purpose of making journalism a force for good in society. That underlying purpose developed as much from the Methodist concept of mission as from the progressive's notion of reform.

In his study of the development of social responsibility in the Methodist Episcopal Church, Tuveson points out that the period between the end of the Civil War and the beginning of World War I is usually depicted as an age of secularism and scientific realism, "but it was also the last time in history when responsible thinkers thought of human life and history as dominated or at least strongly affected by angels and demons."[60]

Methodism of the era was a "confident and aggressive" faith engaged in an "aggressive mission to Christianize every aspect of society." Its mission was shaped by the belief that the very size and prominence of the Methodist Church in America was "a sign of divine favor" that carried with it a special responsibility. This mission came to be seen as a duty to "educate, emancipate and permeate society with religion and finally to convert the world."[61]

To accomplish these aims, Methodists were taught that people are sinful, but they can be made better through instruction in right living. As a corollary, society, too, can be perfected so that it will become more God-pleasing and more conducive to the kind of right living that will make it easier to convert others and help them live in accord with their faith. But for that kind of perfectionism to occur, good Christians must set an example in their private and public lives because "doing the Gospel" is more effective than overt evangelizing.[62] Therefore, Methodists of the era were also counseled to "adjust their views to newly discovered facts" because "Truth can never be hurt by new light."[63]

Sermons and articles in religious periodicals effectively spread the idea that secular vocations are "calls" from God[64] and that science and scientific method-

---

[57]Christian, Schultze and Sims, "Community...," 34-5.

[58]See, for example: "What Should Have Been," *DePauw Daily*, 11 February 1908, 1; "Press Club to Meet," *DePauw Daily*, 10 April 1908, 1.

[59]"Prof. Gough Deplores News Writing," *DePauw Daily*, 10 November 1908, 1; "Meredith Nichols," *DePauw Daily*, 22 January 1909, 1; "A Decline in Editorial Standards," *DePauw Daily*, 24 April 1909, 2.

[60]Ernest Lee Tuveson, *Redeemer Nation* (Chicago: University of Chicago Press, 1968), 205.

[61]Donald G. Jones, *The Sectional Crisis and Northern Methodism: A Study in Piety, Political Ethics and Civil Religion* (Metuchen, N.J.: The Scarecrow Press, 1979), 3, 30, 123.

[62]Daniel Dorchester, *The Why of Methodism*, quoted in Frederick A. Norwood, *The Story of American Methodism* (New York: The Abingdon Press, 1974), 321-2.

[63]Milton S. Terry, *Biblical Dogmatics*, quoted in Norwood, *The Story...*, 319-20.

[64]See, for example, P. H. Swift, "The Problem of Religious Life in the City," *Methodist Review*, May-June

ology are proper tools for understanding religion and for fulfilling their missionary responsibilities by setting a good example.[65]

At DePauw this Methodist understanding of mission and purpose was part of
the academic climate and the student culture. In 1832 the Indiana Conference of
the Methodist Episcopal Church voted to establish the school in order to provide education that would be both classical and practical because "next to the religion of the Son of God, the lights of science [are] best calculated to lessen human woe and increase the sum of human happiness."[66] The same writer who declared turn-of-the-century DePauw as a school split by campus political factions
where students, nevertheless, "meant business," was also careful to note: "And
one may say the DePauw spirit is essentially religious. The average student has
not the prayer meeting sort of religion, perhaps; but the YMCA and YWCA
thrive, filling Plato Hall, and the University service always is crowded."[67]

This was the "theology of doing."[68] If the students engaged in a service project, took the pains to use the latest scientific methodology appropriately in their
work, or spoke of the need to improve the world, the underlying connection to
religion was clear to them as Methodists of their era. They assumed there was
no need to cite Bible verses or make explicit statements linking methodology
and social responsibility to the ultimate purpose of mission to make the connection clear to others. From their background and their education, they knew they
could perfect people and society and that true religion, buttressed by science and
the scientific method, was the way to do it.

Edwin Holt Hughes used the occasion of his 1904 inauguration as president
of DePauw to discuss DePauw's purpose. Christian schools, he said, must provide a classical education grounded in religion and also practical vocational and
scientific training because all vocations are sacred. Only this combination of
"classical and modern" education could provide citizens who are strong in their
faith, able to stand up against "error," and use their vocations as a "force for
good in society."[69] Three years later he inaugurated a chapel series devoted to
life work and Christian duty.[70] Picking up on the idea, Professor Barnes invited
the editor of the *Indianapolis Star* to make the connection between journalism
and Christian responsibility explicit in a lecture to members of the new
journalism class.[71]

*A METHODIST UNDERSTANDING OF JOURNALISM*

Methodist periodicals promoted the idea that the press is a force for good in so-

---

1900, 405-17; W. L. McLennan, "The Place and Work of the Laity in the Church," *Methodist Review*, November-December 1902, 924-38; R. T. Stevenson, "The Missionary Interpretation of History," *Methodist Review*, July-August 1905, 534-47.

[65]See, for example, T. McK. Stuart, "Evolution and the Miraculous," *Methodist Review*, May-June 1903, 360-72; J. B. Young, "The Argument for Mathematical Order," *Methodist Review*, September-October 1903, 729-43; William Love, "Science and Science Falsely So-Called," *Methodist Review*, January-February 1905, 108-11.

[66]"Introduction," *Bulletin*, Greencastle, Ind., DePauw University. New Series 4(2):1. May 1907.

[67]"A Student's Description of Life at DePauw," *Bulletin*, 3(1).

[68]Dorchester, *The Why*, 321-2.

[69]Hughes, *The Message*, 28-30.

[70]"Dr. Hughes Announces Series," *DePauw Daily*, 7 November 1907, 1.

[71]"Get Results Says Fisher," *DePauw Daily*, 28 January 1908, 1.

ciety and that by using proper methodology the press can be a "secular pulpit."[72] Those themes also appeared frequently in the *DePauw Daily*.[73]

On the two occasions during this period that the *Daily* carried complete stories from other newspapers, it was to make an essentially religious connection between journalism and social responsibility. In a 1909 article taken from the Columbia University *Spectator*, Arthur Brisbane of the *New York Journal* was quoted as saying of his work: "... I was imitating the thunderstorms of God. My only regret is that I cannot make thunder; if I could do that, the paper would be perfect."[74] Later in the same year the *Daily* reported that Col. Wilson of the *Ohio State Journal* told students at Ohio Wesleyan University: "A newspaper's business is to tell briefly and clearly for the purpose of elevating and inspiring man. I don't think it has any right to live unless it endeavors to lift up the morals of the people...."[75]

On one level the founding of Sigma Delta Chi was one step in a campaign to make journalism respectable on the DePauw campus. Because of purely local conditions, the students had to find some way to gain the training they felt they needed for their chosen career and that they felt DePauw had promised them. The Press Club and the daily newspaper gave them a laboratory to gain professional skills and also some status on campus. The founding of Sigma Delta Chi assured them that they would be remembered and that the respectable journalism they sought to practice as staff members of the *Daily* would continue at DePauw after they graduated. It also secured DePauw's place among other schools offering journalism training and thus added to their status both on the campus and later when they entered the job market.

But on a second level the founding of Sigma Delta Chi was the first step in bringing a distinctly Methodist understanding of vocation and of proper journalistic methodology and purpose to a broader audience. From the very beginning the students assumed that if they, as reporters and editors, acquired the necessary skills and used them appropriately, the newspaper would be a respectable voice and a force for good. The press could be and should be a secular pulpit, but to be an effective one, there would have to be more trained and dedicated journalists throughout the nation than DePauw alone could provide.

It was the idea of journalism as mission that the founders sought to spread through Sigma Delta Chi and through the example of their own work. The first ritual of the fraternity instructed pledges: "There are world evils to be corrected, there are moral fences to be mended, there are local cesspools to be cleaned ... thieves must be scourged from the temple.... We would secure to you the profession of educators and evangelists, Journalism!"[76] In his history of the fraternity, Clayton wrote: "The explanation of why Sigma Delta Chi grew in size and stature and soon absorbed or outdistanced its rivals can be found in part in the missionary zeal of its founders and early leaders. In retrospect, however, it

---

[72]See, for example: "The ? Election - Its Lessons," *Christian Advocate* (New York), 24 November 1864, 372; Swift, "The Problem...," 414; J.C. Jackson, "The Church and Society: A New Alignment for a New Ideal," *Methodist Review*, January-February 1901, 9-19.

[73]"Good Words of Cheer," *DePauw Daily*, 1 October 1907, 1; "A Freshman," *DePauw Daily*, 15 January 1908, 2; "Journalism Is Important," *DePauw Daily*, 9 January 1909, 1.

[74]Ibid.

[75]"Colonel Wilson," *DePauw Daily*, 22 May 1909, 1.

[76]"Ritual," quoted in Pulliam, "Methodism Shaped...," 35.

appears clear that the driving force of the fraternity was then, as it is now, in its insistence upon journalism as a profession, with definite responsibility of service."[77]

The need for journalism education and the idea of journalism as a profession with a responsibility to society caught on with journalists at other colleges of the era, and this still has meaning today — even though the missionary understanding of education and responsibility that grew out of the academic and religious climate at turn-of-the-century DePauw had meaning primarily for the founders of Sigma Delta Chi. In a letter written to the DePauw Archives, Riddick recalled, "We hoped, but little did we realize that the acorn we brought out on that day would someday become a great oak covering America, its voice heard with influence on some of the nation-wide problems."[78] As editor and publisher of the *LaGrange* [Ind.] *Standard*, his goal was to make the newspaper a voice for morality that would support and uplift the community.[79] In his personal history of Sigma Delta Chi, Glenn wrote, "We were idealists.... We longed dimly for better journalism and a chance to improve and save the world." Throughout his newspaper career and his long association with the fraternity, he attempted to pass on to others his ideas of responsibility, honor, and ethics.[80]

Clippinger, Fisher, Hedges, Hutchens, Lockwood, Millikan, and Sloan had successful careers in journalism, education, and business, but the connection between journalism and mission that grew out of the DePauw experience and that attended the founding of Sigma Delta Chi survived in its clearest form in Pulliam's career as editor and publisher of the *Indianapolis Star* and *News* and the *Phoenix Republic*.

When Pulliam died in 1975, the *Star* and *News* both carried numerous articles and letters that mentioned the influence Pulliam's education at DePauw and the Methodist faith had on his career and on his understanding of the journalistic profession.[81] An *Indianapolis News* editorial writer summed it up: Gene Pulliam yearned to communicate the truth as he saw it, and wisdom as he understood it. His mother, who so wanted him to be a preacher, may not have been disappointed after all.[82] In a tribute to Pulliam, his grandson described the origin of his concept of professionalism: "Methodism was not just another church denomination when Pulliam was growing up.... It was a world view, a philosophy, an ideology that had implications for every area of life.... He apparently never personally embraced the saving faith of his parents, but he absorbed the moral and intellectual aspects of John Wesley's Methodism at home, at Baker [Academy], and at DePauw."[83]

---

[77]Clayton, *Fifty Years...*, 12.

[78]Riddick, "Letters," July 30, 1976 and August 13, 1976.

[79]Ibid., September 10, 1976.

[80]Glenn, *The Sigma Delta Chi Story*, Foreword, 19-22, 68-9, 162.

[81]See, for example, "Eugene C. Pulliam Dies at 86," *Indianapolis Star*, 24 June 1975, 1; "Star Special Report," *Indianapolis Star*, 25 June 1975, 1.

[82]"Pulliam Lauded as Brave, Steadfast," *Indianapolis News*, 27 June 1975, 23.

[83]Pulliam, "Methodism Shaped...," 34-5.

# 14

# Journalists and the Great Monkey Trial
by Marvin N. Olasky

WALTER LIPPMANN wrote in 1921 about "the pictures in our head," the phenomena we want to see. "For the most part," he argued, "we do not see first, then define; we define first and then see."[1] He gave one jocular example of how a traveler's expectations dictate the story he will tell upon return:

> If he carried chiefly his appetite, a zeal for tiled bathrooms, a conviction that the Pullman car is the acme of human comfort, and a belief that it is proper to tip waiters, taxicab drivers, and barbers, but under no circumstances station agents and ushers, then his Odyssey will be replete with good meals and bad meals, bathing adventures, compartment-train escapades, and voracious demands for money.

Only four years after Lippmann wrote that, the Scopes "monkey" trial provided a real-life example of the importance of journalists' presuppositions. Reporters from major newspapers who journeyed to Dayton, Tennessee, carried with them an antipathy toward fundamentalist Christianity. Their resultant treatment of Dayton, the Scopes trial participants, and the important issues involved in the trial threw more light on their biases than on the situation that existed in reality.

How did newspaper trial reports compare with trial records? How did reports from those who came to Dayton like anthropologists from afar compare with reports from observers more familiar with local mores? How did non-journalistic observers remember the events? The answers to those questions are provided by trial documents and the daily June and July 1925 pre-trial, trial, and post-trial coverage in eight newspapers: *New York Times, New York American, Chicago Tribune, Washington Post, Baltimore Sun, Los Angeles Times, Arkansas Gazette,* and *Atlanta Constitution.*

---

[1]Walter Lippmann, *Public Opinion* (New York: Macmillan, 1922), 21.

*A BATTLE OF RELIGIONS*

By the 1920s most academic leaders accepted the theory of evolution as scientific fact. Belief in evolution provided new hope for those who no longer accepted biblical Christianity. As the *New York Times* editorialized, modern man needed "faith, even of a grain of mustard seed, in the evolution of life."[2] The *Times* quoted George Bernard Shaw's statement that "The world without the conception of evolution would be a world wherein men of strong mind could only despair" — for their only hope would be in a God to whom such modernists would not pray.[3]

Other newspapers featured more spokesmen for evolutionary beliefs. The *Chicago Tribune* gave front page space to zoologist H. J. Muller's faith concerning man that "so far he has had only a short probationary period. He is just at the beginning of a great epic adventure in the course of world evolution."[4] Belief in evolution had grown ever since Darwin had reinvigorated the age-old concept through his mid-nineteenth century writings, but World War I had given it new impetus. The great and terrible war so decimated hopes for peaceful progress of mankind that millions came to believe in one or other of two ways upward from misery: either God's grace or man's evolution.

The *New York Times'* hope was in evolution. An editorial stated:

If man has evolved, it is inconceivable that the process should stop and leave him in his present imperfect state. Specific creation has no such promise for man.... No Legislation should (or can) rob the people of their hope.[5]

But in Tennessee, legislation that threatened to "rob the people of their hope" was passed, and the *Times* feared other states might follow.

Tennessee legislators, trying to stop usage of, and teacher reliance on, pro-evolution textbooks, made it a misdemeanor for public school teachers to proclaim as truth the belief "that man has descended from a lower order of animals."[6] The legislation made a clash of worldviews inevitable. The battle began when one young Dayton teacher, John T. Scopes, responded to an American Civil Liberties Union plea for someone to agree to be the defendant in a test case, with the ACLU paying all legal expenses. The ACLU hired agnostic Clarence Darrow, probably the most famous lawyer of the era, to head the defense; fundamentalist William Jennings Bryan, thrice-defeated Democratic presidential candidate and former Secretary of State, became point man for the prosecution.[7]

The issue and the luminaries brought out the journalists.[8] More than 100 reporters were dispatched to the trial; they wired 165,000 words daily to their newspapers during the twelve days of extensive coverage in July 1925. The *New*

---

[2]*New York Times*, 11 July 1925, 10.

[3]Ibid., 2.

[4]*Chicago Tribune*, 21 July 1925, 1.

[5]*New York Times*, 26 July 1925, Section II, 4.

[6]Leslie H. Allen, ed., *Bryan and Darrow at Dayton: The Record and Documents of the "Bible-Evolution Trial"* (New York: A. Lee & Co., 1925), 1.

[7]Bryan died one week after the Scopes trial ended.

[8]The Southern small town setting also contributed to the atmosphere of a religious revival. Many reporters knew they would have a colorful backdrop for their trial coverage.

*York Times* itself received an average of 10,000 words per day from its writers on the scene.[9]

In theory, trial coverage was an opportunity to illuminate the theological bases on which both evolutionist and creationist superstructures were built. From books written on the issues of the case, from a few of the news reports, and from the trial transcripts itself, it is clear that there were intelligent people (and not-so-intelligent people) on both sides of the issue. For instance, even a pro-evolution journalist at one point admitted that the man who had proposed the anti-evolutionary legislation was "a sound logician."[10] Another reporter wrote with amazement of a Tennessee mountain man who had, along with his old clothes and unpolished boots, a scholar's knowledge of Greek and the ability to make careful comparisons of New Testament translations.[11]

In practice, though, reporters described the story as one of pro-evolution intelligence vs. anti-evolution stupidity. H.L. Mencken attacked the Dayton fundamentalists (before he had set foot in the town) as "local primates," "yokels," "morons," and "half-wits."[12] He put aside his typical amusement with life to ride Paul Revere-like through the land with dire warnings about the trial:

Let no one mistake it for comedy, farcical though it may be in all its details. It serves notice on the country that Neanderthal man is organizing in these forlorn backwaters of the land, led by a fanatic, rid of sense and devoid of conscience.[13]

Mencken summarized his view of the debate's complexity by noting, "On the one side was bigotry, ignorance, hatred, superstition, every sort of blackness that the human mind is capable of. On the other side was sense."[14]

Other journalists from the Northeast and the urban Midwest shared that view. Nunnally Johnson, who covered the trial for the *Brooklyn Eagle* and then became a noted Hollywood screenwriter, remembered years later, "For the newspapermen it was a lark on a monstrous scale.... Being admirably cultivated fellows, the were all of course evolutionists and looked down on the local fundamentalists."[15] Acid-tongued Westbrook Pegler, who covered the trial briefly, admired Mencken and imitated his coverage, but noted years later concerning the anti-evolutionists:

They were intelligent people, including a fair proportion of college graduates. Nevertheless, the whole Blue Ridge country was ridiculed on religious

[9]*New York Times*, 22 July 1925, 2.

[10]Ibid., 7 and 18 July, 1925.

[11]Ibid., 19 July 1925, Section VIII, 3.

[12]L. Sprague de Camp, *The Great Monkey Trial* (Garden City, N.Y.: Doubleday, 1968), 274.

[13]*Baltimore Sun*, 18 July 1925, 1.

[14]de Camp, *The Great Monkey Trial*, 436. Mencken was echoing the intolerance of many anti-evolution spokesmen. For instance, Columbia University dean Henry H. Rusby demanded that universities not recognize degrees from universities that did not accept evolution. A leading liberal minister, Charles Francis Potter, argued that "educated and enlightened men ought not to rest until the possibility of such dense mental darkness is removed." The *New York Times* then editorialized against "the mental and moral infection which has been let loose upon the land..." ( *New York Times*, 12 July 1925, section I, 2; *Arkansas Gazette*, 16 June 1925, 2.) Fundamentalists had some justification for believing that they were being told not "live and let live," but "your diseased religion does not deserve to exist."

[15]*New York World Telegram & Sun*, 9 July 1956, 19.

grounds by an enormous claque of supercilious big town reporters.[16]

Such ridicule was not a function of politics; it underlay the politics of both liberal and conservative newspapers. The liberal *New York Times* editorialized that the anti-evolutionist position represented a "breakdown of the reasoning powers. It is seeming evidence that the human mind can go into deliquescence without falling into stark lunacy."[17] The conservative *Chicago Tribune* sneered at fundamentalists looking for "horns and forked tails and the cloven hoofs."[18] Two weeks before the trial began, the *Arkansas Gazette* could note, "These days a newspaper that does not contain a barbed thrust aimed directly or otherwise at Tennessee is fully as difficult to find as a needle in a haystack ... or more to the point, a link in the chain of evolution."[19]

Nor did coverage simply reflect journalistic preference for urban civilization over rural living conditions. When Mencken first arrived in Dayton he was so surprised that he produced his only non-acidic description of Dayton, calling it:

a country town full of charm and even beauty.... The cool houses are surrounded by pretty gardens, with cool green lawns and stately trees. The two chief streets are paved from curb to curb. The stores carry good stocks and have a metropolitan air.... [T]he Evolutionists and the Anti-Evolutionists seem to be on the best of terms and it is hard in a group to distinguish one from the other.[20]

One reporter mentioned with surprise that a Dayton drug store had gleaming counters and packaged goods similar to those available on Fifth Avenue.[21]

The ridicule primarily reflected reporters' outrage at fundamentalist theology, in part because their cultures had only recently "outgrown" that theology. The *New York Times* noted at one point:

A certain unexpectedness in the behavior and talk of the Dayton people. The unexpectedness comes from the absence in these Dayton people of any notable dissimilarity from the people elsewhere except in their belated clinging to a method of Scriptural interpretation that not long ago was more than common in both North and South.[22]

The *Times* writer in those two sentences understood that the fundamentalist beliefs were far from bizarre; in fact, it was the newer method of Scriptural interpretation that had been regarded as bizarre in Times Square as well as Tennessee only a short time before.

---

[16]*New York Journal-American*, 11 September 1960, 19.

[17]*New York Times*, 13 July 1925, 16.

[18]*Chicago Tribune*, 19 July 1925, 5.

[19]*Arkansas Gazette*, 7 July 1925, 6.

[20]*Baltimore Sun*, 9 July 1925, 1.

[21]*Atlanta Constitution*, 8 July 1925, 4: "Robinson's drug store, where the argument took place that started the trial, is a modern emporium with a palatial soda foundation. The same chain store drugs are displayed on the counter that you see in the drug store at Forty-second and Broadway."

[22]*New York Times*, 20 July 1925, 14.

## PRESUPPOSITION AND ERRORS IN DESCRIPTION

When journalists actually arrived in Dayton and began daily reportage, their first job was to describe accurately the legal issues of the trial. That was more difficult than it might have seemed because some correspondents presented the trial as one involving free speech. The *Chicago Tribune*'s Philip Kinsley wrote that the Tennessee law, if upheld, would make every work on evolution "a book of evil tidings, to be studied in secret."[23]

Kinsley's statement was nonsense: Hundreds of pro-evolution writings were on sale in Dayton. Even a drug store had a stack of materials representing all positions. John Butler, the legislator who introduced the anti-evolution bill, had a copy of Darwin's *The Origin of the Species* for his teenage children to read, and told reporters, "I am not opposed to teaching of evolution, but I don't think it ought to be taught in state-supported schools."[24]

The key issue was not free speech, but parental control over school curricula. Even in Tennessee, Christian parents already sensed exclusion of their beliefs from schools they funded. William Jennings Bryan spoke for them when he said he "never advocated teaching the Bible in public schools," but believed

There is no reason why school children should not hear of Bible characters as well as other characters. In other words, there is no reason why the reading of the Bible should be excluded while the reading of books about other characters in history, like Confucius, should be permitted.[25]

Tennessee legislators viewed their anti-evolution bill not as a way of putting Christian religion into the schools, but of forbidding proselyzing for what they considered a trendy but unproved evolutionary faith. Tennessee Governor Austin Peay opposed the uncritical acceptance of evolutionary material "that no science has established."[26] One anti-evolutionary organization called itself the Defenders of True Science versus Speculation, contending that evolution "is a theory not yet approved by science," particularly since species-transitional fossils ("missing links") had not been found.[27] "Demonstrated truth," Bryan insisted, "has no terrors for Christianity."[28]

It would have been difficult but not impossible for journalists to explain these issues, had they the ability to go beyond the pictures in their own heads, or the willingness to do so. But, with rare exceptions, they did not. The *New York American* began one trial story with the sentence, "Tennessee today maintained its quarantine against learning."[29] The battle pitted "rock-ribbed Tennessee" against "unfettered investigation by the human mind and the liberty of

[23]*Arkansas Gazette*, 18 July 1925, 5.

[24]*Baltimore Sun*, 10 July 1925, 1. Also see *Atlanta Constitution*, 9 and 10 July 1925.

[25]*Arkansas Gazette*, 12 July 1925, 1. Also see *Arkansas Gazette*, 23 June 1925, 1, and 28 June 1925, 1; and *Washington Post*, 16 July 1925, 6.

[26]*Arkansas Gazette*, 27 June 1925, 1. Ray Ginger, in *Six Days or Forever?* (Boston: Beacon Press, 1958), writes that Governor Peay thought the anti-evolution bill absurd. Ginger's comment may be an example of an historian projecting his own views onto his subjects.

[27]*Atlanta Constitution*, 2 July 1925, 1.

[28]Ibid., 8 July 1925, 22.

[29]*New York American*, 18 July 1925, 1.

opinion which the Constitution makers preached."[30] Reporters from the *New York Times* and the *Chicago Tribune* regularly attacked Christian faith and "this superheated religious atmosphere, this pathetic search for the 'eternal truth.'"[31]

Columnist Bugs Baer wrote with lively viciousness. He depicted Scopes as an imprisoned martyr, "the witch who is to be burned by Dayton."[32] (Actually, Scopes did not spend a second in jail and regularly ate dinner at the homes of Dayton Christians.) Baer described Bryan's face as "a panorama of curdled egotism."[33] The columnist predicted that a fundamentalist victory would turn "the dunce cap" into "the crown of office."[34] He called residents of Dayton "treewise monkeys" who "see no logic, speak no logic and hear no logic." When William Jennings Bryan Jr., an attorney, arrived for the trial, Baer wrote, "Junior is bound to be a chip off the old blockhead.... Like father, like son, and we don't like either."[35]

The Dayton jurors, who following the trial gave thoughtful accounts of the proceedings, were described in one New York headline: INTELLIGENCE OF MOST LOWEST GRADE." It seemed that

All twelve are Protestant churchgoers.... Hickory-shirted, collarless, suspendered, tanned, raw-boned men are these.... The grade of intelligence as revealed by the attitudes and words of the twelve indicates to this observer that at least nine of the Scopes jurors had never used a four-syllable word in their lives until the term "evolution" was crowded into the local vocabulary.[36]

One prospective juror even had "a homemade hair cut and ears like a loving cup."[37]

Newspapers ran humorous comments about Dayton similar to today's ethnic jokes; the *New York Times*, though, worried that the situation was serious, and trumpeted of "CRANKS AND FREAKS" in a front page headline. The *Times* worried about the belief in creationism by "thousands of unregulated or ill-balanced minds,"[38] and depicted as zombies Tennesseans entering the courthouse: "All were sober-faced, tight-lipped, expressionless."[39] The *Chicago Tribune* news service sometimes criticized anti-evolutionists more subtly:

At regular intervals loud, ringing tones from the courthouse steeple announce the hour to Dayton folk — and announce it consistently thirty-five minutes ahead of central standard time. This little town, object of scorn to residents of

---

[30]Ibid., 14 July 1925, 1.

[31]*Arkansas Gazette* ( *New York Times/Chicago Tribune* news service), 16 July 1925, 3. Not only fundamentalists saw such news coverage as an attack on Christianity generally. The Catholic Press Association telegrammed Bryan, "There is a vast amount of sympathy for Mr. Bryan and the State of Tennessee among the Catholics of America. A great many of us are highly indignant at the ribald abuse which has been heaped upon your splendid stand by the newspapers and non-religionists of certain sections." (*Arkansas Gazette*, 10 July 1925, 1.)

[32]*New York American*, 13 July 1925, 1.

[33]Ibid., 15 July 1925, 4.

[34]Ibid., 16 July 1925, 2.

[35]Ibid., 17 July 1925, 2.

[36]Ibid., 12 July 1925, 1.

[37]Ibid.. See also *Arkansas Gazette*, 11 July 1925, 1.

[38]*New York Times*, 11 July, 13 July, 16 July 1925.

[39]Ibid., 11 July 1925, 1.

great cities, is far from being backward in counting the hours.[40]

*PRESUPPOSITIONS AND BIASED TRIAL COVERAGE*

The typical major newspaper reporter's cartoon version of the Dayton issues wasted an opportunity to explain vital issues. Yet, since newspapers were (and are) event-oriented, perhaps they could not be expected to clarify theological questions. Readers, though, at least should have been able to expect accurate news coverage of the actual trial events.

The former judicial proceedings were not the main show. The Scopes case was open-and-shut, with the ACLU desiring conviction on obvious law-breaking so that the decision could be appealed to the U.S. Supreme Court for a ruling on the Tennessee act's constitutionality. (Ironically, after Scopes' conviction, the Tennessee Supreme Court upheld the anti-evolution law but overturned the conviction on a technicality involving the imposition of a $100 fine without jury approval; the U.S. Supreme Court never heard the case.) The importance of the Dayton trial, for both prosecution and defense, lay in the chance to debate issues.

Accurate coverage of the great debates, however, was not forthcoming. Comparison of news reports on the trial's two most dramatic confrontations with other descriptive information reveals journalistic bias.

The first of the great debates pitted Bryan against Darrow's associate Dudley Malone on July 16. The court transcript shows strong and intelligent orations by both sides. Bryan, within biblical presuppositions, made a logical and coherent argument. He stressed the evolutionary theory's lack of scientific proof and emphasized its inability to answer questions about how life began, how man began, how one species actually changes into another, and so on. He pointed out the irreconcilability of Darwinian doctrines of extra-species evolution with the Biblical account of creation, original sin, and the reasons for Christ's coming. Malone, within evolutionist presuppositions, argued in a similarly cohesive way. On the face of the written record, both sides did well.

Of course, reading the written record of a speech is not the same as hearing a speech. Yet the favorable remarks of many Daytonites indicate the impact of Bryan's oratory. Even the defendant himself, John T. Scopes, said that the speech "was well received by the audience.... Every gesture and intonation of [Bryan's] voice blended so perfectly that it was almost like a symphony; and yet, the impression was that it was all extemporaneous. The longer he talked (a little more than an hour), the more complete was the control he had over the crowd."[41]

Remarks of that kind did not get into major newspapers. Instead, the typical report tracked Mencken's gibe that Bryan's speech "was a grotesque performance and downright touching in its imbecility."[42] W. O. McGeehan of the *New York Herald Tribune* wrote that Bryan "was given the floor and after exactly one hour and ten minutes he was lying upon it horizontally — in a figura-

---

[40]*Arkansas Gazette*, 9 July 1925, 1.

[41]Jerry R. Tompkins, ed., *D-Days at Dayton: Reflections on the Scopes Trial* (Baton Rouge: Louisiana State University Press, 1965), 26.

[42]*Baltimore Sun*, 17 July 1925, 1.

tive sense." (McGeehan, regularly a sportswriter, did not often get to write about figurative self-knockouts.) He used his mind-reading talents to note that "The brethren and sisters in the rear of the courtroom looked sorrowful and disappointed," and he used his awareness of body language to point out that "Mr. Bryan sat in his corner in the attitude of the defeated gladiator."[43]

Many reporters loaded their Bryan coverage with sarcastic biblical allusions: "Unleash his thunder," "make this jury the recording angels of a great victory for revealed religion," or "The sun seemed to stand still in the heavens, as for Joshua of old, and to burn with holy wrath against the invaders of this fair Eden of fundamentalism." Sometimes, sentence after sentence mixed biblical metaphors: "Dayton began to read a new book of revelations today. The wrath of Bryan fell at last. With whips of scorn, he sought to drive science from the temples of God and failed."[44]

The *Chicago Tribune*'s Kinsley, though, predicted that Malone's speech would lead to imminent victory, not in the courtroom but in the hearts and minds of fundamentalists:

Dayton is awakening — more especially the mass of the younger people who heard the great debate. It was evident that the leaven was working.... there is on the streets and in the homes here tonight a new opinion, not universal but of formidable proportions. Bryan is great, but the truth is greater, and the truth as applied to man's origin was not locked in a book in the days of Moses.[45]

Kinsley provided no evidence of this evident awakening, but "news coverage" suggesting similar attacks on the book of Genesis became a staple of reporting from Dayton as the trial wore on.

The second major confrontation came on the trial's last day, when Bryan and Darrow battled in a debate bannered in newspapers across the country: "BRYAN AND DARROW IN BITTER RELIGIOUS CLASH."[46]

The trial transcript shows a presuppositional debate in which both sides enunciated their views with occasional wit and frequent bitterness. If the goal of the antagonists in the Tennessee July heat was to keep their cool, both slipped; but it was Darrow who showed extreme intolerance, losing his temper to talk about "fool religion" and to call Christians "bigots and ignoramuses."[47]

Once again, the question needs to be asked: Was the oral actuality different from the written record? Not according to an anti-evolution writer on one Oklahoma paper who proclaimed, "Mr. Bryan came out more than victorious. He made a monkey out of the defense counsel and left them gasping."[48] That bias is to be expected. More useful is a report from the generally neutral (on this issue) *Los Angeles Times*, which concluded that "Bryan emerges in a better light than his rival."[49] Also useful is a report from the pro-evolution (but attuned to local culture) *Arkansas Gazette*, which reported that Bryan

---

[43] *Los Angeles Times*, 17 July 1925, Section I, 2.
[44] *Arkansas Gazette*, 12 July 1925, 1; 13 July, 1; 17 July, 3.
[45] *Chicago Tribune*. See also *Arkansas Gazette*, 14 July 1925, 5.
[46] *Atlanta Constitution*, 21 July 1925, 1.
[47] *Washington Post*, 21 July 1925, 2.
[48] de Camp, *The Great Monkey Trial*, 435-6.
[49] *Los Angeles Times*, 23 July 1925, Section II, 4.

stood up before Darrow at times and defied him to do his worst.... [Bryan] struck the hearts of many of those who sat in front of him.... today's performance puts the defense of this case where Mr. Bryan has tried to maneuver it — into the field of opposition to the Bible, among the scientific agnosticism that follows Darrow....

[Bryan] set his face to the one goal — the defense of revealed religion, as he and his followers believe it. They number millions and they will applaud him in this struggle. He will be a brave figure to them after today. He emerges as a hero.[50]

Once again, though, New York and Chicago-based reporters declared Bryan a humiliated loser. The *New York Times* called Bryan's testimony "an absurdly pathetic performance, with a famous American the chief creator and butt of a crowd's rude laughter."[51] The next day the *Times* observed, "It was a Black Monday for him [Bryan] when he exposed himself.... It has long been known to many that he was only a voice calling from a poorly-furnished brain-room."[52] The *Herald-Tribune*'s McGeehan wrote that Bryan was "losing his temper and becoming to all intents and purposes a mammal."[53]

A few observations from years later may be helpful. Pro-evolutionist L. Sprague de Camp, after reading contemporary accounts by journalists and spectators, concluded: "The newspaper reporters may have depicted the speech as less effective than it was, because most of them were city men, hostile to the speaker. To them, the Great Commoner [Bryan] was the leader of organized ignorance, the modern Torquemada. They would not have liked his speech no matter how eloquent or stirring it was."[54]

Some predisposed reporters were so far off in their understanding of the other side's beliefs that their stories became ludicrous. For instance, one journalist wrote that "the humiliation of being called 'an ignoramus' and a 'fool and a Fundamentalist' ... cut Bryan to the quick."[55] Bryan, though, knew and quoted two biblical verses from Paul's first letter to the Corinthians:

If any one of you thinks he is wise by the standards of this age, he should become a "fool" so that he may become wise. For the wisdom of this world is foolishness in God's sight.[56]

Bryan also was unashamed about being a "fundamentalist," one who viewed the Bible as inerrant. Those who called Bryan a fool and a fundamentalist in one phrase were unknowingly offering him not a slap but a badge of honor.

Even after the trial ended with a verdict against Scopes, some reporters persisted in mind-reading journalism. The *Chicago Tribune* news service stressed Scopes' "intangible victory.... [Tennesseans] have begun to think and talk free-

---

[50]*Arkansas Gazette*, 21 July 1925, 1.
[51]*New York Times*, 21 July 1925, 2.
[52]Ibid., 22 July 1925, 18.
[53]*Los Angeles Times*, 21 July 1925, 1.
[54]de Camp, *The Great Monkey Trial*, 327.
[55]*Outlook*, 29 July 1925, 443.
[56]I Corinthians 3:18-19 (New International Version translation).

ly."[57] But the *Arkansas Gazette* pointed out that Tennesseans already had thought and talked freely, and noted: "Darrow's agnosticism enabled Bryan and other lawyers for the prosecution to represent the whole proceeding as an attack on religion and the Bible.... [T]he odium with which the prosecution invested the defense of Scopes will cling to it to the end."[58]

Overall, most major newspaper reporters produced so much unobservant coverage that it often seemed as if they were watching the pictures in their head rather than the trial in front of them.[59] The ultimate example of journalistic blindness caused by presupposition came when one New York scribe, under the headline "Scopes is Seen as New Galileo At Inquisition," wrote that the

> sultry courtroom in Dayton, during a pause in the argument, became hazy and there evolved from the mists of past ages a new scene. The Tennessee judge disappeared and I racked my brain to recognize the robed dignitary on the bench. Yes, it was the grand inquisitor, the head of the inquisition at Rome.
>
> Lawyers faded from view, all except the evangelical leader of the prosecution, Mr. Bryan, who was reversely incarnated as angry-eyed Pope Urban.... I saw the Tennessee Fundamentalist public become a medieval mob thirsty for heretical blood.... [It was] 1616. The great Galileo was on trial.[60]

Many journalists in Dayton did not want to see real pictures. They became notorious for spending as little time with the local people as possible. H.L. Mencken, according to Pegler, had minimal contact with Dayton: "He had an airy suite on Lookout Mountain in Chattanooga, with a tub of ice and a fan blowing a cool breeze as he sat in his shorts after an hour or two a day in Dayton." McGeehan, Pegler wrote, did become friendly with a local doctor who, during those days of prohibition, could offer documents more precious than rubies: prescriptions for valid liquor.[61]

Reporters' desire to get away from the physical and spiritual head of Dayton created particularly severe problems on the last day of the trial, which turned from *pro forma* wrap-up to sensation when Bryan and Darrow had their famous confrontation. Many reporters were off swimming or carousing, with the result that other reporters, after telegraphing their own stories, hastily rewrote parts and sent them to the missing reporters' newspapers in order to cover for their friends. Several reporters asked Scopes himself to write parts of the new articles; so journalistic coverage of the trial concluded with a bizarre touch: the defendant reporting on his own case under someone else's byline.[62]

*NO ESCAPE*

Ironically, reporters who praised "open-mindedness" in their stories showed

---

[57]*Arkansas Gazette*, 19 July 1925, 5; see also *New York Times*, 19 July 1925, Section VIII, 3; *Atlanta Constitution*, 22 July, 6.

[58]*Arkansas Gazette*, 23 July 1925, 6.

[59]*Baltimore Sun*, 16 July 1925, 1.

[60]*New York American*, 14 July 1925, 1.

[61]*New York Journal-American*, 11 September 1960, 5.

[62]John T. Scopes and James Presley, *Center of the Storm: Memoirs of John T. Scopes* (New York: Holt, Rinehart and Winston, 1967), 183.

great close-mindedness when confronted with a world view opposed in many ways to their own. The experience of one Scopes trial reporter, Raymond Clapper, shows the pattern.[63] Olive Clapper, his wife, provided in her autobiography a portrait of the journalist as a young Bible-believer in 1912:

> Even though I had known Ray for years, it was not until I was sixteen that I fell in love with him. I can actually pinpoint the evening when his great dark piercing eyes glowed at me as he led the Christian Endeavor meeting at the Presbyterian Church. He read the Bible lesson, announced the hymns we would sing, and opened the discussion.[64]

Four years later, as both were ready to graduate from the University of Kansas, beliefs had changed:

> We owed a lot all our lives to this great state-supported University. It gave us knowledge and confidence in our capacity to learn and to do.... We were beginning to question the rigid beliefs of our parents and needed a more reasonable belief.... We particularly enjoyed Dr. E.C.A. Smith of the Unitarian Church in Lawrence when he discussed evolution and religion.[65]

By 1923, when the Clappers' first child was born, they were firm in their new faith:

> We outlined and agreed upon certain fundamentals to be taught to our children. Chief among these was our attitude toward religion. We had long since discarded the orthodox teachings of our youth. We could not believe the Old Testament prophets, whose teachings no doubt fitted well the savage age in which they lived but suited our world no better than the Greek oracles. The story of Christ we thought was moving and beautiful but we could not accept the virgin birth or the resurrection.[66]

There was no surprise in 1925, therefore, when Ray Clapper told his editor that he just *had to* cover the Scopes trial; as Olive Clapper argued, Bryan would show the world that "the whole case of fundamentalism [was] ridiculous." According to her autobiography:

> Not even chains could have kept Ray from covering that famous trial. In his story of July 17 near the end of the trial, Ray wrote, "Fundamentalist justice has plugged up the ears of this Tennessee mountain jury." ... And so it was. Unbelievable as the trial was to intelligent people, it did have value because the end result was greater enlightenment of people on the subject of evolution.[67]

---

[63]Clapper, a United Press reporter, became a respected Washington correspondent during the 1930s. He died in a plane crash while covering the end of the war against Japan.

[64]Olive Clapper, *One Lucky Woman* (Garden City, N.Y.: Doubleday, 1961), 34.

[65]Ibid., 59.

[66]Ibid., 109.

[67]Ibid., 99.

Other journalists went through similar processes of theological change. Over-all, Scopes trial coverage provides an example of philosopher Cornelius Van Til's contention that all views are essentially religious, in that they are based on certain convictions as to the nature of the universe. Readers of every news story are receiving not only information but are being taught, subtly or explicitly, a particular world view. In Kantian terms, newspapers offer not only phenomena, but noumena; not only facts learned from study, but an infrastructure that gives meaning to those facts.[68]

A Van Tilian perspective on journalism does not mean that reporters are never able to sense that there is a different way of looking at things. Frank Kent, a perceptive *Baltimore Sun* correspondent, generally joined the hunt at Dayton with the other reporters, but one day he was given the poetic gift Robert Burns wrote of, to see ourselves as others see us. The headlines and lead on Kent's July 15 article (after a day without a trial session) were:

DAYTON TO HAVE VARIED VIEW OF ALIEN CULTURE/Impressions Made By Visitors Will Not Be Altogether Favorable ... A lot has been written since the trial began about what the outside world thinks of Dayton. Nothing has been written about what Dayton thinks of the outside world. It would be interesting to know.[69]

Then Kent described some incidents: "On one corner a traveling atheist spoke in a loud voice to a gaping crowd of the absurdity of the Bible," then came to a "horribly hysterical climax." Nearby, "a ribald, jeering crowd of photographers, journalists" and others were "scattering abroad a brand of profanity and a species of joke rather new to the natives." The journalistic mob soon moved:

Someone tipped the gang off that the Holy Rollers were having another meeting two miles away. A score of cars jammed with visitors rushed to the grove. They drove almost into the meeting, turned the glare of their headlights on the pitiful little group ... laughed and joked until, abased and afraid, the Holy Rollers abandoned their prayers and slunk off to their homes in the hills.

Kent also told of

an out-of-town man who, with a number of others, is boarding in the Dayton home of a little bride and groom doing their level best to make everybody comfortable and feed them well. On the table for breakfast were bacon and

---

[68]For an excellent discussion of presuppositionalism, see Cornelius Van Til, *The Defense of the Faith* (Philadelphia: Presbyterian Reformed Publishing Co., 1974). The *Atlanta Constitution* in 1925 showed awareness of the trial coverage's potential effect when it editorialized: "Thousands of columns of newspaper debate have been published under Dayton date lines in the past two weeks, and from it all the cause of the religion of Jesus Christ has not been helped, but the world has been broadcast with the seeds of doubt and skepticism, and only the future can tell what the harvest will be.... [A]mong the millions of people who congest the bumper ground between science and the Bible there may be thousands who will now find themselves drifting into the easy-going channels of agnosticism." (22 July 1925, 6). Nevertheless, when Clarence Darrow revisited Dayton a few years after the trial, he saw a newly-built church (Cumberland Presbyterian) and commented, "I guess I didn't do much good after all."

[69]*Baltimore Sun*, 15 July 1925, 1.

eggs, fruit, hot biscuits, coffee. Said this man in a terrible tone to the little bride, who waits on the table: "Have you no corn flakes?" Unhappily she replied: "I am very sorry, sir, but we haven't any." "Hell!" said this metropolitan gentleman, and, pushing his chair over, he stalked from the room, slamming the door behind him with a bang.

Yet, after showing such perception, the very next day Kent returned to watching the pictures in his head. He heaped ridicule on the fundamentalists and wrote that "Bryan sits in his corner silent and watchful.... You can shut your eyes and imagine him leading them [Daytonites] to burn the unbelievers at the stake. The words 'sacrilegious dogs' seem quivering on his lips."[70] Journalists could not escape presuppositions for long.

---

[70]Ibid., 16 July 1925, 1.

# 15

# The Church and the Debate over Radio /
*1919-1949*
by Robert S. Fortner

PERHAPS WHAT DOOMED the Christian church's involvement in public policy debates during the first thirty years of radio was the so-called Scopes Monkey Trial that took place in Tennessee in 1925. Although the trial, which resulted in the conviction (later overturned) of John Scopes for teaching the theory of evolution in violation of Tennessee's Butler Act, did not ignite the dispute between "modernists" and "fundamentalists" in the church, it certainly crystallized the issues that lay before it. Science seemed to be pitted against Scripture, accommodation with secularism against remaining separate and holy. As an editorial in *Eternity* magazine put it in 1957, "American Protestantism still suffers from the battle that fundamentalism and modernism have been waging for more than a quarter of a century. In a sense, they continue the fight as certain sections of the country are still fighting the Civil War."[1]

This trial took place only six years following the date usually selected as the beginning of the radio era, and still one year before the creation of the National Broadcasting Company by RCA. So it occurred early on in radio's history. But it is difficult to see the event as a defining one for the dispute within the Christian church, even while it was a pivotal moment in a church grappling with the implications of modernity. Radio, of course, was one of the technologies that came during this period to be seen as a primary representation of modernity. Control of it, and of the church's use of it, was crucial to the nature of Christianity's grappling with the world.

One side of the debate over how radio ought to be used came from the "modernists." Their vehicle was the Federal Council of the Churches of Christ in America (FCCCA). Its approach was to provide a kind of generic religious programming over the facilities of the American radio networks, programming that was not sectarian, that would attract large audiences regardless of people's

---

[1]Editorial. "Who's Putting Religion Off the Air?" *Eternity* (1957 April), 14.

particular faiths, and that would assure that religion would be seen as part of the public service obligation of broadcasters — rather than as a basis for profit.[2]

On the other side of the debate were the "fundamentalists," a group that advocated the freedom of individuals and denominations to use radio to evangelize, and included such programs as *The Lutheran Hour*, Charles E. Fuller's *Pilgrim's Hour* and M. R. DeHaan's *Radio Bible Class*. Eventually this group of independent religious radio broadcasters would be instrumental in founding the National Association of Evangelicals and National Religious Broadcasters.

An editorial in *Eternity* magazine summed up the two positions well. The wide cleavage between the different Protestant factions had a long background. It said in 1957: "The NAE stands for freedom to buy time on any station.... The NCC represents the principle that religion is not to be handled on a commercial basis.... Neither of these groups tries very hard to see itself from the other's viewpoint."[3]

The existence of these two strong and opposing points of view meant that the dispute that was crystallized in the Scopes trial would apply to the use of radio by the church as well. Church organizations that used radio in its early history (1919-1949) tended to define their positions using similar arguments and make dire pronouncements based on similar assumptions as were articulated in the "Monkey Trial" affair. What, after all, was more Christian — engagement with the world on the world's terms to guarantee a "place at the table," or use of the world's technology, while simultaneously avoiding formal connection and using the techniques of commercialism and differentiation on sectarian grounds? So pre-occupied was the church with how to make use of this new communications medium in cooperation with the obvious institutional powers of the land, and how to make a place for sectarian positions by avoiding such entanglements, that it failed to contribute to the crucial issues surrounding the application of radio in American life. A potentially significant ethical voice was thus not only largely silent on the issues raised by the peculiar development of American broadcasting as a commercial medium over this period, but the church — through its own internal squabbling and policy inaction — left itself in the unenviable position of being merely a reactionary moral critic, oblivious to the commercial dynamics that it had failed to recognize. Both Christians and the society at large were the losers by the church's ethical failure.

It is important to recognize at the outset that the introduction of radio into American life introduced a variety of what eventually became serious ethical issues. One issue was raised by the enormous investment that Americans made in radio equipment, with the number of radio sets increasing from 2.5 million in 1924 to 45 million by 1939, and investments increasing from $60 million in 1922 to $446 million by 1927.[4] And it was not merely financial investment. By

---

[2]The 13th Annual Institute for Education by Radio, held in 1942, reiterated these tenets of the modernist approach to radio. See "Radio Urged to Fan War Hate," *The Christian Century*, 20 May 1942, 677. Lenox R. Lohr, president of NBC, endorsed these tenets in his speech to the FCCCA in 1938, too. Lenox R. Lohr, *The Partnership of Religion and Radio*, Address to the biennial meeting of the Federal Council of Churches of Christ in America, Buffalo, New York, December 7, 1938. (New York: FCCCA, 1938), 10-1.

[3]Editorial. *Eternity*, 15.

[4]J. L. Ray, "The Distribution and Merchandising of Radio Equipment," in *The Radio Industry: The Story of Its Development* (Chicago: A. W. Shaw, 1928), 254.

1941 Americans were spending nearly a billion hours a week listening to radio.[5]

The principal ethical questions raised by this investment were two. First, what did radio broadcasters "owe" listeners? The industry claimed it was "eager to meet the popular will and quick to sense changes in sentiment as to programs." It was mindful of its responsibilities, it said, recognizing that the tuning knob was a silent weapon in the hands of listeners. "So public approval, an integral fundamental part of a democratically organized society, is the most important factor in deciding what shall or shall not go upon the air of this country."[6]

Second was the issue of listeners' privacy. Since radio broadcasters sensed themselves as invited guests into people's homes, they were eager to avoid offense. For instance, Lenox R. Lohr told the biennial meeting of the FCCCA in 1938 that "the obligation of the National Broadcasting Company to the public is to enforce the simple code of civilized behavior, respect of one man for another, honorable dealing and honest intention, served with courtesy, good manners, and good taste." This worked itself out, he said, with the criteria the network applied to its programs: "the essence of which is to guard the privacy and feelings of our hosts — the millions who have invited us into their homes."[7]

Tied inextricably to his issue was that of commercialism, the sale of advertising to fund the radio industry. To the industry the use of advertising meant that listeners got something for nothing. To others, such as the Radio League of America, the National Committee on Education, even Secretary of Commerce Herbert Hoover and the federal courts, advertising was fraught with danger, cheapening radio, wooing the public with questionable products, interrupting entertainment with advertising chatter.[8] The Ventura, California, *Free Press* claimed in *Empire of the Air* that the excesses of advertising were "tying the noose around its brazen throat," and leading to popular resentment.[9]

What did this have to do with the church's approach to radio? In a word, everything. The radio industry during its first thirty years had to figure out how to pay for what it provided. The original expectations that programming would be paid for by subsidies from the sale of radio receivers turned out to be unworkable. The federal government was not eager to be involved with the radio business, even to regulate it until asked to sort out frequency assignments by the industry itself, and even then it engaged the questions half-heartedly, creating the Federal Radio Commission in 1927 as a temporary agency. The option offered by the European services of creating a license fee to pay for broadcasting was never a serious option. That seemed to suggest advertising, with the stations and networks attracting audiences that advertisers wished to reach.

The church and all non-industry institutions in the society had a choice: to

---

[5]Hadley Cantril and Gordon W. Allport, *The Psychology of Radio* (New York: Peter Smith, 1941), 21.

[6]National Association of Broadcasters, *Broadcasting in the United States* (Washington, D.C.: NAB, 1933), 16.

[7]Lohr, *The Partnership*, 8, 10.

[8]See "The Story of the Radio League of America," Library of Congress, Manuscript Division, Calvin Coolidge Papers; Armstrong Perry, "Education's Rights on the Air," *Education and Radio 1931*, 120-1; "Advertising on Radio is No Good in Opinion of Expert," news clipping forwarded with a letter from James F. Weeland to the Department of Commerce, January 4, 1931, National Archives, RG 40, Box 276, 70133; Herbert Hoover, "Statement by the Secretary of Commerce at the Opening of the Radio Conference on February 27, 1922," National Archives, RG 40, Box 131, 67032/31; Charles N. Lischka, "A Brief for the Freedom of Radio Education," *The Catholic Educational Review* (1932 June), 322.

[9]*Free Press, Empire of the Air* (Ventura, Calif: Ventura Free Press, 1932), 92.

accept this financial arrangement as legitimate or to object to its implications for the family, society, the economy or politics. Despite the deep differences between the two factions in the church, both opted to accept this means of financing the radio industry as legitimate. By the end of the 1940s both the modernists and the fundamentalists were using language to defend their own activities, and attack those of their opposition, that echoed the language developed within the radio industry itself to defend its own practices. In essence the industry was able to co-opt the institution of the church, muting any potential criticism from it as the moral issues raised by radio were debated.

The church might have weighed in as the future of radio was being created by such vested interests. NBC's Advisory Council, for instance, included Charles S. Macfarland, Secretary of the Federal Council of Churches; and some of its earliest programs — along with those of CBS — were church services. Some religious programs, such as Hugh Barrett Dobbs's *Ship of Joy*, even found sponsorship — in this case, the Shell Oil Company. Many well-known religious figures, including S. Parkes Cadman, Harry Emerson Fosdick, Donald Grey Barnhouse, Robert P. Shuler, Aimee Semple McPherson, and Charles E. Fuller, preached sermons on radio during its first two decades. The Lutheran Layman's League was created to assure the presence of the Lutheran perspective — represented by Walter A. Maier — on the airwaves. By 1938 the Federal Council of Churches was reporting receipt of 800,000 letters annually in response to religious radio programs carried over the NBC networks alone.[10] So the church was active in the radio industry, even had a "seat at the table" in the person of Macfarland, but failed to raise any alarm bells as the industry commercialized and then rhetorically legitimized its activities. Any impact on public policy pertaining to radio that the church may have had over this period — the period in which the essential character of American broadcasting was defined — was dulled by this failure.

Why did this happen? There are at least two significant reasons for the church's failure. Both were outcomes of being caught up in what James W. Carey has called the "mythos" of technology. This mythos captures the public imagination as the possibilities of a technology become apparent, either through what appear to be its inherent characteristics, or through the promises of the institutions that control or regulate it.[11] The first reason, then, was the fact that the church, like most of the rest of the country, was caught up in the romance and promise of radio. That radio was able to reach across the sea without the use of wires, to connect people in rural areas to the cultural centers of American life, or to quicken political life and enhance economic life through the creation of national markets, seemed reasons enough to embrace it. And the developing radio industry, first through AT&T's and Westinghouse's involvement, and then through that of RCA, CBS, and eventually ABC, along with that of newspa-

---

[10]NBC actually operated two networks, dubbed "red" and "blue," until the FCC's chain broadcasting rules required it to divest one of these in 1941. This decision was affirmed by the United States Supreme Court in 1943. The divestiture created ABC.

[11]One example of this mythos in action is the comment by Frederick E. Drinker and James G. Lewis: "In the complicated scheme of civilization [radio] may serve as a protector of human life, a companion of the pioneer, an aid to education, a world-wide entertainer and perhaps a means of communication through which other worlds may be reached." Frederick E. Drinker and James G. Lewis, *Radio: Miracle of the 20th Century* (National Publishing Co., 1922), 3-4. [No publication city listed.]

pers, universities, labor unions, and the church, provided a rich mix of expectation for this new technology. The FCCCA recognized this possibility in its annual report in 1925, saying that radio opened up "great possibilities," including
"the presentation of the great questions of moral and religious life."[12] By 1929
the Federal Council was claiming that religious programming on radio had become, not only a "religious educational factor" in American life, but also "a
spiritual force in the family life of the Nation."[13] And Alfred Grant Walton, writing nearly twenty years later, although criticizing the church for its failure to use
radio effectively, reinforced the sense of radio's power by reciting what by then
had become a familiar mantra about the medium: "Business men invest millions in radio advertising. Politicians find radio the best available means for
bringing their message to voters. Cultural forces rely on it continually to foster
programs for community betterment. Meanwhile Protestantism has lagged."[14]
The vision for the use of this powerful new medium was there, in other words, if
only the church would grasp it effectively for the Gospel. As William Hiram
Foulkes succinctly put it, "There is something so uncanny and so far-reaching
in the persuasiveness of the radio waves that to the Christian it might well become another Pentecost — a potential Pentecost at least."[15]

The second reason was what might almost be described as the giddiness of
involvement in this technology itself. For instance, the FCCCA recognized "the
amazing response to religious programming" it sponsored and seemed awed that
"Protestant forces" had control of so much airtime "when the radio industry was
witnessing many kaleidoscopic changes." It was not only profoundly grateful for
the opportunity, but the response confirmed for the FCCCA "the wisdom of the
adoption, early in the decade, of definite principles and policies which have governed its activities."[16]

S. Parkes Cadman perhaps best expressed these principles and policies in a
speech to the Joint Religious Radio Commission, hosted by NBC, on February
23, 1936. "It seems to me," he said, "that we shall have to use radio along
these lines [emphasizing the one eternal voice of God rather than religion's
manifold forms] for to undertake an explanation of all the different varieties and
forms of religion, would be one of the worst and most strategic blunders we
could possibly make. It is bad enough to have these confusions, in which religion, instead of being, as it is meant by God to be, the cement of human society, becomes dynamite to blow it apart."[17]

And it was not merely the modernists who were caught up in this giddiness.
Walter A. Maier, the Lutheran Hour's first radio preacher, told those assembled
at the dedication of station KFUO, whose construction was paid for by the

---

[12]Federal Council of the Churches of Christ in America, *Annual Report 1925* (New York: FCCCA, 1925),
26.

[13]FCCCA, *Annual Report 1929* (New York: FCCCA, 1929), 52.

[14]Alfred Grant Walton, "Reconsider Religious Radio!," *The Christian Century*, 10 September 1947,
1079.

[15]William Hiram Foulkes, "Radio Evangelism," in *The Message and Method of New Evangelism: A Joint
Statement of the Evangelistic Mission of the Christian Church*, ed. Jesse M. Bader (New York: Round Table
Press, 1937), 230.

[16]"The Federal Council: A Review and Forecast" and the report of the "Department of Religious Radio,"
FCCCA, *Biennial Report, 1936.*

[17]S. Parkes Cadman, Speech at Radio City to the Joint Religious Radio Commission, hosted by NBC, in
FCCCA, *Biennial Report 1936* (New York: FCCCA, 1936), 102.

Lutheran Layman's League, that, "In our church today only these towers transmit the Christian message on a regular basis. God grant that this is only the beginning, that someday many other spires of steel may radiate Christ even as structurally they point to heaven."[18] And Holman Day's discussion of the "Shell Ship of Joy," a religious program hosted by Hugh Dobbs, claimed that, "It is known that daily in hundreds of thousands of homes men, women and children stand and broadcast concentrated beneficence at the summons, 'Everybody wish!'.... [When this is done in a theater,] the faces of the people were serious, even reverent. Indubitably they were realizing the power that is exerted by concentrated human thought."[19]

But these two versions of the mythos, one celebrating the ability of radio to cross the demographic boundaries and bind people together, the other arguing for the ecstasy that would come from the particularity of the Christian evangelistic message, were the reasons that the church failed to make a long-lasting or explicit impact on public understanding of the significance of radio for their lives, or to influence public policy that developed during this period. Even during the formative period of radio regulation, out of which came expectations of public service and the legitimacy accorded to the "American system" of advertising-supported commercial radio, the church became caught up in its own internal disputes over the relative value of these two points of view. The churches and denominations that did not belong to the FCCCA, for instance, railed against what they saw as a watered-down gospel that was untrue because it was generic. As James de Forest Murch explained it in 1946, "When NEWSWEEK spoke of the Federal Council as 'a virtual monopoly' in American Protestantism it expressed a common belief among evangelicals. Many hold that it not only restrains the freedom of non-cooperating denominations but often promotes liberalism at the expense of all Bible-believing, Christ-honoring Protestants."[20] And Ernest Gordon called the FCCCA an "ecclesiastical octopus" in 1948, one that was designed to drive "Gospel programs off the air."[21]

This theme of the "conservative" Protestant churches — that the FCCCA was not "Christ-honoring" — peppered much of their rhetoric in the 1940s. Donald E. Hoke wrote in 1944, for instance, that as a result of the arrangement the FCCCA had with CBS and NBC, "the gospel of Christ was never heard on these stations." The salvation for these churches originally had been the Mutual Broadcasting System, which carried the *Old Fashioned Revival Hour, Lutheran Hour, Radio Bible Class,* and *Children's Bible Hour.* But in 1944 Mutual prohibited solicitation of funds over the air and banned all paid religious programs after noon on Sunday, leaving such programs the responsibility for forming their own syndicate to organize time on non-network-affiliated stations.[22]

Throughout the period, however, the modernist churches were ebullient

---

[18] Quoted by Paul L. Maier, *A Man Spoke, A World Listened: The Story of Walter A. Maier* (New York: McGraw-Hill, 1963), 85.

[19] Holman Day, *The Ship of Joy: Hugh Barrett Dobbs Commander* (San Francisco: Schwaabacher-Frey, 1931), 41.

[20] James de Forest Murch, in *United Evangelical Action* (1946 November), 15, quoted in Chester E. Tulga, *The Case Against the Federal Council of Churches* (Chicago: Conservative Baptist Fellowship, 1948), 39-40.

[21] Ernest Gordon, *An Ecclesiastical Octopus* (Boston: Fellowship Press, 1948), 88.

[22] Charles M. Crowe, "Religion on the Air," *The Christian Century,* 23 August 1944, 973.

about their relationship with the broadcasting networks and how that relation-ship had increased the audiences (and legitimacy) of Christianity. NBC's Advisory Council adopted a policy in 1928 that religious messages "should interpret religion at its highest and best," and that they "should be non-sectarian and non-denominational in appeal.[23] John W. Langdale, Chairman of the Joint Religious Radio Commission of the Federations of Churches and the FCCCA, told the FCC in 1934 that the "practical results" of the church attempting to own its own stations would have been "far less satisfactory" than what had been achieved by using network facilities.[24] The value of this approach and the close relationship with network radio was confirmed for the modernists, too, by what others said about it during this period, often in the most surprising places.[25]

But this strange debate had little to do with the moral issues that were being raised by other institutions and individuals in America. On these issues the church was largely mute. In 1926 E. L. Parsons wrote in the *Federal Council Bulletin* that "we must take a definite position in regard to laws and legislation. The position of the State must again and again come under review."[26] It never happened. The FCCCA remained interested in topics such as prohibition, education, war and international justice, and race relations, but was not interested in public policy on radio, the developing commercialism, and its subsequent claims about creating an "American" system of broadcasting meeting industry-defined notions of "public interest." The church was absent, too, on the issue of whether radio should be declared a "natural monopoly" and should thus be operated as a public utility. Even the 1938 effort of the Department of Research and Education of the FCCCA to deal with "social ethics" as it applied to the relationship of radio and the public, failed to take on this structural question. Although the Department's report claimed that the church had both a legitimate and essential role in helping define the functional organization of society as affected by the radio industry, it said that this role was "not primarily one of constituting pressure groups or exercising direct political influence," but rather of helping church members "translate moral principles of Christianity into effective vocational action." The Department decided not to recommend any drastic changes in the control of the American broadcasting system, but to "put every confidence in voluntary group action on a local and national scale, to make high standards operative in the industry."[27] But its focus was on the moral content of radio, not on the implications of radio for social and cultural life. When the

---

[23]Quoted in *Broadcasting: Religion – Education – Agriculture*, Vol. 3 (New York: National Broadcasting Co., 1935), 8.

[24]Quoted in ibid., 11.

[25]See Edgar H. Felix, *Using Radio in Sales Promotion: A Book for Advertisers, Station Managers and Broadcasting Artists* (New York: McGraw-Hill, 1927), 229; Clifford Kirkpatrick, *Report of a Research into the Attitudes and Habits of Radio Listeners* (St. Paul: Webb Book Publishing Co., 1933), 45; Frank A. Arnold, "Radio, A Social Force," in *Radio and Education: Proceedings of the Third Annual Assembly of National Advisory Council on Radio in Education, Inc.* (Chicago: University of Chicago Press, 1933), 68; Spencer Miller, Jr., "Radio and Religion," *The Annals of the American Academy of Political and Social Science*, 177 (1935): 139; Merlin H. Aylesworth, "Broadcasting in the Public Interest," *The Annals of the American Academy of Political and Social Science*, 177 (1935): 117; and Thomas Porter Robinson, *Radio Networks and the Federal Government* (New York: Columbia University Press, 1943), 79-89.

[26]E. L. Parsons, "How Shall the Church Deal With Social Questions?," *Federal Council Bulletin* 9 (1926 May-June), 17.

[27]Department of Research and Education of the FCCCA, *Broadcasting and the Public: A Case Study in Social Ethics* (New York: Abingdon Press, 1938), 195-6.

Protestant Radio Commission was formed, too, in 1948, by amalgamating the Religious Radio Committee formed by several denominations and the FCC-CA's Department of Religious Radio, it focused its efforts on encouraging more discriminating radio listening, standards of decency and good taste in programming, and encouraging the use of radio for educating clergy and church representatives, not in changing the economic basis of the industry or the effects of commercialization that had been heightened through radio advertising since the end of the Depression.[28]

The FCCCA was apparently so enamored by its position within the radio industry that it was able to put a positive spin even on what it apparently recognized as a slight by the industry itself. In 1936 at an observance of the tenth anniversary of the beginnings of chain broadcasting, no mention was made of the role of the Department of Religious Radio. The FCCCA's *Biennial Report* noted that no special "public notice" was made in the celebration, but did say that officials of NBC had commended the Department "in personal and group conferences," and then went on to claim that the extent of Protestant broadcasting "confirmed the wisdom of the adoption, early in the decade, of definite principles and policies which have governed its activities in these years."[29] However, by 1949 Charles M. Crowe perhaps was able to see the implications of FCCCA's "hands-off" posture concerning the wider implications of this cozy relationship. The treatment of religion by the radio industry, he said, had resulted in a situation in which religion "was largely ... on the outside looking in as far as big-time radio is concerned."[30] And only a few years later Charles P. Taft claimed that religious leaders had "recognized that the ethical problems of economic life [had] become increasingly urgent" and that, "what earlier generations took for granted, such as the value and integrity of the individual, the character of government as a tool for service of the people, the capacity of human life for essential dignity and justice — these are now challenged by conflicting assumptions also claimed to be moral or at least essential for an efficient society."[31] By then it was too late.

So, while vested interests struggled to have their own stakes protected through legislation, the church remained preoccupied with its own internal conflicts. Occasionally a church-operated radio station would run afoul of the technical parameters for broadcasting (as Aimee Semple McPherson did in Los Angeles in 1925).[32] The International Bible Students (Jehovah's Witnesses) had difficulties with their broadcasts in the U. S. (their leader, J. F. Rutherford, referred to religion as a "racket" and Christianity as "the most subtle, fraudulent and injurious to humankind"), making his broadcasts "controversial."[33] In 1932 the

---

[28]See William W. Clemes, "From Protestant Radio Commission," *Federal Council Bulletin* (1948 April), 10. Information on the amalgamation can bee seen in William F. Fore's "A Short History of Religious Broadcasting," in *Religious Television Programs: A Study of Relevance*, ed. A. William Bluem (New York: Hastings House, Publishers, 1969), 204-5.

[29]FCCCA, *Biennial Report 1936*, 100.

[30]Charles M. Crowe, "Television Needs Religion," *The Christian Century*, 10 August 1949, 938. Only a few years after the end of this examination there seemed to be a recognition, too, of the failure.

[31]Charles P. Taft, "Foreword" in *Responsibility in Mass Communication*, ed. Wilbur Schramm (New York: Harper & Brothers, 1957), vii-viii.

[32]See Erik Barnouw, *A Tower in Babel: A History of Broadcasting in the United States to 1933* (New York: Oxford University Press, 1966), 179-80.

[33]The IBS was philosophical about their difficulties with licensure or carriage by the networks, explaining

District of Columbia Circuit Court ruled against Trinity Methodist Church in its appeal of an FRC decision not to renew its license. As the court's decision put it, the church's minister, Rev. Dr. Robert Shuler, "alluded slightingly to the Jews as a race, and made frequent and bitter attacks on the Roman Catholic religion and its relations to government. However inspired Dr. Shuler may have been by what he regarded as patriotic zeal, however sincere in denouncing conditions he did not approve, it is manifest, we think, that it is not narrowing the ordinary conceptions of 'public interest' in declaring his broadcasts ... not within that term."[34]

There were extended battles, too, between the radio networks and "religious" broadcasters, such as Father Charles Coughlin, the so-called "radio priest." Coughlin began broadcasting a radio program for children from station WJR, Detroit. He became a national broadcaster in 1930, carried by CBS to an estimated weekly audience of forty million. In October 1931 he changed programming tactics, taking on the "so-called" leaders of the United States, especially President Herbert Hoover, who were indifferent, he said, to "the miserable plight of millions...."[35] Coughlin's church, the Shrine of the Little Flower, was the first Catholic Church in the United States to have its own radio program. WJR's manager said in 1933 that Coughlin was "doing more to break down religious prejudice than any single factor in the United States."[36] Coughlin's broadcasts became so heated, however, that CBS asked him to avoid topics that would lead to political controversy. Although he agreed to do so, he then used his next broadcast to ask listeners whether CBS should be allowed to muzzle him — leading to an estimated 1.25 million letters of protest. The networks then instituted their rotation of speakers representing various religious traditions and eased Coughlin off the air (although he then purchased time on stations not controlled by the networks).

The mainline Protestant churches benefited from Coughlin's difficulties and CBS's efforts to silence him. Given the network's experience with Coughlin, it is not surprising that it, along with NBC, looked for an official and presumably safe means to continue religious broadcasts. "This meant," according to one scholar, "avoiding non-ecclesiastically sanctioned preachers on the network, and creating a body that would oversee the rotating pulpit offered without charge. From the networks' point of view, this would reduce the possibilities of demagoguery and the internecine warfare that, by the 1930s, had engulfed the church."[37]

The networks chose to work through the FCCCA or through consultation

---

that it was due to the continuing control of Satan. See Milton Stacey Czatt, *The International Bible Students Jehovah's Witnesses,* Yale Studies in Religion, No. 4 (New Haven: Yale University Press, 1933), 26. See also J. F. Rutherford, *Enemies* (Brooklyn: Watch Tower Bible and Tract Society, 1937).

[34]F. J. Kahn, "The Shuler Case: Trinity Methodist Church v. Federal Radio Commission, 62 F.2d 850 (D.C. Circuit). November 28, 1932." *Documents of American Broadcasting.* 2d ed. (Englewood Cliffs: Prentice-Hall, 1973), 148.

[35]Quoted by C. J. Tull, *Father Coughlin and the New Deal* (Syracuse: Syracuse University Press, 1965), 1.

[36]R. Mugglebee, *Father Coughlin and the Shrine of the Little Flower: An Account of the Life, Work and Message of Reverend Charles E. Coughlin* (Boston: L. C. Page, 1933), 163.

[37]See L. S. Saunders, "The National Religious Broadcasters and the Availability of Radio Time" Ph.D. dissertation, University of Illinois, 1968, 15-6, 24-6. This result was not without its champions in the evangelical camp. For instance, Walter Maier criticized both Coughlin and Judge Joseph Rutherford. Maier, *A Man Spoke,* 187-8.

with various denominations and local federations of churches. This amounted to an endorsement of a concept the FCCCA had approved in 1929 but that had never before been operational.

This strategy, of course, did not satisfy the more "fundamentalist" or evangelical churches. They saw the strategy as one aimed at keeping them off the air. Later apologists for the non-FCCCA broadcasters would write of the National Association of Evangelicals' rescue of evangelical broadcasting in 1944. The NAE (or more properly the NAE for United Action, NAEUA, at that time) had taken up the issue of religious radio within two months of its formation in 1942, and one of its spokesmen had addressed the Institute for Education by Radio, denying that religious broadcasts ought to serve "a cross-section of the public ... if by that is meant that these addresses should be so diluted in content that they will cease to have the power to bring conviction of spiritual need, or neglect to show very definitely how the need be met." He also disagreed entirely with the recommendation that paid religious broadcasting be eliminated. Any fair division of time among the faiths in America, he said, would divide the available time into four, not three (Protestant, Catholic, Jewish) segments. Protestantism, he argued, was composed of two equal strains: the FCCCA group of "so-called liberal or modernist groups," and a non-cohesive "evangelical or conservative" group. The NAEUA was likely to become the representative of this fourth group. Because the networks were unlikely to provide adequate non-sponsored time for the presentation of religion, the organization thought, groups that were financially able to do so should be permitted to purchase time.[38] So, what the modernists thought of as an excuse for racketeering the fundamentalists defined as one essential characteristic of evangelical Christianity — an uncompromising ability to preach the gospel on each preacher's own terms.[39]

Although the NAEUA action occurred in the 1940s, it was the result of a festering resentment that had been building since the Federal Council's 1929 proposal to have the radio networks assign sustaining time to religious groups through consultations with it rather than with individual denominations. It would be unfair to suggest that there was no justification for the evangelical/fundamentalist attack on the Council, as it did seem to exclude them from radio. A scholar who researched the topic, L. S. Saunders, concluded, however, that the facts do not support the view that the Council was attempting to drive evangelicals off the air. This claim, though, continued to be a rallying cry for evangelicals, a declaration that had powerful results throughout the period.[40]

In one respect these differences of opinion between the two wings of Protestantism were irrelevant. Both perspectives were rooted in the same economic as-

---

[38] Executive Committee, *Evangelical Action: A Report of the National Organization of Evangelicals for United Action.* Compiled and edited volume. (Boston: United Action Press, 1942), 120-1, 122.

[39] Charles M. Crowe claimed in 1944 that, "Many insincere and unauthorized 'evangelists' are making a handsome living from such programs" and that the public's view of religion was distorted by them because they followed "the ultraconservative fundamentalist pattern." Crowe, "Religion on the Air," 973. Even the National Association of Evangelicals, soon after its founding in 1942, urged that "racketeering in religious radio programs be checked by refusing broadcast time to organizations or persons ... not affiliated with regularly incorporated church groups." "Radio Urged to Fan War Hate," 677.

[40] Saunders, *The National Religious Broadcasters,* 33; see also Eugene R. Bertermann, "The Radio for Christ," *United Evangelical Action* (1949 March 1), 3-4; Glenwood Blackmore, "Shall the NCC Control Religious Broadcasting?" *United Evangelical Action* (1956 July 1), 5-6; "Broadcasters Defend 'Liberty,'" *Christianity Today* (1957 February 18), 28-9; James Deforest Murch, *Cooperation without Compromise: A History of the National Association of Evangelicals* (Grand Rapids: Wm. B. Eerdman's, 1956), 73.

sumptions, assumptions that legitimized the commercial basis of American broadcasting. On the one hand, the FCCCA's arguments that it wanted to protect free access to the airwaves and its criticism that the NAEUA's arguments might lead the networks to eliminate free time for religion altogether if they thought there was profit to be made turned out to be true. But The NAEUA argued that "the policy of refusing to sell time for religious programs ... constitutes a major discrimination against religion to which other types or classes programs are not subjected."[41] This was also true. But neither point of view challenged the dominant commercial orthodoxy of the radio networks in the way, for instance, that Levering Tyson did in 1937 in defending the necessity of reserving frequency space for educational uses, or that Charles N. Lishka did in his critique of the activities of the Federal Radio Commission for *The Catholic Educational Review*.[42]

More significant than the economic arguments, however, was the difference between "fundamentalists" and "modernists," or "conservatives" and "liberals." There were three elements to this dispute. First was the fact that FCCCA's 1929 action did not result in any change in the policies of the radio networks or of independent stations insofar as broadcasting religious programs was concerned. Their declared preference for sustaining (or free) time merely endorsed a policy already in effect, one that resulted in rather less access to the airwaves than evangelicals wanted. Second, what did cause a reorientation in the thinking of the networks was the Coughlin affair. That was not a modernist versus fundamentalist issue, but rather of demagogue versus network. Third, the antics of some independent preachers, who claimed ties to the fundamentalist wing of Protestantism, did not encourage the networks to exchange one demagogue for another. Evangelicals may have appeared to be unfortunately indiscriminate in their defense of unlimited access to the airwaves.[43]

What was missing in the approaches of both wings of Protestantism, as well as that of the Roman Catholics, was a sustained concern for the developing federal policies governing broadcasting, the rise and dominance of the commercial networks, the intrusive character of advertising into the American home, and the social effects of this new medium of communication. Modernists and evangelicals alike were too busy trying to use the medium to be bothered with how its organization, financing, or control might ultimately affect the audiences they wished to reach, or even compromise their own use of it. This failure constituted the "politico-orthodox" dimensions of the church's failure.

Despite the claims within FCCCA publications about making "the Christian attitude toward life prevail over such wide areas as to make its application to specific social situations possible," and "setting standards for society,"[44] the Council did little to consider the actual impact of radio or the nature of its con-

---

[41]Eugene R. Bertermann, "Plea for More Time for Gospel Broadcasts," *United Evangelical Action* (15 August 1947), 51.

[42]See Levering Tyson, "Preface," in *Education's Own Stations*, by S. E. Frost, Jr. (Chicago: University of Chicago Press, 1937), viii; Lischka, "A Brief for the Freedom of Radio Education," 323-4; see also Charles N. Lischka, "Radio and Education," *The Catholic Educational Review* (1932 February), 77, 82.

[43]*United Evangelical Action* did speak out against "money-raising rackets by publicity-seeking, get-rich-quick preachers" on the radio in 1946. "A Radio Conspiracy," (April 15, 1946).

[44]W. A. Brown, "Church and State in Contemporary America," FCCCA, *Biennial Report* (New York: FCCCA, 1936), 26-7.

trol. Rather the Council was busy toting up the "amazing response to religious broadcasting."[45]

Fundamentalists and modernists alike agreed on one score: the power of radio and the necessity of harnessing it for religious broadcasting. As Murch explained later, "Evangelicals were in the forefront of the forces of religion which recognized radio broadcasting as an effective means of propaganda.... Radio reached out everywhere; it carried its messages at a speed of 186,000 miles a second; it leaped over boundaries, penetrated walls and touched people never before accessible to the Gospel."[46] And this agreement was actually what freed the radio industry from a sustained critique by the church and led the church itself to leap into internecine warfare — whose Gospel was to be preached?

No Christian publication addressed the issue of radio more broadly. *Christian Century* devoted more space to radio than others, but its emphasis began, and remained, on the issue of religious radio. Only one article, "Freedom of the Radio Pulpit," published in 1932, argued more broadly from a First Amendment perspective on the problem of radio religion.[47]

The church committed two fundamental errors in dealing with this new technology and its supporting institutions (the industry and the government). First, it confined itself to issues as defined by broadcasters. The boundaries set by the networks remained unquestioned. The churches remained dependent on the broadcasters to tell them when their counsel was needed and to determine when to heed it. They failed to reflect on the significance of broadcasting on the social fabric, or on the policies constructed to govern its practice. There is little evidence, either, that the churches gave broadcasting much thought in ecclesiastical assemblies (beyond affirming the "good works" of broadcasters), or that they attempted to give significant voice to faith as it applied to the public debate carried on before Congressional committees, national assemblies, or in the popular press. For the most part — with the exception of seeking broadcasting time or protesting against another's use of time — the churches ignored radio. If debate existed, it occurred at the congregational level. The result of this error was that the interests of the church were defined for them and confined to religious programming alone. Given the immensity of broadcasting, and the rapid changes it was surviving over this period, this confinement resulted in relatively insignificant levels of participation.

Even while the churches were being co-opted, either by their cozy relationship with the radio networks or by their ability to organize alternative syndicates and pay their own way using independent stations – which reduced the necessity of protesting against the direction of the industry – voices in other quarters were being raised to protest the commercialization of American life, commerce's invasion of privacy and the sanctity of the home, and the growing material values in the culture.[48] In 1927, only a year after the creation of NBC, Edgar H. Felix warned broadcasters who wanted to use advertising for support of their station

[45]"Department of Religious Radio," FCCCA, *Biennial Report* (New York: FCCCA, 1936), 103.

[46]Murch, *Cooperation Without Compromise: Evangelicals*, 72.

[47]"Freedom of the Radio Pulpit," *The Christian Century* (27 January 1932), 64.

[48]Merlin H. Aylesworth called radio's "remarkable advertising service" a system "calculated to maintain the American standard of living in a land of plenty." Merlin H. Aylesworth, "Broadcasting in the Public Interest," *The Annals of the American Academy of Political and Social Science*, 177 (1935), 117.

that listeners regarded any attempt to use radio for advertising "an affront."[49] A few years later Frank A. Arnold, in another book on broadcast advertising, complained that programs were broadcast daily "in which the element of good taste apparently never enters."[50] Levering Tyson argued in 1933 that even government control was preferable to "the blatant and nauseating commercialism which some unthinking and ill-advised broadcasters persist in inflicting upon the American public,"[51] and James Rorty a year later claimed that, "the vulgarity and commercial irresponsibility of advertising-supported broadcasting have been greatly complained about." He added that the radio culture that existed in the United States was "acquisitive, emulative, neurotic and disintegrating." Rorty also quoted Lee De Forest, the "father of radio," who complained of the "blatant sales talk, meaningless but maddening station announcements, impudent commands to buy or try" that characterized radio.[52] And Warren B. Dygert, in another book examining the role of radio advertising, put the public objections to it most bluntly: "The advertiser must realize that this 'braying of wares' in the radio market place is as pleasing to many listeners as the hawk of the itinerant huckster under a sickroom window."[53] Even the FCCCA's Department of Research and Education recognized that the public "was beginning to rebel against the avalanche of advertising with exaggerated claims which could not possibly be substantiated."[54] But this recognition caused no substantial critique or re-assessment of the stance of the Federal Council on advertising or the commercialization of American life. It was an opportunity missed, one that was recognized — as previously mentioned — only after it was too late to raise fundamental objections.

Second, having accepted their limited role, churches then set out to protect "orthodoxy" on the airwaves. This was already a rear-guard action. Although the dispute between evangelicals and fundamentalists, on the one side, and modernists and mainliners, on the other, may have appeared to make sense, the real issues had escaped both sides. Once the industry was allowed to define its activities fundamentally on the basis of a commercial orientation, it was easy for either of these two antagonistic camps to be marginalized. The modernists were marginalized by the decision of the networks to eliminate sustaining time for religious programming, while the decision of the NAE and NRB to champion the application of free speech rights as the justification for allowing paid religious

---

[49]Edgar H. Felix, *Using Radio in Sales Promotion: A Book for Advertisers, Station Managers and Broadcasting Artists* (New York: McGraw-Hill, 1927), 211-2.

[50]Frank A. Arnold, *Broadcast Advertising: The Fourth Dimension* (New York: John Wiley & Sons, 1931), 140.

[51]Levering Tyson, *Radio and Education: Proceedings of the Third Annual Assembly of National Advisory Council on Radio in Education, Inc.* (Chicago: University of Chicago Press, 1933), 32.

[52]James Rorty, *Our Master's Voice: Advertising* (1934; reprint ed., New York: Arno Press, 1976), 266. Rorty also put this problem in perspective: "Advertising has to do with the shaping of the economic, social, moral and ethical patterns of the community into serviceable conformity with the profit-making interests of advertisers and of the advertising business," 16.

[53]Warren B. Dygert, *Radio as an Advertising Medium* (New York: McGraw-Hill, 1939), 14-5. Other criticisms came from Anthony B. Meany, *America Handcuffed by Radio C-H-A-I-N-S* (New York: Daniel Ryerson, 1942), 16; Thomas Porter Robinson, *Radio Networks and the Federal Government* (New York: Columbia University Press, 1943), 220; and Joy Elmer Morgan, "Education's Rights on the Air," *Education and Radio 1931*, 120-1, quoted by Robert W. McChesney, "Senator C. C. Dill and the Communications Act of 1934," Paper presented to the Broadcast Education Annual Conference, Dallas, Texas, March 1987, 6.

[54]Department of Research, *Broadcasting and the Public*, 88-9.

programs made it difficult for them to police orthodoxy and opened the airwave to religious hucksters, who would eventually create a succession of scandals that would rock the religious broadcasting community. Their apparent "victory" over the modernists was pyrrhic: it opened the field to those who would pay — devout and charlatan alike. What non-Christian elements in the society saw was a basket of dirty laundry hung out for inspection. It was probably too much to expect the two sides to make common cause, particularly after the bitter dispute in the Scopes trial. But it is not too much to suggest that the two sides, had they been willing to engage in more self-examination about the roots of their dispute, should have recognized that its basis was only tangentially theological. Fundamentally, the dispute was over cultural legitimacy and whose definitions of the nature of the relationship between the church and the culture would prevail. Such a recognition would not have solved the division between these two elements of the church, but it would at least have deepened the debate and perhaps have led to a more prophetic stance vis-à-vis the radio industry, even if not from a single perspective.

Ultimately, however, the church became irrelevant in the creation of broadcasting policy. Its potentially prophetic voice in public policy remained still. It spent its energy in-fighting about orthodoxy, beating back assaults from the fringe (such as Jehovah's Witnesses), and complaining about the moral quality of programming. This critique was easy enough for the radio industry to ignore, though, as its source was never willing to critique the basis for decisions within the industry: what would pay. In the end, then, the church failed to make any significant difference in radio. It failed to secure guarantees for religious programs and failed to bring religious values to bear on the significant social and moral issues raised by the developing radio industry. It was thus nearly irrelevant as an institution confronting the rewritten culture that came in radio's wake.

It was during this period that the nature of broadcasting was defined in America. The definitions adopted then have remained largely intact. During this thirty-year period, too, the mass media became one of the principal architects of public consciousness, the principal tool of consumer material culture, and the principal arbiter of social relations between races, sexes, and age groups. It was a period when reflective Christian involvement was crucial. The squabbles over orthodoxy, however, left the church crippled insofar as significant participation was concerned. Without recognizing it, the church was co-opted by the culture it sought to redeem.

The system of relevances constructed in America over this period, then, came to be largely without responsible participation from the church. Whether blinded by the mythos of the technology, enamored by its potential for evangelization, or struggling for legitimacy as they redefined their identity in the inter-war environment, the church and communities of faith failed to seize the broadcast opportunities afforded them to make a difference in the society they served.

# 16

# The Foundations of Evangelical Publishing / *1900-1942*
by Michael A. Longinow

IN EARLY FEBRUARY OF 1910, A YOUNG GIRL named Eunice Leaming was likely one of the first to open her rural mailbox in Woodward, Iowa. Inside, on page 14 of a newspaper known to her family as the *Pentecostal Herald*, Eunice's letter to "Aunt Flora" appeared at the bottom of the second column, telling a nationwide audience she had recently moved to a farm where there were "lots of chickens, some ducks, and several calves and colts." Eunice's letter also noted that she had "two pets, a big blue hen and a baby sister" and that she attended a one-room schoolhouse shared by sixty other children. The letter, apparently not the first Eunice had gotten published in the *Herald*, may have eluded the newsroom wastebasket not only because of its simple freshness, but because it announced that this girl's family had subscribed to the *Herald* for twelve years — and that she had received eleven postcards from children around the nation who had seen her letters and address.[1] Not long afterward, on a different page, a letter-writer from Princeton, Indiana, said his regular reading list included "my good old Bible and the *Pentecostal Herald* and the Free Methodist paper."[2]

Untold numbers of similar letters — published and unpublished — to revivalist Christian newspapers like the Kentucky-based *Pentecostal Herald*, and the scores of similar periodicals circulating in the late nineteenth and early twentieth century stand as quiet evidence of what was to become a firmly entrenched culture of Christian media — indeed, a kind of literacy of evangelical culture — which helped nurture images of rapid change in American Protestantism between 1880 and 1940. As American Protestants separated themselves along a continuum of conservative and liberal thought in this period, they did so by means of semantic labels either generated or disseminated by print media. For revivalist evangelicals, the battle was the Lord's and the weapons were words — those

---

[1] "Aunt Flora's Hour with the Young Folks," *Pentecostal Herald*, 9 February 1910, 14.
[2] "Letters From the People," from William Warner, *Pentecostal Herald*, 29 June 1913, 10.

they could quote from Scripture and those they could read or write in mass-published form. This chapter examines the phenomenon of evangelical Christian print media in the first half of this century — focusing in particular on revivalist newspapers – for these would pave the way for floods of evangelical book publishing and magazine distribution after World War II and remain a bulwark of Christian evangelical culture at the end of this century, fueling the growth of such popular revivalist movements as Promisekeepers.[3] Such media had an amazing ability to position themselves, for more than a century, in as high a standing in the minds of American Protestants as the family Bible. Indeed, over time Christian media would nearly eclipse the Scriptures as evangelical Christians' guide to navigating post-Christian Western culture – a culture fraught with media many evangelicals found increasingly objectionable.

*THE RELIGIOUS MEDIA MARKETPLACE: NETWORKS ACROSS A NATION*

A tracing of the growth of revivalist American Protestantism requires inquiry into the roots and circulation of its media — and, by extension, the reading habits of those at which it aimed. First, contrary to established research, it must be noted that media development among Protestant evangelicals was more than an urban movement and more than a better marketing of religion — though revivalism touched America's greatest cities and from its earliest inception involved a degree of what would later be labeled marketing theory. Pre-Industrial America's deepest roots of socio-cultural power lay in the vast array of small towns scattered across the continent. Between 1800 and 1830, greater and greater numbers of Americans in rural areas had begun reading periodicals regularly — a large measure of these religious — fed by a growing postal system and a publishing explosion that pumped more varieties of newspapers, pamphlets and books into circulation than was thought possible a generation earlier. In Vermont alone, the percentage of households subscribing to a newspaper jumped from 36 per cent in 1800 to 54 per cent in 1829.[4] Though general histories of journalism devote most attention to the successes of secular print media in this period,[5] evangelical Christian publishing was at least keeping pace, if not leading, this explosion of popular media interest. By 1840, Methodists throughout New York — some 15,000 strong — were subscribers to the *Western Christian Advocate*, while the *Western Methodist Book Concern* in Cincinnati, in 1850, had twenty-five printers and forty-six binders cranking out five different periodicals with combined circulation of 85,000. Adventists, in one 1843 estimate,

---

[3]Richard N. Ostling, "Evangelical Publishing and Broadcasting," in *Evangelicalism and Modern America*, ed. George M. Marsden (Grand Rapids: Eerdmans, 1984), 46-55; Bob Sumner, "Male Spirituality on the Move," *Publisher's Weekly* 243:11 (March 11, 1996): 28-31; Steve Robey, "Promisekeepers Inspires Look-alikes," *Christianity Today* 40:5 (April 29, 1996): 46-9; John Swomley, "Cashing in for Christ," *The Humanist* 56:5 (September 1996): 39-41; R. Laurence Moore, *Selling God: American Religion in the Marketplace of Culture* (New York: Oxford University Press, 1994), 5-8.

[4]William J. Gilmore, *Reading Becomes a Necessity of Life: Material and Cultural Life in Rural New England, 1780-1835* (Knoxville: University of Tennessee Press, 1989), 98-9.

[5]See, for example, Wm. David Sloan and James D. Startt, eds., *The Media in America: A History*, 4th ed. (Northport, Ala.: Vision Press, 1999); Alfred McClung Lee, *The Daily Newspaper in America: The Evolution of a Social Instrument* (New York: Octagon Books, 1973), 18-20; Frank Luther Mott, *American Journalism: A History of Newspapers in the United States Through 250 Years, 1690-1950* (New York: Macmillan, 1950), 321-2.

were spreading their literature across the frontier by the millions.[6] By 1800 the phenomenon of religious publishing was clearly visible in publications like Boston's *Congregational Recorder*, Philadelphia's *Episcopal Recorder*, and the *Presbyterian Observer*, of New York.[7] These, along with Cincinnati's *Western Christian Advocate*, Chicago's *Northwestern Christian Advocate*, and Kentucky's *Pentecostal Herald* helped form what Timothy Smith has called a "vast river of Bibles, books, magazines, pamphlets and religious periodicals."[8] Figures varied, but most states had at least a handful of religious publications to choose from. In 1883, smaller states such as Connecticut had three; Alabama had five; but states with larger populations or those along rail routes such as Michigan and Virginia had more than a dozen; Ohio had 49; Illinois had 56; New York and Pennsylvania had 78 and 79 respectively. Circulation of these publications ranged from 400 in western territorial states such as Oregon to more than 100,000 in New York.[9]

But for such media to be meaningful required willing readers. And while literate Americans were still a minority, their numbers were growing. Literacy paid – in more ways than one. Research into liberalism, popular education, and American media indicates that an interesting combination of both publisher-shrewdness and generous philanthropy in the early 1900s brought increasing numbers of adults into secular reading classes;[10] meanwhile, American Sunday Schools and other church-related educational programs had long been places where people of all ages learned to read as Christians placed education alongside spiritual nurture in their advancement of the gospel.[11] If cultural expansion was a function of language, and language was to be grasped by readers, such a dual propagation of literacy and literature was crucial – and not unexpected. It has been said that the very story of American culture is that of advancing communication within given groups in ever-widening patterns and paths of discourse.[12]

But why were people reading? And how were they reading it? Some have argued that if church-going people read at all in this period, they may not have been reading carefully or critically – particularly in the South, where their often overworked, non-professional ministers were known to publicly disdain the reading of any book not found in the Bible – except their hymnal or *Farmer's Almanac*.[13] Such an assessment carries validity for pockets not only of the South but of the Midwest and other regions of the territorial U.S. in the early 1900s.[14]

---

[6]John C. Nerone, "The Press and Popular Culture in the Early Republic: Cincinnati, 1793-1843," unpublished Ph.D dissertation, University of Notre Dame, 1982.

[7] Mott, *American Journalism...*, 206.

[8]Timothy L. Smith, *Revivalism and Social Reform: American Protestantism on the Eve of the Civil War* (Baltimore: Johns Hopkins Press, 1957, 1980), 39.

[9]*American Newspaper Catalog* (Cincinnati: Edwin Alden & Brothers Advertising Agency, 1883), 489-94.

[10]James M. Wallace, *Liberal Journalism and American Education: 1914-1941* (New Brunswick: Rutgers University Press, 1991), 59-60.

[11]William J. Gilmore, "Elementary Literacy on the Eve of the Industrial Revolution: Trends in Rural New England, 1760-1830," *Proceedings of the American Antiquarian Society* 92 (April 1982): 87-171.

[12]James W. Carey, *Communication as Culture: Essays on Media and Society* (Boston: Unwin Hyman, 1989), 2-3.

[13]Martin E. Marty, *Righteous Empire: The Protestant Experience in America* (New York: The Dial Press, 1970), 222-5.

[14]Burton J. Bledstein, *The Culture of Professionalism: The Middle Class and the Development of Higher Education in America* (New York: W.W. Norton & Co., 1978), 278.

But any arguments about Americans' literacy, or lack thereof, in those decades has proven difficult for many reasons. Scholars have noted a lack of reliable statistics as to who was able to read;[15] and if pinpointing who was capable of reading raises questions, still more complicated is what Americans chose to read if they could, and why they chose to. Could evangelicals' hunger for information be itself a source of socio-cultural power for them? Possibly so. Cultures formed of orality throughout U.S. history – as revivalist strands of American Protestantism certainly were – have often brought about print culture to further themselves.[16] For whatever reason, media readership and revival appear to have gone hand in hand through the late nineteenth and early twentieth century. Moreover, studies of evangelical Christian media indicate that during the nation's great spiritual awakenings both laity and clergy – some of whom were writers and editors – were a more informed lot than commonly portrayed.[17] For church-members of this era, reading was a kind of self-help – an assistance publishers of Christian mass media were more than willing to provide.

It should be noted here that consumers of Christian media were not unaware of the secular news and commercial media that surrounded them. An 1825 edition of the *Methodist Magazine*, published in New York but circulated widely, commented on a report from a British newspaper about war in Europe, saying, "what Christian can read it, and not pour forth the desires of his inmost soul to God that he would restrain the madness of the nations?"[18] Given the advancing technology of presses, rail systems and the U.S. Postal Service, there were plenty of secular news media to go around. In the 1880s, while states like Kentucky, with a population of about 1.7 million, had 14 religious newspapers, there were 211 commercial newspapers selling advertisements across that commonwealth's 790 counties with circulations ranging from 500 to 100,000. Each of Kentucky's counties had at least one newspaper while some, such as Fayette and Jefferson – home of Lexington and Louisville respectively – had dozens.[19] The astute editor of a Christian newspaper in this era made it a practice to scan as many of these as possible – particularly as fodder for editorials on controversial topics such as slavery. One study of religious newspapers in the nineteenth century upper Midwest estimated that the typical editor read scores of newspapers – secular and religious – before each edition of his own, seeking material suitable for inclusion alongside contributed material from staff writers.[20]

Empowerment gained by reading served many purposes for Protestant Evangelicals. Most obviously, it would seem to have served as a tool of upward social mobility from the late 1890s onward – if one views reading as a means of gaining economic advantage in an urbanizing America. The attention of many was indeed on the new cities. One census official in the 1890s declared that the

---

[15]Daniel J. Boorstin, *The Americans: The National Experience* (New York: Vintage/Random House, 1965), 217.

[16]Walter J. Ong, *Rhetoric, Romance and Technology: Studies in the Interaction of Expression and Culture* (Ithaca: Cornell University Press, 1971), 290-9.

[17]David Paul Nord, "The Evangelical Origins of Mass Media in America," chapter 5 of this book; Nathan O. Hatch, *The Democratization of American Christianity* (New Haven: Yale University Press, 1989), ch. 2.

[18]"Horrors of War," letter in *Methodist Magazine* (Methodist *Review*) 8:1, January 1825, 29.

[19]Alden & Brothers, *American Newspaper Catalog...*, 375-7.

[20]Wesley Norton, *Religious Newspapers in the Old Northwest to 1861: A History, Bibliography, and Record of Opinion* (Athens: Ohio University Press, 1977), 34, 43-4.

frontier no longer existed.[21] But as noted earlier, an urban-elite approach to understanding America's cultural development in the early 1900s misses the important influence of grassroots approaches to readership, particularly among the conservative, religious population of areas well away from urban centers. The resilient language of the frontier, in fact, can be seen as an extension of the declamatory language of the pulpit – even for those seldom in church. Such readers, no less than their urban counterparts, needed a handle on the changing world. Christian periodicals provided it in a manner so close to home as to be nearly family-like. Thomas Leonard's insights into reading culture indicate Americans differed in this period from their British counterparts in that rather than picking up a newspaper for group discussion at the local pub or tavern, Americans tended to take theirs home, often gathering by families around a warm hearth where printed text meshed with oral commentary.[22] Readers of Christian periodicals followed a similar pattern. One minister, commenting on Christian reading in 1825, said Christian literature was suitable for reading and comment both "at the table" and "in the fireside circle" and was of "importance in carrying on the work of God."[23]

*HENRY CLAY MORRISON: EDITOR AND REVIVALIST IMAGE-MAKER*

Logistics of literacy alone do not fully explain why Christian newspapers and similar literature mattered as much as they did to grassroots Protestant evangelicals in the late-nineteenth and early-twentieth centuries. Something deeper had apparently been happening among readers to shape their expectations about printed media. To keep touch with reality, language surrounding something such as Holiness Methodist culture could not stop with mere language. Action had to result. And so it did – or was strongly encouraged. Action urged by Christian evangelical newspapers was often aimed at reform – personal or sociocultural – and revivalist newspapers were unique in their aggressive, reformist stance on culture within and outside Christendom. But active reading was a learned response; and it can be argued that editors of religious newspaper quite effectively urged readers, upon putting down their newspaper, to pick up their Bible, their lesson plans for Sunday School, or a pen and paper for letter-writing to a Congressman or Methodist bishop. Hence, newspapers like the *Pentecostal Herald* can be seen as an outgrowth of a massive media movement within evangelicalism to inform and educate laity – a movement, with reference to Methodists in 1865, called "the most energetic religious element in the social development of the continent."[24]

Published in Louisville, Kentucky, for most of its existence, the *Pentecostal Herald* was an arm of Pentecostal Publishing Company, which spread books, tracts and Sunday School curricula from the early 1900s through the inter-war years along the Upper South, lower Midwest and across a wide swath of territory

---

[21]Frederick J. Turner, "The Significance of the Frontier in American History," *Annual Report, for 1893, of the American Historical Association* (Washington, D.C.: Government Printing Office, 1894).

[22]Thomas C. Leonard, *News For All: America's Coming of Age with the Press* (New York: Oxford University Press. 1995), 19-28.

[23]Extract of letter from Rev. W. Case, *Methodist Magazine* 8:3, March 1825, 109-10.

[24]Abel Stevens, *The Centenary of the American Methodism: A Sketch of its History, Theology, Practical System and Success* (New York: Carlton & Porter, 1865), 126.

stretching from upstate New York to San Francisco.[25] Wherever the *Pentecostal Herald* went, revivalism and the culture of experiential, Bible-based faith went as well, acting as a voice aimed at reforming not only American Protestantism but American popular culture itself: from local saloons to state legislatures. To the degree that they compelled readers into the public sphere, religious newspapers like the *Pentecostal Herald* paralleled the many socially committed commercial newspapers and magazines of the era. Much in the pattern of other religious newspapers of the nineteenth century, the *Pentecostal Herald's* founding editor, Henry Clay Morrison, was a clergyman with no apparent journalistic training. Born in 1857 in Western Kentucky, Morrison's entry into American journalism and American Protestantism bridged two important eras: the Second Great Awakening and the Progressive Era. Each movement would leave indelible marks on both American Protestantism and America's media landscape – both secular and Christian. Morrison, perhaps sensing the historic apex he had been born into, lived out the revivalist image – even into the 1940s – of the white-collared, black-booted circuit-riding preacher of the nineteenth century.[26] For Morrison, revival was not merely a concept but a way of life. Though Morrison was a master at corporate-organizational detail and had served urban congregations, he became widely known among evangelical Methodists – and many Fundamentalist Christian leaders – through a reputation for lively preaching along the camp-meeting circuit that stretched from California to New York through the late nineteenth century.

Much in the pattern of the earlier revivalist Charles Grandison Finney, Morrison was known not only for his writing and oratory, but for leadership of a college – Asbury College, southwest of Lexington, between 1910 and 1940. Through this college presidency and by means of his media and camp-meeting connections, Morrison also helped nurture a seminary – named, like the college, after Methodist Bishop Francis Asbury – out of roots in Asbury College's Bible Department. By combining publishing and education in this way, Morrison believed, advancing liberalism within Methodism and Protestant evangelicalism as a whole could be routed in the twentieth century.[27]

Morrison's newspaper originated in 1888 as *The Old Methodist*, a monthly periodical with home offices in Frankfort, Kentucky. Several name changes in its history do not reflect changes in its purpose, for it was a publication from the outset designed as a rhetorical weapon of revivalist faith and practice.[28] "Ask for the Old Paths," appeared under the tiny newspaper's first nameplate. In editorial purpose, Morrison's newspaper flew in the face of what by the 1880's were more doctrinally liberal denominational papers such as Cincinnati's *Western Christian Advocate*. In overall design, however, the *Pentecostal Herald* fit the pattern of these publications from its English-script nameplate to its front-page editorial

[25]G. Wayne Rogers, "A Study of Henry Clay Morrison and His Fundraising Technique in *The Pentecostal Herald* for Asbury Seminary, 1939-1942," unpublished Master's thesis, The University of Kentucky, 1981, 69-72.

[26]Joseph A. Thacker, Jr., *Asbury College: Vision and Miracle* (Nappanee, Ind.: Evangel Press, 1990), 171.

[27]Ibid., 90, 134.

[28]Douglas M. Strong, "Fighting Against Worldliness and Unbelief: Henry Clay Morrison and the Transformation of the Holiness Movement Within Methodism," Conference proceedings, Methodism and the Fragmentation of American Protestantism, 1865-1920, Wesleyan/Holiness Studies Center at Asbury Theological Seminary, Wilmore, Kentucky, September 29-30, 1995.

and multi-column formats. It also followed its competitors' pattern of phenomenal circulation growth in the late nineteenth century.

Founded as a weekly newspaper in 1834, *the Western Christian Advocate*
had 5,500 subscribers within a year of its first issue, and by 1840 claimed
15,000 regular readers — an extensive number by standards of the day.[29] Morrison's *Pentecostal Herald* grew from a 500-copy press-run in 1888 to 15,000 in
1893; 30,000 in 1920; 38,000 in 1934, and nearly 55,000 — the newspaper's
peak circulation — in 1942, the year Morrison died. Historian Wayne Rogers
estimates that in Morrison's fifty-three years editing the newspaper, nearly sixty-
five million copies were distributed.[30] The real reach of Morrison's newspaper,
however – much as any Christian newspaper of this period – is impossible to
measure because of distribution possibilities arising from the "share it with a
friend" admonitions and circulation contests that editors inserted frequently into
these newspapers.

Though other denominations had popular and growing publications in this
period, Methodists were leaders in the Christian newspaper movement, having
established a reputation among America's larger Protestant denominations, beginning in the colonial era, as those most prone to re-examine and re-discover
themselves – in a pattern set by John Wesley himself – through new histories
and proliferating literature.

*MORRISON'S NICHE WITHIN EVANGELICALISM: HOLINESS CULTURE*

Though begun in Kentucky, the *Pentecostal Herald* within ten years had taken
over the first of two religious newspapers in the Southeast that it would buy out.
By 1900, it had readers from Georgia to California;[31] and over the years,
through several name changes, the emerging revivalist culture surrounding the
*Pentecostal Herald* would help it take on a life of its own. By Morrison's death
in 1942, the newspaper had become a primary emblem and rallying point[32] for
the Holiness Movement — that populist-oriented strand of revivalist followers of
John Wesley scattered across the continent and in many parts of the world.[33]

---

[29]Norton, *Religious Newspapers in the Old Northwest...*, 10.

[30]Rogers, "A Study of Henry Clay Morrison...," 45.

[31]Percival A. Wesche, "The Life, Theology and Influence of Henry Clay Morrison," unpublished Ph.D.
dissertation, University of Oklahoma, 1954, 79, 86. See also, *Pentecostal Herald*, 25 March 1908, 2; *Pentecostal Herald* 44, 24 February 1932, 8; and Thomas B. Talbot, "The *Pentecostal Herald* to Date — A Brief
Outline," *Pentecostal Herald*, 25 March 1908, 1. The *Old Methodist* became the *Kentucky Methodist* and
then, on August 11, 1897, took the *Pentecostal Herald* for its nameplate, "Peneteost signifying the outpouring of the Holy Ghost sanctifying the soul, and *Herald* signifying our purpose to carry the good news
of full salvation into every nook and corner of our denomination...," Morrison wrote. *Pentecostal Herald*, 11
August 1897, 1. The newspaper bought out *The Way of Life* in 1895 and *The Way of Faith* in 1932.

[32]Charles Edwin Jones, ed., *A Guide to The Study of the Holiness Movement* (Metuchen, N.J.: Scarecrow
Press, 1974), 74-80; Howard Glenn Spann, "Evangelicalism in Modern American Methodism: Theological
Conservatives in the "Great Deep" of the Church, 1900-1980," unpublished Ph. dissertation, Johns Hopkins University, 1995, 76-9. Holiness believers within the ranks of evangelical Methodists already had scattered press outlets prior to Morrison's newspaper before 1900, though editors of some were becoming theologically suspect afterward. Examples were *The Way of Faith*, eventually taken over by the *Pentecostal Herald*, the northern *Christian Witness* and *Advocate of Bible Holiness*, *Little Methodist*, *God's Revivalist*,
*Guide to Holiness*, *Guide to Perfect Love*, *Holiness Evangel*, *Michigan Holiness Record*, *Standard of Holiness*, and *Way of Life*.

[33]Rogers, "A Study of Henry Clay Morrison...," 53; see also Paul Frederick Abel, "An Historical Study of
the Origin and Development of Asbury Theological Seminary," unpublished Ph.D. dissertation, Columbia
University, 1951, 109-10; An interdenominational holiness camp meeting at Vineland, N.J., is considered

Holiness believers could be found not only in branches of the Methodist Church, but also the Wesleyan Church, United Church of the Brethren, Church of the Nazarene, and Church of God. The movement would also develop strong links, through the nineteenth and twentieth centuries, with the international Salvation Army, the Keswick Movement and scores of national and international evangelistic associations and missionary societies.[34] The Holiness Movement also built ties to the controversial Fundamentalist Movement, and the *Pentecostal Herald's* connections with such high-profile figures as William Jennings Bryan, "Fighting Bob" Shuler, and institutions such as Chicago's Moody Bible Institute, helped establish the newspaper socio-politically in the conflict against modernism and in defense of Creation – both as a scientific premise and as a philosophical foundation – into and beyond the 1930s.

Morrison's ties to Fundamentalism, through his writing and editing, are easily misunderstood. Holiness believers were fundamentalist before and during the rise of Christian Fundamentalism in North America, but cannot be classified — in the strict doctrinal sense — as Fundamentalists. Though the two movements are distinct, the smaller Holiness Movement was one whose rise, decline and socio-cultural agenda paralleled the growth of Christian Fundamentalism in America.[35] One key to the *Pentecostal Herald's* longevity across several decades, also an explanation for Morrison's legacy as a non-denominational leader in both media and education, was his willingness to cooperate with any Christian committed to revivalism and its outworking in the culture of the Church and society. He saw to it that those who would outlive him in the *Pentecostal Herald* newsroom carried this same commitment. The result was that by the time Morrison died, he had in one sense worked himself out of a job as media protagonist. On the other hand, he left behind a newspaper crafted irretrievably in his image.[36]

*MORRISON'S MEDIA AS SHAPERS OF SOCIO-RELIGIOUS SELF-IDENTITY*

Letters to the *Pentecostal Herald* and tributes to Morrison and his publication upon his death indicate this was a newspaper whose principles and images readers used to measure themselves on a socio-religious scale that remained as fixed over the years as the photo image of the newspaper's editor. Such self-measurement by readers was a pattern well-known among religious periodicals tracing to the individualism and pursuit of ideas born in the eighteenth-century press of Europe. Perhaps as important, it provided readers a sense of place in the rapidly changing socio-cultural landscape of American Protestantism. Indeed, the era of Protestant domination of American culture had changed radically by the 1890s. But though some would argue that Protestant evangelical attention was shifting

---

the beginning of the modern Holiness Movement.
    [34]Jones, *A Guide to the Study of the Holiness Movement*, 9, 96, 97, 98, 103, 105, 106-8, 123-4, 129-32, 134, 203, 205, 207-8, 211-4, 216, 258, 274, 276-461.
    [35]Rose, *A Theology of Christian Experience: Interpreting the Historic Wesleyan Message* (Minneapolis: Bethany Fellowship, 1965), 23-78; Douglas A. Foster, "Sectarian Strife in the Midst of the Fundamentalist-Modernist Crisis: The Premillienial Controversy in the Churches of Christ, 1910-1940," Conference Proceedings, Methodism and the Fragmentation of American Protestantism, 1865-1920.
    [36]Wesche, "The Life, Theology and Influence of Henry Clay Morrison...," 88-90. Morrison's *Herald* employees, from press workers to top editors tended to stay with the publication for decades at a time. Wesche notes that through more than fifty years of operation, only three workers were dismissed.

from the American frontier to American cities – thus marginalizing rural Protestants – those who shunned the Big City, in turn being shunned by urbanites, had all the more reason to seek out media to support their notions of socio-religious stability. And as noted earlier, the argument can also be made that those evangelical church-goers who remained non-urban comprised a staunchly conservative and amazingly well-networked element of American Protestantism, the stability of which stemmed from its far-flung, yet resilient cohesion. Central to this cohesion was a resistance among common churchgoers to much of what mainline denominations were calling mainstream socio-religious culture. Christian newspapers could uniquely articulate this resistance.

Hence, the *Pentecostal Herald*, though published in downtown offices most of its publication life, cannot be seen entirely as a city publication. Its larger appeal was to the camp-meeting circuit: that network of people willing to gather faithfully from June to September each year under big-top style tents or open-air tabernacles, at varying distances from urban centers, from California to New York. The readership of the *Pentecostal Herald* of the early 1900s roughly follows the locations of these camp-meetings – seen most vividly in a 1923 subscription map published in the *Pentecostal Herald* showing strongest concentrations of readers in Kentucky, Ohio, Indiana, Michigan, Georgia, Texas and Kansas, with lesser concentrations in Virginia, West Virginia, Pennsylvania, North Carolina, Florida, Arkansas, Missouri, Oklahoma and California. According to the map, every state on the continent had *Pentecostal Herald* readership, though Utah, Arizona, Nevada, New Hampshire, Connecticut, and Rhode Island apparently had the lowest numbers.[37]

In these camp meetings music, preaching, and Christian literature and media coalesced in a common theme of revivalist socio-religious experience.[38] Rules of membership in camp meeting culture were simple: regular attendance and public expression of genuine faith experience. Preaching was ferocious; singing was robust; repentance was up front and personal. Francis Asbury, a camp-meeting promoter, found them so intense that he rarely slept during the multiple days they lasted.[39] Camp meetings embodied a lifestyle and culture all their own[40] as places where toddlers first learned about God, young people found their mates, and the elderly conferred about leaving this life.[41]

Immersion in camp meeting life necessarily involved exposure to Biblical teaching – mixed with healthy doses of folk culture – becoming a self-perpetuating means of the camps' continuation over the years. "These holiness camp meetings are great Bible schools," wrote Morrison in 1924. "The holiness camp

[37]"The Cooperative Plan" map, *Pentecostal Herald*, 14 February 1923, 16. The map appears with an admonition "To Cooperate in getting a Virile, Aggressive, Orthodox, Religious Paper into the hands of 100,000 more readers."

[38]Kenneth Scott Latourette, *A History of Christianity: Reformation to the Present*, vol. 2, rev. ed. (San Francisco: Harper & Row, 1975), 1037, 1231, 1266.

[39]Hatch, *The Democratization of American Christianity...*, 49.

[40]Jones, *A Guide to the Study of the Holiness Movement...*, 336-8; Charles Edwin Jones, "A Study of the Modern Camp Meeting," unpublished Th.M. thesis, Louisville Presbyterian Theological Seminary, 1962; Percival A. Wesche, "The Revival of the Camp Meeting by the Holiness Groups," unpublished M.A. thesis, Divinity School, University of Chicago, 1945.

[41]Rev. J.C. McPheeters, D.D., "Camp Sychar," *Pentecostal Herald*, 25 September 1940, 3. The *Pentecostal Herald* promoted camp meetings through long listings of meetings that, by the 1930s, had become so large that they were printed in classified-style type. The meetings were listed by state. Individual evangelists were also listed alphabetically and by larger advertisements and review articles.

meeting is one of the greatest means of a powerful propaganda in this nation."[42] The *Pentecostal Herald* became inseparably linked to such camp meetings – and suffered with them as popularity of camp meetings declined after World War II – both because the newspaper was distributed at them, and because the newspaper served as an informal guide to camp preachers and musicians through extensive listings of nationwide camp meeting schedules in its back pages and feature stories about camp meeting events.

*TALKING BACK TO MORRISON'S NEWSPAPER: LETTERS AND LONGINGS*

One of the more convincing proofs that the *Pentecostal Herald's* readers did more than passively scan its pages was the manner in which so many talked back, by means of letters, to this newspaper. By writing back to the *Pentecostal Herald*, readers reached out, sometimes in tones of lonely desperation, to what they apparently believed were among the few sympathetic leaders available who shared their faith convictions and socio-cultural values. The reach, at times, was across state lines or across the continent, though some sought such long-distance leadership despite being surrounded by church-going neighbors or family. For *Pentecostal Herald* readers – particularly those well-versed in such religious media – there was no replacing the people about whom they read and with whom they attended camp meetings.[43]

Part of the readers' devotion for the *Pentecostal Herald* and its culture might have sprung from the newspaper's insistence that the only acceptable believers were Holiness believers, and Holiness literature the only acceptable Christian literature. Still another appeal might have been the socio-cultural language that this newspaper modeled – a language comprised of Biblical themes and metaphor, hymn texts, camp-meeting images, and Wesleyan theological terms – whose syntax and vocabulary might not have been easily navigable to those not familiar with the *Pentecostal Herald*. Those who knew it were insiders, and liked it that way.

Research in general on letters to newspapers has shown a variety of relationships between letter-writers and their favorite publications throughout American media history.[44] A common theme that emerges, however, is that letters chosen for print in a publication reflect readers' perception not only of that publication's staff and content, but of fellow-readers. An analysis of *Pentecostal Herald* letters examined for this chapter – and letters appeared in nearly every issue from 1910-1942[45] – suggests that this newspaper produced a socio-cultural bond between readers and their newspaper that was at once simple and complex. The simplic-

---

[42]H.C. Morrison, "Great Bible School with Revival Power," *Pentecostal Herald*, 25 June 1924, 1, 8.

[43]H.C. Morrison, "All Hail to the Great *Herald* Family for 1934!" *Pentecostal Herald and Way of Faith*, 3 January 1934; Mrs. H.C. (Bettie Whitehead) Morrison, "Our *Herald* Family," *Pentecostal Herald and Way of Faith*, 12 September 1945, 5.

[44]Ernest C. Hynds, "Editorial Page Editors Discuss Use of Letters," *Newspaper Research Journal* 13:1-2 (Winter/Spring 1992): 124-36; Steven Pasternak, "The Open Forum: A Study of Letters to the Editor and the People who Write Them," paper presented at the annual convention of the Association for Education in Journalism and Mass Communications, Portland, Ore., July 2-5, 1988; Francisco Vasquez, "Newspapers' Letters to the Editor as Reflectors of Social Structure," paper presented at the annual convention of the Association for Education in Journalism and Mass Communications, Corvallis, Ore., August 6-9, 1983.

[45]Research on letters to the newspaper involved analysis of every other month's issues in the period 1910-1942, with extra analysis of 1943-1945.

ity of the bond came down to the faith readers put in the principles they learned and the persons they read about. The complexity concerned why that faith was so easily planted and how it was lived out. Referring to this bonding of his newspaper's Holiness constituency, Morrison wrote in 1919, that the Holiness Movement – by means of the *Pentecostal Herald* – had produced "the closest brotherhood in all the world" and "a union, a fellowship, a spirit of oneness and cooperation which cannot possibly be secured otherwise."[46]

Examination of *Pentecostal Herald* letters suggests, too, that readers shared not only a common socio-religious language, but shared symbols of their common socio-cultural values. Children's letters are perhaps the most compelling example of this. In such letters, those too young to tidy their thoughts wrote letters of amazing consistency in theme: generally asking to join the "happy band" of child writers to the paper — and avoid W.B. (the waste basket). Children's letters make mention consistently of such socio-cultural badges of honor as long-running family subscriptions to the *Pentecostal Herald*; positive regard for Asbury College or Dr. Henry Clay Morrison; regular attendance at a local Sunday School; faithful reading of the Bible; or a doctrinally accurate profession of faith. The latter, however, was not required for a child's letter to be published. "I go to Sunday School every Sunday," wrote Bessie Sullivan in 1914. "My school teacher's name is Mrs. Anderson, and my Sunday school teacher's name is Mrs. Wilkins. I am not a Christian girl but hope to be one soon."[47] In nearly every child's letter – evidence perhaps that they were so instructed, but perhaps also because they wrote seeking connection with other readers – children described themselves by height, weight, hair color, eye color and complexion. In listing their birthdays children would often ask, as did this one in 1943, "Do I have a twin? If so, please write me.... I would like to hear from boys and girls all over the world."[48]

Most adult letters were placed on the editorial page immediately following the jump section (continuation) of Morrison's front-page editorial. Depending on content – and at times, apparently as space-filler – adult letters were sprinkled through other pages. Among adult letter-writers, the most common socio-cultural symbol of shared values was upkeep of a regular subscription to the *Pentecostal Herald* – evidence, perhaps, that Morrison and his staff chose letters to sway subscribers wavering over cancellation. In any case, there does appear a pattern, over the years, of a kind of hubris surrounding long duration on the *Herald* subscription list. Faithfulness to the *Herald* was apparently seen by some as bordering on reverential, engendering a kind of media sibling rivalry among readers. One Kentucky woman, writing in 1910, traced her readership of the *Herald* back into years it carried another title, remarking, "I presume I am one of the oldest subscribers."[49]

Readers not only followed the ideas and seemed to feel the pain of *Herald* editors and writers, but like the children seeking pen-pals, many adult readers of the *Herald* wrote seeking personal help and affirmation from editors and fellow-

---

[46]H.C. Morrison, "The *Herald* Family," *Pentecostal Herald*, 19 March 1919, 1.
   [47]Letter from Bessie Sullivan, Ava, Mo., in "Our Boys and Girls," ed. Mrs. Bettie Whitehead, *Pentecostal Herald*, 13 May 1914, 14.
   [48]Cf. letter from Muriel Leonard, Rt. 1, Box 29, Cantonment, Fla., "Our Boys and Girls," *Pentecostal Herald and Way of Faith*, 6 January 1943, 10.
   [49]Letter to *Pentecostal Herald* from Amanda Johnson, Cane Valley, Kentucky, 2 November 1910, 11A-B.

subscribers alike. A degree of loneliness – perhaps out of self-isolation – can be seen in these who had so immersed themselves in the revivalist culture of the *Pentecostal Herald* that outsiders became foreign and suspicious. One mother's letter to the *Herald* in 1910 said, "We have no holiness people around here but I wish some would come this way for we need their help.... I have four boys and I desire the prayers of the *Herald* readers that they may be saved and live pure lives."[50]

## SOCIAL POLITICS OF MORRISON'S MEDIA: AGITATION FOR CHANGE

The emergence of Morrison's newspaper came at the end of a century of widespread Protestant influence – partly by means of influence over democratic processes – of cultural definitions of public vice. But such influence was on the wane. The *Old Methodist's* adamant stand in initial editions against liquor – and later, against such other practices as tobacco use,[51] gambling, social dancing and the wearing of immodest clothing placed it in ever-diminishing company among Protestants as the twentieth century unfolded. To the *Pentecostal Herald's* editors, and at least those readers whose letters were printed, such vices were to be forbidden not so much as actions but for what they meant to the culture of revivalism and the Holiness constituency.

By 1910, when the *Pentecostal Herald* had developed more vigor through both nurture of, and support from, its Holiness camp-meeting network and a growing college constituency, its stand on prohibition and the other social vices was stronger than ever.[52] Meanwhile, however, leaders of Methodism had begun asking new questions about social symbols and practices – like the drinking of alcohol and teaching of evolution – that many had formerly frowned upon. Indeed, mainstream Protestantism as a whole had begun pursuing social reform by means other than a demand for public policy favoring formerly dominant Protestant cultural norms. Parenthetically, but significant to their opponents, some of these new social pursuits were done in the company of those not traditionally associated with American Protestantism. The formation, in 1907, of the Methodist Federation for Social Service and later founding of the American Civil Liberties Union by a Methodist cleric in Chicago were but two events in a widening stream of social reforms that went beyond temperance to a questioning of the very economy and agencies of government under which practices such as the liquor trade were possible.[53]

The *Pentecostal Herald*, at times, attacked social injustices in tones similar to its more liberal Protestant counterparts, singling out issues like child labor and prostitution[54] for suggested public-policy attention. Passing references can

---

[50]Letter from Mrs. W.M. Bush, *Pentecostal Herald*, 2 November 1910, 11a.

[51]William A McKeever, "How to Fight the Tobacco Evil" and "The Kansas Anti-Cigarette Law," reprinted from *Baptist World* (Manhattan, Kan.) and *Pentecostal Herald*, 2 February 1910, 13.

[52]John Paul, "The *Herald's* Introduction to the Sunday School Lesson: The World's Temperance Lesson, for November 13, 1910," in *Pentecostal Herald*, 2 November 1910, 11.

[53]George D. McClain, "Pioneering Social Gospel Radicalism: An Overview of the History of the Methodist Federation for Social Action," ch. 25 in Russell E. Richey, et al., eds., *Perspectives on American Methodism: Interpretive Essays* (Nashville: Abingdon Press, 1993), 371-9.

[54]Rev. I.M. Hargett, "A Note of Alarm," *Pentecostal Herald*, 10 February 1910. "The rich man clamors for larger profits," this piece claims, as the "two million child labor slaves" suffer in urban factories; Advertisement, "For God's Sake Do Something," showed a drawing of an anguished woman behind bars, under which

even be found denouncing activity of the Ku Klux Klan.[55] In one instance, a staff correspondent answered a readers' question as to whether socialism was an acceptable view for Christians by saying, "we give our American socialists credit for reputable aims. We answer readily that whatever may be said about their claims, most of their aims are moral, and the church should and I believe does support them."[56]

Amid all such questioning, though, the *Pentecostal Herald* urged aggressive evangelism and rock-ribbed adherence to such social disciplines as frugality[57] and abstinence not only from liquor and tobacco,[58] but also the viewing of motion pictures.[59] Language surrounding these moral disciplines, by the time of Morrison's death, was framed in military terminology, spinning off whatever current warfare phrases were pertinent in the national news. That these military metaphors did not end with Morrison's death indicates not only that *Pentecostal Herald* editors were intent on milking current events in Europe and Asia for literary value, but also that these images were images ingrained in the newspaper's approach to socio-cultural conflicts.[60]

Underlying the *Pentecostal Herald*'s audience-targeting was a stony editorial commitment to the lifestyle of simplicity. Perhaps due to the newspaper's roots in the far-flung camp-meeting movement, but perhaps more so out of challenge to an increasingly mercantilist mass-media within Protestantism in the early 1900s, the *Herald* depicted the poor as the elite. "Who are in great need of employment, at a bare living wage, to secure the actual necessities to support life?" declared one editorial. "The common people."[61] Thrifty farmers or virtuous laborers were heroes while the wealthy were portrayed with suspicion — possessing a thing almost to be feared. Affluence was a quality more often linked, in the paper's columns, with influences of corruption than with potential for redeeming either society or Protestantism. Wealth linked to the liquor trade was the worst type in the *Pentecostal Herald's* view – and part of the reason why religious media were to be preferred over secular. A Morrison editorial in 1934 attacked "millionaires who have foisted upon this nation the liquor traffic" and added a rejoinder against "millionaires who have spent vast sums of money on purchase

---

are the words "God, if I could only get out of here." The advertisement seeks sales of the book that was a collection of essays by attorneys and others against prostitution called "Fighting the Traffic in Young Girls." *Pentecostal Herald*, 10 June 1910.

[55]J.O.A. Vaught, "The Tobacco Question," *Pentecostal Herald*, 28 September 1910. The reference here is to "night riders" in an address in Asheville, N.C. "Under the cover of night men were being whipped, driven from home and, in several instances, killed outright." The article refers to "this clan," as being influential over judges and juries through death threats.

[56]John Paul, "Question Bureau," to question from Arkansas, "Are the claims of the present Socialist party now being taught, moral, and should they be supported by the church?" *Pentecostal Herald*, 13 July 1910, 5.

[57]H.C. Morrison, "Facts Which Call for Serious Thought," *Pentecostal Herald*, 19 September 1934, 1. This rather extreme example is Morrison's claim that automobiles, both as a national spending habit and as vehicles of travel, were dangerous to the moral fiber and general safety of the modernizing nation.

[58]Anonymous, "Pastor Refuses to Oust Smoking Teachers," *Pentecostal Herald*, 13 March 1935.

[59]Rev. Henry F. Pollock, "What's Wrong with the Movies?" *Pentecostal Herald*, 30 September 1936.

[60]J.C. McPheeters, "Totalitarianism of Alcohol," *Pentecostal Herald and Way of Faith*, 1 November 1944, 1."King alcohol has seized upon the present war as his greatest opportunity in the course of human history for the creation of new alcoholic addicts," wrote the editor.

[61]H.C. Morrison, "The Common People," box inserted in page called "With Our Young People," *Pentecostal Herald*, 9 November 9 1932.

of conscienceless newspapers and magazines."[62]

## BLIND SPOTS ON THE LENS: RACIAL STEREOTYPING

A tragic irony of the *Pentecostal Herald's* socio-cultural voice of reform is that while the publication called for sinners to be made "white as snow" in their consciences, it made little effort to make the ethnicity of the Holiness Movement anything but white – at least on this continent. Morrison's own writing and that of contributors to the *Herald* reveal, at best, a misunderstanding of African-American culture in the U.S., and strong evidences of condescension toward cultures of overseas regions. Between 1910 and 1942 no other contributor was so explicitly condescending of African-Americans as Morrison. Put simply, he seemed to believe – at least in early years of his editorial work – in the superiority of European white heredity,[63] a belief that apparently undergirded his writing about both social justice for, and evangelism of, African-Americans and other ethnic groups in the United States and overseas.[64]

Problems such as the lack of vision in the *Pentecostal Herald* toward racial equality in the culture of the Holiness Movement were oversights not unnoticed by leaders surrounding Morrison. John Paul, a key editorial contributor to the *Pentecostal Herald* and eventually vice president of Asbury College under Morrison, described the Holiness Movement, in 1904, as being in danger of compromising its ends by a "lack of tact and wisdom," by "looseness of conscience at some points, such as business matters and social behavior,..." and "lack of touch with humanity and its practical needs."[65] It must be noted, however, that the *Pentecostal Herald* – at its beginning in 1888 and still so through the 1930s – was working within a solidly segregationist culture. Klan membership surged in at least the early part of this era. Red-lining of African-American districts in urban centers was common, coupled with widespread police brutality toward minority groups.[66]

No firm judgment can be made from afar as to what the *Pentecostal Herald's* readership believed about the race question, but, in a coldly practical sense, Morrison's targeting of mainly white readers within the grassroots camp-meeting constituency of the *Pentecostal Herald* was accurate demographic tracking. Morrison, after all, was a reader and pursuer of social attentions and no doubt aware of how closely tied the African Methodist Episcopal Church and other similar denominations in the South were to their own local church leadership

---

[62]H.C. Morrison, "The New Year," *Pentecostal Herald and Way of Faith*, 11 January 1933, 1, 8. See also Morrison, "Making the World Safe for Millionaires," *Pentecostal Herald*, 23 November 1932, 8.

[63]H.C. Morrison, "The Foundation of God Standeth Sure." *Pentecostal Herald*, 4 November 1914, 1. This front-page editorial lamenting the coming of war to Europe worries that the war "will fearfully check the birth rate of the white race, of the most enlightened and progressive peoples, while the oriental populations grow by leaps and bounds."

[64]H.C. Morrison, editorial: "A Startling Combinaton," *Pentecostal Herald*, 29 March 1911, 1. Morrison, in reference to battle over liquor use in Nicholasville, a town ten miles from Wilmore, said he hoped it would become clear "that the men who take a stand with negroes and bloated brewers and whiskey toughs in Louisville and Cincinnati will be relegated from their position and forever retired from places of trust.... "

[65]Rev. John Paul, "What Has Most Hindered the Progress of the Holiness Movement," *Pentecostal Herald*, 9 June 1904, 9.

[66]Benjamin Quarles, *The Negro in the Making of America*, rev. ed. (New York: Macmillan/Collier Books, 1964, 1969), 148, 190-4.

and media culture.[67] Furthermore, an exodus of African-American Baptists from white churches had been ongoing for decades and was nearly complete in areas like Virginia by the year Morrison's first newspaper issue was printed. Hence, African-American church-goers, from before Morrison's birth, had comprised a separate religious culture; white Christians south of the Ohio River for the most part simply did not worship or interact socially with African-American Christians – and rarely questioned the arrangement.

*IMAGES AND ENDINGS: REVIVALISM OUTLIVES A NEWSPAPER*

If Henry Clay Morrison was not a living socio-cultural legend in his own time when he began his newspaper, he eventually became one – partly through his own efforts seen in the *Pentecostal Herald*. He lived image. Evidence in his newspaper in the early 1900s and into the 1940s shows him strictly controlling his appearances in public – and always in *Herald* photos – to highlight his starched white collar, white bow tie, and black Prince Albert coat – his longish white hair over and behind his ears in the style of nineteenth-century Methodist circuit-riders. Though such photos fit surrounding culture early in his career, they stood him in stark contrast to those, in the inter-war period, who appeared beside him with short haircuts and Windsor knots in striped ties under double-breasted suits.[68] Morrison walked the image, preached the image, wrote the image of austere nineteenth century-style revivalism in a sustained resistance to cultural innovation in society at-large and within Protestantism in particular.[69] His *Pentecostal Herald*, from start to finish, was a catalyst to cultural warfare. Morrison urged readers to see themselves as unrelenting soldiers in a fight not likely to be won until they reached heaven. Under one editorial segment deploring tobacco-use by clergy – titled "Fight On" – Morrison wrote, "Let those sneer and fear who will, but meantime remember that the best womanhood of the South does not want her boy to use tobacco and she does not want her pastor's example to counteract her influence and teachings on the subject."[70] Two years later, Morrison wrote that "without doubt those who would enjoy spiritual victories must have the hardihood to declare war on sin; they must have the courage to give and take the killing strokes of real battle."[71] Morrison's first editorial, in 1888, had used language of alarm and conflict that called for action. Penned on a sleepless night during a series of revival services, the piece warned against what he saw as dangerous liberal opinion and teaching in the pulpits and publications of mainline Southern Methodism. That Morrison wrote this initial piece for a publication not yet begun bespoke a visionary editorial approach that would characterize the next fifty years of Morrison's publishing career.

A strong case can be made, however, that the *Pentecostal Herald* and its

---

[67]Mary Francis Berry and John W. Blassingame, *Long Memory: The Black Experience in America* (New York: Oxford University Press, 1982), 96-7, 107-8.

[68]Cf. photos in the *Pentecostal Herald*, 5 January 1938, 1, 3, 4, 5, 6.

[69]Z.T. Johnson, "The Warrior," *Pentecostal Herald*, 20 May 1942, 6; E. Stanley Jones, "Dr. H.C. Morrison's Passing," *Pentecostal Herald*, 27 May 1942.

[70]Henry Clay Morrison, "Fight On," under "Thoughts for the Thoughtful," *Pentecostal Herald*, 20 April 1910, 1.

[71]Henry Clay Morrison, "Victories Do Not Come Without Battle," editorial, *Pentecostal Herald*, 4 September 1912, 1.

constituency should have dispensed more quickly with the Morrison era than they did. The early century had brought new opportunities for media growth and innovation that Morrison had shunned. Followers of the *Pentecostal Herald* and the Wilmore institutions had seen less and less of Morrison after his resignation from the college in 1940, due to Morrison's preaching schedule and increasingly frequent illnesses. His writing, while unchanged in its placement in the newspaper, had tended to become repetitive, with a vague, reminiscent quality.[72] He delegated more and more work to associate editor Bettie Whitehead Morrison – whom he had married after the death of his second wife – or sub-editors.[73] But in 1942 the future apparently looked daunting enough for this newspaper, the college and seminary it had funded, and the wider Holiness Movement, that *Pentecostal Herald* editors opted for tradition. Morrison's image was propped up and carried forward. On the night Morrison died enroute to preaching a service March 24, 1942, the *Pentecostal Herald* was being shipped across the country with his latest editorial and monthly sermon.[74] His front-page editorials continued in two issues after his death, and a column of fresh material — apparently written during his many illnesses – called "He Being Dead Yet Speaketh," ran on page nine of each issue for more than three years afterward. Front pages or inside columns of March or April issues through the 1940s memorialized Morrison in some way.[75]

Morrison's editorial tone was aggressive and visionary to the very end. In the same issue as the initial obituary notice about him – in fact on the same inside page – the *Pentecostal Herald* carried a box containing a terse note from Morrison answering "annoyed" critics as to why the newspaper had taken on a new printing format and page size several issues earlier. "Be patient," Morrison wrote, "Pray for us, stand by us and watch The *Herald* as we enter a new era of usefulness in its wide field of service."[76] And pray readers did, all the while retaining a commitment to informing themselves about their revivalist culture and its surrounding worlds in periodicals like the *Pentecostal Herald* through mid-century and beyond.

R. Laurence Moore argues that as the twentieth-first century begins, one of the few bright points of flame in the hearth of American Protestantism is on college and university campuses.[77] Perhaps Morrison sensed this in the 1940s, for a key segment of his will turned over all assets of the Pentecostal Publishing

---

[72]Henry Clay Morrison, editorial, "Looking Backward," multi-part series in *Pentecostal Herald and Way of Faith*, begun March 18, 1942, 1. Repetition of Morrison's story about the founding of the newspaper appeared more regularly on anniversaries of the paper's start-up, cf. *Pentecostal Herald*, "Fiftieth Birthday of the Pentecostal Herald*," 5 January 1938, 1; "The Fifty-Second Year," *Pentecostal Herald*, 21 June 1939, 1.

[73]Evidence for this comes from the repeated references in the newspaper to Bettie Morrison as the person to contact with correspondence or to connect with details of various programs or events. Other editors wrote for the newspaper in increasing amounts through later years of the newspaper. See especially "Fiftieth Anniversary" issue, *Pentecostal Herald*, 5 January 1938.

[74]Solon McNeese, "The Passing of a Great Warrior," *Pentecostal Herald and Way of Faith*, 8 April 1942, 4.

[75]C.F. Wimberly, "Dr. Morrison — Not an Old Man," *Pentecostal Herald and Way of Faith*, 10 March 1943, 3 cf. E.A. Seamands, "I Am A Debtor to Dr. Morrison," on "Asbury Alumni Page," *Pentecostal Herald and Way of Faith*, 14 April 1943, 6; J.C. McPheeters, "Henry Clay Morrison," *Pentecostal Herald and Way of Faith*, 27 September 1944, 8; McPheeters, "Henry Clay Morrison," editorial, *Pentecostal Herald and Way of Faith*, 7 March 1945, 1.

[76]H.C. Morrison, "Be Patient!" *Pentecostal Herald and Way of Faith*, 1 April 1942, 6.

[77]Moore, *Selling God...*, 143.

Company and *Pentecostal Herald* – by means of a trust agreement – not to his
family, nor to the United Methodist Church, but to Asbury Theological Seminary. By rules of Morrison's will, the *Pentecostal Herald* remained in operation
until 1976, after which it was folded, minus the word Pentecostal in its title,
into the seminary's operations as a public relations magazine.[78] Though the
newspaper's official era as purveyor of revivalist culture was over, the transition
was fairly smooth for in function the newspaper had been an unofficial promoter
of both Asbury College and Asbury Seminary for decades previous.

No clear indication is available as to why Morrison chose a graduate theological institution for this funding, nor why his fortunes did not remain with a publication that had touched so many lives through half a century across the American continent and around the world. But it must be remembered that Morrison's
was a cultural vision. His media power had rested not in presses or campus
buildings but in people – the faces and hearts of common revivalist folk who had
huddled year after year on rude wooden benches under camp-meeting tabernacles
on hot summer days and nights. By Morrison's conception, the future of revivalism was in the churches – notably those in scattered byways of places like
Iowa and Florida, Texas and Kentucky.[79] Cultural excesses of secular media, he
knew, could be answered effectively by Christian media of the type he had maintained for half a century. But perhaps Morrison sensed, given the power and re-
siliency he had experienced in leadership of both a Christian liberal arts college
and evangelical Christian publishing empire, that conservative theological study
and an informed clergy – one trained to pick up and perhaps even publish insightful media – was the most likely of the two to bolster sustained revivalism
among the common folk of North America in the face of what would become
rigorous challenges from Post-Modernism and Post-Christian thought in the
waning twentieth century.

---

[78]"Proceedings and Articles of Incorporation of Morrison Theological Trust," 14 May 1942; "Minutes of
the Special Committee Appointed to Consider Continuation of the *Herald*," 19 September 1974; "Special
Meeting Concerning the Future of *Herald* Magazine," 1 April 1975, Records of the Pentecostal Publishing
Company, Archives, B.L. Fisher Library, Asbury Theological Seminary.
[79]Wesche, "The Life, Influence and Theology of Henry Clay Morrison...," 333-57.

# 17

## Protestant Press Relations / *1930-1970*
by John P. Ferré

SCARCELY A MONTH AFTER THE STOCK MARKET CRASHED in 1929, twenty-one church publicists gathered at the Hotel Washington in Washington, D.C. They met to address what Dartmouth philosophy professor William Kelley Wright had described as "a period of religious depression not less severe than the concomitant moral and economic depression."[1] Just as President Hoover and his advisers were looking for ways to restore the national economy, these publicists were looking for ways to recapture the preeminence of Protestantism. So they established themselves as the Religious Publicity Council, an organization of Protestants called by God "to translate Christian ideals into terms which the average man can understand." They adopted a constitution and elected Herbert D. Rugg, a Congregationalist, as chairman, Dorothy P. Cushing, another Congregationalist, as vice-chairman, and Mabel M. Sheibley, a Presbyterian, as secretary-treasurer. Then they turned their attention to five pressing questions:

1. How can we get newspapers to get the church angle?
2. How can newspapers be brought to recognize the great field there is for news in church life?
3. How can we keep informed as to what our own organizations are doing?
4. What methods can be suggested for getting news before the public through the newspapers?
5. What is the value of newspaper publicity and newspaper advertising?[2]

This agenda shows that they were preoccupied with reaching the American public through the most effective means they knew — the secular media. Church publicists had very little faith in the Protestant press, their traditional means of

---

[1]Quoted in Robert T. Handy, "The American Religious Depression, 1925-1935," *Church History* 29 (March 1960): 3.

[2]George Dugan, Caspar H. Nannes, and R. Marshall Stross, *RPRC: A 50-Year Reflection* (New York: Religious Public Relations Council, 1979), 1-2.

outreach.

The fact that there were enough church publicists in 1929 to form an association shows just how seriously denominations in the twentieth century were taking the secular media. In the nineteenth century, Protestant churches needed no intermediary to reach the public. The few who did not hear sermons in church or read Protestant publications at home were not far from the many who did. Protestant denominations were ubiquitous and authoritative, and the public listened carefully to what they had to say. But Protestant churches lost ground in the twentieth century. By 1930, Protestant periodicals had lost 80 per cent of the circulation they had had in 1900. Daily newspapers stopped covering sermons as a matter of course, and mass circulation periodicals became increasingly critical of traditional Christianity. Recognizing their need for another media strategy, Protestants settled on public relations.[3]

One denomination after another opened public relations offices run by persons experienced in press relations. Their rationale to do so was typically pragmatic. One minister compared church publicity with publicity for the Columbian Exposition in Chicago and found church publicity wanting. Churches had failed to evangelize the world because, he said, churches were long on prayers and sermons and resolutions and short on media publicity. By contrast, the directors of the Columbian Exposition had evangelized the world in just two years. "Africa's obscurest tribe had been told the story of the great Fair," he complained. "'Chicago' is a familiar word in corners of the world where the name of Christ is unknown. Sad is it to think that a passing exhibition of human skill should reach the ears of human beings who have never heard the tidings of Love's infinite sacrifice."[4] So hire they did. The Seventh-day Adventist Church established its Press Bureau in 1912. The following year, the Committee of the General Convention of the Protestant Episcopal Church hired George F. Parker, the former partner of the renowned publicist Ivy Lee, as its secretary for press and publicity. By the time that the Religious Publicity Council formed in Washington, D.C., Baptists, Congregationalists, Lutherans, Methodists, Presbyterians, and United Bretherans had all hired press liaisons.[5]

This chapter covers the first forty years of organized Protestant press relations. It begins in 1929, when the Religious Publicity Council was formed, and it ends in 1970, when the organization, now called the Religious Public Relations Council, Inc., decided to admit Jews and other non-Christians just as it had allowed Roman Catholics to join only three years before. This period of growth from exclusionist beginnings to interfaith cooperation serves as an historical case study of Protestant persistence to gain third-party endorsement from daily newspapers across the United States.

The contemporary accounts of church publicists over this forty-year period show that they self-consciously set out to revive the preeminence of Protestant churches in a prodigal America, a goal that ultimately proved to be elusive. Protestants did succeed in establishing a place for religion news, but as later ob-

---

[3]Hornell Hart, "Changing Social Attitudes and Interests," in *Recent Social Trends of the United States: Report of the President's Research Committee on Social Trends* (New York: McGraw-Hill, 1933), 398-403.

[4]Joseph Wilson Cochrane, "The Law of Publicity," *The Homiletic Review* 50 (1905), 299.

[5]John P. Ferré, "Protestant Press Relations in the United States, 1900-1930," *Church History* 62 (1993): 514-27.

servers would point out, this place was more or less marginal. Slowly, after cycles of church growth and decline, a more daunting task became apparent. By 1970, Protestants and their new partners from other faiths began to understand that their struggle was not to gain a place just in a world becoming increasingly secular, but in a world in which institutions, including religious ones, were being viewed with increasing skepticism. These church publicists were, in other words, trying to stake a claim on modern public life during a time of tremendous ambivalence toward the social dimensions of mainline religious institutions. As they used the secular media to restore the stature that Protestantism had lost by the turn of the century, Protestants between 1930 and 1970 were hopeful, despairing, self-critical — and remarkably acquiescent.

*RATIONALES*

By the 1930s, Protestants both assumed and accepted the preeminence of the secular media. To be sure, they criticized the media, but they criticized the media's performance, not the media's role. Protestants understood well that their own media had long ago lost their nineteenth-century importance. Protestant journalists in the mid-nineteenth century, as Dennis Voskuil has observed, "took all of society to be their beat."[6] Pitting their evangelical slant on politics, economics, and social news against competitive secular publications, church publications reached three-fourths of the American reading public. But in the latter half of the nineteenth century religious periodicals lost out to secular magazines and newspapers, which could claim, as the *New York Tribune* did in 1890, to "treat religious questions and news with an ability and fullness that no religious paper can hope to excel."[7] Protestant newspapers folded, and Protestant magazines turned into house organs or niche publications. By the mid-twentieth century, the church press had only a tenth of the circulation of secular daily newspapers.[8] Protestant groups were lucky to gain the attention of their own members, much less permeate the broader world.

According to sociologist Hornell Hart, religion had been experiencing stiff competition for limited editorial space for some time, and it had been losing the contest. Using the *Readers' Guide to Periodical Literature* as his data base, Hart calculated that in the twentieth century religion had declined steadily as a subject in American magazines. The rate of decline was 2.1 per cent per year from 1905 to 1931 and 2.5 per cent per year from 1931 to 1941.[9] This trend had led one writer to despair:

With thousands of Christian young people every year undergoing weakening if not complete destruction of their faith through the circulation in the homes and libraries of America of magazines containing vast quantities of antichris-

---

[6]Dennis N. Voskuil, "Reaching Out: Mainline Protestantism and the Media," in William R. Hutchison, ed., *Between the Times: The Travail of the Protestant Establishment in America, 1900-1960* (Cambridge: Cambridge University Press, 1989), 73.

[7]Christopher Walters-Bugbee, "The Sad State of the Religious Press," *Books & Religion*, January-February 1985, 4.

[8]Alfred McClung Lee, "The Press and Public Relations of Religious Bodies," *Annals of the American Academy of Political and Social Science* 256 (1948): 120-31.

[9]Hornell Hart, "Religion," *The American Journal of Sociology* 47 (1942): 888.

tian material, there can be no justification of Christians taking an attitude of indifference toward the contents of magazines which they and their neighbors support. *Christian public opinion should make itself felt.* It is the only medium whereby the rising flood of antichristian propaganda in periodical literature can be stemmed.[10]

What needed to be done was clear: To stay in contact with the American public, Protestant churches needed savvy media liaisons.

One reason that reaching the public was so important was that Protestants in mid-century watched nervously as Roman Catholics beat them in terms of growth and commitment. From 1940 until 1960, American Protestant church membership grew from 37,814,606 to 63,668,835, a 68 per cent increase. Meanwhile, Roman Catholic church membership in America nearly doubled, growing from 21,284,455 to 42,104,900, a 98 per cent increase. Roman Catholic growth beat Protestant growth by a full third. Adding to Protestant dismay was the fact that 74 per cent of Roman Catholics went to church every week, as compared with only 40 per cent of Protestants. So it was that in any given week, more Roman Catholics than Protestants went to church — 5.7 million more in 1960, for example. Protestants could take little comfort in the greater size of their church rosters.[11]

Protestants also shared the perception that Roman Catholics received better news coverage. According to Ralph Stoody of the Commission on Public Relations and Methodist Information:

> It often seems to Protestants that Catholic news is overplayed. The reason is quite understandable, of course — New York, Chicago, etc., have large Catholic populations, and the smaller papers tend to follow the lead of the big city papers. I wouldn't want you to get the idea we're anti-Catholic, however. We just want things presented in their right proportions.[12]

Although Protestants agreed that Catholics received better news coverage, many were not as prone as Stoody was to holding the press accountable for the inequity. Leach blamed Protestants for their shortsighted stinginess. He told the story of Bishop William Burt of the Methodist Episcopal Church, who had paid a press agent $100 to issue news releases from a conference over which he was presiding in Buffalo. When someone complained about the needless expense, Bishop Burt simply said, "Rome does it." That silenced the critic. Leach went on to contrast that conference, which received good coverage in the Buffalo press, with a subsequent meeting of the Presbyterian Synod of New York that relied upon volunteer publicity and local reporters and was hardly mentioned in the papers at all.[13]

Walter W. Van Kirk, host of the network radio program *Religion in the*

---

[10]Dan Gilbert, "Pitfalls for Faith in Modern Magazines," *The Sunday School Times*, 24 July 1937, 524.

[11]Benson Y. Landis, ed., *Yearbook of American Churches: Information on All Faiths in the U.S.A.* (New York: National Council of the Churches of Christ in the U.S.A., 1958), 296-7; and 1961 edition, 277-8.

[12]Quoted in Irwin Ross, *The Image Merchants: The Fabulous World of Public Relations* (Garden City, N.Y.: Doubleday, 1959), 213.

[13]William H. Leach, *Church Publicity: A Complete Treatment of Publicity Opportunities and Methods in the Local Church* (Nashville: Cokesbury, 1930), 246.

*News*, said that Roman Catholics received better press coverage because of their "vast and competent press organization that knows what it wants and knows, too, how to get what it wants."[14] He offered three lessons that Protestants could learn from Catholics. First, he said that Protestants tended to avoid fanfare, choosing instead to meet quietly away from crowds. This modesty was counterproductive, Van Kirk said. Protestants should follow the Catholic lead and take religion to the public. Second, he said that the fact that Protestantism was splintered into numerous denominations made Protestant causes seem narrowly sectarian. He recommended that Protestants present a more united front by setting up an interdenominational press bureau to serve the interests that all Protestants shared. Third, he said that Protestants reproved the press less often and much less aggressively than Roman Catholics did. "You may be sure that when Roman Catholics are misrepresented in the press the editors in question hear about it," he said. "But our Protestant people do this, if at all, only rarely."[15] According to Van Kirk, Protestants would get their fair share of press coverage only when they took public relations as seriously as Roman Catholics did.

For their part, Roman Catholics hardly believed that they received superior news coverage. One Catholic writer complained that Protestants received better coverage because one denomination after another was creating a public relations office. "Where does the Catholic Church stand in the midst of this tremendous growth?" she asked. "Away down at the bottom. Paradoxically, while it is the largest single religious body in this country, its secular press relations are far behind the times."[16] The perception among Roman Catholics that their public relations lagged behind that of Protestantism was partly responsible for the Jesuit Thomas Burke writing the first doctoral dissertation on the subject of religion and PR in 1963.[17]

But Roman Catholicism presented only one of two challenges to Protestant authority. Even more threatening than Catholicism was secularism. Christian faith seemed to have become increasingly irrelevant to social and personal life in America. At least this was how many Protestants interpreted Supreme Court decisions throughout the 1940s that defined religious faith and practices as private affairs that had no place in public schools. "The First Amendment has erected a wall between Church and State. That wall must be kept high and impregnable," wrote the Court in *Everson v. Board of Education* (1947). To the Supreme Court, the high and impregnable wall between church and state meant that tax monies could be used to bus children to Catholic schools in New Jersey but that Protestant groups could not use the public schools in Champaign, Illinois, for religious education. The Court's interpretation of the establishment clause of the First Amendment removed faith from the public square, making faith legally irrelevant, or so thought Protestant leaders such as Charles Clayton Morrison. He responded by writing a provocative anthology that called for united Protestant militancy with the revealing title *Can Protestantism Win America?*[18]

---

[14]Walter W. Van Kirk, "Protestantism in the News," *Christian Century*, 10 January 1940, 48.

[15]Ibid., 49.

[16]Jo-Ann Price, "Religion is Making the News," *Information* 73 (1959): 36-7.

[17]Thomas J. M. Burke, "Public Relations of Religious Institutions in a Pluralistic Society," Ph.D. dissertation, New York University, 1963.

[18]Charles Clayton Morrison, *Can Protestantism Win America?* (New York: Harper and Brothers, 1948); Martin E. Marty, *Modern American Religion*, vol. 3: *Under God, Indivisible, 1941-1960* (Chicago: Univer-

Protestant decline was also evident in church records. One PR handbook from the 1930s pointed out that church sanctuaries were more than half empty. Although churches could seat 53 million persons, only 25 million persons, it said, were church members, which left 28 million seats vacant.[19] This statistical reasoning reappeared in 1950: "The nation's two hundred and fifty thousand churches have over seventy-nine million members, and yet, never, except on Easter, do more than thirty-eight million of us go to church."[20] Even the fact that church membership was growing faster than the U.S. population was not completely good news for Protestant churches. Dayton McKean used a poll from 1954, the year that Congress inserted "under God" into the Pledge of Allegiance, to show that the apparent religiousness of Americans belied widespread ignorance in what they confessed to believe:

> Although 96 per cent of Americans say that they believe in God, this near-unanimity does not ... accompany a high level of information about religion; for example, 51 per cent could not name the first book of the Bible, 60 per cent could not give the names of the Holy Trinity, 66 per cent did not know who delivered the Sermon on the Mount, and 79 per cent could not name one prophet mentioned in the Old Testament.[21]

Because much religion seemed to have become little more than uninformed vestiges of a previously vital faith, something new had to be done. Carol Towers Toussaint told members of the National Council of Churches to face facts:

> If only three in every ten church members hear the preacher from the pulpit, how are we going to reach the remaining seven and the unchurched? By meeting the people where they are.... If Mr. Average Individual is sitting in front of his television set, listening to his radio, attending a movie or reading a daily paper, then the church must present its case through these systems of communication.[22]

James Supple made the same recommendation in *The Christian Century*: "[T]hrough the newspaper, magazine and radio the church can reach that twentieth century phenomenon — the American pagan who can be won back to the Christian faith only through a growing awareness of that faith's relevance to life."[23]

Public relations offered both a carrot and a stick to Protestantism. The stick was the threat of social oblivion that many Protestants felt. Sophisticated PR would be key to maintaining any sort of presence on the public agenda. Indeed, public relations and church presence were often used synonymously, as in John

---

sity of Chicago Press, 1996), 130-56, 211-30.

[19]Lewis A. Myers, *Principles and Techniques of Religious Publicity* (Fort Worth: Taylor-Lowe, n.d.), 46.

[20]Willard A. Pleuthner, *Building Up Your Congregation: Help from Tested Business Methods* (Chicago: Wilcox & Follett, 1950), 73.

[21]Dayton D. McKean, "The State, the Church, and the Lobby," in James Ward Smith and A. Leland Jamison, eds., *Religious Perspectives in American Culture*, Vol. 2 (Princeton, N.J.: Princeton University Press, 1961), 124-5.

[22]Carol Towers Toussaint, "Public Relations and the Churches," *National Council Outlook*, December 1953, 12.

[23]James O. Supple, "Church and Press — Enemies or Allies?" *Christian Century*, 17 August 1949, 961.

Fortson's definition of public relations as "the task of keeping the Church at the center of modern life" and in Stewart Harral's claim that the very survival of churches depended upon how well they competed with other institutions to gain and maintain public favor.[24]

In *The New Emphasis on Promotion in Protestant Churches*, Norman Richardson said that churches had largely ignored public relations, which he defined as the obligation "to discover, create, and conserve a growing and intelligently sympathetic constituency, outside of its own membership."[25] Ignoring public relations had cost the churches their standing before the public. Churches had fallen behind commercial, educational, and political institutions in captivating public attention and sympathy because these competing agencies had been willing to experiment with promotions until they reached the audiences they sought. Richardson predicted that unless the churches made every effort to keep Protestantism on the public agenda, they would be vulnerable to legislation and other forms of structural interference to their operation and mission. The hour was already late; churches were well on their way to becoming socially irrelevant. Richardson pointed out that religion was missing from the literature of politics, economics, social science, and education, and that communities operated as if the various Protestant organizations in their midst did not matter. Effective press relations would give the churches a strong public voice that society could not easily ignore or misinterpret.[26]

But if PR's stick was social oblivion, its carrot was evangelism, a sure way of winning over the wayward. The evangelical promise of the secular press was pointed out repeatedly during this period. Typical of these endorsements was the claim that effective press relations would not only draw outsiders to the church, but it would also motivate church members to worship in church on Sundays and to return to church for other activities during the week.[27] Indeed, evangelism seemed nearly impossible without media publicity: "[I]n the case of most churches that are having outstanding success in reaching and enlisting people, it will be found that they are the churches that receive frequent and wholesome news coverage."[28]

*A Model Program of Church Public Relations*, published by the Baptist General Convention of Texas in the late 1950s, gave testimony to the evangelical promise of press relations. A six-month public relations project at the First Baptist Church of Greenville, Texas, which employed a panoply of techniques from questionnaires to press releases, caused church attendance to rise and offerings to increase. This project showed just how strategic public relations could produce measurable results for churches. "The pastor now looks to skilled communications experts to help him keep the church's program before the congregation and the general public as well," the report concluded.[29]

---

[24]John L. Fortson, *How to Make Friends for Your Church: A Manual on Public Relations* (New York: Association Press, 1943), 7; Stewart Harrel, *Public Relations for Churches* (New York: Abingdon-Cokesbury, 1945), 7.

[25]Norman E. Richardson, *The New Emphasis on Promotion in Protestant Churches* (Chicago: Presbyterian Theological Seminary, 1941), 22-3.

[26]Ibid., 57.

[27]Richmond O. Brown, *Practical Church Publicity* (Nashville: Broadman, 1953), v.

[28]Erwin L. McDonald, *The Church Using the Newspaper* (Nashville: Broadman Supplies, n.d.), 2.

[29]Leonard L. Holloway, *A Model Program of Church Public Relations* (Dallas: Public Relations Depart-

*IMPEDIMENTS*

Wanting the third-party endorsement that news coverage in the secular media could bestow was one thing, but actually getting it was another. For Protestants, the twentieth century can be seen as a period of transition from reliance upon the church press to reliance upon the secular media as a primary means of communication with the American public. Getting the third-party endorsement of the secular media meant changing budgets and offices and customs. But most importantly, getting the third-party endorsement of the secular media meant convincing Protestants, for whom churches were intrinsically important and interesting, that churches were associations with beliefs and activities that had to compete on level ground with all other social, business, and professional groups for the attention of the public and its gatekeepers.

Although some church publicists thought that the press slighted Protestantism, most were inclined to believe that poor news coverage was less the fault of journalists than of the churches themselves. "The reason that more and better church news fails to be included in the columns of the daily newspaper, when space is available, is due in large measure to errors in news judgment and lack of ability on the part of those charged with the responsibility of placing it," wrote W. Austin Brodie in *Keeping Your Church in the News*.[30] Richmond Brown personalized the point in *Practical Church Publicity*: "When I hear a preacher complaining that his local paper won't publish church news, I immediately suspect that he doesn't prepare his news stories properly."[31]

The most common explanation for poor news coverage was also the easiest to remedy. Church people simply did not have a developed sense for news and did not know how to prepare press releases that would attract media attention. One writer after another followed the lead of William Leach, who in 1930 pleaded with church leaders for more sophistication in their dealings with the press. He pointed out that newspapers were flooded with editorial material, three-quarters of which had been prepared by professionals. According to Leach, churches failed to get space in large city dailies because their submissions to newspapers lacked polish. According to this explanation, the only stumbling block that newspapers placed before churches was a matter of appearance.[32]

The amateur character of the news coming from churches was captured in a study of two daily newspapers in Charleston, South Carolina. Less than a third of the church news that appeared in these papers was entertaining or informative enough to be considered news; the rest was largely irrelevant to everyone not immediately involved in the events being reported.[33] And these were the stories that the dailies published! Fundamentalist theologian Carl F. H. Henry told the story from his early years in journalism of receiving a report of a visiting speaker's church address. The report was as far from standard press release form as one might imagine. Not only was it a hand-written, chronological report that was

ment, Baptist General Convention of Texas, n.d.), 62.

[30]W. Austin Brodie, *Keeping Your Church in the News: How to Inform the Public about Your Church in Action* (Philadelphia: Blakiston, 1942), 16.

[31]Brown, *Practical Church Publicity*, 10.

[32]Leach, *Church Publicity...*, 243.

[33]Anna Louise Murchison, "Church Publicity in the Service of Southern Baptist Churches," M.R.E. thesis, Woman's Missionary Union Training School, 1939, 37-8.

twelve pages long, but the twelve pages had been pasted together and then rolled up like a scroll that unwound to a length of nine or ten feet. Henry saved this missive in a scrapbook marked with the caption "Why Newspapermen Drink!"[34]

The lack of professionalism in submitting news to the press was often blamed on the complacency of ministers. They had their hands full running their churches in traditional ways; they had neither the time nor the inclination to learn and practice press relations. In the 1930s, the *Detroit News* planned a series of seminars to teach ministers how to turn religious news into published newspaper stories, but the series was canceled after fewer than twenty ministers attended the second meeting. *Detroit News* church editor Henry G. Hoch complained of the "*complete lack of interest* on the part of those who are supposed to be interested in church news."[35]

The story was the same for the religion editor of the *Chicago Tribune*, William Norton. Some time after a minister had complained to Norton that the *Tribune* was ignoring both him and his church, Norton read a report about the church's twenty-fifth anniversary, an occasion celebrated with a special program with a keynote address by a distinguished clergyman, in a denominational publication. Norton later asked him why he had not notified the *Tribune*. "I was too busy," he said. Norton replied, "Yet you complain that the paper does not notice your work. Do you expect us to practice telepathy?"[36]

Salem Kirban described similar experiences with Bible schools in his *Church Promotional Handbook.* "I cannot understand how any school can devote so much time to acquainting young men and women about the Bible (the Product) and so little, if any, time in showing them how to move the product," he complained. "Schools are spending all their time on the 'manufacture' of Bible scholars and none in showing the scholar how to move his product (God's Word) off the showroom floor and into the hearts of men and women for whom Christ died."[37]

Kirban's business metaphor is appropriate here because critics were calling for more salesmanship in church work. Willard Pleuthner, vice-president of Batten, Barton, Durstine & Osborne advertising agency in New York, found fault with the churches' professional mind-set, saying that churches were accustomed to people seeking them out instead of reaching out themselves:

On the boards of urban churches there are often too many bankers, lawyers, doctors, and retired businessmen, and too few sales managers, advertising men, and active business executives on the way up the ladder of success. As a result, there is little aggressive salesmanship-thinking to "season" the conservatism of men who have to be conservative to succeed in their non-selling professions. Yet, today our churches need aggressive selling leadership more than any organization in the world. The yearly gains in membership show that many churches are not keeping abreast of national growth. They are being

---

[34]Carl F. H. Henry, *Successful Church Publicity: A Guidebook for Christian Publicists*, 2nd ed. (Grand Rapids, Mich.: Zondervan, 1943), 136-7.

[35]Brodie, *Keeping Your Church in the News...*, 117-8.

[36]William Bernard Norton, *Church and Newspaper* (New York: Macmillan, 1930), 115.

[37]Salem Kirban, *Church Promotional Handbook* (Huntingdon Valley, Pa.: Kirban Associates, 1963), i.

by-passed by competing activities which grow bigger and bigger through successful methods of selling.[38]

The apparent preference for face-to-face personal communication, particularly on
church property, would make Protestantism less and less relevant in a world in
which other social agencies sought public attention aggressively.

Even when a denomination recognized the value of regular, professional associations with the news media and went so far as to establish a press bureau, it
would hold back. Professional conservatism would cast the press bureau as an
agency designed to serve the other, more important agencies of the denomination. Its subservient role meant that it would not be funded or staffed at a level
adequate to perform the very outreach it was created to do.[39] Kenneth Underwood said that this reticence led to bringing coals to Newcastle: "Understaffed
and underbudgeted, [our present publicity workers] have decided that they must
first inform loyal church members about missions work. That done, they have
had little time or money to initiate a wide-scale publicity program."[40]

Low funding levels were criticized for being counterproductive in one other
respect. Journalism scholar Alfred McClung Lee pointed out that low salaries for
Protestant public relations meant that the most talented persons would be lured
away by higher paying secular positions. He gave as an example a denomination's director of public relations who left for a position in an advertising agency
that paid more than the head of his well-to-do denomination made. "Noncom-
mercial appeals finally failed to hold him," Lee said.[41]

This criticism of the clergy and the denominations for inwardness, naïveté,
and arrogance was common among advocates of strong press relations. There
was, however, another, more severe line of thought that held that Protestants received poor press because that is what they deserved. Most churches were not
newsworthy, some critics charged, because they had become social clubs, apos-
tate, salt without savor. According to a newspaper editor, "The trouble is that
the church's activities do not make sufficient impact on the communities they
serve to attract general public attention."[42] PR professor Stanley Stuber agreed,
saying that churches would receive favorable publicity when they earned it by
practicing what they preached.[43]

Stuber went on to give an exception that proved the rule. A group of devout
people living in the New Jersey suburbs of New York learned that several black
families were being forced to vacate a building where they had lived for many
years and could find no other place to live. So the group figured out a way to
buy the property so that it could rent the apartments to the same families. This
group deserved the public approval and newspaper publicity it won because it
actually acted on the principles it professed.[44]

---

[38]Pleuthner, *Building Up Your Congregation...*, 5-6.

[39]Edward L. Grief, "Communications: The New Ministry," in *Crisis in the Church: Essays in Honor of
Truman B. Douglass*, ed. Everett C. Parker (Philadelphia: Pilgrim, 1969), 85-95.

[40]Kenneth Underwood, *Our Story and How to Tell It* (New York: Home Missions Council of North America, 1943), 4.

[41]Lee, "The Press and Public Relations of Religious Bodies," 126.

[42]Wilbur Elston, "Social, but Little Action," *Christian Century*, 24 January 1962, 107.

[43]Stanley I. Stuber, *Public Relations Manual for Churches* (Garden City, N.Y.: Doubleday, 1951), 33.

[44]Ibid.

To be sure, most advocates of church press relations saw the press simply as a conduit through which the light of Protestant truth could shine. But others were beginning to see public relations in terms of change, not just in others, but in the churches themselves. This conception of public relations represented a departure from a one-way, paternalistic model of publicity for a two-way, democratic conception of public relations as a means of constructive dialogue between church and society. By the late 1950s, it was a commonplace that, as Leonard L. Holloway wrote in *A Model Program for Church Public Relations*, "Information must flow from church leaders to congregation to community, and then back from community to congregation to leaders."[45]

*STRATEGIES*

However they may have felt about the need for change within American Protestantism, a sizable portion of press relations specialists were optimists who believed that the secular press was taking the coverage of religion more seriously than ever before. Carl F. H. Henry, a former journalist and lifelong observer of the press, said that improved Protestant press relations was the silver lining behind the clouds of the Great Depression and two world wars, a period of crisis that had led newspapers to become more responsive to religion. Henry believed that the press's responsiveness to religion would endure because it had developed gradually and so was likely to be more than a passing fancy. Secular editors had grown to appreciate news about religion, not because they wanted to promote the interests of the churches, but because they believed that religious activities interested their readers.[46]

Henry listed some specific developments that he believed would leave religious news coverage neither to chance nor to the changing fancies of editors and reporters:

*The Religious News Service:* Begun in 1934 under the auspices of the National Conference of Catholics and Jews, this agency gathered news of religion without denominational interference. Both the Associated Church Press (Protestant) and the Catholic Press Association praised RNS for its objectivity and evenhandedness. By 1960, RNS had 742 clients: 45 per cent were church publications, 30 per cent were radio and television stations, and 25 per cent were secular newspapers and magazines.[47]

*Courses in colleges and seminaries:* The formal study of communications continued to expand. By mid-century, courses in religious journalism and public relations were being taught at Andover-Newton Theological School, Candler Seminary, Chicago Theological Seminary, Oklahoma Baptist University, and Southern Baptist Theological Seminary; and the School of Journalism at Syracuse University had established a graduate program in religious journalism.

---

[45]Holloway, *A Model Program of Church Public Relations*, 5.
[46]Henry, *Successful Church Publicity...*, 91-9.
[47]Ray Erwin, "Religious News Now Often Makes Good Page 1 Copy," *Editor & Publisher*, 24 November 1951, 52; Dugan, Nannes, Stross, *RPRC: A 50-Year Reflection*, 26.

*Denominational press bureaus:* The expanding roster of the Religious Public Relations Council, together with the establishment of the Baptist Public Relations Association in 1954, illustrates that Protestant groups were hiring great numbers of media liaisons. They were also supporting communications with increased funding. The Methodist Commission on Public Relations began in 1940 as a one-person operation with a budget of $25,000. By 1959, the expanded Commission on Public Relations and Methodist Information had several staff members and a budget of $110,000.[48]

Most books and articles written about Protestant public relations between 1930 and 1970 agreed with Henry's positive assessment of religious news reporting. In 1930, for instance, Christopher Leach, the editor of *Church Management*, wrote,

There is a growing interest in religious news, and more of it is appearing in the papers every month. This is due not to any unseen moving of the spirit. The able publicists who in the past decade have handled denominational and cooperative Church publicity as well as local Church publicists have been selling the Church and religion as necessary public commodities.[49]

This observation was echoed in 1943: "In the last ten years," wrote John Fortson in *How to Make Friends for Your Church*, "there has been great improvement in the quality of religious news reporting."[50] These upbeat observations continued throughout the 1950s. In 1953, Religious News Service managing editor Louis Minsky said that religious news had reached a new peak.[51] Later that year, Donald C. Bolles, Director of Public Relations for the National Council of the Churches of Christ, reported the results of a survey that found that editors of sixteen Wisconsin daily newspapers rated religion as a primary interest of their readers and that these newspapers actually published more religious news than they had ten years before.[52] According to Bolles, "The media are more and more bothering about heaven. The news about religion in the last decade has moved from the obit page to the front page."[53] More than a decade after Henry sensed an increase in the religious news reporting, Edwin J. Mitchell, church editor of the Seattle *Post-Intelligencer*, was still able to say that local papers were "more and more ... opening their columns to religion."[54]

*MIXED RESULTS*

Had the founders of the Religious Publicity Council been able to see forty years into the future, they would have taken pride in the fact that four of the five questions they set out to answer had been settled quite favorably to the interests of

---

[48]Ross, *The Image Merchants...*, 209.
[49]Leach, *Church Publicity...*, 51.
[50]Fortson, *How to Make Friends for Your Church...*, 145.
[51]"The Religion Beat," *Newsweek*, 18 May 1953, 100.
[52]Toussaint, "Public Relations and the Churches," 12.
[53]Quoted in Ross, *The Image Merchants...*, 210.
[54]Quoted in Florence Gordon, "More Effective Christian Communication," *National Council Outlook*, May 1956, 11.

Protestants. Denominational press offices learned how to "keep informed as to what [their] own organizations [were] doing." And through the church page, newspapers did "get the church angle," they had been "brought to recognize the great field there is for news in church life," and they had gotten church "news before the public." Protestants had spent more than four decades integrating public relations offices into church structures and honing their media relations skills, and the secular press had responded by reserving a place for news from the churches. Commitment to press relations had paid off.

This success with newspapers was good for Protestant churches whose options for public communication were few. Radio had held great promise in the 1920s, but it grew increasingly commercial, which left little — and undesirable — time for most Protestants. Most groups were unwilling to devote the considerable resources to running their own stations or to creating their own programs, which attracted small audiences of the already committed anyway. Because television was like radio in this respect, only far more expensive, most Protestant groups focused their media relations efforts on getting news coverage. Broadcast news would come to matter more; but from 1930 to 1970, newspapers were the major sources of news. Protestant churches thus could take satisfaction in the page that many newspapers reserved mainly for them.

But the fifth question lingered. *What is the value of newspaper publicity and newspaper advertising?* The answer was depressing. Protestant denominations had devoted organizational resources to press relations with the primary result of the Saturday religion page. By 1949 there would be enough reporters on the church beat to form the Religious Newswriters Association. In the early 1950s, these reporters were joined by AP and UPI staffers who were assigned full-time to religion.[55] A survey of religion editors on daily newspapers in 1958 revealed that more than 90 per cent of newspapers had a weekly religion page and that 44 per cent of them had been started after World War II.[56] The religion page was filled with material from press releases, ideal copy to accompany the adjacent church advertising. Not surprisingly, religion news became tame — nice, but insubstantial. "We get many thank-you notes and no complaints," said Catherine Melniker, editor of the Saturday religion page in the *New York Journal-American.*[57] Eighty-three per cent of ministers surveyed in 1960 in Michigan said that religion news was fair or very complete.[58] Other research found that a third of newspaper subscribers read the religion page. Most were female church members who enjoyed the feature stories, church reports, and notices.[59] To be sure, there was some religion elsewhere in the news — civil rights reporting and Vatican II are two examples — but a sizable portion of religion news was soft enough for the Saturday religion page.[60]

---

[55]Roland E. Wolseley, *Interpreting the Church through Press and Radio* (Philadelphia: Muhlenberg Press, 1951), 36-7.

[56]John Martin Meek, "Press is Keeping Pace with Religious Interest," *Editor & Publisher*, 5 July 1958, 43.

[57]Ray Erwin, "Religious News Now Often Makes Good Page 1 Copy," *Editor & Publisher*, 24 November 1951, 52.

[58]Vernon Wanty, "Where the Churches Go to Newspapers," *Editor & Publisher*, 16 April 1960, 39.

[59]Judith M. Buddenbaum and Stewart M. Hoover, "The Role of Religion in Public Attitudes Toward Religion News," in Daniel A. Stout and Judith M. Buddenbaum, eds. *Religion and Mass Media: Audiences and Adaptations* (Thousand Oaks, Calif.: Sage, 1996), 136.

[60]Mark Silk, *Unsecular Media: Making News of Religion in America* (Urbana: University of Illinois Press,

Whatever satisfaction Protestants could take in the religion page would be short-lived, given the increasing value of editorial space in the competitive newspaper market. Even in the halcyon 1950s, the religion page did not seem headed for eternity. In 1957, Edward J. Hughes, vice president and editorial director of Westchester County Publishers, Inc. in New York, warned that the amount of news about religion would likely decrease as American social life became more and more complex and competition for limited space increased.[61] Five years later, Barrows could say that "the average American newspaper carries little or no reference to the church and its impact on our modern day."[62] The rose-water religion page was no match for social turbulence.

Nor would it be able to adapt to fundamental changes in American religion. The religion page was ideal for the publicity releases of religious establishments, but it was ill-suited to the diversity of faith outside the Protestant-Catholic-Jewish trinity. Religion would be defined less by traditional institutions and more by individual spiritual and ethical awakenings outside traditional institutions. The traditional religions would endure, to be sure, but religion news would need a venue suitable to deinstitutionàlized American religion.

So it was that by 1970 denominational Protestantism had every reason to shore up its media relations by working together with Roman Catholic and Jewish PR personnel. Protestantism was weathering social upheaval, and the religion page was beginning to seem like a luxury from a bygone era. Why not work with personnel from the other religious traditions for a place in an increasingly unconventional world?

Indeed, by the time the Religious Public Relations Council issued its belated welcome to Roman Catholics and Jews, Protestants had learned to take the media seriously because the media covered who they believed to be important or interesting in some way, perceptions that were highly susceptible to the influence of professional liaisons. Protestants were also beginning to learn that the news media would assist them less in their evangelism than in the maintenance of their legitimacy. And the maintenance of legitimacy is why the beginnings of interfaith organization is so significant. By 1970, Protestants realized that the struggle for stature in the society was not among the major institutions of religion. The quest for legitimacy was more ultimate. It was a contest between religion and non-religion. Interfaith cooperation had become a matter of survival.

---

1995), 24-8.

[61]Stanley G. Matthews, "Communicating the Church's Message," *National Council Outlook*, May 1957, 27.

[62]William J. Barrows, Jr., *How to Publicize Church Activities* (Westwood, N.J.: Revell, 1962), 43.

# 18

# The *National Courier,* News, and Religious Ideology

by John D. Keeler, J. Douglas Tarpley, and Michael R. Smith

THE *NATIONAL COURIER* was a bi-weekly, national newspaper with a decidedly Christian mission in its relatively brief history. Between 1975 and 1977, the two lean years of the its existence, its succinct mission statement below its front-page nameplate changed often. At first, it announced it would be the newspaper that was "speaking the truth in love."[1] In later months, its slogan told its approximately 100,000 readers it was "bringing the mind of Christ to bear on events of our time."[2] It changed three more times and finally ended with just "America's Christian Newspaper."[3]

The changing slogans reflect the struggle inside the newsroom in framing what was a noble experiment, dedicated to the ideal of a non-denominational newspaper committed to the highest journalism standards while reporting all types of news from a Christian perspective. It was an experiment distinctly shaped by and a strategic response to unsettling, changing conditions that characterized the American culture generally and the Christian community specifically in the late 1960s and 1970s. Yet its pursuit of an idealistic mix of Christian purpose and journalistic quality was wrought with tensions that are bound to arise when religious ideology is used to organize a news media venture.

The history of the *National Courier* is to a large extent a discovery of how these tensions were at work in this Christian news organization. They were tensions articulated in the form of provocative questions that, to those who gave a portion of their lives to the experiment, often seemed unanswerable: What is the specific mission of this publication? How can we be a meaningful voice for those in the Christian community who believe that America's Judeo-Christian heritage, traditions, values, and beliefs were being lost in the changing culture of the 1960s and 1970s? How can we be distinct from, yet competitive with main-

---

[1]*National Courier,* 4 November 1975, 1.
[2]*National Courier,* 12 December 1975, 1.
[3]*National Courier,* 8 July 1977, 1.

stream publications and other news media? How can we provide an alternative to the liberal worldview that dominates much of the news media? What is the role of faith in news reporting? Can newsroom cultures and the cultures of faith coexist? Can people of diverse Christian backgrounds be compatible in a news organization with a Christian mission? Should the publication be devoted to advocacy journalism or traditional standards of journalistic neutrality or "objectivity?" How can we balance editorial staff desires for excellence in content with publication owners' insistence on financial solvency? How do we mix the inevitably conflicting goals of profitability and involvement in Christian ministry? How do we attract a reading audience within a Christian community best characterized by it diversity, divisions, different levels of spiritual maturity, theological differences and various degrees of interest in, need for and sophistication related to news? If we focus the publication on a particular segment of the Christian community, or even the Christian community as a whole, can we develop a broad enough base of readers to attract advertising support?

The *National Courier* ultimately succumbed without fully resolving these issues. Yet the strenuous effort on the part of its staff to do so serves as an excellent historical example of the formidable task involved in launching a successful Christian news publication in recent times.

The *National Courier* was clearly an effort to respond strategically to changes that were occurring in United States in the 1960s and 1970s — fundamental changes in the American culture, changes in religious attitudes, beliefs and activities and changes in the press.

## *CHANGES IN CULTURE, RELIGION, AND THE PRESS*

The *National Courier* emerged as a national voice for primarily conservative elements of the Christian community during a period of tremendous social upheaval. Traditional values, political and social institutions and icons were challenged as Americans experienced and clashed over the assassinations of John F. Kennedy, Bobby Kennedy and Martin Luther King, the Vietnam war, the Watergate scandals during the Nixon administration, the civil rights movement, the abortion debate, relaxed attitudes and behavior regarding drugs, sex and rock music and even theological dialogue about the "death of God."

The editorial pages reflected the *National Courier's* efforts to deal with these trends, issues, and their aftermath. For example, as the 200th anniversary of the United States approached, an editorial declared that "a nation founded by God's grace in a mood of freedom and independence" had not "followed the God in whom we trust" and had "looked to man as our source" rather than God. A call for national prayer and repentance was the nation's only hope.[4] Another editorial page contained a plea against racism that advised readers to "take Mr. King's advice about speaking out, preaching out, praying out and living out the Gospel and loving and praying for both people discriminated against, but also people who     discriminate."[5] "Moral values should be taught at home not in the schools" suggested another editorial speaking out against sex education in

---

[4]"Call for Humility," *National Courier*, 21 October 1975, 26.
[5]"Pray about Racism," *National Courier*, 6 February 1976, 18.

schools.[6] A question-and-answer column in another edition declared homosexuality a "sexual perversion" that can be overcome only through God and a loving, rather than a self-righteous body of Christian believers who are failing to help those with the problem.[7] Amid growth in the number of state-operated lotteries and other forms of gambling, the *National Courier* called this government activity "a blight on our country and a threat to its vulnerable citizens."[8] Recognizing that abortion was a difficult issue, the paper still stated that it "wishes to make plain that it is opposed to abortion on demand."[9] "Christians must become more active in combating the darkness of the pornography with the light of the Gospel," still another editorial declared.[10]

Stands such as these in response to the cultural climate that developed in the 1960s and 1970s were primarily confined to the editorial section, but the newspaper used this vehicle to address at one time or another the full spectrum of moral issues that were raised during the era.

Amid these cultural changes, many Americans groped for some direction in their lives that had lost their moral compass. Growing numbers of them turned to religion. Moreover, a great many of them turned to the faith of their fathers, mothers and grandparents. Specifically, an orthodox revival in both Catholic and Protestant denominations occurred. The ranks of the Roman Catholic church swelled to more than 48 million people, but with changed people who were no longer content to obey quietly every edict handed down by the church. More than seventy-two million American Protestants also were among this great throng of men and women moving back toward God and similarly demanding more dialogue with church leaders. Many polls documented that religion was increasing its influence on American life. The "born again" experience became popularized in American culture as former President Jimmy Carter and many others tried to articulate their religious faith.

It was more conservative, evangelical denominations and organizations that prospered most during this time period, while many "mainline" churches lost members, often as a result of church splits over liberal interpretations of Scripture, a move toward ecumenism, and the ordination of homosexuals and women. *Christianity Today*, a leading Christian thought magazine, named 1976 the "Year of the Evangelical" because of the rise of religious conviction and practice.[11] At the same time, some Americans were attracted to eastern religions, concepts, and practices that were being introduced into the national culture.

The *National Courier* was both the product of this renewed interest in Christianity and a response to old and new issues that Christians needed resolved in this era of religious revival. "We were responding to the changes going on," declared the newspaper's founder, Dan Malachuk.[12] In a retrospective editorial written by a member of the publisher's board, Jamie Buckingham, the paper's "evangelical" purpose was made clear. "Stories were written to glorify God, edify the body, tell the whole truth, and lead persons to faith in Jesus Christ," he

[6]Sex and the Schools," *National Courier*, 6 February 1976, 18.

[7]Dennis and Rita Bennett, "Should Church Ordain Gays?" *National Courier*, 9 January 1976, 19.

[8]"The Blight of Gambling," *National Courier*, 23 January 1976, 26.

[9]"Abortion on Demand," *National Courier*, 26 December 1975, 18.

[10]"Fighting Pornography," *National Courier*, 5 March 1976, 18.

[11]David Kucharsky, "The Year of the Evangelical," *Christianity Today*, 22 October 1976

[12]Dan Malachuk, personal telephone interview, 26 April 1997.

stated, yet "the *National Courier* never took sides — it was written to bless the entire body."[13] This attempt to speak to a variety of Christians was evidenced in an editorial that focused on the fundamental issue of "activism v. salvation," historically a source of contention in the Christian community. "Neither personal salvation nor social activism can be stressed as the message of the Gospel in its entirety," the editorial concluded.[14] However, the newspaper was quick to warn its readers about religious beliefs that were contrary to the tenets of the Christian faith. For example, it enlightened its audiences about the wave of eastern religion gurus, groups, ideas, and practices that had permeated parts of American society during the time period through a series of articles[15] and at the same time pronounced in an editorial the dangers of involvement with them.[16] In effect, it attempted to respond accurately and fairly to events and issues of interest to an American culture seemingly interested in religious news and news from a religious perspective, but ultimately the desire was to point people to fundamental tenets of the Christian faith.

The *National Courier* also was launched as an alternative voice to both the mainstream press and Christian publications of its day. In the pursuit of truth about Watergate, Vietnam, the civil rights fight, and other major issues and events of the 1960s and 1970s, the mainstream press honed investigative, in-depth journalistic practices and responded to the public's growing demand for the press to be an aggressive "watchdog" and interpreter of events in the worlds of government, business, sports, religion, and other areas of interest. The *National Courier* viewed itself as a "watchdog" with a special point of view, stating that it would "undertake investigative stories [that] are aimed at plots or schemes — governmental, business or otherwise — that intentionally victimize people, not at the isolated mistakes or failures by individuals. The paper, like its Lord, must have the quality of mercy."[17]

In the 1970s, religion became news. In addition to the traditional local church news, print journalists began chronicling the major events of regional, national and international religious movements. Some developed religion sections and began running stories in other parts of the newspaper that recognized that religion, as interpreted by the press, had a bearing on presidential elections, foreign diplomacy, Supreme Court decisions, and other national affairs. Yet these news media were criticized by many in the Christian community for their uncertainty or ignorance about religious matters and the tendency by some to treat religion primarily as a private, personal experience. They also were chastised for their inability to adequately interpret how religion impacted public policy issues and news events and how these, in turn, affected religious communities and beliefs. Church publications, most produced by church organizations, preferred to focus on "church news" exclusively.

The *National Courier* attempted to fill the void. "We are keenly aware that

---

[13]Jamie Buckingham, "With tears in our eyes, we say farewell," *National Courier*, 16 September 1977, 1, 18.

[14]"Activism v. Salvation," *National Courier*, 20 February 1976, 26.

[15]Jack and Betty Cheetham, "The Transcendental Experience: Paradise or Self-Destruction," *National Courier*, 7 October 1975, 24-5; Jack and Betty Cheetham, "The Spiritual Dilemma: Who Really Has the Answers?" *National Courier*, 21 October 1975, 24-5, 28.

[16]"Not for Christians," *National Courier*, 21 October 1975, 26.

[17]"Looking at the Record," *National Courier*, 2 December 1975, 26.

large numbers of people have lost faith in the reliability of much of the national media, in terms of impartiality and fairness, and we desire to bring relief to this credibility crisis," an early editorial proclaimed. The newspaper desired to pursue "the main themes of integrity, accuracy and fairness" remembering that it "belongs to the entire Body of Christ, not to any particular movement or branch of the Christian community" and through these ideals "reach into non-Christian homes far and wide."[18]

It was amid their concerted efforts to respond effectively to the changes in culture, religion and the press that characterized the 1960s and 1970s that those involved with the *National Courier* were confronted with many fundamental questions and issues about the purpose and nature of Christian journalism.

*STRUGGLES WITH ISSUES OF CHRISTIAN JOURNALISM:
THE* NATIONAL COURIER *EXPERIENCE*

The *National Courier* was a publication of Dan Malachuk's Logos International Fellowship, the world's largest charismatic book publisher of the 1970s. It released its first issue on September 30, 1975, under the leadership of Bob Slosser, then the assistant national editor and assistant news editor of the *New York Times*. In a promotional brochure, Slosser said the *National Courier* would perform the surveillance function of the press, by looking for trends and insisting on telling the truth, even about fellow Christians. It also would carry out the interpretation function of the press, by explaining to readers what stories meant.[19]

The publication hired a mix of experienced and younger journalists, contributing columnists, and stringers. It had bought facilities, including a printing press, in Plainfield, New Jersey, from the Gannett Corporation, raised financial support from the Christian community to launch the publication and counted on targeted subscription sales, supermarket sales, and advertising revenues to finance it in the future. The newspaper quickly discovered its printing press was outdated, experienced difficulty in reaching optimistic subscription projections, and had to abandon the idea of supermarket distribution because of cost and ethical factors. The *National Courier's* newness, its Christian purpose, and problems in defining its audience clearly hindered obtaining advertising support.

Faced with the harsh realities of the news business, Malachuk, the publisher, was suggesting a more "charismatic" quality for the periodical by the second year of the publication's existence, in part to attract more readers.[20] The neo-Pentecostal or charismatic movement, developed in both mainline Protestant and Roman Catholic denominations in the mid-20th century, was characterized by the belief in outward manifestations of the Holy Spirit's indwelling, often in demonstrative activities. Thus throughout its relatively short life, the *National Courier* staff struggled to achieve ambitious, yet ambiguous goals; develop a distinctive format and editorial content; carve out a niche in the news media marketplace; and attract a critical mass of loyal readers.

In early 1977, Malachuk informed the staff that he would take over leadership

---

[18]Ibid.

[19]Rough copy of promotional brochure for the *National Courier*, 20 May 1975.

[20]Jane Henry, Secretary, minutes from *National Courier* business retreat, 19-20 November 1976.

of the editorial side of the publication.[21] Staff members, including John Lawing, formerly the features editor and later national editor, formally registered their sense of disappointment with the new directions the newspaper was taking. He particularly took issue with its change from a publication devoted to a Christian perspective of all news and events to one concerned primarily with happenings in the Christian community that were of interest mainly to a narrow segment of it. "The *National Courier* has a better and higher calling," he concluded.[22]

While the staff tried its best to accommodate Malachuk, ambiguity about the publication's basic purpose remained to the end. By late August 1977, the Logos trustees who oversaw the work voted to stop publication of the newspaper.[23] Although by then the paper had generated a promising base of advertising support and at one point had reached a subscription peak of about 110,000, it could not handle the indebtedness a new publication requires to make a profit.

Many of the challenges the *National Courier* faced are common to all developing news organizations; however, the newspaper's history is still most characterized by its inability to satisfactorily answer basic philosophical questions related to institutionalizing Christian ideology. Among these questions were: What is the publication's Christian mission? What does Christian journalism really mean? Is the publication a business or a ministry? How can the newspaper balance what has been termed "faith and fact;"[24] that is, optimistic religious faith with realistic assessment of conditions within and external to the news operations? To what extent can the publication differ from both mainstream and Christian news organizations and their publications? Is there really a sufficient audience for a Christian interpretation of news events and issues?

## DIFFICULTIES IN ESTABLISHING A CHRISTIAN MISSION

Conventional wisdom suggests than in order for a news or any other organization to succeed, it must have a clear, distinct overriding mission, one that is understood and supported by both the organization and its outside publics. In a retrospective assessment of the *National Courier* contained in its August 1977 final edition, Logos board member and contributing columnist Jamie Buckingham noted that the newspaper was the result of a "word from God" given to Logos publisher Dan Malachuk and that, "There is no reason, even now, to believe it was anything other than that."[25] In Christian circles, the idea that a new venture can be God-inspired is generally accepted; so those involved with the development of the publication had little trouble dealing with the notion that it came from a compelling yet cloudy spiritual revelation given to its founder.

"I didn't do this newspaper on my own," Malachuk once said.[26] Before launching the publication, he had sought counsel from an impressive array of about twenty Christian journalists at a meeting in his Plainfield, New Jersey, home in March 1975. The group had warned him about the great financial risks

---

[21]Dan Malachuk, letter to Jim Talley, National Editor, *National Courier*, 24 January 1977, 1.

[22]John Lawing, memo to Dan Malachuk, 10 February 1977, 1.

[23]Jamie Buckingham, "There is No Hope Outside of This," *National Courier*, 16 September 1977, 19.

[24]Judith Buddenbaum and D. Stout, *Religion and the Mass Media* (Thousand Oaks, Calif.: Sage Publications, 1996).

[25]Jamie Buckingham, "With Tears in Our Eyes," *National Courier*, 16 September 1977, 1.

[26]Dan Malachuk, telephone interview, 26 April 1997.

associated with starting such a publication.[27] At the same time, they confirmed that a national newspaper that offered some form of Christian perspective of issues and events could provide something conspicuously missing in the mass media. It also had the potential to attract journalists capable of developing it and sizeable audiences interested in reading it. Those who later joined the *National Courier* or in other ways actively participated in this venture seemed to share this general vision. However, it was a vision that was never precisely defined. As a result, although some sort of vision was "carried around in people's heads," recalled John Lawing,[28] the specific nature of the mission was shaped more by events and circumstances than by predetermined agreement among all those who were involved.

On the surface, Malachuk and Slosser shared similar visions. The *National Courier* was to be "a refined *Christian Science Monitor*, but with a broader audience," explained Malachuk.[29] It was, Slosser said, to be "a newspaper addressing contemporary stories and issues with a Christian perspective, not predominantly religious in content — except in editorials."[30] "We are not a Jesus paper, but a religious journal," he was fond of saying.[31]

But beneath the apparent harmony of visions, these two principals held disparate views regarding what the publication should be. Drawing from his extensive journalism background, including editorial roles with the *New York Times*, Slosser envisioned a *National Courier* that would "examine trends, activities, and actions affecting substantial segments of the population, and human-interest stories with broad reader appeal."[32] It would be a blend of religious news, general news columns, and editorials. In-depth coverage of happenings and issues within and related to the Christian community would provide readers with something largely missing in the mainstream press, but much more emphasis would be placed on stories, analysis, and commentary about contemporary political, social, and other issues and events that would appeal to a much broader reading audience. Honesty, accuracy, fairness, and other traditional journalistic standards would temper a conservative, but not necessarily obvious Christian treatment of this type of news.

As a successful Christian book publisher, Malachuk pictured a newspaper directed toward a Christian audience, discovering or rediscovering Christianity amid the "charismatic renewal" and "Jesus" movements prominent in the 1970s. Logos books reflected and were in part credited with stimulating these movements. The *National Courier* was to be modeled after supermarket tabloids such as the *National Inquirer*, featuring stories with a Christian flavor on money, sex, celebrities, miracles, and other aspects of the supernatural.

While Malachuk's religious tabloid and Slosser's "hard news" visions did not initially generate a hostile atmosphere at the *National Courier*, the editorial staff, recruited by Slosser and with his general vision in mind, quickly noticed the incompatibility between the two perspectives. From the onset, "[Malachuk

---

[27]Dan Malachuk, telephone interview conducted by Cheryl Hoffman, 13 April 1990.

[28]John Lawing, personal interview conducted in Virginia Beach, Virginia, 22 April 1997.

[29]Dan Malachuk, telephone interview conducted by Cheryl Hoffman, 13 April 1990.

[30]Bob Slosser, interview conducted by Cheryl Hoffman in Virginia Beach, Virginia, 11 April 1990.

[31]Kenneth A. Briggs, "Religious Paper is Planned in Jersey," *New York Times*, 23 June 1975, sec. 5, 4.

[32]Rough copy of promotional brochure for the *National Courier*, 20 May 1975.

and Slosser] were doing a lot of talking *by* each other," observed Lawing. "I don't think they were listening *to* each other."[33] Slosser recalled that "Dan and I never fought over vision, but I might have changed the vision. I just don't know."[34] However, Lawing recalled that after questioning Slosser at an early stage about how Malachuk's Christian tabloid model could be implemented, he replied, "'We're not going to do that.' I assumed he had carte blanche from the publisher."[35]

Crises tend to reveal whether an organization has a well-defined mission that is comprehended and subscribed to by all significant parties. The *National Courier*'s first major crisis came in the spring of 1976. Logos International Fellowship had previously been incorporated as a non-profit church organization affiliated with the Independent Assemblies of God denomination. This gave both Logos and the *National Courier* special second-class rate mailing and other privileges afforded to non-profit organizations.[36] Facing Internal Revenue Service inquiries about some of its operations and fearing its tax-exempt status would be lost, the denomination pressured Malachuk to reduce the newspaper's emphasis on political and social news and issues that had characterized the first dozen or so editions of the publication. To Slosser, Malachuk's subsequent request to the editorial staff that the newspaper should primarily focus on news pertaining to the Christian community and the work God was doing throughout the world constituted a drastic change from the "vision [I] thought everybody agreed with" to one that involved a "blatant religiousness" he found unbearable.[37]

*CHALLENGE OF DEFINING CHRISTIAN JOURNALISM*

Laboring under conflicting interpretations of the *National Courier*'s mission, its staff found it difficult to define what Christian journalism is and what it is not. Among the provocative defining questions that the paper understood on a latent level but failed to answer on the manifest level were these: Should a Christian news publication pursue traditional standards of "objectivity" or concentrate on being advocates for the Christian faith? What is a workable mix of religious and general news that will attract readers? What is a Christian view of news and entertainment? How can diverse theological perspectives among those involved in a Christian news organization be accommodated? Furthermore, how can a Christian newspaper please a potential audience comprised of many denominational and theological backgrounds and at the same time reach nonbelievers?

"The aim of the *Courier* is to report, analyze, and comment with absolute Christian integrity, fairness and compassion in the hope of providing edification and illumination in these difficult times," an editorial in a preliminary, promotional, sample edition of the paper proclaimed.[38] The editorial pages were earmarked as the "place to which we will confine our 'preaching' and attempt to shed full light on events."[39] Lawing recalled, "On features or anything with a

---

[33]John Lawing, interview conducted by Cheryl Hoffman in Virginia Beach, Virginia, 10 April 1990.
[34]Slosser interview, 11 April 1990.
[35]Lawing interview, 10 April 1990.
[36]Dan Malachuk, Letter to Mail Classification Division, U.S. Post Office, 31 October 1975.
[37]Slosser interview, 11 April 1990.
[38]"Here We Stand," *National Courier*, 12 August 1975, 2.
[39]Rough copy of promotional brochure, 20 May 1975.

point of view, we could advocate a Christian perspective but in news, we were fairly traditional and used an objective approach, the middle of the road standard."[40]

However, there was some question at the *National Courier* about whether the goal of objectivity extended to providing readers with the truth about fellow Christians, good or bad. The editorial staff, experienced with traditional journalism standards and practices, thought it did. But its editorial freedom, first challenged by publisher Malachuk's spring 1976 directive to "relinquish [its] set journalistic patterns" in order to discover and incorporate more spiritual happenings, truths, and perspective into the newspaper's content,[41] was put to a dramatic test in February 1977. Moments before printing, the publisher pulled a front-page story dealing with a Better Business Bureau report that criticized 120 Christian organizations, many of them highly respected, for failing to disclose how they spent funds or for managing them poorly. Malachuk cited the story as reflecting a problem with the "philosophy of the editors." "The editorial board never checked with me until after the fact," he explained. "Of [the] organizations named in the article, about eight of them were checked. The rest had no chance to respond — [and] the Better Business Bureau wouldn't tell us where they got their information." In his mind, this represented "poor editorial work," reprehensible for a staff that "came from reputable newspapers." "I don't think they liked me after that," he acknowledged.[42]

The staff also had difficulty in settling the issue of what was an effective blend of religious and general news. Initially, articles focused on both the U.S. presidential campaign, racism, homosexuality, and other events and issues of general interest as well as issue-oriented and human interest features specifically pertaining to the church. The first full edition of the newspaper on September 30, 1975, contained editorials on school busing to achieve racial integration, a peace accord in the Middle East, New York City's financial crisis, maintaining a fair, pluralistic perspective in the public school classroom, and an assessment of Gerald Ford's presidency. Secular and religious news would be brought together because "Jesus Christ is the Lord of all creation, and of all situations," declared editor Slosser. But when asked by the publishers to revise his original delineation of the *National Courier* in May 1976, he stated that the newspaper "will become more Christian, both in subject matter and in approach to articles. We will concentrate on articles with definite Christian overtones and we will approach the articles spiritually.... If a story does not have an overt Christian dimension, we will leave it to the secular press." From that time on, the *National Courier*'s focus was to concentrate on "reporting the Lord's Work."[43]

The staff wrestled with what it means to "approach articles spiritually." Former news editor Rick Kauffman explained that it was an effort "to take secular news and present if from a biblical perspective, to draw attention to Christ."[44] It was "looking for the perspective behind the news," according to

---

[40]John Lawing, personal interview, 26 April 1997.

[41]John Lawing, unpublished notes from *National Courier* meeting about its vision, April 1976.

[42]Dan Malachuk, telephone interview, 26 April 1997.

[43]Rough copy of promotional brochure, 20 May 1975.

[44]Rick Kauffman, telephone interview conducted by Cheryl Hoffman, 12 April 1990.

Dorianne Perrucci, who served as a feature editor for the publication.[45] Dave Wimbish, another news editor and columnist, put it this way: "Our idea was not to just present stories of what was going on in the church. If this is God's world, then everything going on here is Christian in that sense. Our idea was to give a truthful view of what's going on in the world."[46] Contributing columnist and Logos board member Jamie Buckingham described his rendition of a Christian perspective of news as looking "at facts and events from a spiritual perspective — I'm one of those persons who can't help but see the hand of God in everything around me. Thus, when I write, I look at things from God's eye — [but] I don't have a view of God from any sectarian perspective."[47]

When Slosser moved to another role at Logos in March 1977, Malachuk provided an even narrower interpretation of what a Christian perspective of news entailed. "The vision for an international Christian newspaper, given a more spiritual thrust only nine months ago, is clearer now than ever before," he stated. It was "to inform, to edify, to correct, to support, to entertain God's people, and to seek souls for Him."[48]

The daunting task of establishing an effective "Christian journalism" formula was perhaps best exemplified by the *National Courier*'s experience with a lengthy "miracles" feature it regularly included. A news version of "Christian witnessing," it reported and to some degree documented miraculous healings and other works of God experienced by individuals deemed credible by the editorial staff. Although such testimonies were a good means of enticing a variety of readers and fit Malachuk's tabloid concept for the newspaper, some members of the editorial staff were uncomfortable with treating such difficult-to-verify experiences as news stories. When an amazing healing reported in the October 15, 1976, edition turned out to be fabricated, the *National Courier* lost some of the credibility with readers and supporters it desperately needed to survive. It also soon carried such stories under the banner of "testimonies" and tried to avoid the appearance of directly endorsing them as factual.[49]

Efforts to develop an adequate definition of Christian journalism were thwarted by the fact that the *National Courier*'s key staff came from a number of different denominational backgrounds. Staff members had worldviews, shaped by their specific religious traditions, which they brought into the ongoing newsroom debate over what Christian journalism really was. Although they were an "eclectic" group, they were supportive of each other, according to Lawing.[50] Their faith in God and agreement with the core elements of Christian doctrine and common dedication to journalistic professionalism allowed them to support, in unity, a broad vision for a national Christian newspaper.

At the same time, despite their varying denominational experiences, they were largely conservative, evangelical, and at least somewhat aligned to the "charismatic" element of the Church in that time period. In effect, they may have been collectively too narrow in perspective to define Christian journalism effec-

---

[45]Dorianne Perrucci, telephone interview conducted by Cheryl Hoffman, 9 April 1990.

[46]David Wimbish, telephone interview conducted by Cheryl Hoffman, 8 April 1990.

[47]Jamie Buckingham, "Views from Heaven and Hell," *National Courier*, 12 August 1975, 2.

[48]Daniel Malachuk, "Lifting Jesus Higher," *National Courier*, 4 March 1977, 1.

[49]Alice Pattico, "The doctor rushed to the intercom and yelled, 'the Jesus girl' — something has happened to her," *National Courier*, "Miracles" section, 15 October 1976, 32.

[50]Lawing interview, 22 April 1997.

tively. Lawing, the former feature and national editor of the newspaper thought so. "Almost from the beginning, we got derailed," he said. "We had a group of hard core charismatics [but] we never had a body of talent."[51]

## THE CHALLENGE OF FINDING A MARKET NICHE

The *National Courier* found it equally problematic to develop a unique position in the marketplace of media vying for the attention of audiences. As with all young media organizations, briskly establishing this distinctiveness was essential for the newspaper's survival. "We will not be an awful lot different from some other newspapers. But if we establish a reputation for credibility I believe we will attract many non-Christians," Slosser declared before the initial printing of the publication.[52] However, the more the publication paralleled the offerings of the secular press, it was in danger of failing to be distinct enough for readers, advertisers, and supporters. It could be too secularized for some but too Christianized for others.

When Malachuk demanded in April 1976 a shift in editorial focus toward more religious content and spiritual emphasis, he noted that the *National Courier* had been modeled too much after secular publications and was attempting to compete too much with "the world," thus becoming "interesting, but not much more."[53] James Talley, the national editor at the time, dutifully responded by calling for a revitalized *National Courier* that stopped looking "like the *New York Daily News* with all its Boraxy brashness" and sounding "like the *New York Times* with all its stiltedly prissiness." "Our readers are not interested in our experiments," he observed. "They just expect a good, sharp, accurate, God-fearing and God-loving newspaper."[54] But as it moved in this direction, the *National Courier* may have lost any uniqueness it may have had among Christian publications. Although disappointed about these changes, columnist Dave Wimbish noted that this revised mandate did allow the organization to pursue "what we were best at."[55] In the end, however, the publication may have become no more than "*Christianity Today*'s news section, but with a narrow charismatic approach," as Lawing put it.[56]

The *National Courier*'s difficulties in establishing a unique position in the marketplace were closely tied to its problems in clearly profiling target audiences for the publication. The basic issue those involved with the publication struggled to resolve was whether they were primarily trying to reach Christians or non-Christians. "We were hoping to attract the nominal Christian," Malachuk later stated. "That's who we were shooting for. In the first edition, we wrote something about the New Age. We wanted to reach out for that element that was looking for other religions."[57] The *National Courier* name itself implied that there was an attempt to attract broader audiences than typically sought by other

---

[51]Lawing interview, 26 April 1997.
[52]Kenneth Briggs, "Religious Newspaper is Planned in New Jersey," *New York Times*, 23 June 1975, sec.5, 4.
[53]John Lawing, unpublished notes from meeting on the vision of the *National Courier*, April 1976.
[54]Ibid., 8-9.
[55]Wimbish interview, 8 April 1990.
[56]Lawing interview, 10 April 1990.
[57]Dan Malachuk, telephone interview, 26 April 1997.

Christian publications. A short salvation message that was often included in the editorial pages was indicative of a desire to evangelize nonbelievers. Yet, Lawing recalled, "I didn't know who the audience was. We thought that if we started a publication, we could attract committed Christians and by being so brilliant and perceptive, we could get non-Christian readers, too."[58] Necessary preliminary and ongoing formal audience research was never conducted.

With content aimed at nominal Christians or unbelievers, the *National Courier* might have developed a larger circulation than was typical of other Christian publications. On the other hand, it risked gaining the support of or being misunderstood by those more devoted to the Christian faith. Not surprisingly, in the fifth issue of the publication, the editors were compelled to explain what they were attempting to accomplish to readers in the wake of letters to the editor from those who anticipated a greater Christian flavor and/or minimal criticism of Christian organizations and ministries.[59] The editorial staff's desire not to avoid controversy in religious news coverage and be comprehensive in its coverage was bound to offend those whose particular brand of Christianity seemed to be slighted. At the same time, the newspaper depended on a 325,000-person Logos mailing list to attract initial readers. Many of these people identified with the "charismatic renewal" community. Some inside the organization wondered if attempts to curry favor with this group would unduly antagonize other segments of the Christian subculture.

The *National Courier*'s peak circulation of 110,000 was far below what was needed to become financially solvent and even further below the expectations of its publishers. These expectations were in part built on questionable assumptions about Christians such as: (1) They would read a news publication with a Christian perspective as a substitute for or in addition to other sources of news and entertainment utilized in their lives. (2) They would be drawn to a purely national publication that could not provide them with news of *local* interest. (3) They would prefer to read a nondenominational publication rather than publications that appealed to the particular segment of the Church of which they were a part. (4) They liked to read at all. "We have 80 million Christians in the United States but they don't read," publisher Malachuk later lamented.[60]

*THE PROBLEM IN DISTINGUISHING BETWEEN BUSINESS AND MINISTRY*

Many of the *National Courier*'s complications can be traced to its failure to discover a balance between being a business and a ministry. The publication was produced by the same organization, Logos, that had successfully published inspirational Christian books that not only attracted but ministered to readers. Its board expected a newspaper that would similarly minister to the needs of its audiences yet be operated in businesslike fashion. Logos was tied to the Independent Assemblies of God, a non-profit ministry and one of the four Pentecostal denominations that include the Pentecostal Holiness Church, the United Pentecostal Church Inc., and the International Church of the Foursquare Gospel. When the newspaper struggled to find a sizeable audience and become financially

---

[58]Lawing interview, 26 April 1997.
[59]"Looking at the Record," *National Courier*, 2 December 1975, 26.
[60]Malachuk interview, 26 April 1997.

stable, Logos increasingly questioned whether the *National Courier* was either economically viable or able to serve existing or potential audiences. At its retreat in November 1976, Logos board member and executive vice-president of the newspaper Allan Rundle urged the *Courier* staff to pursue sound business principles yet evangelize, prophesy to, and disciple the publication's readers regarding the Christian faith.[61] Looking back on his experience with the publication, he later observed, "I've never heard of any changed lives because of the newspaper. Spiritual fruit was born from Logos [its books]; I don't know of any spiritual fruit from the newspaper."[62]

The newspaper was started with ministerial zeal but with some understanding of the exorbitant costs associated with launching a new, national publication. "The question was: Is there a viable market for a bi-weekly Christian newspaper? The general feeling was yes, do it, but it will cost a lot of money," recalled Rundle.[63] But when circulation manager Roy Coffman joined the organization, he quickly found that a well-thought-out business plan was missing, and the newspaper was greatly underfinanced, including insufficient funds devoted to marketing and promotion.[64] Its costly printing press was never adequate. Its plans for grocery, drugstore, and newsstand distribution were undermined by prohibitive costs. Logos' 325,000-person mailing list did not generate anticipated subscribers. The effort to build suitable circulation through prepaid subscriptions, Christian bookstores, and word of mouth was a painfully slow, inadequate process for a young news organization with limited resources and high hopes. The publication attracted advertisers, mainly Christian organizations with products and services for Christians. However, with a limited national audience, a gray black-and-white tabloid look, and no market research data that could be used to profile the special nature of its readers or potential readers, success in securing a variety of advertisers was quite limited.

The staff all arrived under the assumption that the publication had a Christian purpose and atmosphere but was still a business. They were fundamentally like-minded in faith and came with a sense of Christian "calling" and a desire to touch people's lives through the newspaper. As a group, the staff prayed together, met twice a week for corporate worship at work, donated money to the effort, and participated in retreats that combined business and spiritual activities. While these same activities are evident in most Christian organizations, the *National Courier* staff often experienced a blurring of lines between ministry and business.

For the staff, the distinctions between business and ministry became even less clear when it was revealed, at the time the organization feared losing special tax and postal service privileges, that the publication had from the start been legally and for practical purposes incorporated as a non-profit "church" organization, with the publisher, editor, and executive vice-president serving as "elders." The newsroom personnel were unaware of this provision until 1977.

The content of the newspaper, with its Christian perspective of general news,

---

[61]Jane Henry, minutes, *National Courier* retreat, 19-20 November 1976, 3-4.

[62]Allen Rundle, telephone interview, 26 April 1997.

[63]Ibid.

[64]Kenneth Eugene Waters, "Toward the Successful Christian Publication," Ph. D. dissertation, University of Southern California, 1982.

its thoughtful religious news, its editorials and columns with biblical and spiritual undertones, its reports of miracles and testimonies, and its public expression of the needs of the poor, sick, needy, and persecuted around the world all reflected the ministerial purpose and nature of the organization. Nonetheless, the impatient desire for solvency placed strains on both the editorial and business sides of the organization. While the editorial staff looked for newsworthy stories that would inform, minister to, and change the world in some way, those most concerned with the financial well being of the organization asked for content that would sell. Contrary to what founding editor Slosser had intended, the editorial staff was sometimes directly pressured to produce certain types of content. The *National Courier*'s business was often mixed with Logos Publishing's bookselling operations. "The advertising guys hassled us," remembered John Lawing. "They wanted us to review books exclusively."[65] Even Slosser was drawn away from his editorial duties to help write a book on presidential candidate Jimmy Carter, *The Miracle of Jimmy Carter*. The lure of a probable moneymaking publication, coupled with Carter's public declaration that he was a "born again" Christian, was too great for Malachuk and others to resist.[66]

In the end, the *National Courier* venture proved to be a very costly experiment. Although the newspaper showed some signs of developing sufficient readership and advertising revenues, the latter particularly after its purpose and content became more blatantly Christian, clearly it was not a financial success. "When we went bankrupt, we were $4 million in the hole. The paper caused the organization [Logos] to collapse," recalled Malachuk.[67]

*DIFFICULTIES IN SEPARATING FAITH VS. FACT*

Problems associated with balancing business and ministry were symptomatic of deeper tensions and confusion at the *National Courier* that greatly contributed to its demise. Its staff placed their hopes in God, his sovereign intervention, and in biblical promises of provision, and, according to Malachuk, "God supplied."[68] "We are not disappointed in the faithfulness of God," wrote Jamie Buckingham in the publication's last issue.[69] Such faith enabled the staff to deal with extreme uncertainties, battle seemingly insurmountable odds, and weather crises, conflicts, and disappointments associated with trying to establish a publication of this nature and scale.[70] It also was partly responsible for unrealistic expectations, ignoring facts, circumstances, and problems that needed to be remedied, and even failure to plan adequately and use sound management principles, or as former foreign editor Rick Kauffman described it, "Throw a newspaper together and thousands of people will want it, and everything else, because it's God's will."[71]

A high level of faith was *expected* of the staff. For example, Malachuk once criticized them for "negative thought patterns [that] can stop the flow of God's

[65]Lawing interview, 26 April 1997.
[66]Malachuk interview, 13 April 1990.
[67]Malachuk interview, 26 April 1997.
[68]Malachuk interview, 13 April 1990.
[69]Buckingham, "With Tears," 18.
[70]Lawing interview, 22 April 1997.
[71]Rick Kauffman, telephone interview conducted by Cheryl Hoffman, 12 April 1990.

inspiration to us as He does not work in a negative climate."[72] It was regularly implied that the *National Courier's* situation would improve if the staff would repent or be more spiritual.[73] The editorial staff came to believe that those at Logos were suspicious of journalists and investigative journalism and viewed questioning and legitimate criticism of *National Courier* leadership, affairs, and circumstances as "negativism" or a threat to spiritual unity.[74]

The spiritual climate, established at the *National Courier* primarily through its visionary, prophetic publisher and ties to Logos, was predominantly Pentacostal, with strong belief in the manifestation, workings, and direction of the Holy Spirit in the individual and corporate lives of Christians. Some staff members were uncomfortable with this atmosphere.[75] This discomfort reached its peak after Malachuk assumed more control over the editorial direction of the newspaper in January 1997 declaring that he had been "disobedient to the Lord in having delegated too much authority and spiritual leadership to others at the newspaper."[76] In a letter to a colleague, editorial staff member Perrucci blamed "the pentacostal" nature of Logos for fostering a perspective of journalism that tended to "overlook reality."[77]

Attempts to reconcile differences in vision, conflicts between publisher and editorial staff, and varying interpretations of matters of faith marked the final months of the *National Courier* experiment. "We're all going the same place," national editor Talley tried to reason with the publisher. "The only question before us is how we get there. And as the Lord leads you, I trust you will share with us — then we, together, can think on these things, and write these things with integrity and with spiritual, professional, and intellectual honesty."[78] However, the publication's management apparently never understood that a staff made up of people from a variety of Christian cultures were held together by the idea of "devotion to all and to the Lord, listening to others within the parameters of basics [i.e., elements of Christian doctrine]."[79] They required steadfast adherence to a nebulous, often shifting vision for the publication. They expected all obstacles to success to be overcome by faith alone. "They were not keyed into reality," observed circulation manager Roy Coffman. "They looked to their faith to bail them out."[80]

*THE LEGACY OF THE* NATIONAL COURIER

The failure of the *National Courier* to survive beyond two years can be attributed to a variety of intermingled factors. In his analysis of the paper, scholar Ken Waters suggests one reason: The newspaper, or any other Protestant publication for that matter, that hoped to offer content attractive to and compatible

---

[72]Dan Malachuk, Special Memorandum, "Remember the Landmarks," 20 January 1977, 1-2.

[73]Wimbish interview, 8 April 1990.

[74]Lawing interview, 10 April 1990.

[75]Wimbish interview, 8 April 1990; Lawing interview, 22 April 1997; Perrucci interview, 9 April 1990; Kauffman interview, 12 April 1990.

[76]Malachuk, Special Memorandum, "Remember the Landmarks."

[77]Dorrianne Perrucci, letter to Stephen Noll, book reviewer for the *National Courier*, 4 February 1977.

[78]James Talley, memorandum to Dan Malachuk, 10 February 1977.

[79]Talley interview, 9 April 1990.

[80]Roy Coffman, telephone interview conducted by Cheryl Hoffman, 12 April 1990.

with the beliefs of a large, national audience could not overcome the reality that the Christian community is divided into countless numbers of small segments, each with its own leaders, theological perspectives, organizations and concerns. In effect, Christians, to a large extent, are only able to agree on basic components of Christian doctrine, thus potentially ruining any issue-oriented news endeavor aimed at them. Only Christian news media that gear their efforts toward a particular group of Christians or that advocate a specific cause could achieve success in the cultural climate of the 1970s or thereafter.[81]

Malachuk recognized this problem when he wrote to readers that Christian journalists, writers, publishers, and audiences needed to recognize that, "we build walls" that prevent seeing "the Lord at work" around the world. "Sometimes he shows up in some very strange places indeed. But that just means we have to keep our eyes open to see what he's *really* doing — especially if it is outside our own small islands."[82]

David Aikman, a *Time* magazine correspondent from 1971 to 1994 and now a free-lance media critic, believes evangelical Christians do not subscribe to as many periodicals as others, and certainly this was an important audience the *National Courier* generally was trying to reach. "The *National Courier* was balanced, honest, insightful, with lots of news," he said. "Sadly, evangelical Christians didn't want to buy it."[83]

However, this alone does not fully account for why the *National Courier* was unable to endure. It fell prey to poor management, severe distribution problems, lack of a clear, agreed-upon mission, conflicts between management and editorial staff, difficulties in distinguishing between business and ministry, drastic and constant shifts in editorial philosophy, failure to clearly identify, profile, and develop potential readers before and after launching the publication, limited advertising support, failure to find a distinct position in the media marketplace and in people's minds, an inability to fully define what "Christian journalism" should be, troubles in discriminating between faith and presumption, and much more.

The *National Courier* acted as a stimulating forum for wrestling with issues about religious journalism. It produced a professional product, with many good articles, columns, and commentary that are provocative and still read well today. Although circulation projections were never fully met, it attracted a sizable number of loyal readers. It provides media historians with a picture of some of the issues of the era, viewed from a Christian perspective. It offers Christian and other religious groups interested in developing news media organizations many valuable lessons in what to expect and barriers to success that must be hurdled.

---

[81]Ken Waters, "Christian Journalism's Finest Hour?" *Journalism History* 20:2 (Summer 1994): 62.
[82]Dan Malachuk, "Do We Say What We Mean?" *National Courier*, 16 April 1976, 22.
[83]David Aikman, personal interview, 31 August 1997.

# Editor

WM. DAVID SLOAN is the founder of the American Journalism Historians Association and served a five-year term as editor of its research journal, *American Journalism*. He has published eighteen other books, among them *The Media in America: A History*; *Historical Methods in Mass Communication*; *The Significance of the Media in American History*; *American Journalism History: An Annotated Bibliography*; *Perspectives on Mass Communication History*; *The Early American Press, 1690-1783*; *The Age of Mass Communication; Great Editorials*; and *Masterpieces of Reporting*. He also is co-editor of the seven-volume series "History of American Journalism," a work in progress. He has authored more than eighty articles and papers on history and journalistic writing and has been recognized with several research awards for his work in media history. In 1998 he received the AJHA's Kobre Award for lifetime achievements. He is national president (1998-2000) of Kappa Tau Alpha, the mass communication honor society, and of the AJHA (1999-2000). A professor of journalism at the University of Alabama, he received the Ph.D. in mass communication and United States history from the University of Texas.

# Authors

JUDITH M. BUDDENBAUM, professor of journalism at Colorado State University, is author of *Reporting News about Religion: An Introduction for Journalists* and co-editor of *Religion and Mass Media: Audiences and Adaptations*. She also has written a number of book chapters and journal articles on religion and the media. She received her Ph. D. in mass communication from Indiana University.

DAVID COPELAND is the author of *Colonial American Newspapers: Character and Content* and *Colonial Newspapers as Journals of Opinion*. He is also co-editor of *Media History Monographs*. The author of numerous journal articles, book chapters, and research presentations, he is president-elect of the American Journalism Historians Association. He received his Ph.D. in mass communication research from the University of North Carolina and a Th. M. in church history from Southeastern Baptist Theological Seminary. He teaches mass communication at Emory & Henry College.

BRUCE J. EVENSEN is the author of *When Dempsey Fought Tunney* and *Truman, Palestine and the Press* and editor of *The Responsible Reporter*, now in its second edition. He has written more than seventy articles in research journals. He received his Ph. D. in mass communication from the University of

Wisconsin-Madison and is a professor of communication at DePaul University.

JOHN P. FERRÉ is an associate professor communication at the University of Louisville, where he studies ethical, religious, and historical dimensions of mass media in the United States. In addition to numerous articles and reviews, he has written several books, including *Good News: Social Ethics and the Press* with Clifford G. Christians and P. Mark Fackler. He received his Ph. D. degree from the University of Illinois.

ROBERT S. FORTNER, professor of communication arts and sciences at Calvin College, is the author of two books, *International Communication* and *Public Diplomacy and International Politics*, and a number of articles in scholarly and professional journals in communication. Before entering teaching, he worked in radio and public relations. He received his Ph. D. in mass communication research from the University of Illinois.

KYLE HUCKINS received his Ph. D. in mass communication from the University of Texas and teaches at Regent University.

CAROL SUE HUMPHREY is the author of the books *"This Popular Engine": The Role of New England Newspapers During the American Revolution* and *The Press of the Young Republic, 1783-1833*. She also has authored a variety of articles and book chapters on journalism of the Revolutionary era. She received her Ph. D. in history from the University of North Carolina and teaches history at Oklahoma Baptist University.

J. D. KEELER, a professor of communication at Regent University, has published articles and presented numerous research papers at academic conferences. He received the Ph. D. in mass communication from the University of Texas.

MICHAEL A. LONGINOW, associate professor and coordinator of the journalism program at Asbury College, received his Ph. D. from the University of Kentucky.

DAVID PAUL NORD, a professor of journalism and American Studies at Indiana University, is author of *Newspapers and New Politics: Midwestern Municipal Reform, 1890-1900*, and of numerous articles on the history of American journalism, religious publishing, and reading and readership. He is acting editor of the *Journal of American History*. He received the Ph. D. in mass communication from the University of Wisconsin.

MARVIN OLASKY, a professor of journalism at the University of Texas, is the author of thirteen books, including *Prodigal Press*; *Telling the Truth*; *The Press and Abortion, 1938-1988*; *The Tragedy of American Compassion*; and *Fighting for Liberty and Virtue*. He also has written more than 100 articles. He received the Ph. D. in American Culture from the University of Michigan.

MICHAEL R. SMITH is an associate professor of communication at Regent University, where he received his Ph. D. degree. Prior to joining the Regent faculty, he taught at Taylor University. He is the author of two books on community history.

J. DOUGLAS TARPLEY is chairman of the School of Journalism at Regent University. He has served as national president of the Society of Collegiate Journalists and has received a variety of national awards for his teaching and academic service. He received the Ph. D. in journalism at Southern Illinois University.

BERNELL ELIZABETH TRIPP, associate professor of journalism at the University of Florida, is the author of *The Origins of the Black Press* and numerous book chapters and papers on the nineteenth-century black press. She received her Ph.D. in mass communication from the University of Alabama.

STEPHEN J. WHITFIELD, professor of American Studies at Brandeis University, has published eight books, most recently *In Search of American Jewish Culture*. He has served as Fulbright visiting professor at the Hebrew University of Jerusalem and at the Catholic University of Leuven in Belgium. He received the Ph. D. in the History of American Civilization at Brandeis University.

JULIE HEDGEPETH WILLIAMS is author of *The Significance of the Printed Word in Early America* and co-author of *The Early American Press, 1690-1783* and of *The Great Reporters: An Anthology of News Writing at Its Best*. She also has authored chapters on colonial journalism, media and religion, and women in the media for several other books and has presented numerous research papers at academic conferences. She is a member of the Board of Directors of the American Journalism Historians Association and chair of its Publications Committee. She received her Ph.D. in mass communication at the University of Alabama and received the AJHA's first award for the nation's outstanding doctoral dissertation. She teaches journalism at Samford University.